WEBSTER'S
RHYMING
DICTIONARY ALPHABETICAL GUIDE TO
RHYMING SOUNDS

WEBSTER'S RHYMING DICTIONARY

ALPHABETICAL GUIDE TO RHYMING SOUNDS

CREATED IN COOPERATION WITH THE EDITORS OF

MERRIAM-WEBSTER

Dalmatian Press

This 2013 Edition published by arrangement with Federal Street Press,
a division of Merriam-Webster, Incorporated

Distributed by **Dalmatian Press**
113 Seaboard Lane
Franklin, TN 37067

CE13844/1212

Printed in Ithaca, NY, USA

Contents

How to Use This Book   **vi**

Pronunciation Symbols   **viii**

Rhyming sounds that begin with **A**   **1**

Rhyming sounds that begin with **E**   **60**

Rhyming sounds that begin with **I**   **105**

Rhyming sounds that begin with **O**   **144**

Rhyming sounds that begin with **U**   **193**

Rhyming sounds that begin with **Y**   **211**

How to Use This Book

Welcome to this new rhyming dictionary, where you'll find over 40,000 rhyming words—enough to last you the rest of your life.

We've tried to make this book as easy as possible to use. However, it works quite differently from an ordinary dictionary, so please read these brief instructions to be sure you make the best use of it you can.

All the entries in this book are for *rhyming sounds*. All rhyming sounds begin with a vowel, so every entry begins with *A, E, I, O, U,* or *Y.*

All rhyming sounds also begin with an accented syllable. The rhyming sounds listed here all have one syllable, two syllables, or three syllables.

If a word has only one syllable, that syllable is always accented (as in *bee* and *sea*). A two-syllable word may be accented on either its first syllable (as in *beta* and *data*) or its second syllable (as in *agree* and *must-see*). A three-syllable word may be accented on its first syllable (*attitude, gratitude*), its middle syllable (*illusion, seclusion*), or its last syllable (*anymore, tug-of-war*).

Though the rhyming sounds in this dictionary are never more than three syllables long, the words themselves may have six or more syllables. In every entry, the words are divided into sections according to number of syllables; each section begins with a small bullet (•). So, for instance, the **y¹** entry starts with a group of one-syllable words, which is followed by five more bulleted sections, the last one consisting of six-syllable words.

Some words have two accented syllables, with one of them almost always stronger than the other. Notice that when you say the word "middle," you put no accent at all on the second syllable, but when you say "schoolkid," you put a strong accent on its first syllable and a weaker accent on its second syllable. In this book, the rhyming sound always begins with the *last* accented syllable, whether or not that syllable is the one with the strongest accent. So *schoolkid* is shown at the **id¹** entry—that is, the entry for its weakly accented syllable.

Many rhymes can be spelled in several different ways. For example, the rhyming sound that is often spelled *-eek* (as in *creek*) can also be spelled *-eak* (as in *peak*), *-ique* (*mystique*), *-ic* (*chic*), or *-ik* (*batik*). So how do you find a rhyme for a particular word? Just look up the spelling of its rhyming sound.

Let's suppose you need a rhyme for *equator*. All you need to do is notice how its rhyming sound is spelled. Since the rhyming sound always begins with the last accented syllable and always begins with a vowel, the rhyming sound of *equator* is obviously spelled *-ator*. And sure enough, the entry **ator** shows all the rhymes for *equator*, no matter how their endings are spelled: *crater, freighter, creator*, etc.

But suppose you had instead wanted a rhyme for *later*, and had looked up the spelling for its rhyming sound, *-ater*. There you would have found two separate entries, **ater**[1] and **ater**[2]. Next to **ater**[1] you would have seen the pronunciation \ȯt-ər\, and next to **ater**[2] you would have seen the pronunciation \ȧt-ər\. Looking at the Pronunciation Symbols table on page viii, you would have seen that only the second pronunciation matched the pronunciation of *later*. But you might not have even needed to look up the pronunciation symbols, since you would have noticed immediately that the words listed at **ater**[1]—words such as *daughter* and *water*—didn't rhyme with *later*. Moving on to **ater**[2], you would have seen that no words are listed there at all, but that it instead simply contains the direction "see ATOR." Turning to **ator**, you would have found all the words that rhyme with *later*, regardless of how they were spelled.

Now suppose you need a word to rhyme with *dance*, and you've found the list you were looking for at **ance**[3]. But maybe none of the words there is quite what you want. This time you're in luck: there are some other possibilities. At the end of the entry, you'll see the following note: "—*also* -s, -'s, *and* -s' *forms of nouns and* -s *forms of verbs listed at* ANT[5]." In other words, at **ant**[5] you can find some nouns and verbs that might do the trick. Turning to **ant**[5], you see that it lists such nouns as *aunt* and *confidan*t, which would rhyme with *dance* in their plural form (*aunts, confidants*), in their possessive form (*aunt's, confidant's*), or in their plural possessive form (*aunts', confidants'*). You would also see such verbs as *enchant* and *gallivant*, which in the first-person singular (*enchants, gallivants*) would also rhyme with *dance*.

Not everyone pronounces all words the same way. So, for example, you will see words like *drawn, gone*, and *yawn* at both **on**[1] and **on**[3]. Usually only one pronunciation will seem right for you.

These few instructions should be all you need to make the best use of the dictionary. We hope you'll keep it close at hand to jog your memory, enlarge your lyrical vocabulary, and expand your poetic ambitions.

Pronunciation Symbols

ə	banana, collide, abut
ᵊ	preceding \l\ and \n\, as in battle, mitten, and eaten; following \l\, \m\, \r\, as in French table, prisme, titre
ər	further, merger, bird
a	mat, gag, sap
ā	day, fade, aorta
ä	bother, cot, father
aủ	now, loud, Faust
b	baby, rib
ch	chin, nature \'nā-chər\
d	did, adder
e	bet, peck, help
ē	fee, easy, media
f	fifty, phone, rough
g	go, big
h	hat, ahead
i	tip, banish, active
ī	site, buy, deny
j	job, gem, judge
k	kin, cook, ache
k̲	German ich, Buch
l	lily, pool
m	murmur, dim
n	no, own
ⁿ	preceding vowel or diphthong is pronounced with the nasal passages open, as in French un bon vin blanc \œⁿ-bōⁿ-vaⁿ-bläⁿ\
ŋ	sing \'siŋ\, finger \'fiŋ-gər\, ink \'iŋk\
ō	bone, know, beau
ȯ	saw, all, caught
ȯi	coin, destroy
p	pepper, lip
r	red, car, rarity
s	source, less
sh	shy, mission, machine, special
t	tie, attack, late
th	thin, ether
t̲h̲	then, either
ü	rule, fool, union \'yün-yən\, few \'fyü\
ủ	pull, would, book
v	vivid, give
w	we, away
y	yard, cue \'kyü\, mute \'myüt\
z	zone, raise
zh	vision, azure \'a-zhər\

A

a¹ \ä\ aah, ah, baa, bah, blah, bra, fa, ha, la, ma, moi, nah, pa, rah, shah, ska, spa • aha, Allah, blah-blah, Casbah, chutzpah, Degas, faux pas, feta, gaga, goombah, grandma, grandpa, ha-ha, hoopla, hurrah, huzzah, oompah, pooh-bah, ta-ta, Utah, voilà • Akita, aloha, baklava, brouhaha, Chippewa, coup d'état, guarana, la-di-da, ma-and-pa, Mardi Gras, Omaha, Ottawa, panama, Panama, polenta, Shangri-la, tempura • ayatollah, je ne sais quoi, phenomena

a² \ā\ see AY¹

a³ \ȯ\ see AW¹

aa¹ \a\ see AH³

aa² \ä\ see A¹

aag \äg\ see OG¹

aal¹ \āl\ see AIL

aal² \ȯl\ see ALL¹

aal³ \äl\ see AL¹

aam \äm\ see OM¹

aan \an\ see AN⁵

aans¹ \äns\ see ANCE²

aans² \änz\ see ONZE

aard \ärd\ see ARD¹

aari \är-ē\ see ARI¹

aaron \ar-ən\ see ARON²

aarten \ärt-ᵊn\ see ARTEN

aas \äs\ see OS¹

aatz \ätz\ see OTS

ab¹ \äb\ see OB¹

ab² \äv\ see OLVE²

ab³ \ab\ blab, cab, crab, dab, drab, fab, flab, gab, grab, jab, lab, Lab, nab, scab, slab, stab, tab • Ahab, backstab, confab, prefab, rehab, smack-dab • baobab, taxicab

aba \äb-ə\ casaba • Ali Baba

abah \äb-ə\ see ABA

abard \ab-ərd\ clapboard, scabbard —*also* -ed *forms of verbs listed at* ABBER²

abbard \ab-ərd\ see ABARD

abbas \ab-əs\ see ABBESS

abbat \ab-ət\ see ABIT

abbed¹ \ab-əd\ crabbed, rabid

abbed² \abd\ blabbed, stabbed —*also* -ed *forms of verbs listed at* AB³

abber¹ \äb-ər\ see OBBER

abber² \ab-ər\ blabber, crabber, gabber, grabber, jabber, stabber • backstabber, land-grabber

abbess \ab-əs\ abbess • Barabbas

abbet \ab-ət\ see ABIT

abbey \ab-ē\ see ABBY

abbie¹ \äb-ē\ see OBBY

abbie² \ab-ē\ see ABBY

abbit \ab-ət\ see ABIT

abbitt \ab-ət\ see ABIT

abble¹ \äb-əl\ bauble, cobble, gobble, hobble, Kabul, squabble, wobble

abble² \ab-əl\ Babel, babble, dabble, gabble, rabble, scrabble, Scrabble • hardscrabble • psychobabble, technobabble

abbler \ab-lər\ babbler, dabbler, scrabbler

abbly \ab-lē\ see ABLY

abbot \ab-ət\ see ABIT

abby \ab-ē\ abbey, Abby, blabby, cabbie, crabby, flabby, gabby, grabby, scabby, shabby, tabby

abe¹ \āb\ babe, nabe

abe² \ab\ see AB³

abe³ \ä-bə\ see ABA

abel \ā-bəl\ see ABLE

aben \äb-ən\ see OBIN

aber¹ \ā-bər\ see ABOR
aber² \äb-ər\ see OBBER
abes \ā-bēz\ see ABIES
abi¹ \äb-ē\ see OBBY
abi² \əb-ē\ see UBBY
abi³ \ab-ē\ see ABBY
abid \ab-əd\ see ABBED¹
abies \ā-bēz\ rabies, scabies • antirabies
—also -s, -'s, and -s' forms of nouns listed at ABY
abile \ab-əl\ see ABBLE²
abit \ab-ət\ abbot, habit, rabbit • cohabit, inhabit, jackrabbit
able \ā-bəl\ Abel, able, Babel, cable, fable, gable, label, Mabel, sable, stable, table • disable, enable, round table, timetable, turntable, unable, unstable, worktable
abled \ā-bəld\ fabled, gabled
—also -ed forms of verbs listed at ABLE
ablis \ab-lē\ see ABLY
ably \ab-lē\ chablis, drably
abor \ā-bər\ labor, neighbor, saber • belabor
abot \ab-ət\ see ABIT
abre \äb\ see OB¹
abul \äb-əl\ see ABBLE¹
abulous \ab-yə-ləs\ fabulous • fantabulous
aby \ā-bē\ baby, maybe • crybaby
ac¹ \ak\ see ACK²
ac² \äk\ see OCK¹
ac³ \o̊\ see AW¹
aca¹ \äk-ə\ see AKA¹
aca² \ak-ə\ alpaca • Strait of Malacca
acable \ak-ə-bəl\ see ACKABLE
acao \ō-kō\ see OCO
acas \ak-əs\ fracas • Caracas
acca¹ \ak-ə\ see ACA²
acca² \äk-ə\ see AKA¹
accent \ak-sənt\ accent • relaxant
acchus \ak-əs\ see ACAS
accid \as-əd\ see ACID

acco¹ \ak-ə\ see ACA¹
acco² \ak-ō\ see AKO²
ace¹ \ās\ ace, base, bass, brace, case, chase, face, grace, Grace, lace, mace, Mace, pace, place, race, space, Thrace, trace, vase • abase, airspace, backspace, birthplace, boldface, bookcase, bootlace, briefcase, crankcase, debase, deface, disgrace, displace, dogface, efface, embrace, encase, erase, fireplace, footrace, lactase, misplace, nutcase, outpace, outrace, paleface, replace, retrace, shoelace, showcase, showplace, slipcase, someplace, staircase, suitcase, typeface, unlace, wheelbase, workplace, worst-case • about-face, aerospace, anyplace, commonplace, cyberspace, database, double-space, everyplace, hyperspace, interface, interlace, interspace, lowercase, marketplace, pillowcase, single-space, steeplechase, triple-space, uppercase
ace² \ā-sē\ see ACY
ace³ \äs\ see OS¹
ace⁴ \as\ see ASS³
ace⁵ \äch-ē\ see OTCHY
ace⁶ \äs-ə\ see ASA¹
aceable \ā-sə-bəl\ placeable, traceable • embraceable, erasable, replaceable, untraceable • irreplaceable
acean \ā-shən\ see ATION¹
aced \āst\ based, baste, chaste, faced, haste, laced, paste, taste, waist, waste • bald-faced, barefaced, bold-faced, distaste, foretaste, lambaste, moonfaced, rad waste, shamefaced, snailpaced, slipcased, stone-faced, straight-faced, straitlaced, toothpaste, two-faced • aftertaste, poker-faced • scissors-and-paste
—also -ed forms of verbs listed at ACE¹

aceless \ā-sləs\ baseless, faceless, graceless

aceman \ā-smən\ baseman, spaceman

acement \ā-smənt\ basement, casement, placement • displacement, replacement • bargain-basement

acency \ās-ᵊn-sē\ adjacency, complacency

acent \ās-ᵊnt\ adjacent, complacent

aceor \ā-sər\ see ACER¹

aceous \ā-shəs\ see ACIOUS

acer¹ \ā-sər\ pacer, racer, spacer, tracer • defacer, eraser • steeplechaser

acer² \as-ər\ see ASSER

acet \as-ət\ asset, facet, tacit

acewalking \ās-wȯ-kiŋ\ racewalking, spacewalking

acey \ā-sē\ see ACY

ach¹ \äk\ see OCK¹

ach² \ak\ see ACK²

ach³ \ach\ see ATCH³

acha \äch-ə\ cha-cha, gotcha

ache¹ \āk\ see AKE¹

ache² \ash\ see ASH³

ache³ \äch-ē\ see OTCHY

ache⁴ \ach-ē\ see ATCHY

ached \acht\ attached, detached • unattached
—*also* -ed *forms of verbs listed at* ATCH³

acher \ā-kər\ see AKER¹

achet \ach-ət\ see ATCHET

achi \äch-ē\ see OTCHY

achian \ā-shən\ see ATION¹

achm \am\ see AM²

achment \ach-mənt\ see ATCHMENT

acho \äch-ō\ macho, nacho • gazpacho

acht \ät\ see OT¹

achtsman \ät-smən\ see OTSMAN

achy \ā-kē\ see AKY

acia \ā-shə\ geisha • acacia, Croatia, Dalmatia

acial \ā-shəl\ facial, glacial, racial,

spatial • biracial, palatial • interracial, multiracial

acian \ā-shən\ see ATION¹

acias \ā-shəs\ see ACIOUS

acid \as-əd\ acid, flaccid, placid • antacid, nonacid

acie \ā-shə\ see ACIA

acier¹ \ā-shər\ see ASURE¹

acier² \ā-zhər\ see AZIER

acile \as-əl\ see ASSEL²

acing \ā-siŋ\ bracing, casing, facing, lacing, racing, spacing, tracing • all-embracing, self-effacing
—*also* -ing *forms of verbs listed at* ACE¹

acious \ā-shəs\ gracious, spacious • audacious, bodacious, capacious, curvaceous, fallacious, flirtatious, Ignatius, loquacious, mendacious, pugnacious, rapacious, sagacious, tenacious, ungracious, vivacious, voracious • disputatious, efficacious, ostentatious, perspicacious

acis \as-ē\ see ASSY

acist \ā-səst\ see ASSIST

acit \as-ət\ see ACET

acity¹ \as-tē\ see ASTY²

acity² \as-ət-ē\ audacity, capacity, pugnacity, rapacity, sagacity, tenacity, veracity, vivacity • incapacity • overcapacity

acive \ā-siv\ see ASIVE

ack¹ \äk\ see OCK¹

ack² \ak\ back, black, Braque, clack, crack, flak, hack, jack, Jack, knack, lack, Mac, Mack, pack, plaque, quack, rack, sac, sack, shack, slack, smack, snack, stack, tach, tack, thwack, track, wack, whack, wrack, yak • aback, Amtrak, attack, backpack, backtrack, Balzac, bareback, blackjack, blowback, bushwhack, buyback, callback, carjack, coatrack, cognac, come back, comeback, cossack, cut back, cutback,

drawback, fall back, fallback,
fastback, fast-track, fatback,
feedback, flapjack, flashback,
fullback, greenback, halfback,
half-track, hardback, hatchback,
hayrack, haystack, hijack, hold
back, horseback, humpback,
hunchback, Iraq, jam-pack, jet-
black, kayak, Kazak, kickback,
knapsack, knickknack, laid-back,
macaque, Muzak, one-track,
outback, payback, pitch-black,
play back, playback, racetrack,
ransack, restack, roll back, roll-
back, runback, sad sack, set back,
setback, shellac, sidetrack, six-
pack, skyjack, slapjack, Slovak,
smokestack, snap back, snow-
pack, softback, sumac, swayback,
swept-back, switchback, tarmac,
throwback, thumbtack, ticktack,
touchback, unpack, wisecrack,
wolf pack • almanac, applejack,
back-to-back, bivouac, bric-a-
brac, canvasback, cardiac, crack-
erjack, cul-de-sac, diamondback,
gunnysack, Kodiak, lumberjack,
maniac, medevac, mommy track,
moneyback, multitrack, off-the-
rack, paperback, piggyback,
Pontiac, quarterback, running
back, single-track, Union Jack,
zodiac • Adirondack, biofeed-
back, counterattack, demoniac,
insomniac • egomaniac,
hypochondriac, pyromaniac, sal
ammoniac • megalomaniac

ackable \ak-ə-bəl\ packable, stack-
able

ackal \ak-əl\ see ACKLE

acked \akt\ see ACT

acken \ak-ən\ blacken, slacken

ackened \ak-ənd\ blackened,
slackened

acker \ak-ər\ backer, clacker,
cracker, hacker, jacker, lacquer,
packer, slacker, stacker, tracker

• attacker, backpacker, bush-
whacker, carjacker, firecracker,
graham cracker, hijacker,
kayaker, linebacker, nutcracker,
safecracker, skyjacker,
wisecracker • soda cracker
—*also* -er *forms of adjectives listed
at* ACK²

acket \ak-ət\ bracket, jacket,
packet, racket • dust jacket, flak
jacket, life jacket, straitjacket
• bomber jacket, dinner jacket,
yellowjacket

ackey \ak-ē\ see ACKY

ackguard \ag-ərd\ see AGGARD

ackie \ak-ē\ see ACKY

acking \ak-iŋ\ backing, blacking,
cracking, packing, smacking,
tracking, whacking • bushwhack-
ing, kayaking, meatpacking,
nerve-racking, safecracking,
skyjacking
—*also* -ing *forms of verbs listed at*
ACK²

ackish \ak-ish\ blackish, brackish

ackle \ak-əl\ cackle, crackle,
grackle, jackal, shackle, tackle
• debacle, ramshackle • block and
tackle, tabernacle

ackly \ak-lē\ blackly, slackly • ab-
stractly, compactly, exactly • in-
exactly • matter-of-factly

acko \ak-ō\ see AKO²

ackson \ak-sən\ see AXON

acky \ak-ē\ Jackie, khaki, lackey,
tacky, wacky • Nagasaki, ticky-
tacky

acle¹ \ik-əl\ see ICKLE

acle² \äk\ see OCK¹

acle³ \äk-əl\ see OCKLE

acle⁴ \ak-əl\ see ACKLE

aco \äk-ō\ see OCCO

acon¹ \ā-kən\ see AKEN

acon² \ak-ən\ see ACKEN

acque¹ \ak\ see ACK²

acque² \äk\ see OCK¹

acquer \ak-ər\ see ACKER

acques \äk\ see OCK[1]

acre[1] \ā-kər\ see AKER[1]

acre[2] \ak-ər\ see ACKER

act \akt\ act, backed, bract, cracked, fact, packed, pact, stacked, tact, tracked, tract • abstract, attract, class act, compact, contact, contract, crookbacked, detract, distract, enact, exact, extract, humpbacked, hunchbacked, impact, intact, outact, playact, protract, react, refract, retract, subtract, swaybacked, transact • artifact, cataract, counteract, eye contact, inexact, interact, noncontact, overact, reenact, subcompact, subcontract, vacuum-packed • matter-of-fact, overreact, ultracompact
— also -ed forms of verbs listed at ACK[2]

actable \ak-tə-bəl\ compactible, contractible, distractible, exactable, extractable, intractable, retractable

acte[1] \äkt\ see OCKED

acte[2] \akt\ see ACT

acted \ak-təd\ abstracted, impacted
—also -ed forms of verbs listed at ACT

acter \ak-tər\ see ACTOR

actery \ak-trē\ see ACTORY

actible \ak-tə-bəl\ see ACTABLE

actic \ak-tik\ tactic • climactic, didactic, galactic • chiropractic • anticlimactic, intergalactic

actical \ak-ti-kəl\ practical, tactical • impractical

actice \ak-təs\ cactus, practice • malpractice

actics \ak-tiks\ tactics
—also -s, -'s, and -s' forms of nouns listed at ACTIC

actile \ak-t°l\ tactile • pterodactyl

acting \ak-tiŋ\ acting • exacting, self-acting

—also -ing forms of verbs listed at ACT

action \ak-shən\ action, faction, fraction, traction • abstraction, attraction, contraction, diffraction, distraction, extraction, inaction, infraction, live-action, reaction, refraction, retraction, subtraction, transaction • benefaction, chain reaction, counteraction, interaction, satisfaction • dissatisfaction, overreaction, self-satisfaction • affirmative action

actional \ak-shnəl\ factional, fractional

active \ak-tiv\ active • attractive, inactive, proactive, reactive • hyperactive, interactive, overactive, psychoactive, retroactive, unattractive • radioactive

actly \ak-lē\ see ACKLY

actor \ak-tər\ actor, factor, tractor • contractor, detractor, fudge factor, protractor, reactor, subtracter • benefactor, chiropractor, malefactor, subcontractor

actory \ak-trē\ factory • olfactory, refractory • satisfactory • unsatisfactory

actous \ak-təs\ see ACTICE

actress \ak-trəs\ actress • benefactress

actual \ak-chəl\ actual, factual • contractual

acture \ak-chər\ fracture • compound fracture, manufacture, simple fracture

actus \ak-təs\ see ACTICE

actyl \ak-t°l\ see ACTILE

acular \ak-yə-lər\ oracular, spectacular, vernacular • unspectacular

acy \ā-sē\ Basie, lacy, racy, spacey, Stacy, Tracy • prima facie

acyl \as-əl\ see ASSEL[2]

ad[1] \ä\ see A[1]

ad² \äd\ see OD¹

ad³ \ad\ ad, add, bad, bade, brad, cad, Chad, clad, dad, fad, gad, glad, grad, had, lad, mad, pad, plaid, rad, sad, scad, shad, tad, trad • Baghdad, Belgrade, comrade, Conrad, crash pad, crawdad, doodad, dryad, egad, footpad, forbade, gonad, granddad, ironclad, keypad, launchpad, maenad, mouse pad, naiad, nomad, notepad, reclad, scratch pad, Sinbad, touch pad, triad • armorclad, Galahad, Iliad, legal pad, Leningrad, lily pad, Stalingrad, Trinidad, undergrad, Volgograd • jeremiad, olympiad, Upanishad

ada¹ \äd-ə\ nada • armada, cicada, Granada, Masada, Nevada, tostada • empanada, enchilada, yada yada • Sierra Nevada

ada² \ād-ə\ Ada • armada, cicada, Grenada

adable \ād-ə-bəl\ gradable, tradable • persuadable, upgradable • biodegradable

adah \äd-ə\ see ADA²

adal \ad-ᵊl\ see ADDLE

adam \ad-əm\ Adam, madam • macadam

adan¹ \ad-n\ see ADDEN

adan² \äd-n\ see ODDEN

add \ad\ see AD³

adden \ad-ᵊn\ gladden, madden, sadden • Aladdin

adder \ad-ər\ adder, bladder, gladder, ladder, madder, sadder • air bladder, fish ladder, gallbladder, puff adder, stepladder • Jacob's ladder

addie \ad-ē\ see ADDY¹

addik \äd-ik\ see ODIC

addin \ad-ᵊn\ see ADDEN

adding \ad-iŋ\ padding
—also -ing forms of verbs listed at AD³

addish¹ \äd-ish\ see ODDISH

addish² \ad-ish\ see ADISH

addle \ad-ᵊl\ addle, paddle, saddle, straddle • astraddle, dog paddle, sidesaddle, skedaddle, unsaddle

addler¹ \äd-lər\ see ODDLER

addler² \ad-lər\ paddler, straddler

addock¹ \ad-ik\ see ADIC

addock² \ad-ək\ haddock, paddock

addy¹ \ad-ē\ baddie, caddie, caddy, daddy, faddy, laddie, paddy • granddaddy, tea caddy

addy² \äd-ē\ see ODY¹

ade¹ \ād\ aid, aide, bade, blade, braid, fade, glade, grade, jade, laid, made, maid, paid, raid, rayed, shade, spade, staid, suede, they'd, trade, wade • abrade, afraid, air raid, arcade, Band-Aid, barmaid, Belgrade, blockade, bridesmaid, brigade, brocade, cascade, Cascade, charade, clichéd, cockade, crusade, decade, degrade, dissuade, downgrade, evade, eyeshade, fair-trade, first aid, grenade, handmade, handmaid, homemade, housemaid, inlaid, invade, limeade, low-grade, man-made, mermaid, milkmaid, nightshade, nursemaid, old maid, parade, persuade, pervade, postpaid, repaid, sacheted, self-made, stockade, sunshade, switchblade, tirade, unbraid, unmade, unpaid, upbraid, upgrade, waylaid • accolade, Adelaide, aquacade, balustrade, barricade, cannonade, cavalcade, centigrade, chambermaid, colonnade, custom-made, dairymaid, escapade, esplanade, everglade, foreign aid, hearing aid, legal aid, lemonade, marinade, marmalade, masquerade, Medicaid, meter maid, motorcade, orangeade, palisade, promenade, ready-made, renegade, retrograde, serenade, tailor-made, unafraid, underlaid, visual aid

—*also* -ed *forms of verbs listed at* AY[1]

ade[2] \äd\ *see* OD[1]

ade[3] \ad\ *see* AD[3]

ade[4] \äd-ə\ *see* ADA[2]

adely \ad-lē\ *see* ADLY

aden[1] \ād-ᵊn\ laden, maiden • handmaiden • overladen

aden[2] \äd-ən\ Aden • Baden-Baden

ader \ād-ər\ aider, blader, grader, Nader, nadir, raider, seder, trader • crusader, day trader, evader, fair trader, free trader, horse trader, invader • masquerader, serenader

ades[1] \ād-ēz\ ladies, Hades

ades[2] \ādz\ AIDS • Cascades • Everglades • jack-of-all-trades —*also* -s, -'s, *and* -s' *forms of nouns and* -s *forms of verbs listed at* ADE[1]

adge \aj\ badge, cadge, hajj, Madge

adger \aj-ər\ badger, cadger

adh \äd\ *see* OD[1]

adhe \äd-ē\ *see* ODY[1]

adian \ād-ē-ən\ Acadian, Arcadian, Barbadian, Canadian, circadian • French Canadian, Trinidadian

adic \ad-ik\ haddock • nomadic, sporadic • seminomadic

adie \ād-ē\ *see* ADY

adies \ād-ēz\ *see* ADES[1]

ading \ād-iŋ\ braiding, shading • degrading, unfading —*also* -ing *forms of verbs listed at* ADE[1]

adir \ād-ər\ *see* ADER

adish \ad-ish\ faddish, radish • horseradish

adium \ād-ē-əm\ radium, stadium • palladium

adle \ād-ᵊl\ cradle, dreidel, ladle

adley \ad-lē\ *see* ADLY

adly \ad-lē\ badly, Bradley, gladly, madly, sadly • comradely

adness \ad-nəs\ badness, gladness, madness, sadness

ado[1] \äd-ō\ bravado, mikado • avocado, Colorado, Coronado, desperado, El Dorado • aficionado • incommunicado, Llano Estacado

ado[2] \ād-ō\ credo • Alfredo, Laredo, tornado • desperado, El Dorado

ados \ā-dəs\ *see* ADUS

adrate \äd-rət\ *see* ODERATE

adrian \ā-drē-ən\ Adrian, Adrienne, Hadrian

adrienne \ā-drē-ən\ *see* ADRIAN

adt \ät\ *see* OT[1]

adual \aj-əl\ *see* AGILE

adus \ā-dəs\ Barbados —*also* -s, -'s, *and* -s' *forms of nouns listed at* ADA[2]

ady \ād-ē\ lady, Sadie, shady • bag lady, first lady, landlady, milady, old lady, saleslady • dragon lady, leading lady, painted lady

ae[1] \ā\ *see* AY[1]

ae[2] \ē\ *see* EE[1]

ae[3] \ī\ *see* Y[1]

aea \ē-ə\ *see* IA[1]

aean \ē-ən\ *see* EAN[1]

aedal \ēd-ᵊl\ *see* EEDLE

aedile \ēd-ᵊl\ *see* EEDLE

aegis[1] \ā-jəs\ *see* AGEOUS

aegis[2] \ē-jəs\ *see* EGIS

ael \āl\ *see* AIL

aeli \ā-lē\ *see* AILY

aelic \al-ik\ *see* ALLIC

aemon \ē-mən\ *see* EMON[1]

aen \äⁿ\ *see* ANT[1]

aena \ē-nə\ *see* INA[2]

aenia[1] \ē-nē-ə\ *see* ENIA[1]

aenia[2] \ē-nyə\ *see* ENIA[2]

aens \äⁿs\ *see* ANCE[1]

aeon \ē-ən\ *see* EAN[1]

aera \ir-ə\ *see* ERA[2]

aere[1] \er-ē\ *see* ARY[1]

aere[2] \ir-ē\ *see* EARY

aerial[1] \er-ē-əl\ *see* ARIAL

aerial[2] \ir-ē-əl\ *see* ERIAL

aerie   **8**

aerie¹ \ā-rē\ airy, fairy
aerie² \er-ē\ see ARY¹
aerie³ \ir-ē\ see EARY
aero¹ \er-ō\ see ERO²
aero² \ar-ō\ see ARROW²
aeroe¹ \ar-ō\ see ARROW²
aeroe² \er-ō\ see ERO²
aery¹ \ā-rē\ see AERIE¹
aery² \er-ē\ see ARY¹
aesar \ē-zər\ see EASER²
aestor \ē-stər\ see EASTER
aet \āt\ see ATE¹
aetor \ēt-ər\ see EATER¹
aeum \ē-əm\ see EUM¹
aeus \ē-əs\ see EUS¹
af \af\ see APH
afe¹ \āf\ chafe, safe, strafe, waif
  • fail-safe, unsafe, vouchsafe
  • supersafe
afe² \af\ see APH
afel \äf-əl\ waffle • falafel • Belgian
  waffle
afer \ā-fər\ strafer, wafer
aff \af\ see APH
affable \af-ə-bəl\ affable, laughable
affe \af\ see APH
affed \aft\ see AFT²
affer¹ \äf-ər\ see OFFER¹
affer² \af-ər\ laugher, staffer
affic \af-ik\ see APHIC
affick \af-ik\ see APHIC
affir \af-ər\ see AFFER²
affle¹ \äf-əl\ see AFEL
affle² \af-əl\ baffle, raffle
affy \af-ē\ daffy, taffy
afic \af-ik\ see APHIC
afir \af-ər\ see AFFER²
aft¹ \āft\ waft
  —*also* -ed *forms of verbs listed at*
  OFF¹
aft² \aft\ aft, craft, daft, draft, graft,
  haft, raft, shaft, Taft, waft • abaft,
  aircraft, campcraft, camshaft,
  crankshaft, downdraft, driveshaft,
  handcraft, life raft, redraft, skin
  graft, spacecraft, stagecraft, state-
  craft, updraft, witchcraft, wood-

craft • fore-and-aft, handicraft,
hovercraft, landing craft, under-
staffed, watercraft • antiaircraft
—*also* -ed *forms of verbs listed at*
APH
after \af-tər\ after, crafter, drafter,
  grafter, laughter, rafter • here-
  after, thereafter • handicrafter
aftsman \af-smən\ craftsman,
  draftsman, raftsman • handcrafts-
  man • handicraftsman
afty \af-tē\ crafty, drafty
ag \ag\ bag, brag, crag, drag, fag,
  flag, gag, hag, jag, lag, mag, nag,
  rag, sag, shag, slag, snag, stag,
  swag, tag, wag • air bag, beanbag,
  brown-bag, dirtbag, dishrag, dog
  tag, do-rag, fleabag, flight bag,
  gasbag, grab bag, handbag, ice
  bag, jet lag, mailbag, mixed bag,
  outbrag, phone tag, price tag,
  ragtag, red flag, sandbag, school-
  bag, sight gag, sleazebag, tea bag,
  time lag, tote bag, washrag, wind-
  bag, zigzag • carpetbag, doggie
  bag, duffel bag, garment bag,
  litterbag, lollygag, punching bag,
  saddlebag, scalawag, shopping
  bag, shoulder bag, sleeping bag
  • capture the flag, overnight bag
aga¹ \ä-gə\ bodega, omega
  • rutabaga
aga² \eg-ə\ see EGA¹
agan \ā-gən\ see AGIN
agar¹ \äg-ər\ see OGGER¹
agar² \əg-ər\ see UGGER¹
agate \ag-ət\ see AGGOT
age¹ \äj\ dodge, lodge, raj • barrage, collage, corsage, dislodge,
  garage, hodgepodge, massage
  • camouflage • espionage
age² \äzh\ barrage, collage, corsage, dressage, garage, massage,
  mirage, montage, portage • as-
  semblage, bon voyage, camouflage, decoupage, fuselage,
  sabotage • espionage

age³ \āj\ age, cage, gage, gauge, page, rage, sage, stage, wage • assuage, backstage, birdcage, engage, enrage, front-page, ice age, Iron Age, new age, off-stage, onstage, Osage, outrage, rampage, rib cage, road rage, school age, soundstage, space-age, teenage, uncage, upstage • batting cage, center stage, disengage, legal age, mental age, middle age, multistage, under-age • coming-of-age, minimum wage

age⁴ \āg\ see EG¹

age⁵ \äg-ə\ see AGA¹

aged \ājd\ aged, gauged • engaged • middle-aged
—*also* -ed *forms of verbs listed at* AGE³

agel \ā-gəl\ bagel, Hegel • finagle, inveigle

ageless \āj-ləs\ ageless, wageless

agen¹ \ā-gən\ see AGIN

agen² \ä-gən\ see OGGIN

ageous \ā-jəs\ aegis • courageous, contagious, outrageous • advantageous, noncontagious • disadvantageous

ager¹ \ā-jər\ major, pager, sager, wager • New Ager, teenager • golden-ager, middle-ager, preteenager, Ursa Major

ager² \äg-ər\ see OGGER¹

agey \ā-jē\ see AGY

agga \äg-ə\ see AGA¹

aggar \äg-ər\ see OGGER¹

aggard \ag-ərd\ blackguard, haggard, laggard

agged \ag-əd\ cragged, jagged, ragged

agger \ag-ər\ bagger, dagger, lagger, stagger, swagger, • three-bagger, two-bagger • carpetbagger, cloak-and-dagger

aggie \ag-ē\ see AGGY²

agging \ag-iŋ\ bagging, flagging, lagging, nagging • unflagging • carpetbagging
—*also* -ing *forms of verbs listed at* AG

aggle \ag-əl\ gaggle, haggle, straggle, waggle

aggly \ag-lē\ scraggly, straggly

aggot \ag-ət\ agate, maggot

aggy¹ \äg-ē\ see OGGY¹

aggy² \ag-ē\ baggy, craggy, scraggy, shaggy

agh \ä\ see A¹

agi¹ \äg-ē\ see OGGY¹

agi² \ag-ē\ see AGGY²

agian \ā-jən\ see AJUN

agic \aj-ik\ magic, tragic

agile \aj-əl\ agile, fragile, gradual

agin \ā-gən\ pagan, Reagan • Copenhagen

aging \ā-jiŋ\ aging, raging, staging • unaging
—*also* -ing *forms of verbs listed at* AGE³

agion \ā-jən\ see AJUN

agious \ā-jəs\ see AGEOUS

agm \am\ see AM²

agman \ag-mən\ bagman, flagman

agne \ān\ see ANE¹

ago¹ \äg-ō\ Chicago, farrago • Santiago

ago² \ā-gō\ farrago, Tobago, virago • San Diego • Tierra del Fuego

ago³ \äŋ-gō\ see ONGO

agon \ag-ən\ dragon, flagon, wagon • bandwagon, chuck wagon, Pendragon, snapdragon • covered wagon, paddy wagon, station wagon

agonal \ag-ən-ᵊl\ diagonal, hexagonal, octagonal, pentagonal

agoras \ag-ə-rəs\ Protagoras, Pythagoras

agot \ag-ət\ see AGGOT

agrance \ā-grəns\ flagrance, fragrance

agrant \ā-grənt\ flagrant, fragrant, vagrant

agster \ag-stər\ dragster, gagster
agua \äg-wə\ Managua
• Aconcagua, Nicaragua
ague[1] \āg\ see EG[1]
ague[2] \äg\ see OG[1]
aguey \eg-ē\ see EGGY
agy \ā-jē\ cagey, stagy
ah[1] \ä\ see A[1]
ah[2] \ȯ\ see AW[1]
ah[3] \a\ baa, nah
aha \ä-hä\ aha, Baja
aham \ā-əm\ see AHUM
ahd \äd\ see OD[1]
ahdi \äd-ē\ see ODY[1]
ahdom \äd-əm\ see ODOM
ahib \äb\ see OB[1]
ahl \äl\ see AL[1]
ahler \äl-ər\ see OLLAR
ahlia \ä-lē-ə\ see ALIA
ahma[1] \äm-ə\ see AMA[1]
ahma[2] \am-ə\ see AMA[2]
ahman[1] \äm-ən\ see OMMON
ahman[2] \am-ən\ see AMMON
ahn \än\ see ON[1]
ahms \ämz\ see ALMS
ahnda \än-də\ see ONDA
ahr \är\ see AR[3]
aht \ät\ see OT[1]
ahua \ä-wə\ see AWA[1]
ahum \ä-əm\ Graham, mayhem
ahveh \ä-vä\ see AVE[1]
ai[1] \ā\ see AY[1]
ai[2] \ē\ see EE[1]
ai[3] \ī\ see Y[1]
ai[4] \ȯi\ see OY
a'i \ī\ see Y[1]
aia[1] \ā-ə\ Hosea, Isaiah, Judea
• Himalaya, Mauna Kea
aia[2] \ī-ə\ see IAH[1]
aiad \ī-əd\ see YAD
aiah \ā-ə\ see AIA[1]
aic \ā-ik\ archaic, Hebraic, Judaic, mosaic, prosaic • algebraic, formulaic
aice \ās\ see ACE[1]
aiche \esh\ see ESH[1]
aid[1] \ād\ see ADE[1]

aid[2] \ed\ see EAD[1]
aid[3] \ad\ see AD[3]
aida \ī-də\ see IDA[2]
aide[1] \ād\ see ADE[1]
aide[2] \īd-ē\ see IDAY
aiden \ād-ᵊn\ see ADEN[1]
aider \ād-ər\ see ADER
aiding \ād-iŋ\ see ADING
aido \ī-dō\ see IDO[1]
aids \ādz\ see ADES[2]
aiety \ā-ət-ē\ see AITY
aif \āf\ see AFE[1]
aig \āg\ see EG[1]
aight \āt\ see ATE[1]
aighten \āt-ᵊn\ see ATEN[1]
aightly \āt-lē\ see ATELY[1]
aign \ān\ see ANE[1]
aigne \ān\ see ANE[1]
aignment \ān-mənt\ see AINMENT
aik \īk\ see IKE[2]
aika \ī-kə\ see ICA[1]
ail \āl\ ail, ale, bail, bale, braille, Braille, dale, Dale, fail, flail, frail, gale, Gale, Gayle, grail, hail, hale, jail, kale, mail, male, nail, pail, pale, quail, rail, sail, sale, scale, shale, snail, stale, tail, tale, they'll, trail, vale, veil, wail, whale, Yale
• airmail, assail, avail, bake sale, betrayal, bewail, blackmail, bobtail, broadtail, bud scale, cattail, chain mail, Clydesdale, coattail, cocktail, contrail, curtail, derail, detail, dovetail, downscale, ducktail, e-mail, entail, exhale, fan mail, female, fire sale, fishtail, folktale, full-scale, guardrail, handrail, hangnail, impale, inhale, junk mail, mainsail, outsail, passfail, pigtail, portrayal, presale, prevail, renail, resale, retail, right whale, Scottsdale, shirttail, slop pail, small-scale, snail mail, sperm whale, strong gale, tag sale, telltale, thumbnail, timescale, toenail, toothed whale, topsail, travail, unveil, upscale, voice

mail, wage scale, wassail, white sale, white whale, wholesale, yard sale • Abigail, altar rail, antimale, Chippendale, Chisholm Trail, coffin nail, cottontail, express mail, fairy tale, fingernail, garage sale, ginger ale, Holy Grail, humpback whale, killer whale, monorail, nightingale, old wives' tale, paper trail, pilot whale, ponytail, Richter scale, rummage sale, supersale, swallowtail, tattletale, tooth and nail, vapor trail • certified mail, Fort Lauderdale, Oregon Trail, registered mail, Santa Fe Trail, self-betrayal, sixpenny nail, tenpenny nail

ailable \ā-lə-bəl\ mailable, sailable, salable, scalable • available, resalable, unsalable • unassailable, unavailable

ailand \ī-lənd\ see IGHLAND

aile \ī-lē\ see YLY

ailed \āld\ mailed, nailed, sailed, scaled, tailed, veiled • detailed, pigtailed, unveiled • ponytailed
—*also* -ed *forms of verbs listed at* AIL

ailer \ā-lər\ bailer, baler, jailer, mailer, sailor, scaler, tailor, Taylor, trailer, wailer, whaler • blackmailer, derailleur, detailer, e-mailer, house trailer, retailer, self-mailer, wholesaler • semitrailer
—*also* -er *forms of adjectives listed at* AIL

ailey \ā-lē\ see AILY

ailie \ā-lē\ see AILY

ailiff \ā-ləf\ bailiff, caliph

ailing \ā-liŋ\ failing, mailing, railing, sailing, veiling, whaling • boardsailing, prevailing, retailing, unfailing • parasailing
—*also* -ing *forms of verbs listed at* AIL

aille[1] \āl\ see AIL

aille[2] \ī\ see Y[1]

aille[3] \īl\ see ILE[1]

aille[4] \ä-yə\ see AYA[1]

ailles \ī\ see Y[1]

ailleur \ä-lər\ see AILER

ailment \āl-mənt\ ailment • derailment

ailor \ā-lər\ see AILER

ails \ālz\ see ALES[1]

aily \ā-lē\ daily, gaily, scaly • Israeli • ukulele

aim \ām\ see AME[1]

aimable \ā-mə-bəl\ see AMABLE

aiman \ā-mən\ see AMEN[1]

aimant \ā-mənt\ see AYMENT

aiment \ā-mənt\ see AYMENT

aimer \ā-mər\ framer, gamer, lamer, tamer • disclaimer, proclaimer • Hall of Famer

aimless \ām-ləs\ see AMELESS

ain[1] \ā-ən\ see AYAN[1]

ain[2] \ān\ see ANE[1]

ain[3] \en\ see EN[1]

ain[4] \in\ see IN[1]

ain[5] \īn\ see INE[1]

ain[6] \a^n\ see IN[4]

aina \ī-nə\ see INA[1]

ainable \ā-nə-bəl\ stainable, trainable • attainable, containable, explainable, obtainable, restrainable, sustainable • unattainable, uncontainable, unobtainable

aine[1] \ān\ see ANE[1]

aine[2] \en\ see EN[1]

ained \ānd\ brained, caned, craned, drained, grained, pained, stained, strained, veined • birdbrained, bloodstained, coarsegrained, contained, harebrained, ingrained, lamebrained, restrained, tearstained, unfeigned, unstained, untrained • featherbrained, multipaned, scatterbrained, self-contained, unexplained, unrestrained
—*also* -ed *forms of verbs listed at* ANE[1]

ainer \ā-nər\ drainer, gainer,

planer, stainer, strainer, trainer
• abstainer, campaigner, complainer, container, explainer, nobrainer, obtainer, retainer
• aquaplaner, entertainer
—*also* -er *forms of adjectives listed at* ANE[1]

ainful \ān-fəl\ baneful, gainful, painful • disdainful

aininess \ā-nē-nəs\ braininess, graininess

aining \ā-nin\ complaining, sustaining, weight training • selfsustaining, uncomplaining
—*also* -ing *forms of verbs listed at* ANE[1]

ainless \ān-ləs\ brainless, painless, stainless

ainly \ān-lē\ mainly, plainly, sanely, vainly • humanely, insanely, profanely, ungainly • inhumanely

ainment \ān-mənt\ arraignment, attainment, containment, detainment • edutainment, entertainment, infotainment, self-containment

aino \ī-nō\ see INO[1]

ains \ānz\ reins • cremains, Great Plains, remains
—*also* -s, -'s, *and* -s' *forms of nouns and* -s *forms of verbs listed at* ANE[1]

aint \ānt\ ain't, faint, feint, mayn't, paint, quaint, saint, taint • acquaint, complaint, constraint, greasepaint, oil paint, repaint, restraint, war paint • head restraint, patron saint, plaster saint, self-restraint • Latter-Day Saint, luminous paint

ain't \ānt\ see AINT

ainting \ān-tin\ oil painting, wall painting • finger painting
—*also* -ing *forms of verbs listed at* AINT

aintly \ānt-lē\ faintly, quaintly, saintly

ainy \ā-nē\ brainy, grainy, rainy, zany • Khomeini • Allegheny

ainz \īnz\ see INES[3]

aipse \āps\ see APES

air[1] \er\ see ARE[4]

air[2] \īr\ see IRE[1]

aira \ī-rə\ see YRA

aird \erd\ see AIRED

aire[1] \er\ see ARE[4]

aire[2] \ir\ see EER[2]

aire[3] \īr\ see IRE[1]

aired \erd\ laird • fair-haired, impaired, long-haired, prepared, shorthaired, unpaired, wirehaired
• multilayered, underprepared, unimpaired
—*also* -ed *forms of verbs listed at* ARE[4]

airer \er-ər\ see EARER[1]

aires[1] \er\ see ARE[4]

aires[2] \ar-ēs\ see ARES[2]

airess[1] \er-əs\ see ERROUS

airess[2] \ar-əs\ see ARIS[2]

airie \er-ē\ see ARY[1]

airing \er-in\ see ARING[1]

airish \er-ish\ see ARISH[1]

airist \er-əst\ see ARIST

airly \er-lē\ barely, fairly, rarely, squarely

airn \ern\ see ERN[1]

airo \ī-rō\ see YRO[1]

airs \erz\ theirs • downstairs, nowheres, somewheres, upstairs • foreign affairs, musical chairs
—*also* -s, -'s, *and* -s' *forms of nouns and* -s *forms of verbs listed at* ARE[4]

airy[1] \er-ē\ see ARY[1]

airy[2] \ā-rē\ see AERIE[1]

ais \ā\ see AY[1]

aisal[1] \ā-zəl\ see ASAL

aisal[2] \ī-səl\ see ISAL[1]

aisant \ās-³nt\ see ACENT

aise[1] \āz\ see AZE[1]

aise[2] \ez\ see AYS[1]

aiser[1] \ā-zər\ see AZER

aiser² \ī-zər\ see IZER
aisian \ā-zhən\ see ASION
aisin \āz-ᵊn\ see AZON
aising \ā-ziŋ\ blazing, glazing, hazing, phrasing • amazing, appraising, fund-raising, hair-raising, stargazing, trailblazing
 • crystal gazing
—*also* -ing *forms of verbs listed at* AZE¹
aisle \īl\ see ILE¹
aisley \āz-lē\ paisley, nasally
aisne \ān\ see ANE¹
aisse \ās\ see ACE¹
aisson \ās-ᵊn\ see ASON¹
aist¹ \ā-əst\ see AYEST
aist² \äst\ see ACED
aist³ \äst\ see OST¹
aisy \ā-zē\ see AZY
ait¹ \ā\ see AY¹
ait² \āt\ see ATE¹
ait³ \īt\ see ITE¹
ait⁴ \at\ see AT⁵
aite \īt\ see ITE¹
aited \āt-əd\ see ATED
aiten \āt-ᵊn\ see ATEN¹
aiter \āt-ər\ see ATOR
aith \āth\ eighth, faith, Faith, wraith • good faith
aithe \āth\ see AITH
aiti \āt-ē\ see ATY
aitian \ā-shən\ see ATION¹
aiting \āt-iŋ\ see ATING
aitly \āt-lē\ see ATELY¹
aitor \āt-ər\ see ATOR
aitour \āt-ər\ see ATOR
aity \ā-ət-ē\ deity, gaiety • spontaneity
aius \ī-əs\ see IAS¹
aiva \ī-və\ see IVA¹
aive \āv\ see AVE²
aix \ā\ see AY¹
aize \āz\ see AZE¹
aj \äj\ see AGE¹
aja¹ \ä-hä\ see AHA
aja² \ī-ə\ see IAH¹
ajan \ā-jən\ see AJUN

ajj \aj\ see ADGE
ajor \ā-jər\ see AGER¹
ajun \ā-jən\ Cajun • contagion
ak¹ \äk\ see OCK¹
ak² \ak\ see ACK²
aka¹ \äk-ə\ Dhaka, Oaxaca, Osaka • Lake Titicaca
aka² \ak-ə\ see ACA²
akable \ā-kə-bəl\ breakable, shakable • mistakable, nonbreakable, unbreakable • unmistakable
akan \ak-ən\ see ACKEN
akar \äk-ər\ see OCKER
ake¹ \āk\ ache, bake, Blake, brake, break, cake, drake, Drake, fake, flake, Jake, lake, make, quake, rake, sake, shake, sheikh, slake, snake, spake, stake, steak, take, wake • air brake, awake, backache, beefsteak, caretake, cheesecake, cheesesteak, clambake, cupcake, daybreak, disc brake, earache, earthquake, fast break, firebreak, fish cake, forsake, fruitcake, green snake, hand brake, handshake, headache, heartache, heartbreak, hotcake, housebreak, intake, jailbreak, keepsake, king snake, milk snake, mistake, muckrake, namesake, opaque, outbreak, outtake, pancake, partake, pound cake, prebake, rat snake, remake, retake, rewake, seaquake, sea snake, shortcake, snowflake, sponge cake, toothache, uptake, windbreak • bellyache, coffee break, coral snake, Crater Lake, double take, garter snake, give-and-take, Great Salt Lake, Great Slave Lake, griddle cake, hognose snake, johnnycake, make-or-break, minute steak, overtake, parking brake, patty-cake, piece of cake, plumber's snake, rattlesnake, station break, stomachache, undertake, water snake,

wedding cake • Salisbury steak, tension headache, upside-down cake • emergency brake, Lady of the Lake, potato pancake

ake² \ak\ see ACK²

ake³ \äk-ē\ see OCKY

aked \ākt\ awaked, half-baked, sunbaked
—*also* -ed *forms of verbs listed at* AKE[1]

aken \ā-kən\ bacon, Macon, shaken, taken, waken • awaken, forsaken, mistaken, retaken, unshaken • godforsaken, over-taken, undertaken

aker¹ \ā-kər\ acre, baker, breaker, faker, maker, Quaker, shaker • backbreaker, caretaker, car-maker, dressmaker, filmmaker, gill raker, glassmaker, heartbreaker, homemaker, house-breaker, icebreaker, jawbreaker, kingmaker, lawbreaker, lawmaker, mapmaker, match-maker, muckraker, noisemaker, pacemaker, peacemaker, print-maker, sailmaker, saltshaker, shirtmaker, shoemaker, snow-maker, steelmaker, strikebreaker, tiebreaker, toolmaker, watch-maker, windbreaker, winemaker, wiseacre • automaker, bellyacher, circuit breaker, coffee maker, moviemaker, papermaker, pepper shaker, troublemaker, undertaker • cabinetmaker, policymaker

aker² \ak-ər\ see ACKER

akery \ā-krē\ bakery, fakery

akes \āks\ cornflakes, Great Lakes, sweepstakes
—*also* -s, -'s, *and* -s' *forms of nouns and* -s *forms of verbs listed at* AKE[1]

ake-up \ā-kəp\ break up, breakup, make up, makeup, rake up, shake-up, shake up, take up, wake-up

akey \ā-kē\ see AKY

akh \äk\ see OCK[1]

aki¹ \äk-ē\ see OCKY

aki² \ak-ē\ see ACKY

akian \äk-ē-ən\ see OCKIAN

aking \ak-iŋ\ see ACKING

ako¹ \äk-ō\ see OCCO

ako² \ak-ō\ wacko • tobacco

aky \ā-kē\ achy, cakey, flaky, shaky, snaky • headachy

al¹ \äl\ doll, loll, sol • atoll, Baikal, cabal, chorale, Nepal, real • aerosol, femme fatale, parasol, Portugal, protocol, Senegal • Ne-anderthal

al² \el\ see EL[1]

al³ \ȯl\ see ALL[1]

al⁴ \al\ gal, pal, Val • canal, chorale, corral, decal, locale, morale • femme fatale, rationale • Guadalcanal

ala¹ \äl-ä\ à la, Allah, gala

ala² \äl-ə\ Allah, gala • Kampala, koala, Valhalla • ayotollah, Guatemala

ala³ \ā-lə\ gala • Venezuela

ala⁴ \al-ə\ Allah, gala • Valhalla

alable \ā-lə-bəl\ see AILABLE

alace \al-əs\ see ALIS²

alad \al-əd\ see ALID²

alam \äl-əm\ see OLUMN

alan \al-ən\ see ALLON

alance \al-əns\ balance, valance • imbalance, rebalance • counter-balance, overbalance, platform balance

alap \al-əp\ see ALLOP²

alar \ā-lər\ see AILER

alary \al-ə-rē\ calorie, gallery, salary, Valerie • rogues' gallery

alas \al-əs\ see ALIS²

alate \al-ət\ see ALLET²

ald¹ \ȯld\ bald, scald, walled • so-called • Archibald, Buchenwald, coveralled
—*also* -ed *forms of verbs listed at* ALL[1]

ald² \ólt\ see ALT
alder \ól-dər\ alder, balder
ale¹ \ā-lē\ see AILY
ale² \āl\ see AIL
ale³ \äl\ see AL¹
ale⁴ \al\ see AL⁴
ale⁵ \äl-ē\ see OLLY¹
ale⁶ \al-ē\ see ALLY⁴
alea \ā-lē-ə\ see ALIA
aleck¹ \el-ik\ see ELIC
aleck² \al-ik\ see ALLIC
aled \āld\ see AILED
aleigh¹ \äl-ē\ see OLLY¹
aleigh² \ól-ē\ see AWLY
alement \āl-mənt\ see AILMENT
alen \ä-lən\ see OLLEN⁵
alent \al-ənt\ see ALLANT
alep \al-əp\ see ALLOP²
aler¹ \ā-lər\ see AILER
aler² \äl-ər\ see OLLAR
alerie \al-ə-rē\ see ALARY
ales¹ \ālz\ sales, Wales • entrails
 • New South Wales, Prince of
 Wales • cat-o'-nine-tails
 —also -s, -'s, and -s' forms of
 nouns and -s forms of verbs listed
 at AIL
ales² \äl-əs\ see OLIS
alet \al-ət\ see ALLET²
alette \al-ət\ see ALLET²
aley \ā-lē\ see AILY
alf \af\ see APH
alfa \al-fə\ see ALPHA
algia \al-jə\ neuralgia, nostalgia
ali¹ \äl-ē\ see OLLY¹
ali² \al-ē\ see ALLY⁴
ali³ \ó-lē\ see AWLY
ali⁴ \ā-lē\ see AILY
alia \ā-lē-ə\ Australia, azalea, re-
 galia • bacchanalia • parapherna-
 lia
alian¹ \ā-lē-ən\ alien • Australian,
 mammalian • bacchanalian
 • Episcopalian
alian² \al-yən\ see ALLION
alic \al-ik\ see ALLIC
alice \al-əs\ see ALIS²

alid¹ \äl-əd\ see OLID
alid² \al-əd\ ballad, pallid, salad,
 valid • invalid • Caesar salad,
 Waldorf salad
alien \ā-lē-ən\ see ALIAN¹
aling \ā-liŋ\ see AILING
alinist \äl-ə-nəst\ see OLONIST
alinn \al-ən\ see ALLON
alion¹ \ā-lē-ən\ see ALIAN¹
alion² \al-yən\ see ALLION
aliph \ā-ləf\ see AILIFF
alis¹ \ā-ləs\ see AYLESS
alis² \al-əs\ Alice, callous, callus,
 chalice, Dallas, malice, palace
 • aurora borealis
alist \al-əst\ ballast, callused
ality¹ \äl-ət-ē\ jollity, quality
 • equality, frivolity • coequality,
 inequality
ality² \al-ət-ē\ brutality, fatality,
 finality, formality, frugality, legal-
 ity, locality, mentality, morality,
 mortality, neutrality, rascality,
 reality, totality, vitality • abnor-
 mality, actuality, amorality, cor-
 diality, factuality, functionality,
 generality, geniality, hospitality,
 illegality, immorality, immortal-
 ity, informality, joviality, logical-
 ity, musicality, nationality,
 personality, practicality, punctu-
 ality, rationality, sensuality, sexu-
 ality, technicality, triviality,
 unreality • congeniality, eventual-
 ity, impartiality, impracticality,
 irrationality, municipality, origi-
 nality, sentimentality, spirituality,
 split personality, theatricality,
 universality • artificiality, confi-
 dentiality, constitutionality, indi-
 viduality, unconventionality,
 virtual reality
alk \ók\ balk, caulk, chalk, gawk,
 hawk, squawk, stalk, talk, walk
 • back talk, Black Hawk, board-
 walk, cakewalk, catwalk, corn-
 stalk, crosswalk, eyestalk, fish

hawk, jaywalk, leafstalk, marsh
hawk, Mohawk, moonwalk,
nighthawk, Norfolk, outtalk, pep
talk, racewalk, ropewalk,
shoptalk, sidewalk, sleepwalk,
small talk, space walk, sweet-talk,
trash talk • baby talk, double-
talk, Kitty Hawk, pillow talk,
power walk, sparrow hawk, toma-
hawk

alker \ȯ-kər\ gawker, hawker,
squawker, stalker, walker • jay-
walker, sleepwalker, spacewalker
• double-talker

alkie \ȯ-kē\ balky, chalky, gawky,
gnocchi, stalky, talky • Milwau-
kee • walkie-talkie

alking \ȯ-kiŋ\ caulking, walking
• racewalking, spacewalking
—*also* -ing *forms of verbs listed at*
ALK

alkland \ȯk-lənd\ see AUCKLAND

alky \ȯ-kē\ see ALKIE

all¹ \ȯl\ all, awl, ball, bawl, brawl,
call, crawl, doll, drawl, fall, gall,
hall, haul, mall, maul, pall, Paul,
Saul, scrawl, shawl, small, sprawl,
squall, stall, tall, trawl, wall, y'all,
yawl • and all, appall, air ball, at
all, atoll, AWOL, baseball, Baikal,
beach ball, beanball, befall, bird-
call, blackball, brick wall, catcall,
cell wall, close call, cornball,
cure-all, curveball, de Gaulle,
dodgeball, downfall, drywall,
duck call, eight ball, enthrall,
eyeball, fair ball, fastball, fireball,
fire wall, foosball, football, fore-
stall, foul ball, free-fall, game
ball, golf ball, goofball, googol,
hair ball, handball, hardball,
holdall, house call, install, John
Paul, jump ball, landfall, meat-
ball, menthol, mess hall, moth-
ball, Nepal, nightfall, oddball,
paintball, pinball, pitfall, pratfall,
prayer shawl, puffball, rainfall,
rainsquall, recall, roll call, Saint
Paul, screwball, seawall, short-
haul, shortfall, sidewall, sleaze-
ball, slimeball, snowball, snowfall,
softball, sour ball, spitball, stick-
ball, stonewall, stone wall, strip
mall, tell-all, toll call, town hall,
U-Haul, windfall, withdrawal,
you-all • above all, aerosol, after
all, alcohol, all in all, basketball,
borough hall, butterball, cannon-
ball, carryall, caterwaul, city hall,
climbing wall, conference call,
coverall, crystal ball, curtain call,
Donegal, ethanol, free-for-all,
gasohol, judgment call, know-it-
all, knuckleball, methanol, music
hall, Montreal, off-the-wall, over-
all, overhaul, paddleball, parasol,
protocol, racquetball, reinstall,
Senegal, shopping mall, study
hall, superball, tetherball, unin-
stall, urban sprawl, volleyball,
wake-up call, wall-to-wall, warts-
and-all, waterfall, wherewithal
• cholesterol, hole-in-the-wall,
medicine ball, Neanderthal, total
recall

all² \äl\ see AL¹

all³ \al\ see AL⁴

alla¹ \äl-ə\ see ALA²

alla² \al-ə\ see ALLOW⁴

allace \äl-əs\ see OLIS

allad \al-əd\ see ALID²

allage \al-ə-jē\ see ALOGY²

allah¹ \äl-ä\ see ALA¹

allah² \äl-ə\ see ALA²

allah³ \al-ə\ see ALLOW⁴

allan \al-ən\ see ALLON

allant \al-ənt\ gallant, talent

allas \al-əs\ see ALIS²

allast \al-əst\ see ALIST

alle¹ \al\ see AL⁴

alle² \al-ē\ see ALLY⁴

alle³ \äl-ē\ see OLLY¹

alled \ȯld\ see ALD¹

allee \al-ē\ see ALLY⁴

allen \al-ən\ see ALLON
aller¹ \ȯ-lər\ bawler, brawler, caller, crawler, drawler, hauler, mauler, scrawler, smaller, squaller, taller, trawler • installer, night crawler • melon baller
aller² \al-ər\ pallor, valor
alles \ī-əs\ see IAS¹
allet¹ \äl-ət\ see OLLET
allet² \al-ət\ ballot, mallet, palate, palette, pallet, valet • secret ballot
alley \al-ē\ see ALLY⁴
alli \al-ē\ see ALLY⁴
allic \al-ik\ Gaelic, italic • metallic, smart aleck • nonmetallic
allid \al-əd\ see ALID²
allie \al-ē\ see ALLY⁴
alling \ȯ-liŋ\ calling, drawling, falling, galling, hauling, mauling, Pauling, stalling • appalling, name-calling
—also -ing *forms of verbs listed at* ALL¹
allion \al-yən\ scallion, stallion • battalion, Italian, medallion, rapscallion
allis¹ \al-əs\ see ALIS²
allis² \al-ē\ see ALLY⁴
allis³ \äl-əs\ see OLIS
allish \ȯ-lish\ smallish, tallish
allit \ä-lət\ see OLLET
allith¹ \äl-əs\ see OLIS
allith² \äl-ət\ see OLLET
allo \äl-ō\ see OLLOW¹
allon \al-ən\ Alan, Allen, gallon, talon
allop¹ \äl-əp\ see OLLOP
allop² \al-əp\ gallop, scallop • bay scallop, sea scallop
allor \al-ər\ see ALLER²
allory \al-ə-rē\ see ALARY
allot \al-ət\ see ALLET²
allous \al-əs\ see ALIS²
allow¹ \el-ō\ see ELLO
allow² \äl-ə\ see ALA²
allow³ \äl-ō\ see OLLOW¹
allow⁴ \al-ō\ callow, fallow, hallow, shallow, tallow • marsh-mallow
allows \al-ōz\ gallows
—also -s, -'s, *and* -s' *forms of nouns listed at* ALLOW⁴
alls \ȯlz\ Angel Falls • Niagara Falls, Yellowstone Falls • Victoria Falls, Yosemite Falls
—also -s, -'s, *and* -s' *forms of nouns and* -s *forms of verbs listed at* ALL¹
allused \al-əst\ see ALIST
ally¹ \ā-lē\ see AILY
ally² \äl-ē\ see OLLY¹
ally³ \ȯ-lē\ see AWLY
ally⁴ \al-ē\ alley, dally, galley, rally, Sally, tally, valley • blind alley, Death Valley, finale, Nepali • Central Valley, dillydally, Great Rift Valley, Mexicali, shilly-shally, Tin Pan Alley • lily of the valley, Yosemite Valley
allyn \al-ən\ see ALLON
alm \äm\ see OM¹
almar \äm-ər\ see OMBER¹
almer \äm-ər\ see OMBER¹
almily \äm-ə-lē\ see OMALY
almish \äm-ish\ see AMISH¹
almist \äm-ist\ psalmist • Islamist
almon \am-ən\ see AMMON
alms \ämz\ alms, Brahms, Psalms
—also -s, -'s, *and* -s' *forms of nouns and* -s *forms of verbs listed at* OM¹
almy \äm-ē\ see AMI¹
alo \äl-ō\ see OLLOW¹
aloe \al-ō\ see ALLOW⁴
alogist \äl-ə-jəst\ see OLOGIST
alogy¹ \äl-ə-jē\ see OLOGY
alogy² \al-ə-jē\ analogy • mineralogy
alom \äl-əm\ see OLUMN
alon \al-ən\ see ALLON
alop \al-əp\ see ALLOP²
alor¹ \äl-ər\ see OLLAR
alor² \al-ər\ see ALLER²
alorie \al-ə-rē\ see ALARY
alory \al-ə-rē\ see ALARY

alp \alp\ alp, scalp
alpha \al-fə\ alpha • alfalfa
alque \ȯk\ see ALK
alsa \ȯl-sə\ balsa, salsa
alse \ȯls\ false, waltz
alt \ȯlt\ fault, halt, malt, salt, vault, volt, Walt • asphalt, assault, basalt, cobalt, default, exalt, no-fault, pole vault, rock salt • garlic salt, somersault, table salt • San Andreas Fault
alta \äl-tə\ Malta, Yalta
altar \ȯl-tər\ see ALTER
alter \ȯl-tər\ altar, alter, falter, halter, vaulter, Walter • Gibraltar, pole-vaulter
alti \ȯl-tē\ see ALTY
alting \ȯl-tiŋ\ halting, salting, vaulting
  —also -ing forms of verbs listed at ALT
altless \ȯlt-ləs\ faultless, saltless
alto \al-tō\ alto • contralto • Palo Alto
alty \ȯl-tē\ faulty, salty
altz \ȯls\ see ALSE
alus¹ \ā-ləs\ see AYLESS
alus² \al-əs\ see ALIS²
alve¹ \äv\ see OLVE²
alve² \alv\ salve, valve • bivalve • safety valve, univalve
alve³ \av\ calve, halve, have, salve
alvin \al-vən\ Alvin, Calvin
aly \al-ē\ see ALLY⁴
alysis \al-ə-səs\ analysis, dialysis, paralysis
am¹ \äm\ see OM¹
am² \am\ am, clam, cram, dam, damn, damned, Graham, gram, ham, jam, jamb, lam, lamb, ma'am, Pam, ram, Sam, scam, scram, sham, slam, spam, swam, yam • exam, grand slam, imam, logjam, madame, Mailgram, program, webcam • Abraham, Amsterdam, Boulder Dam, cablegram, centigram, cryptogram, diagram, diaphragm, epigram, giant clam, hard-shell clam, hexagram, hologram, Hoover Dam, kilogram, milligram, Minicam, monogram, pentagram, pictogram, reprogram, Rotterdam, self-exam, soft-shell clam, Suriname, telegram, Uncle Sam • Grand Coulee Dam, ideogram, Virginia ham • parallelogram
ama¹ \äm-ə\ Brahma, comma, drama, lama, llama, mama, momma • pajama • Dalai Lama, diorama, docudrama, Fujiyama, melodrama, panorama, Suriname, Yokohama
ama² \am-ə\ Brahma, drama, gamma, mamma • da Gama, Miami, pajama • Alabama, diorama, docudrama, melodrama, panorama
amable \ā-mə-bəl\ blamable, claimable, framable, nameable, tamable
aman¹ \ā-mən\ see AMEN¹
aman² \äm-ən\ see OMMON
amant \ā-mənt\ see AYMENT
amash \äm-ish\ see AMISH¹
amateur \am-ət-ər\ see AMETER
amba \äm-bə\ mamba, samba
ambar¹ \äm-bər\ see OMBER²
ambar² \am-bər\ amber, Amber, clamber, timbre
amber¹ \am-bər\ see AMBAR²
amber² \am-ər\ see AMMER
ambia \am-bē-ə\ Gambia, Zambia
amble¹ \äm-bəl\ see EMBLE
amble² \am-bəl\ amble, bramble, gamble, ramble, scramble • unscramble
ambler \am-blər\ gambler, rambler, scrambler • unscrambler
ambol \am-bəl\ see AMBLE²
ame¹ \ām\ aim, blame, came, claim, dame, fame, flame, frame, game, lame, maim, name, same, shame, tame • A-frame, acclaim,

aflame, airframe, ball game, became, big game, big-name, board game, brand name, code name, declaim, defame, disclaim, exclaim, first name, inflame, last name, mainframe, mind game, misname, nickname, no-name, pen name, place-name, postgame, pregame, proclaim, reclaim, reframe, rename, selfsame, surname, time frame, trade name, war game • all the same, arcade game, counterclaim, domain name, family name, given name, Hall of Fame, just the same, maiden name, overcame, singing game, waiting game • baptismal name, name of the game, video game

ame² \äm\ see OM¹

ame³ \am\ see AM²

ame⁴ \äm-ə\ see AMA¹

ameable \ā-mə-bəl\ see AMABLE

amed \āmd\ named • ashamed
• unashamed
—*also* -ed *forms of verbs listed at* AME¹

amel \am-əl\ see AMMEL

ameless \ām-ləs\ aimless, blameless, nameless, shameless

amely \ām-lē\ gamely, lamely, namely, tamely

amen¹ \ā-mən\ caiman, Cayman, Haman, layman, shaman, stamen, Yemen • Grand Cayman, highwayman

amen² \äm-ən\ see OMMON

ameness \ām-nəs\ lameness, sameness, tameness • selfsameness

ament \ā-mənt\ see AYMENT

amer \ā-mər\ see AIMER

ames \āmz\ James • fun and games
• Olympic Games
—*also* -s, -'s, *and* -s' *forms of nouns and* -s *forms of verbs listed at* AME¹

ameter \am-ət-ər\ amateur • diam-

eter, hexameter, parameter, pentameter, tetrameter

amfer \am-pər\ see AMPER²

ami¹ \äm-ē\ balmy, mommy, palmy, swami, Tommy • pastrami, salami, tsunami • origami

ami² \am-ə\ see AMA²

ami³ \am-ē\ see AMMY

amic¹ \ō-mik\ see OMIC²

amic² \am-ik\ ceramic, dynamic
• panoramic, undynamic • aerodynamic, thermodynamic

amics \äm-iks\ see OMICS

amie¹ \ā-mē\ Amy, Jamie, Mamie
• cockamamy

amie² \am-ē\ see AMMY

amil¹ \äm-əl\ see OMMEL¹

amil² \am-əl\ see AMMEL

amin \am-ən\ see AMMON

amine \am-ən\ see AMMON

aming \ā-miŋ\ flaming, framing, gaming
—*also* -ing *forms of verbs listed at* AME¹

amish¹ \äm-ish\ Amish • schoolmarmish

amish² \am-ish\ Amish, famish

amist \äm-əst\ see ALMIST

amity \am-ət-ē\ amity • calamity

amma \am-ə\ see AMA²

ammable \am-ə-bəl\ flammable
• inflammable, nonflammable, programmable • diagrammable

ammal \am-əl\ see AMMEL

ammar \am-ər\ see AMMER

amme \am\ see AM²

ammel \am-əl\ camel, mammal
• enamel

ammer \am-ər\ clamber, clamor, crammer, glamour, grammar, hammer, jammer, scammer, slammer, spammer, stammer, yammer • clawhammer, enamor, jackhammer, programmer, sledgehammer • ball-peen hammer, yellowhammer

ammes \äm-əs\ see OMISE

ammie \am-ē\ see AMMY

amming \am-iŋ\ damning • programming
—*also* -ing *forms of verbs listed at* AM[2]

ammon \am-ən\ famine, salmon • backgammon, examine • cross-examine

ammy \am-ē\ chamois, clammy, Grammy, jammy, mammy, Sammy, whammy • Miami • double whammy

amn \am\ see AM[2]

amned \am\ see AM[2]

amning \am-iŋ\ see AMMING

amois \am-ē\ see AMMY

amon[1] \ā-mən\ see AMEN[1]

amon[2] \am-ən\ see OMMON

amor \am-ər\ see AMMER

amorous \am-rəs\ amorous, clamorous, glamorous

amos \ā-məs\ see AMOUS

amour \am-ər\ see AMMER

amous \ā-məs\ Amos, famous • ignoramus, Nostradamus

amp[1] \ämp\ see OMP[1]

amp[2] \ä^m\ see ANT[1]

amp[3] \amp\ amp, camp, champ, clamp, cramp, damp, lamp, ramp, scamp, stamp, tamp, tramp, vamp • arc lamp, boot camp, break camp, C-clamp, death camp, floor lamp, food stamp, off-ramp, on-ramp, revamp, sunlamp, tax stamp, time-stamp, unclamp • labor camp, postage stamp, rubber-stamp, writer's cramp

amper[1] \äm-pər\ see OMPER

amper[2] \am-pər\ camper, damper, hamper, pamper, scamper, tamper • happy camper

amphor \am-fər\ see AMFER

ampi[1] \äm-pē\ see OMPY

ampi[2] \am-pē\ see AMPY

ample \am-pəl\ ample, sample, trample • example • for example

ampy \am-pē\ crampy, scampi

amus[1] \ā-məs\ see AMOUS

amus[2] \äm-əs\ see OMISE

amy \ā-mē\ see AMIE[1]

an[1] \ä^n\ see ANT[1]

an[2] \än\ see ON[1]

an[3] \ən\ see UN[1]

an[4] \aŋ\ see ANG[2]

an[5] \an\ an, Ann, ban, bran, can, clan, Dan, fan, Jan, man, Nan, pan, plan, ran, scan, span, Stan, tan, van, Van • adman, afghan, Afghan, ape-man, Batman, bedpan, began, best man, Bhutan, birdman, boss man, caftan, caiman, CAT scan, caveman, Cayman, Cèzanne, chessman, Cheyenne, Chopin, deadpan, Diane, dishpan, divan, doorman, dustpan, flight plan, frogman, game plan, G-man, Greenspan, headman, he-man, Iran, Japan, jazzman, Joanne, Koran, life span, Luanne, madman, mailman, Milan, milkman, newsman, oilcan, oilman, oil pan, old man, oneman, outran, pecan, plowman, point man, postman, Queen Anne, Qur'an, rattan, Roseanne, routeman, Roxanne, Ruthann, Saipan, sandman, saucepan, sedan, snowman, spaceman, Spokane, spray can, straight man, strongman, stuntman, Sudan, suntan, Suzanne, Tarzan, tin can, toucan, trainman, trashman, vegan, Walkman, wingspan, wise man, yes-man • also-ran, anchorman, bogeyman, boogeyman, businessman, cameraman, caravan, cattleman, countryman, defenseman, family man, frying pan, garageman, garbageman, handyman, Julianne, Kazakhstan, Ku Klux Klan, Kurdistan, Kyrgyzstan, leading man, man-to-man, Marianne, master plan, middleman, minivan, minuteman, mountain man, muscleman, om-

anchor

budsman, overran, Pakistan, Parmesan, partisan, Peter Pan, plainclothesman, Ramadan, rather than, repairman, selectman, serviceman, spick-and-span, superman, Superman, Teheran, Turkistan, weatherman, workingman, Yucatan • Afghanistan, attention span, bipartisan, catamaran, cavalryman, committeeman, deliveryman, medicine man, newspaperman, orangutan, radioman, Raggedy Ann, Tajikistan, Turkmenistan, Uzbekistan, watering can

an⁶ \äng\ see ONG¹

an⁷ \änt\ see ANT²

ana¹ \än-ə\ Anna, Donna, fauna, Ghana, Lana • Botswana, iguana, Madonna, mañana, nirvana, piranha, Tijuana • French Guiana, prima donna, Rosh Hashanah • Americana

ana² \ā-nə\ Dana, Lana

ana³ \an-ə\ Anna, Ghana, Hannah, Lana • banana, bandanna, cabana, Diana, Guiana, Guyana, gymkhana, Havana, hosanna, Joanna, Montana, savanna, Susanna • French Guiana, Indiana, Juliana, Mariana, poinciana, Pollyanna, Santa Ana • Americana, Louisiana

anacle \an-i-kəl\ see ANICAL

anagh \an-ə\ see ANA³

anah¹ \ō-nə\ see ONA¹

anah² \än-ə\ see ANA¹

analyst \an-ᵊl-ist\ analyst, panelist • psychoanalyst

anan \an-ən\ see ANNON

anary \an-rē\ see ANNERY

anate \an-ət\ see ANNET

anc¹ \aⁿ\ see ANT¹

anc² \aŋ\ see ANG²

anc³ \aŋk\ see ANK

anca \aŋ-kə\ Sanka • Casablanca

ance¹ \äⁿs\ nuance, Provence, séance • diligence, renaissance • insouciance • pièce de résistance
—*also* -s, -'s *and* -s'*forms of nouns and* -s *forms of verbs listed at* ANT¹

ance² \äns\ Hans • nuance, response, séance • nonchalance, renaissance

ance³ \ans\ chance, dance, France, glance, lance, Lance, prance, stance, trance • advance, askance, barn dance, break-dance, by chance, enhance, entrance, expanse, finance, freelance, line dance, outdance, romance, sideglance, snake dance, square dance, sun dance, sweatpants, tap dance, war dance • at first glance, ballroom dance, belly dance, circumstance, fighting chance, game of chance, happenstance, in advance, Port-au-Prince, refinance, smarty-pants, song and dance, underpants
—*also* -s, -'s, *and* -s' *forms of nouns and* -s *forms of verbs listed at* ANT⁵

ancement \an-smənt\ advancement, enhancement • self-advancement

ancer \an-sər\ answer, cancer, dancer • break-dancer, freelancer, line dancer, lung cancer, nondancer, square dancer, tap dancer • anticancer, ballroom dancer, belly dancer • Tropic of Cancer

ances \an(t)-səs\ see ANCIS

anch¹ \änch\ see AUNCH¹

anch² \ȯnch\ see AUNCH²

anch³ \anch\ blanch, Blanche, branch, ranch, stanch • dude ranch • avalanche, olive branch

anche¹ \anch\ see ANCH³

anche² \an-chē\ see ANCHY

anchi \an-chē\ see ANCHY

anchion \an-chən\ see ANSION

anchor \aŋ-kər\ see ANKER

anchy \an-chē\ branchy
• Comanche

ancial \an-chəl\ see ANTIAL

ancis \an(t)-səs\ Frances, Francis
• Aransas
—*also* -s, -'s, *and* -s' *forms of nouns and* -s *forms of verbs listed at* ANCE³

anck \änk\ see ONK¹

anco \äŋ-kō\ see ONCO

ancor \aŋ-kər\ see ANKER

ancre \aŋ-kər\ see ANKER

anct \aŋt\ see ANKED

ancy \an-sē\ chancy, fancy, Nancy

and¹ \äⁿ\ see ANT¹

and² \änd\ see OND¹

and³ \and\ and, band, bland, brand, canned, gland, grand, hand, land, manned, sand, stand, strand • armband, at hand, backhand, badland, bandstand, brass band, broadband, brushland, cabstand, coastland, command, cowhand, crash-land, cropland, deckhand, demand, disband, dockhand, dreamland, expand, farmhand, farmland, field hand, firebrand, firsthand, forehand, freehand, gangland, grandstand, grassland, handstand, hatband, headband, headstand, heartland, homeland, hour hand, Iceland, inland, kickstand, Lapland, lefthand, longhand, mainland, marshland, newsstand, nightstand, offhand, oil gland, old hand, on hand, parkland, playland, quicksand, rangeland, right-hand, shorthand, stagehand, swampland, sweatband, sweat gland, Thailand, thirdhand, waistband, washstand, wasteland, watchband, wetland, withstand, wristband • baby grand, beforehand, bellyland, borderland, contraband, countermand, Dixieland, fairyland, fatherland, Ferdinand, forestland, garage band, hand in hand, helping hand, high command, Holy Land, meadowland, minute hand, motherland, narrowband, no-man's-land, on demand, one-man band, out of hand, overhand, pastureland, promised land, public land, reprimand, Rio Grande, rubber band, Samarkand, secondhand, sleight of hand, taxi stand, timberland, try one's hand, understand, wonderland • misunderstand, multiplicand, to beat the band, vacationland • never-never land • Alice-in-Wonderland
—*also* -ed *forms of verbs listed at* AN⁵

and⁴ \än\ see ON¹

and⁵ \änt\ see ANT²

anda¹ \an-də\ panda • Amanda, Miranda, Uganda, veranda • giant panda, memoranda, propaganda

anda² \än-də\ see ONDA

andable \an-də-bəl\ expandable
• understandable

andaed \an-dəd\ see ANDED

andal \an-d°l\ see ANDLE

andaled \an-d°ld\ handled • wellhandled
—*also* -ed *forms of verbs listed at* ANDLE

andall \an-d°l\ see ANDLE

andam \an-dəm\ see ANDUM

andar \ənd-ər\ see UNDER

ande¹ \ən\ see UN¹

ande² \an\ see AN⁵

ande³ \an-dē\ see ANDY

ande⁴ \and\ see AND³

ande⁵ \än-də\ see ONDA

anded \an-dəd\ banded, branded, candid, handed, landed, stranded
• backhanded, bare-handed, highhanded, left-handed, one-handed, red-handed, right-handed, shorthanded, two-handed • emptyhanded, evenhanded,

heavy-handed, singlehanded, underhanded
—also -ed *forms of verbs listed at* AND³

andel \an-dᵊl\ see ANDLE
andem \an-dəm\ see ANDUM
ander¹ \en-dər\ see ENDER
ander² \än-dər\ see ONDER¹
ander³ \an-dər\ blander, brander, candor, gander, grander, grandeur, pander, sander, slander • bystander, commander, demander, left-hander, meander, right-hander • Alexander, coriander, salamander, wing commander
anders \an-dərz\ Flanders
—also -s, -'s, *and* -s' *forms of nouns and* -s *forms of verbs listed at* ANDER³
andes \an-dēz\ Andes
—also -s, -'s, *and* -s' *forms of nouns and* -s *forms of verbs listed at* ANDY
andeur \an-dər\ see ANDER³
andhi \an-dē\ see ANDY
andi \an-dē\ see ANDY
andible \an-də-bəl\ see ANDABLE
andid \an-dəd\ see ANDED
anding \an-diŋ\ branding, standing • commanding, crash landing, freestanding, long-standing, outstanding, upstanding • belly landing, mind-expanding, notwithstanding, pancake landing, understanding • instrument landing, misunderstanding
—also -ing *forms of verbs listed at* AND³
andish \an-dish\ blandish, brandish • outlandish
andist \an-dəst\ blandest, grandest • propagandist
andle \an-dᵊl\ candle, Handel, handle, Randall, sandal, scandal, vandal • manhandle, mishandle, panhandle • Roman candle, votive candle

andled \an-dᵊl\ see ANDALED
andly \an-lē\ see ANLY
ando \an-dō\ Brando • commando, Fernando, Orlando • San Fernando
andom \an-dəm\ see ANDUM
andor \an-dər\ see ANDER³
andra \an-drə\ Sandra • Cassandra • Alexandra
andrea \an-drē-ə\ see ANDRIA
andres \an-dərz\ see ANDERS
andria \an-drē-ə\ Andrea, Alexandria
andsome \an-səm\ see ANSOM
andum \an-dəm\ random, tandem • memorandum
andy \an-dē\ Andy, bandy, brandy, Brandy, candy, dandy, handy, Randy, sandy, Sandy • ear candy, eye candy, hard candy, jim-dandy, rock candy, unhandy • cotton candy, Rio Grande
ane¹ \ān\ bane, brain, Cain, cane, chain, crane, Crane, Dane, deign, drain, Duane, feign, gain, grain, Jane, lane, main, Maine, mane, pain, pane, plain, plane, rain, reign, rein, sane, Seine, skein, slain, Spain, sprain, stain, strain, train, vain, vane, vein, wane, Wayne, Zane • abstain, again, air lane, airplane, attain, Bahrain, biplane, birdbrain, bloodstain, brain drain, campaign, champagne, Champlain, choke chain, chow mein, cocaine, complain, constrain, contain, detain, disdain, domain, Elaine, explain, eyestrain, fast lane, floodplain, food chain, germane, Great Dane, Helene, humane, Hussein, inane, ingrain, insane, lamebrain, left brain, lo mein, Lorraine, maintain, membrane, methane, midbrain, migraine, mundane, New Spain, obtain, octane, ordain, pertain, plain-Jane, profane,

propane, ptomaine, raise Cain,
refrain, remain, restrain, retain,
retrain, right brain, sea-lane,
seaplane, sustain, tearstain, ter-
rain, Ukraine, unchain, urbane,
warplane • acid rain, aeroplane,
aquaplane, Aquitaine, ascertain,
bullet train, cell membrane, cello-
phane, Charlemagne, down the
drain, entertain, featherbrain, free
throw lane, high-octane, hurri-
cane, inclined plane, inhumane,
Mary Jane, memory lane, mono-
plane, multigrain, multilane,
Novocain, novocaine, overtrain,
pollen grain, preordain, reattain,
sandhill crane, scatterbrain, Spanish Main, sugarcane, Tamerlane,
toilet train, wagon train, water
main, weather vane, whooping
crane, windowpane • Serengeti
Plain

ane² \an\ see AN⁵

ane³ \än-ə\ see ANA¹

ane⁴ \än\ see ON¹

anea \ā-nē-ə\ see ANIA

anean \ā-nē-ən\ see ANIAN

aned \änd\ see AINED

anee \an-ē\ see ANNY

aneful \ān-fəl\ see AINFUL

anel \an-ᵊl\ see ANNEL

anelist \an-ᵊl-əst\ see ANALYST

aneous \ā-nē-əs\ extraneous, spon-
taneous • instantaneous, miscella-
neous, simultaneous
• contemporaneous, extempora-
neous

aner¹ \ā-nər\ see AINER

aner² \än-ər\ see ONOR¹

anet \an-ət\ see ANNET

aneum \ā-nē-əm\ see ANIUM

aney \ȯ-nē\ see AWNY¹

ang¹ \äŋ\ see ONG¹

ang² \aŋ\ bang, clang, dang, fang,
gang, hang, rang, sang, slang,
sprang, tang, twang • bang-bang,
big bang, chain gang, ginseng,

harangue, meringue, mustang,
shebang, slam-bang • antigang,
boomerang, give a hang, inter-
gang, overhang • orangutan

ang³ \ȯŋ\ see ONG²

anga \äŋ-gə\ see ONGA

angar \aŋ-ər\ see ANGER²

ange \ānj\ change, mange, range,
strange • arrange, chump change,
derange, estrange, exchange, free-
range, long-range, short-range,
shortchange, small change • Cascade Range, disarrange, driving
range, interchange, post
exchange, prearrange, rearrange,
stock exchange, Teton Range,
Wasatch Range • Alaska Range,
Aleutian Range

angel \aŋ-gəl\ see ANGLE

angell \aŋ-gəl\ see ANGLE

angement \ānj-mənt\ arrangement,
derangement, estrangement • pre-
arrangement, rearrangement

anger¹ \ān-jər\ changer, danger,
manger, ranger, stranger
• arranger, endanger, exchanger,
lone ranger, shortchanger • forest
ranger, money changer, Texas
Ranger • dog in the manger

anger² \aŋ-ər\ hangar, hanger
• cliff-hanger, coat hanger, head-
banger • paperhanger

anger³ \aŋ-gər\ anger, clangor

angi \aŋ-ē\ see ANGY²

angie \aŋ-ē\ see ANGY²

anging¹ \ān-jiŋ\ unchanging, wide-
ranging
—*also* -ing *forms of verbs listed at*
ANGE

anging² \aŋ-iŋ\ hanging • paper-
hanging
—*also* -ing *forms of verbs listed at*
ANG²

angle \aŋ-gəl\ angle, bangle, dan-
gle, jangle, mangle, spangle, stran-
gle, tangle, wangle, wrangle
• entangle, quadrangle, rectangle,

right angle, triangle, untangle, wide-angle • disentangle • Bermuda Triangle

angled \aŋ-gəld\ angled, tangled • newfangled, right-angled, star-spangled
—also -ed *forms of verbs listed at* ANGLE

angler \aŋ-glər\ angler, strangler, wrangler

angling \aŋ-gliŋ\ angling, gangling
—also -ing *forms of verbs listed at* ANGLE

angly \aŋ-glē\ gangly, jangly

ango \aŋ-gō\ mango, tango • fandango

angor¹ \aŋ-ər\ see ANGER²

angor² \aŋ-gər\ see ANGER³

angour \aŋ-gər\ see ANGER²

angster \aŋ-stər\ gangster, prankster

angue \aŋ\ see ANG²

anguer \aŋ-ər\ see ANGER²

anguish \aŋ-gwish\ anguish, languish

anguor \aŋ-ər\ see ANGER²

angy¹ \ān-jē\ mangy, rangy

angy² \aŋ-ē\ tangy, twangy

anha \än-ə\ see ANA¹

ani¹ \än-ē\ Bonnie, bonny, Connie, Donnie, Ronnie, tawny • afghani, Irani • Modigliani, Pakistani • mulligatawny

ani² \an-ē\ see ANNY

ania \ā-nē-ə\ mania • Tasmania • egomania, kleptomania, Lithuania, Mauritania, Oceania, Pennsylvania, pyromania, Transylvania • megalomania

anian \ā-nē-ən\ Albanian, Iranian, Jordanian, Romanian, Ukrainian • Lithuanian, Pennsylvanian, subterranean • Mediterranean

aniard \an-yərd\ lanyard, Spaniard

anic \an-ik\ manic, panic • Germanic, Hispanic, mechanic, organic, satanic, titanic, volcanic

• aldermanic, inorganic, messianic, oceanic, pre-Hispanic • transoceanic

anical \an-i-kəl\ manacle • botanical, mechanical, tyrannical • puritanical

anice \an-əs\ see ANISE

anicle \an-i-kəl\ see ANICAL

anics \an-iks\ annex, panics • mechanics

aniel¹ \an-ᵊl\ see ANNEL

aniel² \an-yəl\ see ANUAL¹

anion \an-yən\ banyan, canyon • Bryce Canyon, companion, Grand Canyon, Hells Canyon

anis \an-əs\ see ANISE

anise \an-əs\ anise, Janice, Janis • Johnannes • Scipio Africanus

anish \an-ish\ banish, clannish, mannish, Spanish, tannish, vanish

anister \an-ə-stər\ banister, canister

anite \an-ət\ see ANNET

anity \an-ət-ē\ sanity, vanity • humanity, insanity, profanity • Christianity, inhumanity

anium \ā-nē-əm\ cranium • geranium, titanium, uranium

ank \aŋk\ bank, blank, clank, crank, dank, drank, flank, franc, frank, Frank, hank, lank, plank, prank, rank, sank, shank, shrank, spank, stank, swank, tank, thank, yank, Yank • gangplank, outflank, outrank, point-blank, sandbank, snowbank, state bank, think tank, West Bank • antitank, data bank, draw a blank, Georges Bank, national bank, piggy bank, riverbank, walk the plank • clinkety-clank

anka \aŋ-kə\ see ANCA

anked \aŋt\ tanked • sacrosanct
—also -ed *forms of verbs listed at* ANK

ankee \aŋ-kē\ see ANKY

anker \aŋ-kər\ anchor, banker,

26

canker, flanker, hanker, rancor,
tanker, thanker • supertanker
—also -er *forms of adjectives listed
at* ANK
ankh \äŋk\ see ONK[1]
ankie \aŋ-kē\ see ANKY
ankish \aŋ-kish\ crankish, prank-
ish
ankle \aŋ-kəl\ ankle, rankle
ankly \aŋ-klē\ blankly, frankly
anks \aŋs\ see ANX
ankster \aŋ-stər\ see ANGSTER
anky \aŋ-kē\ cranky, hankie,
lanky, skanky, swanky, Yankee
• hanky-panky
anley \an-lē\ see ANLY
anli \an-lē\ see ANLY
anly \an-lē\ blandly, grandly,
manly, Stanley • unmanly
ann[1] \an\ see AN[5]
ann[2] \än\ see ON[1]
anna[1] \än-ə\ see ANA[1]
anna[2] \an-ə\ see ANA[3]
annah \an-ə\ see ANA[3]
annalist \an-ᵊl-əst\ see ANALYST
annan \an-ən\ see ANNON
anne \an\ see AN[5]
anned \and\ see AND[3]
annel \an-ᵊl\ channel, Daniel,
flannel, panel • impanel • English
Channel
anner \an-ər\ banner, canner,
manner, manor, planner, scanner,
tanner • city planner
annery \an-rē\ cannery, granary,
tannery
annes \an-əs\ see ANISE
annet \an-ət\ granite, Janet, planet
• pomegranate
annexe \an-iks\ see ANICS
annibal \an-ə-bəl\ cannibal, Hanni-
bal
annic \an-ik\ see ANIC
annie \an-ē\ see ANNY
annin \an-ən\ see ANNON
annish \an-ish\ see ANISH
annon \an-ən\ cannon • Buchanan

annous \an-əs\ see ANISE
anns \anz\ see ANS[4]
annual \an-yəl\ see ANUAL[1]
anny \an-ē\ Annie, canny, cranny,
Danny, fanny, granny, Lanny,
nanny • afghani, uncanny • Hin-
dustani, hootenanny
ano[1] \än-ō\ guano • Chicano, piano, soprano • grand piano
• mezzo-soprano, player piano,
upright piano
ano[2] \an-ō\ piano, soprano
• mezzo-soprano
anon \an-ən\ see ANNON
anor \an-ər\ see ANNER
anous \an-əs\ see ANISE
anqui \aŋ-kē\ see ONKY
ans[1] \äns\ see ANCE[2]
ans[2] \änz\ see ONZE
ans[3] \ans\ see ANCE[3]
ans[4] \anz\ Hans
—also -s, -'s, *and* -s' *forms of
nouns and* -s *forms of verbs listed
at* AN[5]
ans[5] \aⁿ\ see ANT[1]
ansard \an-sərd\ see ANSWERED
ansas \an(t)-səs\ see ANCIS
anse \ans\ see ANCE[3]
anser \an-sər\ see ANCER
ansion \an-chən\ mansion • expan-
sion
ansom \an-səm\ handsome, ransom • king's ransom
answer \an-sər\ see ANCER
answered \an-sərd\ answered,
mansard • unanswered
ansy \an-zē\ pansy, tansy • chimpanzee
ant[1] \äⁿ\ croissant, Mont Blanc,
Rouen, savant • aide-de-camp,
denouement
ant[2] \änt\ aunt, can't, flaunt, font,
fount, gaunt, taunt, want • gallant, grandaunt, piedmont, savant, Vermont • commandant,
confidant, debutante, dilettante,
nonchalant, restaurant

ant³ \ənt\ see ONT¹

ant⁴ \ȯnt\ see AUNT¹

ant⁵ \ant\ ant, aunt, can't, chant, grant, Grant, pant, plant, rant, scant, shan't, slant • eggplant, enchant, extant, fire ant, gallant, grandaunt, houseplant, implant, jade plant, land grant, recant, replant, savant, seed plant, supplant, transplant, white ant • adamant, commandant, confidant, confidante, cormorant, covenant, dilettante, gallivant, pitcher plant, power plant, rubber plant, spider plant, sycophant • flowering plant

anta \ant-ə\ Fanta, manta, Santa • Atlanta

antal \änt-ᵊl\ see ONTAL¹

antam \ant-əm\ bantam, phantom

antar \ant-ər\ see ANTER²

ante¹ \än-tā\ Brontë, Dante • andante

ante² \änt\ see ANT²

ante³ \ant\ see ANT⁵

ante⁴ \änt-ē\ see ANTI¹

ante⁵ \ant-ē\ ante, chantey, pantie, scanty, shanty • andante • vigilante

anted \an-təd\ disenchanted
—also -ed forms of verbs listed at ANT⁵

anter¹ \änt-ər\ see AUNTER¹

anter² \ant-ər\ banter, canter, granter, grantor, planter • decanter, enchanter, implanter • tam-o'-shanter

antes \an-tēz\ antes • Cervantes

antey \ant-ē\ see ANTE⁵

anther \an-thər\ anther, panther • Black Panther

anti¹ \änt-ē\ Brontë, jaunty • andante

anti² \ant-ē\ see ANTE⁵

antial \an-chəl\ substantial • circumstantial, insubstantial, nonfinancial, unsubstantial

antic \ant-ik\ antic, frantic • Atlantic, gigantic, pedantic, romantic • North Atlantic, transatlantic, unromantic

antie \ant-ē\ see ANTE⁵

anting¹ \ant-iŋ\ planting • enchanting
—also -ing forms of verbs listed at ANT⁵

anting² \ənt-iŋ\ see UNTING

antis \ant-əs\ mantis • Atlantis

anto \än-tō\ Squanto • Toronto

antom \ant-əm\ see ANTAM

antor \ant-ər\ see ANTER²

antos \an-təs\ see ANTIS

antre \ant-ər\ see ANTER²

ants \ans\ see ANCE³

antus \ant-əs\ see ANTIS

anty \ant-ē\ see ANTE⁵

anual¹ \an-yəl\ annual, Daniel, spaniel • biannual, field spaniel, Nathaniel • cocker spaniel, semiannual, springer spaniel, water spaniel

anual² \an-yə-wəl\ annual, manual, Manuel • biannual, Emmanuel, Immanuel • semiannual • Victor Emmanuel

anuel \an-yəl\ see ANUAL²

anus¹ \ā-nəs\ see AYNESS

anus² \an-əs\ see ANISE

anx \aŋs\ thanks • Fairbanks, Grand Banks, phalanx • Outer Banks
—also -s, -'s, and -s' forms of nouns and -s forms of verbs listed at ANK

any¹ \ā-nē\ see AINY

any² \en-ē\ see ENNY

anyan \an-yən\ see ANION

anyard \an-yərd\ see ANIARD

anyon \an-yən\ see ANION

anz \ans\ see ANCE³

anza \an-zə\ stanza • bonanza • Sancho Panza • extravaganza

anzee \an-zē\ see ANSY

ao¹ \ā-ō\ see EO¹

ao² \ō\ see OW¹
ao³ \au̇\ see OW²
aoighis \āsh\ see ECHE¹
aole \au̇-lē\ see OWLY²
aône \ōn\ see ONE¹
aori \au̇r-ē\ see OWERY
aos¹ \au̇s\ see OUSE²
aos² \ä-äs\ chaos, Laos
aotian \ō-shən\ see OTION
aow \au̇\ see OW²
ap¹ \äp\ see OP¹
ap² \əp\ see UP
ap³ \ap\ cap, chap, clap, flap, gap, gape, hap, lap, Lapp, map, nap, nape, pap, rap, sap, scrap, slap, snap, strap, tap, trap, wrap, yap, zap • bootstrap, burlap, catnap, cell sap, claptrap, death cap, death trap, dunce cap, dewlap, dognap, earflap, entrap, enwrap, firetrap, gift wrap, hubcap, ice cap, jockstrap, kidnap, kneecap, madcap, mishap, mousetrap, mud flap, nightcap, on tap, pace lap, recap, remap, road map, sand trap, shrink-wrap, skullcap, skycap, snowcap, speed trap, stopgap, unsnap, unstrap, unwrap, whitecap, wiretap • baseball cap, beat the rap, blasting cap, booby trap, gangsta rap, giddyap, gingersnap, handicap, leghold trap, on the map, overlap, photomap, rattletrap, relief map, shoulder strap, stocking cap, thinking cap, thunderclap, tourist trap, weather map • Venus flytrap
apable \ā-pə-bəl\ capable • escapable, incapable • inescapable
apal \ā-pəl\ see APLE
apboard \ab-ərd\ see ABARD
ape¹ \āp\ ape, cape, crape, crepe, drape, gape, grape, nape, scrape, shape, tape • agape, cloudscape, duct tape, escape, great ape, landscape, man ape, misshape, moonscape, North Cape, red tape, reshape, Scotch tape, sea grape, seascape, shipshape, snowscape, take shape, townscape, undrape • Barbary ape, cityscape, fire escape, masking tape, ticker tape, waterscape • audiotape, adhesive tape, anthropoid ape, bent out of shape, magnetic tape, videotape
ape² \ap\ see AP³
ape³ \äp-ē\ see OPPY
ape⁴ \ap-ē\ see APPY
apel \ap-əl\ see APPLE
apelin \ap-lən\ see APLAIN
apen \ā-pən\ capon • misshapen
aper \ā-pər\ caper, draper, gaper, paper, scraper, shaper, taper, tapir, vapor • crepe paper, flypaper, graph paper, landscaper, newspaper, notepaper, reshaper, sandpaper, skyscraper, tar paper, term paper, wallpaper, wastepaper, waxed paper • butcher paper, carbon paper, funny paper, tissue paper, toilet paper, tracing paper, writing paper
apery \ā-prē\ drapery, papery, vapory
apes \āps\ traipse
—*also* -s, -'s, *and* -s' *forms of nouns and* -s *forms of verbs listed at* APE¹
aph \af\ calf, chaff, gaffe, graph, half, laugh, staff, staph • bar graph, behalf, carafe, Falstaff, flagstaff, giraffe, half-staff, horselaugh, line graph, riffraff • autograph, bathyscaphe, circle graph, epigraph, epitaph, half-and-half, lithograph, paragraph, phonograph, photograph, polygraph, seismograph, telegraph, understaff • choreograph
aphe¹ \āf\ see AFE¹
aphe² \af\ see APH
apher \af-ər\ see AFFER²
aphic \af-ik\ graphic, traffic • autographic, biographic, demographic,

geographic, lithographic, phono-
graphic, photographic, seismo-
graphic, telegraphic, typographic
• choreographic

api \äp-ē\ see OPPY

apid \ap-əd\ rapid, vapid

apir \ā-pər\ see APER

apist \ā-pist\ rapist • escapist,
landscapist

aplain \ap-lən\ chaplain, Chaplin,
sapling

aple \ā-pəl\ maple, papal, staple
• red maple, rock maple • antipa-
pal, sugar maple

aples \ā-pəlz\ Naples, staples

apless \ap-ləs\ hapless, strapless

aplin \ap-lə-n\ see APLAIN

aply \ap-lē\ see APTLY

apo \äp-ō\ capo • da capo, gestapo

apon \ā-pən\ see APEN

apor \ā-pər\ see APER

apory \ā-prē\ see APERY

apour \ā-pər\ see APER

app \ap\ see AP³

appable \ap-ə-bəl\ mappable • re-
cappable, unflappable

appalli \äp-ə-lē\ see OPOLY

appe \ap\ see AP³

apped \apt\ see APT

apper¹ \äp-ər\ see OPPER

apper² \ap-ər\ clapper, dapper,
flapper, mapper, rapper, snapper,
tapper, trapper, wrapper, yapper,
zapper • backslapper, catnapper,
dognapper, dust wrapper, kidnap-
per, knee-slapper, red snapper,
thigh slapper, wiretapper
• gangsta rapper, whippersnapper

apphic \af-ik\ see APHIC

appie \äp-ē\ see OPPY

appily \ap-ə-lē\ happily, snappily
• unhappily

appiness \ap-ē-nəs\ happiness,
sappiness, snappiness • unhappi-
ness

apping \ap-iŋ\ capping, mapping,
strapping, trapping, wrapping

—*also* -ing *forms of verbs listed at*
AP³

apple \ap-əl\ apple, chapel, dapple,
grapple, scrapple • crab apple,
mayapple, pineapple, thorn apple
• Adam's apple

apps \aps\ see APSE

appy \ap-ē\ gappy, happy, sappy,
scrappy, snappy • serape,
slaphappy, unhappy • trigger-
happy

aps \aps\ see APSE

apse \aps\ chaps, lapse, taps, traps
• collapse, elapse, perhaps, re-
lapse, time-lapse

—*also* -s, -'s, *and* -s' *forms of*
nouns and -s *forms of verbs listed*
at AP³

apt \apt\ apt, rapt • adapt, snow-
capped, untapped

—*also* -ed *forms of verbs listed at*
AP³

apter \ap-tər\ captor, chapter,
raptor • adapter • oviraptor • ve-
lociraptor

aption \ap-shən\ caption • adap-
tion, contraption, miscaption

aptive \ap-tiv\ captive • adaptive

aptly \ap-lē\ aptly, raptly

aptor \ap-tər\ see APTER

apture \ap-chər\ rapture • enrap-
ture, recapture

apy \ap-ē\ see APPY

aq¹ \äk\ see OCK¹

aq² \ak\ see ACK²

aqi \äk-ē\ see OCKY

aque¹ \āk\ see AKE¹

aque² \ak\ see ACK²

aqui \äk-ē\ see OCKY

ar¹ \er\ see ARE⁴

ar² \ȯr\ see OR¹

ar³ \är\ are, bar, car, char, czar, far,
gar, jar, mar, noir, our, par, R,
scar, spar, star, tar, tsar, tzar • afar,
ajar, all-star, bazaar, bizarre,
boudoir, boxcar, Bronze Star, cash
bar, cigar, costar, cougar, crossbar,

crowbar, disbar, Dog Star, feldspar, film noir, five-star, fixed star, flatcar, four-star, guitar, Gunnar, Hagar, handcar, horsecar, hussar, Ishtar, jaguar, Jaguar, Kevlar, leaf scar, lounge car, lumbar, Lamar, lodestar, Magyar, memoir, Mylar, NASCAR, North Star, pace car, pine tar, polestar, prowl car, pulsar, Qatar, quasar, radar, railcar, raw bar, rebar, Renoir, roll bar, sandbar, scout car, shofar, sidecar, slot car, snack bar, solar, sonar, sports bar, sports car, stock car, streetcar, tank car, T-bar, toolbar, town car, unbar • air guitar, arctic char, au revoir, avatar, blazing star, Bolívar, bumper car, cable car, caviar, coffee bar, color bar, command car, commissar, dining car, double star, evening star, exemplar, falling star, giant star, handlebar, Indy car, insofar, isobar, jaguar, Jaguar, Kandahar, Leyden jar, mason jar, megastar, millibar, minibar, minicar, Miramar, morning star, motorcar, multicar, muscle car, Myanmar, neutron star, open bar, registrar, rent-a-car, repertoire, reservoir, rising star, salad bar, samovar, scimitar, seminar, shooting star, Silver Star, sleeping car, steel guitar, superstar, touring car, turbocar, VCR, Zanzibar • anti-roll bar, Doppler radar, Madagascar, Mount Palomar, radio car, radio star • Hawaiian guitar, horizontal bar

ara[1] \är-ə\ Laura • Guevara, Gomorrah, saguaro, tiara • capybara, sayonara • Guadalajara

ara[2] \er-ə\ see ERA[1]

ara[3] \ar-ə\ see ARROW[1]

ara[4] \òr-ə\ see ORA

arab \ar-əb\ Arab, Carib, carob, scarab • pan-Arab • anti-Arab

arable \ar-ə-bəl\ arable, bearable, parable, shareable, wearable • declarable, nonarable, unbearable

aracen \ar-ə-sən\ see ARISON

aracin \ar-ə-sən\ see ARISON

arage \ar-ij\ see ARRIAGE

aragon \ar-ə-gən\ paragon, tarragon

arah[1] \er-ə\ see ERA[1]

arah[2] \ar-ə\ see ARROW[1]

aral[1] \ar-əl\ see ARREL[2]

aral[2] \ər-əl\ see ERRAL

aralee \er-ə-lē\ see ARILY

aran[1] \er-ən\ see ARON[1]

aran[2] \ar-ən\ see ARON[2]

arant[1] \er-ənt\ see ARENT[1]

arant[2] \ar-ənt\ see ARENT[2]

araoh[1] \er-ō\ see ERO[1]

araoh[2] \ar-ō\ see ARROW[2]

aras \är-əs\ see ORRIS[1]

arass \ar-əs\ see ARIS[2]

arat \ar-ət\ carat, caret, carrot, karat, parrot • disparate

arate \ar-ət\ see ARAT

arative[1] \er-ət-iv\ declarative, imperative

arative[2] \ar-ət-iv\ narrative • comparative, declarative

arb \ärb\ barb, carb, garb • rhubarb

arbel \är-bəl\ see ARBLE

arber \är-bər\ see ARBOR

arble \är-bəl\ barbel, garble, marble

arboard \är-bərd\ barbered, larboard, starboard

arbor \är-bər\ arbor, barber, harbor • Ann Arbor, Pearl Harbor

arc[1] \äk\ see OCK[1]

arc[2] \ärk\ see ARK[1]

arce \ärs\ see ARSE[1]

arch \ärch\ arch, larch, march, March, parch, starch • cornstarch, dead march • Gothic arch, horseshoe arch, on the march, wedding march

archal \är-kəl\ sparkle • monar-chal, outsparkle • hierarchal, matriarchal, patriarchal
arche \ärsh\ see ARSH
arched \ärcht\ arched, parched
—*also* -ed *forms of verbs listed at* ARCH
archer \är-chər\ archer, marcher • departure
archic \är-kik\ anarchic, monar-chic • hierarchic, oligarchic
archical \är-ki-kəl\ monarchical • oligarchical
archon \är-kən\ see ARKEN
archy \är-kē\ snarky • anarchy, malarkey, monarchy • hierarchy, matriarchy, patriarchy, oligarchy
arck \ärk\ see ARK[1]
arct \ärkt\ see ARKED
arctic \ärt-ik\ see ARTIC
ard[1] \ärd\ bard, barred, card, chard, guard, hard, lard, shard, yard • Asgard, backyard, bankcard, barnyard, Bernard, blackguard, blowhard, boatyard, bombard, brickyard, charge card, churchyard, coast guard, court-yard, die-hard, diehard, discard, dockyard, dooryard, face card, farmyard, flash card, Gerard, graveyard, green card, ill-starred, junkyard, lifeguard, mudguard, noseguard, off guard, old guard, on guard, phone card, placard, point guard, postcard, punch card, rear guard, rearguard, re-gard, retard, safeguard, scorecard, shipyard, smart card, sound card, steelyard, stockyard, switchyard, time card, unbarred, vanguard, wild card • Abelard, avant-garde, bodyguard, boulevard, business card, calling card, Christmas card, color guard, credit card, debit card, disregard, greeting card, honor guard, ID card, leotard, lumberyard, MasterCard, national guard, navy yard, no-holds-barred, playing card, postal card, report card, Saint Bernard, Scot-land Yard, self-regard, union card, unitard • picture-postcard, video card • identity card
—*also* -ed *forms of verbs listed at* AR[3]
ard[2] \är\ see AR[3]
ard[3] \ȯrd\ see OARD
ardant \ärd-ᵊnt\ ardent • flame-retardant
arde \ärd\ see ARD[1]
arded[1] \ärd-əd\ guarded • retarded, unguarded
—*also* -ed *forms of verbs listed at* ARD[1]
arded[2] \ȯrd-əd\ corded, sordid
—*also* -ed *forms of verbs listed at* OARD
arden[1] \ärd-ᵊn\ garden, harden, pardon • rock garden, roof gar-den, tea garden • kitchen garden, water garden
arden[2] \ȯrd-ᵊn\ cordon, Gordon, Jordan, warden • churchwarden
ardener \ärd-nər\ gardener, pard-ner, partner • landscape gardener
ardent \ärd-ᵊnt\ see ARDANT
arder[1] \ärd-ər\ ardor, guarder, larder
arder[2] \ȯrd-ər\ see ORDER
ardi \ärd-ē\ see ARDY
ardian[1] \ärd-ē-ən\ guardian • Ed-wardian
ardian[2] \ȯrd-ē-ən\ see ORDION
ardine \ärd-ⁿ\ see ARDEN[1]
arding \ȯrd-iŋ\ see ORDING[1]
ardom \ärd-əm\ czardom, stardom • megastardom, superstardom
ardon \ärd-ᵊn\ see ARDEN[1]
ardoner \ärd-nər\ see ARDENER
ardor \ärd-ər\ see ARDER[1]
ardy \ärd-ē\ hardy, tardy • Bacardi, foolhardy
are[1] \er-ē\ see ARY[1]
are[2] \är\ see AR[3]

are³ \är-ē\ see ARI¹
are⁴ \er\ air, bare, bear, Blair,
blare, care, chair, Claire, dare,
e'er, ere, err, fair, fare, flair, flare,
glare, hair, hare, Herr, heir, lair,
mare, ne'er, pair, pare, pear,
prayer, rare, rear, scare, share,
snare, spare, square, stair, stare,
swear, tear, their, there, they're,
ware, wear, where • affair, aglare,
airfare, antbear, armchair, aware,
bakeware, barware, beachwear,
beware, big hair, black bear,
bricklayer, brown bear, bugbear,
carfare, cave bear, clayware,
cochair, coheir, compare, cook-
ware, courseware, day-care, deck
chair, declare, despair, éclair,
elsewhere, ensnare, eyewear,
fanfare, flatware, footwear, for-
bear, forebear, forswear,
foursquare, freeware, giftware,
glassware, Great Bear, groupware,
hardware, health care, hectare,
high chair, horsehair, hot air,
impair, knitwear, life-care, long-
hair, loungewear, menswear,
midair, mohair, neckwear, night-
mare, no fair, nonglare, outstare,
out-there, outwear, playwear,
plowshare, Poor Clare, premiere,
prepare, rainwear, repair, self-
care, shareware, shorthair, Sin-
clair, skiwear, sleepwear, sloth
bear, software, somewhere,
sportswear, stemware, stoneware,
sun bear, swimwear, threadbare,
tinware, unfair, Voltaire, warfare,
welfare, wheelchair • aftercare,
air-to-air, antiglare, anywhere,
arctic hare, Asian pear, billion-
aire, bill of fare, boutonniere,
camel hair, Camembert,
chinaware, compressed air,
county fair, debonair, Delaware,
derriere, dinnerware, disrepair,
doctrinaire, earthenware, easy

chair, étagère, everywhere, germ
warfare, get somewhere, grizzly
bear, here and there, hide or hair,
in one's hair, in the air, ironware,
kitchenware, laissez-faire, legion-
naire, lion's share, Little Bear,
love affair, managed care, market
share, Medicare, metalware,
millionaire, on the square, open-
air, outerwear, overbear, perfect
square, plasticware, polar bear,
potty-chair, prickly pear, ques-
tionnaire, rocking chair, savoir
faire, science fair, self-aware, self-
despair, silverware, snowshoe
hare, solar flare, solitaire, swivel
chair, tableware, tear one's hair,
teddy bear, then and there,
thoroughfare, trench warfare,
Tupperware, unaware, under-
wear, vaporware, wash-and-wear,
wear and tear, woodenware,
world premiere, zillionaire
• breath of fresh air, concession-
aire, devil-may-care, director's
chair, electric chair, enamelware,
hyperaware, intensive care, Kodiak bear, lighter-than-air, out of
one's hair, primary care, ready-to-
wear, social welfare, spectacled
bear, surface-to-air, up in the air
• castle in the air, middle of
nowhere
area \er-ē-ə\ see ARIA
areable¹ \er-ə-bəl\ see EARABLE¹
areable² \ar-ə-bəl\ see ARABLE
areal \er-ē-əl\ see ARIAL
arean¹ \er-ē-ən\ see ARIAN¹
arean² \ar-ē-ən\ see ARIAN²
ared \erd\ see AIRED
aredness \ar-əd-nəs\ see ARIDNESS
arel \ar-əl\ see ARREL²
arely¹ \er-lē\ see AIRLY
arely² \är-lē\ see ARLIE
arem \er-əm\ see ARUM
arence¹ \er-əns\ Clarence, Terence
• forbearance

arence² \ar-ən(ts)\ see ARENTS

arent¹ \er-ənt\ daren't, errant, parent • aberrant, apparent, godparent, grandparent, house parent, knight-errant, nonparent, stepparent, transparent • heir apparent

arent² \ar-ənt\ daren't, parent • apparent, godparent, grandparent, stepparent, transparent • heir apparent

aren't¹ \er-ənt\ see ARENT¹

aren't² \ar-ənt\ see ARENT²

arents \ar-ən(t)s\ Clarence —also -s, -'s, and -s' forms of nouns listed at ARENT²

arer \er-ər\ see EARER¹

ares¹ \erz\ see AIRS

ares² \ar-ēz\ Buenos Aires —also -s, -'s, and -s' forms of nouns and -s forms of verbs listed at ARRY³

ares³ \är-əs\ see ORRIS¹

aret \ar-ət\ see ARAT

arey¹ \ar-ē\ see ARRY³

arey² \er-ē\ see ARY¹

arez \är-əs\ see ORRIS¹

arf¹ \ärf\ barf, scarf

arf² \órf\ see ORPH

argain \är-gən\ bargain, jargon • outbargain, plea-bargain • in the bargain

arge \ärj\ barge, charge, large, Marge, sarge • at-large, depth charge, discharge, enlarge, recharge, surcharge, take-charge • by and large, countercharge, cover charge, overcharge, service charge, undercharge • carrying charge

arger \är-jər\ charger • enlarger, recharger • turbocharger

arget \är-gət\ argot, target • off target, on target

argo \är-gō\ argot, cargo, Fargo, largo, Margot • embargo, Key Largo • supercargo

argon \är-gən\ see ARGAIN

argot¹ \är-gət\ see ARGET

argot² \är-gō\ see ARGO

arh \är\ see AR³

ari¹ \är-ē\ quarry, sari, scarry, sorry, starry • curare, safari • calamari, Kalahari, Stradivari

ari² \er-ē\ see ARY¹

ari³ \ar-ē\ see ARRY³

aria \er-ē-ə\ area • Bavaria, Bulgaria, hysteria, malaria, planaria, Samaria

arial \er-ē-əl\ aerial, burial • malarial • adversarial, secretarial

arian¹ \er-ē-ən\ Marian, Marion • agrarian, Aquarian, barbarian, Bavarian, Bulgarian, Cancerian, cesarean, grammarian, Hungarian, librarian, Maid Marian, ovarian, Rotarian, sectarian, Sumerian • antiquarian, centenarian, libertarian, nonsectarian, Presbyterian, proletarian, Rastafarian, Sagittarian, seminarian, Unitarian, vegetarian • Austro-Hungarian, authoritarian, disciplinarian, egalitarian, humanitarian, octogenarian, parliamentarian, totalitarian, utilitarian, veterinarian

arian² \ar-ē-ən\ carrion, clarion, Marian, Marion, agrarian, Aquarian, barbarian, Bavarian, Bulgarian, cesarean, Hungarian, ovarian, Rastafarian, Austro-Hungarian

ariat¹ \er-ē-ət\ lariat • commissariat, proletariat, secretariat

ariat² \ar-ē-ət\ chariot, lariat • commissariat, proletariat • Judas Iscariot

ariate \er-ē-ət\ see ARIAT¹

arib \ar-əb\ see ARAB

arice \ar-əs\ see ARIS²

aridness \ar-əd-nəs\ aridness • preparedness

aried¹ \er-ēd\ see ERRIED

aried² \ar-ēd\ see ARRIED

ariel \er-ē-əl\ see ARIAL

arier[1] \er-ē-ər\ see ERRIER
arier[2] \ar-ē-ər\ see ARRIER[2]
aries \ar-ēz\ see ARES[2]
arilee[1] \ar-ə-lē\ see ARALEE
arilee[2] \er-ə-lē\ see ARILY
arily \er-ə-lē\ merrily, scarily, warily • primarily • arbitrarily, customarily, legendarily, militarily, momentarily, monetarily, necessarily, ordinarily, secondarily, temporarily, voluntarily • extraordinarily, involuntarily, unnecessarily
arin \är-ən\ foreign, Lauren, Orin, warren, Warren
arinate \ar-ə-nət\ see ARONET
arinet \ar-ə-nət\ see ARONET
aring[1] \er-iŋ\ airing, bearing, Bering, daring, fairing, flaring, glaring, herring, paring, raring, sparing, tearing, wearing • ball bearing, childbearing, seafaring, time-sharing, unerring, unsparing, wayfaring • overbearing, profit sharing
—*also* -ing *forms of verbs listed at* ARE[4]
aring[2] \er-ən\ see ARON[1]
ario \er-ē-ō\ stereo • Ontario
arion[1] \ar-ē-ən\ see ARIAN[2]
arion[2] \er-ē-ən\ see ARIAN[1]
ariot \ar-ē-ət\ see ARIAT[2]
arious \er-ē-əs\ Darius, various • Aquarius, gregarious, hilarious, nefarious, precarious, vicarious • Stradivarius, Sagittarius
aris[1] \är-əs\ see ORRIS[1]
aris[2] \ar-əs\ Clarice, harass, Harris, Paris • coheiress, embarrass, Polaris • plaster of paris
arish[1] \er-ish\ bearish, cherish, garish, perish, squarish • nightmarish
arish[2] \ar-ish\ garish, parish • vinegarish
arison \ar-ə-sən\ garrison, Garrison, Harrison, Saracen • comparison

arist \er-əst\ scenarist
—*also* -est *forms of adjectives listed at* ARE[4]
aritan \er-ət-ᵊn\ see ERATIN
arity[1] \er-ət-ē\ see ERITY
arity[2] \ar-ət-ē\ charity, clarity, parity, rarity • barbarity, disparity, hilarity, polarity, vulgarity • angularity, circularity, familiarity, muscularity, peculiarity, popularity, regularity, similarity, singularity, solidarity • dissimilarity, irregularity, unfamiliarity, unpopularity
arium \er-ē-əm\ aquarium, herbarium, solarium, terrarium, vivarium • honorarium, oceanarium, planetarium, sanitarium
arius \er-ē-əs\ see ARIOUS
ark[1] \ärk\ arc, ark, bark, Clark, dark, hark, lark, Marc, mark, Mark, narc, nark, park, quark, shark, spark, stark • aardvark, airpark, ballpark, benchmark, birchbark, birthmark, Bismarck, blue shark, bookmark, check mark, debark, Denmark, earmark, embark, hallmark, hash mark, landmark, monarch, Ozark, pitch-dark, pockmark, postmark, remark, shagbark, skylark, theme park, tidemark, trademark, whale shark • basking shark, disembark, double-park, Estes Park, great white shark, Joan of Arc, make one's mark, mako shark, matriarch, meadowlark, oligarch, patriarch, question mark, thresher shark, tiger shark, toe the mark, watermark, water park • amusement park, high-water mark, in the ballpark, shot in the dark, vest-pocket park • whistle in the dark
ark[2] \ork\ see ORK[2]
ark[3] \ərk\ see ORK[1]
arke \ärk\ see ARK[1]

arked \ärkt\ marked • ripple-marked
—*also* -ed *forms of verbs listed at* ARK[1]
arken \är-kən\ darken, hearken
arker \är-kər\ barker, darker, marker, Parker, starker • book-marker, Ozarker, skylarker • Magic Marker, nosey parker
arkey \är-kē\ see ARCHY
arkic \är-kik\ see ARCHIC
arking \är-kiŋ\ barking, marking, parking • loan-sharking • valet parking
—*also* -ing *forms of verbs listed at* ARK[1]
arkle \är-kəl\ see ARCHAL
arks \ärks\ Marx • Ozarks
—*also* -s, -'s, *and* -s' *forms of nouns and* -s *forms of verbs listed at* ARK[1]
arky \är-kē\ see ARCHY
arl \ärl\ Carl, gnarl, Karl, quarrel, snarl • ensnarl, unsnarl
arla \är-lə\ Carla, Darla, Marla
arlan \ä-lən\ see ARLINE
arlay \är-lē\ see ARLIE
arle \ärl\ see ARL
arlen \är-lən\ see ARLINE
arler \är-lər\ see ARLOR
arless \är-ləs\ Carlos, starless
arlet \är-lət\ Charlotte, harlot, scarlet, starlet, varlet
arley \är-lē\ see ARLIE
arlie \är-lē\ barley, Charlie, gnarly, Harley, parlay, parley, snarly • bizarrely
arlin \är-lən\ see ARLINE
arline \är-lən\ Harlan, marlin, Marlin • blue marlin, white marlin
arling \är-liŋ\ darling, starling
—*also* -ing *forms of verbs listed at* ARL
arlor \är-lər\ parlor, quarreler
arlos \är-ləs\ see ARLESS
arlot \är-lət\ see ARLET

arlotte \är-lət\ see ARLET
arlous \är-ləs\ see ARLESS
arly \är-lē\ see ARLIE
arlyn \ä-lən\ see ARLINE
arm[1] \ärm\ arm, charm, farm, harm • alarm, disarm, firearm, fish farm, forearm, nonfarm, rearm, schoolmarm, sidearm, strong-arm, tree farm, unarm, wind farm • arm in arm, buy the farm, false alarm, overarm, twist one's arm, underarm • collective farm, shot in the arm
arm[2] \äm\ see OM[1]
arm[3] \órm\ see ORM[2]
arma[1] \är-mə\ karma, Parma
arma[2] \ər-mə\ see ERMA
armed \ärmd\ armed, charmed • unarmed
—*also* -ed *forms of verbs listed at* ARM[1]
arment \är-mənt\ garment, varmint • disbarment • undergarment, overgarment
armer[1] \är-mər\ armor, charmer, farmer • snake charmer • tenant farmer
armer[2] \ór-mər\ see ORMER
armic \ər-mik\ see ERMIC
arming[1] \är-miŋ\ charming, farming • alarming, disarming, Prince Charming
—*also* -ing *forms of verbs listed at* ARM[1]
arming[2] \ór-miŋ\ see ORMING
armint \är-mənt\ see ARMENT
armless \ärm-ləs\ armless, charm-less, harmless
armoir \är-mər\ see ARMER[1]
army \är-mē\ army, smarmy • standing army • Salvation Army
arn[1] \ärn\ barn, darn, yarn
arn[2] \órn\ see ORN[1]
arna \ər-nə\ see ERNA
arnate \är-nət\ garnet • incarnate
arne[1] \ärn\ see ARN[1]
arne[2] \är-nē\ see ARNY

arner \ȯr-nər\ see ORNER
arness \är-nəs\ harness
• bizarreness
arnet \är-nət\ see ARNATE
arney \är-nē\ see ARNY
arning \ȯr-niŋ\ see ORNING
arnish \är-nish\ garnish, tarnish,
varnish
arny \är-nē\ Barney, blarney, carny
• Killarney • chili con carne
aro[1] \er-ō\ see ERO[2]
aro[2] \ar-ō\ see ARROW[2]
aro[3] \är-ə\ see ARA[1]
aro[4] \är-ō\ see ORROW[1]
arob \ar-əb\ see ARAB
aroe[1] \ar-ō\ see ARROW[2]
aroe[2] \er-ō\ see ERO[2]
arol \ar-əl\ see ARREL[2]
arold \er-əld\ see ERALD
arole \ar-əl\ see ARREL[2]
arom \er-əm\ see ARUM
aron[1] \er-ən\ Aaron, baron,
Charon, Erin, heron, raring,
Sharon • sub-Saharan
aron[2] \ar-ən\ Aaron, baron, barren,
Charon, Sharon • sub-Saharan
aronet \ar-ə-nət\ baronet, clarinet
arous[1] \er-əs\ see ERROUS
arous[2] \ar-əs\ see ARIS[2]
arp[1] \ärp\ carp, harp, sharp, tarp
• Jew's harp • Autoharp, super-
sharp
arp[2] \ȯrp\ see ORP
arpen \är-pən\ sharpen, tarpon
arper \är-pər\ carper, sharper
arpie \är-pē\ see ARPY
arpon \är-pən\ see ARPEN
arpy \är-pē\ harpy, sharpie
arque \ärk\ see ARK[1]
arqui \är-kē\ see ARCHY
arrable \ar-ə-bəl\ see ARABLE
arrage \är-ij\ see [1]orage
arragon \ar-ə-gən\ see ARAGON
arrant[1] \ar-ənt\ see ARENT[2]
arrant[2] \ȯr-ənt\ see ORRENT
arras \ar-əs\ see ARIS[2]
arrass \ar-əs\ see ARIS[2]

arrative \ar-ət-iv\ see ARATIVE[2]
arre \är\ see AR[3]
arred \ärd\ see ARD[1]
arrel[1] \ȯr-əl\ see ORAL
arrel[2] \ar-əl\ Aral, barrel, carol,
Carol, Darryl • apparel • cracker-
barrel
arreler \är-lər\ see ARLOR
arrell \ar-əl\ see ARREL[2]
arrely \är-lē\ see ARLIE
arren[1] \ar-ən\ see ARON[2]
arren[2] \ȯr-ən\ see ORIN[1]
arren[3] \är-ən\ see ARIN
arrener \ȯr-ə-nər\ see ORONER
arreness \är-nəs\ see ARNESS
arret \ar-ət\ see ARAT
arrett \ar-ət\ see ARAT
arrh \är\ see AR[3]
arriage \ar-ij\ carriage, marriage
• disparage, miscarriage, mixed
marriage • baby carriage, horse-
less carriage, intermarriage, un-
dercarriage
arrie \ar-ē\ see ARRY[3]
arried \ar-ēd\ harried, married,
varied • unmarried
arrier[1] \ȯr-ē-ər\ see ARRIOR
arrier[2] \ar-ē-ər\ barrier, carrier
• ballcarrier, mail carrier, noncar-
rier, sound barrier, spear-carrier
• aircraft carrier, letter carrier
arrion \ar-ē-ən\ see ARIAN[2]
arrior \ȯr-ē-ər\ sorrier, warrior
• weekend warrior
arris \ar-əs\ see ARIS[2]
arrison \ar-ə-sən\ see ARISON
arro \är-ō\ see ORROW[1]
arroll \ar-əl\ see ARREL[2]
arron \ar-ən\ see ARON[2]
arrot \ar-ət\ see ARAT
arroty \ar-ət-ē\ see ARITY[2]
arrow[1] \ar-ə\ Clara, Kara, Sarah,
Tara • mascara, Sahara, tiara
• capybara, marinara, Santa Clara
arrow[2] \ar-ō\ arrow, barrow, har-
row, marrow, narrow, pharaoh,
sparrow, taro, tarot, yarrow

• bone marrow, house sparrow, Point Barrow, song sparrow, straight-arrow, tree sparrow, wheelbarrow • straight and narrow • Kilimanjaro

arry¹ \är-ē\ see ARI¹

arry² \òr-ē\ see ORY

arry³ \ar-ē\ Barry, Carrie, carry, Cary, chary, Gary, Harry, Larry, marry, nary, parry, Shari, tarry • miscarry, safari • cash-and-carry, hari-kari, intermarry, Stradivari • Tom, Dick, and Harry

arryl \ar-əl\ see ARREL²

ars \ärz\ Lars, Mars, ours • behind bars, Stars and Bars
—*also* -s, -'s, *and* -s' *forms of nouns and* -s *forms of verbs listed at* AR³

arse¹ \ärs\ farce, sparse

arse² \ärz\ see ARS

arsh \ärsh\ harsh, marsh • salt marsh

arshal \är-shəl\ see ARTIAL

arshall \är-shəl\ see ARTIAL

arsle \äs-əl\ see OSSAL

arson \ärs-ᵊn\ arson, Carson, parson

art¹ \ärt\ art, Art, Bart, cart, chart, Chartres, dart, hart, heart, kart, mart, part, smart, start, tart • apart, at heart, bar chart, Bogart, by heart, clip art, depart, dogcart, Earhart, eye chart, false start, fine art, folk art, go-cart, golf cart, handcart, head start, Hobart, impart, in part, jump-start, kick-start, mouthpart, Mozart, outsmart, oxcart, pie chart, pop art, pushcart, rampart, restart, street-smart, Stuttgart, sweetheart, take heart, take part, upstart, voice part • à la carte, applecart, bleeding heart, Bonaparte, change of heart, counterpart, fall apart, flying start, for one's part, heart-to-heart, martial

art, mini-mart, multipart, on one's part, open-heart, poles apart, Purple Heart, running start, set apart, take apart, underpart • for the most part, performance art, state-of-the-art

art² \òrt\ see ORT¹

arta \är-tə\ Marta, Sparta • Jakarta • Magna Carta

artan \ärt-ᵊn\ see ARTEN

artar \ärt-ər\ see ARTER¹

arte¹ \ärt-ē\ see ARTY¹

arte² \ärt\ see ART¹

arted¹ \ärt-əd\ see EARTED

arted² \òrt-əd\ see ORTED

arten \ärt-ᵊn\ carton, hearten, Martin, smarten, Spartan, tartan • dishearten, Saint Martin • kindergarten

arter¹ \ärt-ər\ barter, Carter, charter, garter, martyr, starter, tartar • nonstarter, self-starter, snail darter
—*also* -er *forms of adjectives listed at* ART¹

arter² \òt-ər\ see ATER¹

arter³ \òrt-ər\ see ORTER

artes \ärt\ see ART¹

arth \ärth\ Garth, hearth • open-hearth

arti \ärt-ē\ see ARTY¹

artial \är-shəl\ marshal, Marshal, Marshall, martial, partial • court-martial, earl marshal, field marshal, grand marshal, impartial, sky marshal

artic \ärt-ik\ arctic, Arctic • antarctic, Antarctic, cathartic

article \ärt-i-kəl\ article, particle • alpha particle, beta particle, microparticle

artile \òrt-ᵊl\ see ORTAL

artily \ärt-ᵊl-ē\ artily, heartily

artin \ärt-ᵊn\ see ARTEN

arting \ärt-iŋ\ carting, charting, karting, parting, starting • self-starting

—also -ing *forms of verbs listed at* ART[1]

artisan \ärt-ə-zən\ artisan, partisan • bipartisan, nonpartisan

artizan \ärt-ə-zən\ see ARTISAN

artless \ärt-ləs\ artless, heartless

artly[1] \ärt-lē\ partly, smartly, tartly

artly[2] \ort-lē\ see ORTLY

artner \ärt-nər\ partner • kindergartner, secret partner

arton \ärt-ᵊn\ see ARTEN

artre \ärt\ see ART[1]

artres \ärt\ see ART[1]

artridge \är-trij\ cartridge, partridge

arts[1] \är\ see AR[3]

arts[2] \ärts\ street smarts • private parts • master of arts, principal parts

—also -s, -'s, *and* -s' *forms of nouns and* -s *forms of verbs listed at* ART[1]

arture \är-chər\ see ARCHER

arty[1] \ärt-ē\ arty, hearty, party, smarty • block party, Havarti, tea party, war party • cocktail party, slumber party

arty[2] \ort-ē\ see ORTY

artyr \ärt-ər\ see ARTER[1]

artz[1] \orts\ see ORTS

artz[2] \ärts\ see ARTS[2]

arum \er-əm\ harem • harum-scarum

arus \ar-əs\ see ARIS[2]

arval \är-vəl\ see ARVEL

arve \ärv\ carve, starve

arvel \är-vəl\ larval, marvel

ary[1] \er-ē\ aerie, airy, berry, bury, Carey, Cary, Cherie, cherry, Cherry, dairy, Derry, fairy, ferry, Gary, Gerry, hairy, Jerry, Kerry, Mary, marry, merry, Merry, nary, Perry, prairie, query, scary, Shari, sherry, terry, Terry, vary, very, wary • barberry, bayberry, bearberry, bing cherry, blackberry, black cherry, blueberry, canary, chokeberry, chokecherry, con-

trary, cranberry, dewberry, gooseberry, hackberry, Hail Mary, library, mulberry, nondairy, primary, raspberry, rosemary, Rosemary, soapberry, strawberry, summary, tooth fairy, unwary • actuary, adversary, antiquary, apiary, arbitrary, aviary, beriberi, black raspberry, boysenberry, budgetary, Canterbury, capillary, cautionary, cemetery, centenary, chinaberry, commentary, commissary, corollary, coronary, culinary, customary, dictionary, dietary, dignitary, dromedary, dysentery, elderberry, emissary, estuary, February, fragmentary, functionary, honorary, huckleberry, intermarry, January, lectionary, legendary, legionary, lingonberry, literary, loganberry, luminary, mercenary, military, millinery, missionary, momentary, monastery, monetary, mortuary, necessary, ordinary, partridgeberry, planetary, pulmonary, red mulberry, reliquary, salivary, salmonberry, salutary, sanctuary, sanitary, secondary, secretary, sedentary, seminary, serviceberry, solitary, sour cherry, stationary, stationery, statuary, Stradivari, temporary, Tipperary, Tom and Jerry, tributary, Typhoid Mary, unitary, urinary, Virgin Mary, visionary, voluntary, winterberry • bicentenary, confectionery, contemporary, deflationary, disciplinary, discretionary, extemporary, extraordinary, hereditary, illusionary, imaginary, incendiary, inflationary, insanitary, interlibrary, involuntary, itinerary, judiciary, lending library, nonmilitary, obituary, on the contrary, pituitary, precautionary, preliminary, probationary, reactionary, subsidiary, uncustomary, unnecessary, unsanitary, veterinary, vocabulary • beneficiary, evolutionary, intermediary, interplanetary, paramilitary, penitentiary, revolutionary

ary² \ar-ē\ see ARRY³

ary³ \är-ē\ see ARI¹

aryan¹ \er-ē-ən\ see ARIAN¹

aryan² \ar-ē-ən\ see ARIAN²

aryl \ar-əl\ see ARREL²

as¹ \ash\ see ASH³

as² \as\ see ASS³

as³ \az\ see AZZ

as⁴ \ä\ see A¹

as⁵ \äsh\ see ASH¹

as⁶ \äz\ see OISE¹

as⁷ \əz\ see EUSE¹

as⁸ \äs\ see OS¹

as⁹ \ȯ\ see AW¹

asa¹ \äs-ə\ Lhasa, Ossa • kielbasa

asa² \az-ə\ see AZA¹

asable \ā-sə-bəl\ see ACEABLE

asal \ā-zəl\ Basil, hazel, Hazel, nasal, phrasal • appraisal, witch hazel

asally \āz-lē\ see AISLEY

asca \as-kə\ see ASKA

ascal \as-kəl\ paschal, rascal

ascar \as-kər\ see ASKER

ascent \ās-ᵊnt\ see ACENT

asch¹ \ask\ see ASK

asch² \äsh\ see ASH¹

asch³ \ȯsh\ see ASH²

aschal \as-kəl\ see ASCAL

ascia \ā-shə\ see ACIA

ascible \as-ə-bəl\ see ASSABLE

ascicle \as-i-kəl\ see ASSICAL

asco¹ \äs-kō\ see OSCOE

asco² \as-kō\ fiasco, Tabasco

ascot \as-kət\ see ASKET

ascus \as-kəs\ Damascus, Velázquez

ase¹ \ās\ see ACE¹

ase² \āz\ see AZE¹

ase³ \āz\ see OISE¹

asel \äz-əl\ see OZZLE

ased \āst\ see ACED

aseless \ā-sləs\ see ACELESS

aseman \ā-smən\ see ACEMAN

asement \ās-mənt\ basement, casement • abasement, debasement • bargain-basement, self-abasement

aser¹ \ā-sər\ see ACER¹

aser² \ā-zər\ see AZER

asey \ā-sē\ see ACY

ash¹ \äsh\ gosh, josh, mosh, nosh, posh, quash, slosh, squash, swash, wash • awash, backwash, eyewash, galosh, goulash, kibosh, mishmash, mouthwash, whitewash • acorn squash, hubbard squash, mackintosh, summer squash, winter squash

ash² \ȯsh\ gosh, quash, slosh, squash, swash, wash • awash, backwash, brainwash, car wash, eyewash, hogwash, mouthwash, prewash, whitewash • acorn squash, hubbard squash, summer squash, winter squash

ash³ \ash\ ash, bash, brash, cache, cash, clash, crash, dash, flash, gash, gnash, hash, lash, mash, rash, sash, slash, smash, splash, stash, thrash, thresh, trash • abash, backlash, backslash, cold cash, eyelash, gate-crash, goulash, green flash, heat rash, hot flash, mishmash, moustache, mustache, potash, rehash, slapdash, tongue-lash, unlash, Wabash, whiplash, white ash • balderdash, calabash, diaper rash, mountain ash, nettle rash, petty cash, prickly rash, succotash • settle one's hash

ashan \ash-ən\ see ASSION

ashed¹ \ȯsht\ sloshed • stonewashed, unwashed • acid-washed
—also -ed forms of verbs listed at ASH²

ashed[2] \asht\ dashed, smashed
• unabashed
—*also* -ed *forms of verbs listed at*
ASH[3]

ashen \ash-ən\ see ASSION

asher[1] \äsh-ər\ josher, mosher,
nosher, squasher, washer • dishwasher

asher[2] \òsh-ər\ washer • brain-
washer, dishwasher, whitewasher

asher[3] \ash-ər\ basher, crasher,
rasher, slasher, smasher • gate-
crasher • atom-smasher, haber-
dasher

ashi[1] \äsh-ē\ see ASHY[1]

ashi[2] \ash-ē\ see ASHY[2]

ashing \ash-iŋ\ crashing, dashing,
flashing, mashing, slashing,
smashing • tongue-lashing
—*also* -ing *forms of verbs listed at*
ASH[3]

ashion \ash-ən\ see ASSION

asht \asht\ see ASHED[2]

ashy[1] \äsh-ē\ squashy • wishy-
washy

ashy[2] \ash-ē\ ashy, flashy, splashy,
trashy

asi[1] \äs-ē\ see OSSY[1]

asi[2] \äz-ē\ see AZI[1]

asi[3] \äsh-ē\ see ASHY[1]

asia \ā-zhə\ Asia • Caucasia, Eur-
asia, fantasia, Malaysia • Anasta-
sia, Australasia, euthanasia

asian[1] \ā-shən\ see ATION[1]

asian[2] \ā-zhən\ see ASION

asic \ā-zik\ phasic • euthanasic,
multiphasic

asid \as-əd\ see ACID

asie \ā-sē\ see ACY

asil[1] \as-əl\ see ASSEL[2]

asil[2] \az-əl\ see AZZLE

asil[3] \äz-əl\ see ASAL

asil[4] \äz-əl\ see OZZLE

asin \ās-ᵊn\ see ASON[1]

asing[1] \ā-siŋ\ see ACING

asing[2] \ā-ziŋ\ see AISING

asion \ā-zhən\ Asian • abrasion,
Caucasian, dissuasion, equation,
Eurasian, evasion, invasion, occa-
sion, persuasion • Amerasian,
anti-Asian, Australasian, on occa-
sion

asis \ā-səs\ basis • oasis • home-
ostasis

asive \ā-siv\ abrasive, evasive,
invasive, persuasive, pervasive

ask \ask\ ask, bask, Basque, cask,
flask, mask, task • death mask,
face mask, gas mask, ski mask,
unmask • multitask, take to task,
vacuum flask • oxygen mask

aska \as-kə\ Alaska, Nebraska

asked \ast\ see AST[2]

asker \as-kər\ masker • Madagascar

asket \as-kət\ ascot, basket, casket,
gasket • breadbasket, handbasket,
wastebasket • blow a gasket

asking \as-kiŋ\ multitasking
—*also* -ing *forms of verbs listed at*
ASK

asm \az-əm\ chasm, plasm, spasm
• phantasm, sarcasm • ectoplasm,
protoplasm • enthusiasm

asma \az-mə\ asthma, plasma
• miasma

asn't \əz-ᵊnt\ doesn't, wasn't

aso[1] \as-ō\ see ASSO[1]

aso[2] \äs-ō\ see ASSO[2]

ason[1] \ās-ᵊn\ basin, caisson, chas-
ten, hasten, Jason, mason, Mason
• Freemason, Great Basin, stone-
mason, washbasin

ason[2] \āz-ᵊn\ see AZON

asp \asp\ asp, clasp, gasp, grasp,
hasp, rasp • handclasp, last-gasp,
unclasp

asque \ask\ see ASK

asquer \as-kər\ see ASKER

ass[1] \ās\ see ACE[1]

ass[2] \äs\ see OS[1]

ass[3] \as\ ass, bass, brass, class,
crass, gas, glass, grass, has, lass,
mass, pass, sass • air mass, alas,

Alsace, amass, art glass, beach grass, bear grass, bent grass, black bass, Black Mass, bluegrass, bunchgrass, bypass, crabgrass, crevasse, cuirass, cut glass, degas, eelgrass, en masse, eyeglass, first-class, folk mass, ground glass, harass, high-class, high mass, hourglass, impasse, jackass, jump pass, landmass, Madras, milk glass, morass, oat grass, outclass, plate glass, quack grass, rock bass, ryegrass, salt grass, sand-glass, saw grass, screen pass, sea bass, sheet glass, shortgrass, smart-ass, spun glass, spyglass, stained glass, striped bass, sub-class, sung mass, surpass, sweet-grass, switchgrass, sword grass, tallgrass, teargas, third-class, trespass, turfgrass, wheatgrass, white bass, wineglass, wire grass, wiseass, witchgrass, world-class, yard grass • bottled gas, Brenner Pass, Cajon Pass, channel bass, cocktail glass, come to pass, demitasse, Donner Pass, fiber-glass, forward pass, Khyber Pass, largemouth bass, laughing gas, lemongrass, looking glass, lower-class, middle-class, opera glass, overpass, Plexiglas, safety glass, sassafras, second-class, Simplon Pass, smallmouth bass, solemn mass, tourist class, underclass, underpass, upper-class, water glass, working-class • atomic mass, critical mass, laughing jackass, snake in the grass

assable \as-ə-bəl\ passable • im-passable, irascible • unsurpassable

assail \äs-əl\ see OSSAL

assal \as-əl\ see ASSEL[2]

assar \as-ər\ see ASSER

asse[1] \as\ see ASS[3]

asse[2] \äs\ see OS[1]

assed \ast\ see AST[2]

assee \as-ē\ see ASSY

assel[1] \äs-əl\ see OSSAL

assel[2] \as-əl\ Basil, castle, facile, hassle, passel, tassel, vassal, wres-tle • forecastle

asser \as-ər\ crasser, gasser • amasser, harasser • antimacassar

asset \as-ət\ see ACET

assian \ash-ən\ see ASSION

assible \as-ə-bəl\ see ASSABLE

assic \as-ik\ classic • Jurassic, Triassic • neoclassic, semiclassic

assical \as-i-kəl\ classical, fascicle • semiclassical

assid \as-əd\ see ACID

assie[1] \as-ē\ see ASSY

assie[2] \äs-ē\ see OSSY[1]

assim \äs-əm\ see OSSUM

assin \as-ᵊn\ see ASTEN[2]

assion \ash-ən\ ashen, fashion, passion, ration • compassion, high fashion, impassion, refashion • after a fashion

assis \as-ē\ see ASSY

assist \ā-sist\ bassist, racist • con-trabassist, double bassist

assive \as-iv\ massive, passive • impassive

assle \as-əl\ see ASSEL[2]

assness \as-nəs\ see ASTNESS

asso[1] \as-ō\ basso, lasso • El Paso, Picasso, sargasso

asso[2] \äs-ō\ Picasso • Burkina Faso

assock \as-ək\ cassock, hassock

assus \as-əs\ see ASSIS

assy \as-ē\ brassy, chassis, classy, gassy, glassy, grassy, lassie, sassy • Tallahassee • Haile Selassie

ast[1] \əst\ see UST[1]

ast[2] \ast\ blast, cast, caste, fast, hast, last, mast, past, vast • aghast, at last, avast, Belfast, bombast, broadcast, contrast, downcast, forecast, foremast, full blast, gymnast, half-caste, half-mast, mainmast, miscast, news-cast, offcast, outcast, repast,

sandblast, sportscast, steadfast, topmast, typecast, unasked, webcast, windblast • acid-fast, at long last, colorcast, colorfast, counterblast, flabbergast, hard-and-fast, mizzenmast, overcast, plaster cast, simulcast, telecast, weathercast • enthusiast, iconoclast
—*also* -ed *forms of verbs listed at* ASS[3]

asta \as-tə\ canasta • Mount Shasta
astable \at-ə-bəl\ see ATIBLE
astard \as-tərd\ bastard, dastard, plastered
aste[1] \āst\ see ACED
aste[2] \ast\ see AST[2]
asted \as-təd\ blasted, masted
—*also* -ed *forms of verbs listed at* AST[2]
asteful \āst-fəl\ tasteful, wasteful • distasteful
asten[1] \ās-ᵊn\ see ASON[1]
asten[2] \as-ᵊn\ fasten • assassin, unfasten
aster[1] \ā-stər\ baster, taster • wine taster
aster[2] \as-tər\ aster, Astor, blaster, caster, castor, faster, master, pastor, plaster • bandmaster, brewmaster, broadcaster, choirmaster, disaster, dockmaster, drillmaster, grand master, headmaster, newscaster, past master, paymaster, postmaster, quizmaster, remaster, ringmaster, sandblaster, schoolmaster, scoutmaster, sportscaster, spymaster, surf caster, taskmaster, toastmaster, webcaster • alabaster, burgomaster, China aster, concertmaster, ghetto blaster, harbormaster, quartermaster, stationmaster, telecaster, wagon master, weathercaster
astered \as-tərd\ see ASTARD
astering \as-tə-riŋ\ plastering • overmastering

—*also* -ing *forms of verbs listed at* ASTER[2]
astes \as-tēz\ Ecclesiastes
—*also* -s, -'s, *and* -s' *forms of nouns listed at* ASTY[2]
asthma \az-mə\ see ASMA
astic \as-tik\ drastic, plastic, spastic • bombastic, dynastic, elastic, fantastic, gymnastic, monastic, sarcastic, scholastic • ecclesiastic, enthusiastic, iconoclastic, interscholastic
astics \as-tiks\ gymnastics, slimnastics
astid \as-təd\ see ASTED
astie \as-tē\ see ASTY[2]
astiness \ā-stē-nəs\ hastiness, tastiness
asting[1] \ā-stiŋ\ basting, wasting
—*also* -ing *forms of verbs listed at* ACED
asting[2] \as-tiŋ\ casting, lasting • fly casting, linecasting, surf casting, typecasting • central casting, everlasting
—*also* -ing *forms of verbs listed at* AST[2]
astle \as-əl\ see ASSEL[2]
astly \ast-lē\ ghastly, lastly, vastly • steadfastly
astness \as-nəs\ crassness • steadfastness • colorfastness
astor \as-tər\ see ASTER[2]
astoral \as-trəl\ see ASTRAL
astral \as-trəl\ astral, pastoral
astre \as-tər\ see ASTER[2]
asty[1] \ā-stē\ hasty, pasty, tasty
asty[2] \as-tē\ nasty • capacity, contrasty • angioplasty, overcapacity
asuble \as-ə-bəl\ see ASSABLE
asure[1] \ā-shər\ glacier • erasure
asure[2] \ā-zhər\ see AZIER
asy \as-ē\ see ASSY
at[1] \ä\ see A[1]
at[2] \ät\ see OT[1]
at[3] \ət\ see UT[1]
at[4] \ȯt\ see OUGHT[1]

at[5] \at\ bat, brat, cat, chat, drat, fat, flat, frat, gat, gnat, hat, mat, Matt, matte, pat, Pat, phat, plait, plat, rat, sat, scat, slat, spat, splat, stat, that, vat • all that, at bat, at that, bath mat, begat, bobcat, brickbat, brown rat, Cassatt, chitchat, combat, comsat, coon cat, cowpat, cravat, Croat, defat, dingbat, doormat, fat cat, fiat, fly at, format, fruit bat, get at, go at, hard hat, have at, hellcat, high-hat, house cat, keep at, look at, Manx cat, meerkat, milk fat, mole rat, mudflat, muskrat, nonfat, old hat, pack rat, pick at, place mat, polecat, rug rat, salt flat, silk hat, sneeze at, snowcat, stand pat, tomcat, top hat, trans fat, whereat, white hat, wildcat, wombat • acrobat, alley cat, Ararat, arrive at, autocrat, bell the cat, bureaucrat, butterfat, Cheshire cat, chew the fat, copycat, cowboy hat, democrat, diplomat, habitat, hang one's hat, jungle cat, Laundromat, leopard cat, Norway rat, off the bat, Persian cat, photostat, pit-a-pat, plutocrat, poke fun at, pussycat, rat-a-tat, reformat, scaredy-cat, smell a rat, take aim at, technocrat, thermostat, tiger cat, tit for tat, vampire bat, water rat, welcome mat, where it's at • Angora cat, aristocrat, go to the mat, Jehoshaphat, kangaroo rat, Siamese cat, single combat, talk through one's hat, ten-gallon hat, throw money at, under one's hat • proletariat, secretariat

at[6] \a\ see AH[3]

ata[1] \ät-ə\ cantata, Carlotta, pinata, regatta, ricotta, sonata • terracotta • persona non grata, Rio de la Plata

ata[2] \āt-ə\ beta, data, eta, strata, theta, zeta • peseta, potato, substrata, tomato

ata[3] \at-ə\ data • regatta • persona non grata

atable[1] \āt-ə-bəl\ debatable, inflatable, locatable, relatable, rotatable, translatable • cultivatable, untranslatable

atable[2] \at-ə-bəl\ see ATIBLE

atal \āt-ᵊl\ fatal, natal • nonfatal, postnatal, prenatal

atalie \at-ᵊl-ē\ see ATTILY

atally \āt-ᵊl-ē\ fatally, natally • postnatally, prenatally

atalyst \at-ᵊl-əst\ catalyst • philatelist

atan[1] \āt-ən\ see ATEN[1]

atan[2] \at-ᵊn\ see ATIN[2]

atant[1] \āt-ᵊnt\ blatant, latent, patent

atant[2] \at-ᵊnt\ patent • combatant • noncombatant

atar \ät-ər\ see OTTER

atary \āt-ə-rē\ see OTTERY

atch[1] \ech\ see ETCH

atch[2] \äch\ see OTCH

atch[3] \ach\ batch, catch, hatch, latch, match, natch, patch, scratch, snatch, thatch • attach, crosshatch, detach, dispatch, fair catch, from scratch, mismatch, night latch, nuthatch, outmatch, rematch, Sasquatch, unlatch, Wasatch • booby hatch, coffee klatch, escape hatch, safety match, shoulder patch

atcher[1] \äch-ər\ watcher • birdwatcher, clock-watcher, topnotcher

atcher[2] \ach-ər\ batcher, catcher, stature • cowcatcher, dispatcher, dogcatcher, eye-catcher, flycatcher, head-scratcher • body snatcher, train dispatcher

atchet \ach-ət\ hatchet, ratchet • bury the hatchet

atchily

atchily \ach-ə-lē\ patchily,
scratchily

atching \ach-iŋ\ catching • back-
scratching, cross-hatching, eye-
catching, head-scratching,
nonmatching
—*also* -ing *forms of verbs listed at*
ATCH[3]

atchman \äch-mən\ see OTCHMAN

atchment \ach-mənt\ catchment
• attachment, detachment

atchouli \ach-ə-lē\ see ATCHILY

atchy \ach-ē\ catchy, patchy,
scratchy • Apache

ate[1] \āt\ ate, bait, Cate, crate, date,
eight, fate, freight, gait, gate,
grate, great, hate, Kate, late,
mate, pate, plait, plate, rate, sate,
skate, slate, spate, state, straight,
strait, trait, wait, weight • abate,
aerate, age-mate, airfreight, await,
bandmate, baseplate, Bass Strait,
berate, birthrate, blank slate,
blind date, bookplate, breastplate,
cheapskate, checkmate, citrate,
classmate, collate, create, cre-
mate, curate, cut-rate,
deadweight, death rate, debate,
deflate, dictate, dilate, donate,
elate, equate, estate, filtrate, first-
rate, fixate, floodgate, flyweight,
frustrate, gestate, gyrate, help-
mate, home plate, hot plate,
housemate, hydrate, ice-skate,
inflate, ingrate, inmate, innate,
instate, irate, khanate, Kuwait,
lactate, legate, lightweight, locate,
magnate, mandate, messmate, name-
plate, narrate, negate, nitrate,
notate, of late, orate, ornate,
outwait, placate, playdate, play-
mate, portrait, postdate, predate,
primate, prime rate, probate,
prorate, prostrate, pulsate, rain
date, rebate, relate, restate, room-
mate, rotate, schoolmate, seat-

mate, sedate, shipmate, soul mate,
spectate, stagnate, stalemate,
substrate, tailgate, teammate,
tenth-rate, third-rate, tinplate, to
date, tollgate, translate, tristate,
truncate, update, upstate, V-8,
vacate, vibrate, workmate • abdi-
cate, acclimate, activate, advo-
cate, aggravate, aggregate, agitate,
allocate, alternate, amputate,
animate, annotate, apartheid,
apostate, arbitrate, automate,
bantamweight, Bering Strait,
cabinmate, Cabot Strait, calcu-
late, calibrate, caliphate, candi-
date, captivate, carbonate,
carbon-date, castigate, celebrate,
chief of state, chlorinate, circu-
late, city-state, cogitate, collocate,
compensate, complicate, concen-
trate, condensate, confiscate,
conjugate, consecrate, constipate,
consummate, contemplate, cop-
perplate, correlate, corrugate,
counterweight, culminate, culti-
vate, Davis Strait, decimate, deco-
rate, dedicate, dehydrate,
delegate, demarcate, demonstrate,
denigrate, Denmark Strait, deviate, deprecate, desecrate, desig-
nate, desolate, detonate,
devastate, deviate, dislocate,
dissipate, distillate, dominate,
double date, duplicate, educate,
elevate, elongate, emanate, emi-
grate, emirate, emulate, escalate,
estimate, excavate, exchange rate,
exculpate, explicate, expurgate,
extirpate, extricate, fabricate,
fascinate, fashion plate, feather-
weight, federate, flagellate, fluctu-
ate, formulate, fulminate,
fumigate, generate, germinate,
Golden Gate, graduate, granulate,
gravitate, heavyweight, hesitate,
hibernate, Hudson Strait, hyphen-
ate, illustrate, imitate, immigrate,

immolate, implicate, incarnate, incubate, inculcate, indicate, infiltrate, in-line skate, innovate, instigate, insulate, interstate, intimate, inundate, irrigate, irritate, isolate, iterate, lacerate, laminate, laureate, legislate, levitate, liberate, license plate, liquidate, litigate, lubricate, magistrate, marinate, masticate, mediate, medicate, meditate, middleweight, militate, mitigate, moderate, modulate, mortgage rate, motivate, multistate, mutilate, nation-state, nauseate, navigate, nominate, obfuscate, obligate, obviate, on a plate, operate, orchestrate, oscillate, out-of-date, overstate, overweight, paperweight, penetrate, percolate, perforate, permeate, perpetrate, police state, pollinate, populate, potentate, predicate, profligate, promulgate, propagate, punctuate, radiate, real estate, recreate, re-create, regulate, reinstate, relegate, relocate, renovate, replicate, reprobate, resonate, roller-skate, ruminate, running mate, salivate, saturate, scintillate, second-rate, segregate, self-portrait, separate, ship of state, silver plate, simulate, situate, speculate, stablemate, starting gate, steady state, stimulate, stipulate, subjugate, sublimate, suffocate, sultanate, supplicate, surrogate, syncopate, syndicate, tablemate, tabulate, target date, terminate, tête-à-tête, titillate, tolerate, triplicate, underrate, understate, underweight, vaccinate, vacillate, validate, vegetate, venerate, ventilate, vertebrate, vindicate, violate, vitiate, Watergate, welfare state, welterweight • abbreviate, accel-

erate, accentuate, accommodate, accumulate, adjudicate, adulterate, affiliate, agglomerate, alienate, alleviate, amalgamate, ameliorate, annihilate, anticipate, appreciate, appropriate, approximate, articulate, asphyxiate, assassinate, assimilate, associate, at any rate, attenuate, authenticate, barbiturate, bicarbonate, capitulate, certificate, coagulate, collaborate, commemorate, commiserate, communicate, compassionate, confederate, conglomerate, congratulate, consolidate, contaminate, cooperate, coordinate, corroborate, deactivate, decapitate, decelerate, deescalate, defoliate, degenerate, deliberate, delineate, depopulate, depreciate, desegregate, devaluate, discriminate, disintegrate, disseminate, dissociate, domesticate, elaborate, electroplate, eliminate, elucidate, emaciate, emancipate, emasculate, encapsulate, enumerate, enunciate, equivocate, eradicate, evacuate, evaluate, evaporate, exaggerate, exasperate, exfoliate, exhilarate, exonerate, expropriate, extenuate, exterminate, facilitate, fish or cut bait, gesticulate, hallucinate, humiliate, illuminate, impersonate, inactivate, inaugurate, incarcerate, incinerate, incorporate, incriminate, indoctrinate, inebriate, infatuate, infuriate, ingratiate, initiate, inoculate, insinuate, interpolate, interrelate, interrogate, intimidate, intoxicate, invalidate, investigate, invigorate, irradiate, Italianate, Korea Strait, legitimate, manipulate, necessitate, negotiate, noncandidate, obliterate, officiate, Orange Free State, orientate, originate, oxygenate, participate, perpetuate, pontificate, precipitate, predominate, prefabricate, premeditate, prevaricate, procrastinate, prognosticate, proliferate, proportionate, quadruplicate, quintuplicate, reciprocate, recuperate, redecorate, reduplicate, reeducate, refrigerate, regenerate, regurgitate, reincarnate, reiterate, rejuvenate, repudiate, resuscitate, retaliate, reverberate, Singapore Strait, sophisticate, subordinate, substantiate, vanity plate • adjustable rate, circumnavigate, decontaminate, deteriorate, differentiate, discombobulate, disorientate, disproportionate, excommunicate, expiration date, hyperventilate, incapacitate, intermediate, misappropriate, overcompensate, overeducate, overestimate, overmedicate, overpopulate, overstimulate, recapitulate, rehabilitate, renegotiate, superannuate, underestimate

ate² \at\ see AT⁵

ate³ \ät\ see OT¹

ate⁴ \ät-ē\ see ATI¹

ate⁵ \ət\ see UT¹

ated \āt-əd\ dated, fated, gated, stated • belated, ill-fated, outdated, related, truncated • animated, antiquated, caffeinated, calculated, carbonated, complicated, corrugated, dedicated, educated, elevated, hyphenated, integrated, laminated, liberated, perforated, saturated, simulated, syncopated, understated • affiliated, articulated, coordinated, decaffeinated, domesticated, encapsulated, incorporated, inebriated, interrelated, intoxicated, opinionated, premeditated, sophisticated, uncalculated, uncomplicated, underinflated, unmitigated, unsaturated • unadulterated, unanticipated, undereducated, underpopulated, unsophisticated • underappreciated

—*also* -ed *forms of verbs listed at* ATE¹

ateful \āt-fəl\ fateful, grateful, hateful • ungrateful

atel¹ \ət-ᵊl\ see OTTLE

atel² \ät-ᵊl\ see ATAL

ateless \āt-ləs\ dateless, weightless

atelist \at-ᵊl-əst\ see ATALYST

ately¹ \āt-lē\ greatly, lately, stately • innately • Johnny-come-lately

ately² \at-ᵊl-ē\ see ATTILY

atem \ät-əm\ see ATUM¹

atement \āt-mənt\ statement • abatement, misstatement, restatement • overstatement, reinstatement, understatement

aten¹ \āt-ᵊn\ Dayton, Satan, straighten

aten² \at-ᵊn\ see ATIN²

aten³ \ät-ᵊn\ see OTTEN

atent¹ \āt-ᵊnt\ see ATANT¹

atent² \at-ᵊnt\ see ATANT²

ater¹ \ȯt-ər\ daughter, slaughter, tauter, water • backwater, bathwater, breakwater, deepwater, dishwater, floodwater, forequarter, freshwater, goddaughter, Goldwater, granddaughter, groundwater, headwater, highwater, hindquarter, hold water, hot water, ice water, jerkwater, manslaughter, meltwater, rainwater, saltwater, seawater, self-slaughter, stepdaughter, still water, tap water, tidewater, tread water, wastewater, white-water • above water, holy water, in deep water, mineral water, overwater, running water, soda water, toilet water, underwater • dead in the water, fish out of water, hell or high water

ater² \āt-ər\ see ATOR

atering \ȯt-ə-riŋ\ slaughtering • mouthwatering • overwatering

atery \ät-ə-rē\ see OTTERY

ates¹ \āts\ Yeats • Gulf States • Levant States, Papal States, Trucial States • Persian Gulf States, United States • house of delegates
—*also* -s, -'s, *and* -s' *forms of nouns and* -s *forms of verbs listed at* ATE¹

ates² \āt-ēz\ Euphrates
—*also* -s, -'s, *and* -s' *forms of nouns listed at* ATY

atest \āt-əst\ latest • at the latest
—*also* -est *forms of adjectives listed at* ATE¹

atey \āt-ē\ see ATY

ath¹ \äth\ see OTH¹

ath² \ȯth\ see OTH²

ath³ \ath\ bath, hath, lath, math, path, wrath • birdbath, bloodbath, flight path, footbath, footpath, glide path, half bath, sunbath, towpath, warpath • aftermath, bridle path, psychopath, shower bath, take a bath, telepath, whirlpool bath • sociopath

atha \ät-ə\ see ATA¹

athe¹ \āth\ bathe, lathe, scathe, swathe • sunbathe

athe² \ath\ see ATH³

ather¹ \äth-ər\ bother, father, rather • forefather, godfather, grandfather, Our Father, stepfather • city father, founding father, Holy Father

ather² \əth-ər\ see OTHER¹

ather³ \ath-ər\ blather, Cather, gather, lather, rather, slather • woolgather

athering \ath-ə-riŋ\ woolgathering
—*also* -ing *forms of verbs listed at* ATHER³

athi \ät-ē\ see ATI¹

athlon \ath-lən\ decathlon, pentathlon, triathlon

ati¹ \ät-ē\ Dottie, dotty, knotty, naughty, potty, Scotty, snotty, spotty • karate, Scarlatti • glitterati, Gujarati, literati, manicotti, Maserati • illuminati

ati² \ātē\ see ATTY

ati³ \äts\ see OTS

ati⁴ \as\ see ASS³

atia \ā-shə\ see ACIA

atial \ā-shəl\ see ACIAL

atian \ā-shən\ see ATION¹

atians \ā-shənz\ see ATIONS

atible \at-ə-bəl\ compatible, getatable • incompatible

atic¹ \ät-ik\ see OTIC

atic² \at-ik\ attic, static • aquatic, asthmatic, chromatic, climatic, dogmatic, dramatic, ecstatic, emphatic, erratic, fanatic, lymphatic, phlegmatic, pneumatic, pragmatic, prismatic, quadratic, rheumatic, schematic, Socratic, thematic, traumatic • acrobatic, Adriatic, aerobatic, antistatic, aromatic, Asiatic, autocratic, automatic, bureaucratic, charismatic, cinematic, democratic, diplomatic, emblematic, enigmatic, Hippocratic, nonemphatic, operatic, photostatic, problematic, programmatic, symptomatic, systematic, technocratic, thermostatic, undogmatic, undramatic • aristocratic, axiomatic, diagrammatic, electrostatic, idiomatic, melodramatic, overdramatic, overemphatic, psychosomatic, uncinematic, undemocratic, undiplomatic • semiautomatic

atica \at-i-kə\ hepatica, sciatica, viatica

atical \at-i-kəl\ fanatical, grammatical, sabbatical • mathematical, ungrammatical

atics \at-iks\ dramatics • acro-

batics, mathematics
—*also* -s, -'s, *and* -s' *forms of
nouns listed at* ATIC[2]
atie \ăt-ē\ *see* ATY
atiens \ā-shənz\ *see* ATIONS
atik \at-ik\ *see* ATIC[2]
atile \at-ᵊl-ē\ *see* ATTILY
atim \ăt-əm\ *see* ATUM[1]
atin[1] \ăt-ᵊn\ *see* OTTEN
atin[2] \at-ᵊn\ batten, fatten, flatten,
Latin, Patton, satin • Manhattan,
Mountbatten, pig latin, Powhatan
atin[3] \ăt-ᵊn\ *see* ATEN[1]
ating \āt-iŋ\ grating, plating, rating,
skating • bearbaiting, bullbaiting,
call-waiting, frustrating, race-
baiting, self-hating, self-rating,
speed skating • aggravating, cal-
culating, carbon dating, fascinat-
ing, figure skating, in-line skating,
maid-in-waiting, nauseating,
operating, penetrating, suffocat-
ing, titillating • accommodating,
discriminating, humiliating, lady-
in-waiting, self-deprecating, self-
operating, self-regulating,
self-replicating, subordinating,
undeviating, unhesitating • self-
perpetuating
—*also* -ing *forms of verbs listed at*
ATE[1]
atinous \at-nəs\ *see* ATNESS
ation[1] \ā-shən\ Asian, Haitian,
nation, ration, station, Thracian
• aeration, Alsatian, carnation,
causation, cessation, cetacean,
citation, Claymation, conflation,
C ration, creation, cremation,
Croatian, crustacean, dalmatian,
damnation, deflation, dictation,
dilation, donation, duration,
elation, equation, Eurasian, filtra-
tion, fixation, flirtation, flotation,
formation, foundation, frustra-
tion, gas station, gestation, grada-
tion, gyration, hydration,
inflation, K ration, lactation,

legation, libation, location, migra-
tion, mutation, narration, nega-
tion, notation, oration, ovation,
plantation, privation, probation,
prostration, pulsation, quotation,
relation, rotation, salvation, seda-
tion, sensation, space station,
stagnation, starvation, substation,
summation, taxation, temptation,
translation, truncation, vacation,
vibration, vocation, way station,
workstation • abdication, aberra-
tion, acclamation, accusation,
activation, adaptation, admira-
tion, adoration, adulation, affec-
tation, affirmation, aggravation,
aggregation, agitation, allegation,
allocation, amputation, altera-
tion, altercation, alternation,
Amerasian, animation, annexa-
tion, annotation, Appalachian,
application, approbation, arbitra-
tion, aspiration, attestation, aug-
mentation, automation, aviation,
avocation, calculation, calibra-
tion, cancellation, carbonation,
celebration, chlorination, circula-
tion, coloration, combination,
commendation, commutation,
compensation, compilation,
complication, computation, con-
centration, condemnation,
condensation, confirmation,
confiscation, conflagration, con-
frontation, congregation, conjuga-
tion, connotation, consecration,
conservation, consolation, con-
stellation, consternation,
constipation, consultation, con-
templation, conversation, convo-
cation, coronation, corporation,
correlation, corrugation, crop
rotation, culmination, cultivation,
cumulation, declamation, declara-
tion, decoration, dedication,
defamation, defecation, deforma-
tion, degradation, dehydration,

delegation, demonstration, denigration, deportation, deprivation, derivation, desecration, designation, desolation, desperation, destination, detonation, devastation, deviation, dislocation, dissertation, divination, domination, duplication, education, elevation, emigration, emulation, escalation, estimation, evocation, exaltation, excavation, exclamation, expectation, expiration, explanation, exploitation, exploration, exportation, exultation, fabrication, fascination, federation, fermentation, filling station, fire station, flagellation, fluoridation, fluctuation, forestation, formulation, fragmentation, fumigation, gene mutation, generation, germination, graduation, habitation, heat prostration, hesitation, hibernation, hyphenation, illustration, imitation, immigration, implantation, implication, importation, incantation, incarnation, inclination, incubation, indentation, indication, indignation, infestation, infiltration, inflammation, information, innovation, inspiration, installation, instigation, insulation, integration, intonation, invitation, invocation, irrigation, irritation, isolation, jubilation, laceration, lamentation, legislation, levitation, liberation, limitation, liquidation, litigation, lubrication, medication, meditation, misquotation, mistranslation, moderation, modulation, molestation, motivation, multination, mutilation, navigation, nomination, obfuscation, obligation, observation, occupation, operation, orchestration, ordination, oscillation, ostentation, penetration, percolation, perforation, perspiration, pigmentation, police station, pollination, population, power station, preparation, presentation, preservation, proclamation, procreation, prolongation, propagation, protestation, provocation, publication, punctuation, radiation, recitation, re-creation, recreation, reformation, refutation, registration, regulation, rehydration, relaxation, relocation, renovation, replication, reputation, reservation, resignation, respiration, restoration, retardation, revelation, revocation, ruination, sanitation, saturation, segmentation, segregation, separation, service station, simulation, situation, speculation, stimulation, stipulation, stylization, suffocation, syncopation, syndication, tabulation, termination, T formation, titillation, toleration, transformation, transmigration, transportation, trepidation, tribulation, usurpation, vaccination, valuation, variation, vegetation, veneration, ventilation, vindication, violation, weather station • abbreviation, abomination, acceleration, accommodation, accreditation, accumulation, adjudication, administration, affiliation, alienation, amplification, annihilation, anticipation, appreciation, appropriation, approximation, argumentation, articulation, asphyxiation, assassination, assimilation, association, authentication, authorization, beautification, centralization, certification, civilization, clarification, classification, coeducation, cohabitation, collaboration, colonization, commemoration, communication, confederation, configuration, congratulation, consideration, consolidation, contamination, continuation, cooperation, coordination, cross-pollination, crystallization, de-escalation, deforestation, degeneration, deification, deliberation, demonization, denomination, denunciation, depreciation, deregulation, desegregation, determination, devaluation, digitization, discoloration, discrimination, disinclination, disintegration, dissemination, documentation, dramatization, echolocation, elaboration, elimination, elucidation, emancipation, enumeration, equalization, eradication, evacuation, evaluation, evaporation, exaggeration, examination, exasperation, exhilaration, extermination, falsification, feminization, fertilization, fortification, globalization, glorification, gratification, hallucination, harmonization, humiliation, hyperinflation, illumination, imagination, immunization, impersonation, implementation, improvisation, inauguration, incarceration, incineration, incorporation, incrimination, indoctrination, infatuation, initiation, inoculation, instrumentation, interpretation, interrelation, interrogation, intimidation, intoxication, invalidation, investigation, itemization, justification, legalization, liberalization, magnetization, magnification, manifestation, manipulation, mechanization, memorization, misapplication, miscalculation, misinformation, mobilization, modernization, modification, multiplication, mystification, nationalization, naturalization, negotiation, normalization, notifi-cation, obliteration, organization, origination, orientation, ornamentation, overinflation, oxygenation, participation, pasteurization, perpetuation, polarization, postgraduation, post-Reformation, precipitation, predestination, preoccupation, prepublication, preregistration, prettification, procrastination, proliferation, pronunciation, purification, qualification, ratification, reaffirmation, realization, recommendation, recuperation, redecoration, rededication, reduplication, reforestation, reformulation, refrigeration, regeneration, regimentation, reincarnation, reiteration, rejuvenation, remuneration, renunciation, representation, retaliation, reverberation, sedimentation, Serbo-Croatian, signification, simplification, socialization, solicitation, sophistication, specialization, specification, stabilization, standardization, sterilization, subordination, supplementation, transfiguration, uglification, unification, unionization, urbanization, verification, victimization, vocalization, vulgarization, westernization, x-radiation • characterization, circumnavigation, commercialization, criminalization, cross-examination, decentralization, decontamination, deterioration, differentiation, disorientation, disorganization, disqualification, diversification, electrification, excommunication, experimentation, generalization, homogenization, hospitalization, hyperventilation, idealization, identification, insubordination, intensification, megacorporation, militarization, miniaturization, misappropriation, miscommuni-

cation, misinterpretation, mispro-
nunciation, misrepresentation,
monopolization, overcompensa-
tion, overpopulation, personifica-
tion, popularization,
reconciliation, reconsideration,
rehabilitation, reorganization,
revitalization, solidification, un-
derestimation, visualization

ation² \ā-zhən\ see ASION

ation³ \ash-ən\ see ASSION

ational¹ \ā-shnəl\ sensational • con-
frontational, congregational,
conversational, educational, gen-
erational, gravitational, inspira-
tional, motivational, recreational
• coeducational, improvisational,
organizational

ational² \ash-nəl\ national, rational
• irrational • international, multi-
national

ationist \ā-shnəst\ conservationist,
isolationist, preservationist, segre-
gationist

ations \ā-shənz\ Galatians, rela-
tions • Lamentations, League of
Nations, Revelations • United
Nations

atious \ā-shəs\ see ACIOUS

atis \at-əs\ see ATUS²

atist \āt-əst\ see ATEST

atitude \at-ə-tüd\ see ATTITUDE

atius \ā-shəs\ see ACIOUS

ative \āt-iv\ dative, native • cre-
ative, nonnative • contemplative,
cumulative, decorative, imitative,
innovative, irritative, legislative,
meditative, operative, penetrative,
qualitative, quantitative, spec-
ulative, vegetative • admin-
istrative, appreciative, au-
thoritative, collaborative, com-
memorative, communicative,
cooperative, degenerative,
deliberative, investigative, post-
operative • uncommunica-
tive

atl \ät-ᵊl\ see OTTLE

atlas \at-ləs\ atlas, Atlas, fatless,
hatless

atless \at-ləs\ see ATLAS

atli \ät-lē\ see OTLY

atling \at-liŋ\ rattling • saber rattling
  —also -ing forms of verbs listed at
ATTLE

atly \at-lē\ flatly, rattly

atness \at-nəs\ fatness, flatness
• gelatinous

ato¹ \ät-ō\ auto, blotto, grotto,
lotto, motto, Otto • legato, stac-
cato, tomato, vibrato • moderato,
pizzicato

ato² \āt-ō\ Cato, Plato • potato,
tomato • couch potato, hot potato, plum tomato, sweet potato
• cherry tomato

atom \at-əm\ see ATUM²

aton \at-ᵊn\ see ATIN²

ator \āt-ər\ crater, dater, freighter,
gator, grater, hater, later, satyr,
skater, traitor, waiter • creator,
curator, debater, dictator, dona-
tor, dumbwaiter, equator, first-
rater, headwaiter, ice-skater,
locator, Mercator, migrator,
narrator, pond skater, rotator,
spectator, speed skater, tailgater,
theater, third-rater, translator
• abdicator, activator, agitator,
alligator, alternator, animator,
arbitrator, aviator, calculator,
carburetor, circulator, commen-
tator, cultivator, decorator,
demonstrator, educator, elevator,
escalator, estimator, excavator,
figure skater, fumigator, genera-
tor, gladiator, illustrator, imitator,
incubator, indicator, in-line
skater, innovator, inspirator,
instigator, insulator, liberator,
mediator, moderator, motivator,
navigator, numerator, operator,
orchestrator, percolator, perpe-

trator, pollinator, radiator, regu-
lator, renovator, respirator, roller
skater, second-rater, separator,
simulator, Sunset Crater, termina-
tor, valuator, ventilator, violator
• accelerator, administrator,
annihilator, collaborator, concil-
iator, coordinator, denominator,
emancipator, enumerator, evalua-
tor, exterminator, facilitator,
grain elevator, impersonator,
incinerator, interrogator, investi-
gator, negotiator, perambulator,
procrastinator, refrigerator,
sooner or later
—*also* -er *forms of adjectives listed
at* ATE[1]

atre \at\ see AT[5]

atric \a-trik\ Patrick • theatric
• geriatric, pediatric, psychiatric

atrick \a-trik\ see ATRIC

atrics \a-triks\ theatrics • pedi-
atrics

atrix \ā-triks\ matrix • Beatrix

atron \ā-trən\ matron, patron

ats[1] \äts\ see OTS

ats[2] \ats\ bats, rats • Bonneville
Salt Flats
—*also* -s, -'s, *and* -s' *forms of
nouns and* -s *forms of verbs listed
at* AT[5]

atsa \ät-sə\ see ATZO[1]

atsch \ach\ see ATCH[3]

atsu \ät-sü\ Matsu • shiatsu

atsy \at-sē\ see AZI[3]

att[1] \at\ see AT[5]

att[2] \ät\ see OT[1]

atta \ät-ə\ see ATA[1]

attage \at-ij\ see OTTAGE

attan \at-ᵊn\ see ATIN[2]

atte \at\ see AT[5]

attel \at-ᵊl\ see ATTLE

atten \at-ᵊn\ see ATIN[2]

atter \at-ər\ batter, chatter, clatter,
fatter, flatter, hatter, latter, matter, patter, platter, satyr, scatter,
shatter, spatter, splatter, tatter

• dark matter, gray matter, no
matter, standpatter, the matter
• antimatter, for that matter,
pitter-patter, printed matter,
subject matter

attering \at-ə-riŋ\ scattering, smat-
tering • earth-shattering, unflat-
tering
—*also* -ing *forms of verbs listed at*
ATTER

attern \at-ərn\ pattern, Saturn,
slattern • test pattern • holding
pattern

attery \at-ə-rē\ battery, flattery

atti[1] \ät-ē\ see ATI[1]

atti[2] \at-ē\ see ATTY

attic \at-ik\ see ATIC[2]

attica \at-i-kə\ see ATICA

attice[1] \at-əs\ see ATUS[2]

attice[2] \at-ish\ see ATTISH

attie \at-ē\ see ATTY

attily \at-ᵊl-ē\ cattily, chattily,
Natalie, nattily, rattly • philately

atting \at-iŋ\ batting, matting,
tatting
—*also* -ing *forms of verbs listed at*
AT[5]

attish \at-ish\ brattish, fattish,
flattish

attitude \at-ə-tüd\ attitude, gratitude, latitude, platitude • beatitude, ingratitude, midlatitude

attle \at-ᵊl\ battle, cattle, prattle,
rattle, tattle • beef cattle, death
rattle, embattle, pitched battle,
Seattle • dairy cattle, tittle-tattle

attling \at-liŋ\ see ATLING

attly[1] \at-ᵊl-ē\ see ATTILY

attly[2] \at-lē\ see ATLY

atto[1] \at-ə\ see ATA[3]

atto[2] \ät-ō\ see ATO[1]

atton \at-ᵊn\ see ATIN[2]

atty \at-ē\ batty, bratty, catty,
chatty, fatty, Hattie, natty, patty,
Patty, ratty • nonfatty • Cincinnati

atum[1] \āt-əm\ substratum, verba-
tim • ultimatum

atum² \at-əm\ atom • substratum

atur \āt-ər\ see ATOR

ature¹ \ā-chər\ nature • 4-H'er • force of nature, freak of nature, human nature, Mother Nature, nomenclature, second nature

ature² \ach-ər\ see ATCHER²

aturn \at-ərn\ see ATTERN

atus¹ \āt-əs\ gratis, status, stratus • hiatus • altostratus, apparatus, cirrostratus, nimbostratus

atus² \at-əs\ gratis, lattice, status, stratus • clematis • altostratus, apparatus, cirrostratus, nimbo-stratus

atute \ach-ət\ see ATCHET

aty \āt-ē\ eighty, Haiti, Katie, Leyte, matey, weighty, yeti • Papeete

atyr \āt-ər\ see ATOR

atz¹ \ats\ see ATS²

atz² \äts\ see OTS

atzo¹ \ät-sə\ matzo • piazza

atzo² \ät-sō\ see AZZO

atzu \ät-sü\ see ATSU

au¹ \ō\ see OW¹

au² \ü\ see EW¹

au³ \aù\ see OW²

au⁴ \ò\ see AW¹

aub \äb\ see OB¹

aube \ōb\ see OBE¹

auber \ȯb-ər\ Micawber, mud dauber

auble \äb-əl\ see ABBLE¹

auce \ȯs\ see OSS¹

aucer \ȯ-sər\ see OSSER

auch \äch\ see OTCH

auche \ōsh\ see OCHE²

auckland \ȯk-lənd\ Auckland, Falkland

aucous \ȯ-kəs\ caucus, raucous

aucus \ȯ-kəs\ see AUCOUS

aud¹ \ȯd\ awed, broad, Claude, clawed, flawed, fraud, god, jawed, laud, Maude • abroad, applaud, defraud, maraud • antifraud, wire fraud

—also -ed *forms of verbs listed at* AW¹

aud² \äd\ see OD¹

audable \ȯd-ə-bəl\ audible, laud-able • applaudable, inaudible

aude¹ \aùd-ē\ see OWDY

aude² \ȯd-ē\ see AWDY

aude³ \ȯd\ see AUD¹

audible \ȯd-ə-bəl\ see AUDABLE

audit \ȯd-ət\ audit, plaudit

audy¹ \äd-ē\ see ODY¹

audy² \ȯd-ē\ see AWDY

auer \aùr\ see OWER²

auffeur \ō-fər\ see OFER

auge \āj\ see AGE³

auged \ājd\ see AGED

auger¹ \ȯ-gər\ see OGGER²

auger² \ā-jər\ see AGER¹

augh¹ \af\ see APH

augh² \ä\ see A¹

augh³ \ak̄\ see ACH¹

augh⁴ \ȯ\ see AW¹

aughable \af-ə-bəl\ see AFFABLE

augham \ȯm\ see AUM¹

aughn¹ \än\ see ON¹

aughn² \ȯn\ see ON³

aught¹ \ät\ see OT¹

aught² \ȯt\ see OUGHT¹

aughter¹ \af-tər\ see AFTER

aughter² \ȯt-ər\ see ATER¹

aughty¹ \ȯt-ē\ haughty, naughty • Buonarroti

aughty² \ät-ē\ see ATI¹

augre \ȯg-ər\ see OGGER²

augur \ȯg-ər\ see OGGER²

aui \aù-ē\ see OWIE

auk \ȯk\ see ALK

aukee \ȯ-kē\ see ALKIE

aul \ȯl\ see ALL¹

aulay \ȯ-lē\ see AWLY

auld¹ \ȯl\ see ALL¹

auld² \ō\ see OW¹

auled \ȯld\ see ALD¹

auler \ȯ-lər\ see ALLER¹

aulin \ȯ-lən\ see ALLEN

auling \ȯ-liŋ\ see ALLING

aulish \ȯ-lish\ see ALLISH

aulk \ȯk\ see ALK
aulker \ȯ-kər\ see ALKER
aulking \ȯ-kiŋ\ see ALKING
aulle \ȯl\ see ALL[1]
aulm \ȯm\ see AUM[1]
ault[1] \ȯlt\ see ALT
ault[2] \ō\ see OW[1]
aulter \ȯl-tər\ see ALTER
aulting \ȯl-tiŋ\ see ALTING
aultless \ȯlt-ləs\ see ALTLESS
aulty \ȯl-tē\ see ALTY
aum[1] \ȯm\ qualm • meerschaum
aum[2] \äm\ see OM[1]
aun[1] \än\ see ON[1]
aun[2] \ən\ see UN[1]
aun[3] \ȯn\ see ON[3]
aun[4] \aůn\ see OWN[2]
auna[1] \än-ə\ see ANA[1]
auna[2] \ȯn-ə\ see ONNA[1]
aunch[1] \änch\ conch, paunch,
  stanch
aunch[2] \ȯnch\ haunch, launch,
  paunch, stanch, staunch
aunchy \ȯn-chē\ paunchy, raunchy
aunder[1] \ȯn-dər\ launder, maunder
aunder[2] \än-dər\ see ONDER[1]
aunish \än-ish\ see ONISH
aunt[1] \ȯnt\ daunt, flaunt, gaunt,
  haunt, jaunt, taunt, want • avaunt
aunt[2] \ant\ see ANT[5]
aunt[3] \änt\ see ANT[2]
aunted \ȯnt-əd\ see ONTED
aunter[1] \änt-ər\ saunter, taunter
aunter[2] \ȯnt-ər\ haunter, saunter,
  taunter
aunty[1] \ȯnt-ē\ flaunty, jaunty
aunty[2] \änt-ē\ see ANTI[1]
aunus \än-əs\ see ONUS[1]
aupe \ōp\ see OPE
auphin \ȯ-fən\ see OFFIN
aur[1] \aůr\ see OWER[2]
aur[2] \ȯr\ see OR[1]
aura[1] \ȯr-ə\ see ORA
aura[2] \är-ə\ see ARA[1]
aural \ȯr-əl\ see ORAL
aure \ȯr\ see OR[1]
aurea \ȯr-ē-ə\ see ORIA

aurean \ȯr-ē-ən\ see ORIAN
aurel \ȯr-əl\ see ORAL
auren[1] \är-ən\ see ARIN
auren[2] \ȯr-ən\ see ORIN[1]
aurence \ȯr-ən(t)s\ see AWRENCE
aureus \ȯr-ē-əs\ see ORIOUS
auri \aůr-ē\ see OWERY
aurian \ȯr-ē-ən\ see ORIAN
auric \ȯr-ik\ see ORIC
aurice[1] \är-əs\ see ORRIS[1]
aurice[2] \ȯr-əs\ see AURUS
auricle \ȯr-i-kəl\ see ORICAL
aurie[1] \ȯr-ē\ see ORY
aurie[2] \är-ē\ see ARI[1]
aurous \ȯr-əs\ see AURUS
aurus \ȯr-əs\ Boris, chorus, Doris,
  Horace, Maurice, morris, Morris,
  Norris, porous, Taurus • Centau-
  rus, decorous, Dolores, phospho-
  rous, sonorous, thesaurus
  • allosaurus, brontosaurus,
  stegosaurus • apatosaurus, tyran-
  nosaurus
aury \ȯr-ē\ see ORY
aus[1] \aůs\ see OUSE[2]
aus[2] \ȯz\ see AUSE[1]
ausal \ȯ-zəl\ causal • menopausal
ause[1] \ȯz\ cause, 'cause, clause,
  gauze, pause, yaws • applause,
  because • grasp at straws,
  menopause, Santa Claus
  — also -s, -'s, and -s' forms of
  nouns and -s forms of verbs listed
  at AW[1]
ause[2] \əz\ see EUSE[1]
auseous \ȯ-shəs\ see AUTIOUS
auss \aůs\ see OUSE[1]
aussie[1] \äs-ē\ see OSSY[1]
aussie[2] \ȯ-sē\ see OSSY[2]
aust[1] \aůst\ see OUST[1]
aust[2] \ȯst\ see OST[3]
austen \ȯs-tən\ see OSTON
austin \ȯs-tən\ see OSTON
austless \ȯst-ləs\ costless • ex-
  haustless
aut[1] \ō\ see OW[1]
aut[2] \aůt\ see OUT[3]

aut³ \ät\ see OT¹
aut⁴ \ȯt\ see OUGHT¹
aute \ōt\ see OAT
autics \ät-iks\ see OTICS
autious \ȯ-shəs\ cautious, nauseous • incautious • overcautious
auto¹ \ȯt-ō\ auto, Giotto • risotto
auto² \ät-ō\ see ATO¹
auve \ōv\ see OVE²
auze \ȯz\ see AUSE¹
auzer \au̇-zər\ see OUSER
av¹ \äv\ see OLVE²
av² \av\ see ALVE²
ava¹ \äv-ə\ fava, guava, java, Java, lava • cassava • balaclava, Bratislava, Costa Brava
ava² \av-ə\ java • balaclava
avage \av-ij\ ravage, savage
avan \ä-vən\ see AVEN¹
avant \av-ənt\ haven't, savant
avarice \av-rəs\ see AVEROUS
ave¹ \äv-ā\ clave, grave, Jahveh
ave² \āv\ brave, cave, crave, Dave, fave, gave, grave, knave, lave, nave, pave, rave, save, shave, slave, stave, they've, waive, wave, Wave • airwave, behave, brain wave, close shave, cold wave, concave, conclave, deprave, enclave, engrave, enslave, forgave, Great Slave, heat wave, octave, repave, shock wave, shortwave, sine wave, sound wave, wage slave • after-shave, Fingal's Cave, Mammoth Cave, microwave, misbehave, tidal wave • permanent wave, radio wave
ave³ \av\ see ALVE³
ave⁴ \äv\ see OLVE²
aved \āvd\ waved • depraved, unsaved
—*also* -ed *forms of verbs listed at* AVE²
avel \av-əl\ cavil, gavel, gravel, ravel, travel • unravel • gavel-to-gavel
aveling \av-liŋ\ traveling

—*also* -ing *forms of verbs listed at* AVEL
avement \āv-mənt\ pavement • enslavement
aven¹ \ā-vən\ Avon, craven, graven, haven, maven, raven, shaven • New Haven, night raven • riboflavin, Winter Haven • Stratford-upon-Avon
aven² \av-ən\ see AVIN
aven't \av-ən\ see AVANT
aver¹ \äv-ər\ slaver • palaver
aver² \ā-vər\ braver, caver, favor, flavor, graver, quaver, raver, savor, shaver, slaver, waiver, waver • disfavor, engraver, face-saver, flag-waver, lifesaver, screen saver, time-saver
aver³ \av-ər\ slaver • cadaver, palaver
avern \av-ərn\ cavern, tavern
averous \av-rəs\ avarice • cadaverous
avery \āv-rē\ Avery, bravery, knavery, quavery, savory, slavery • unsavory, white slavery • antislavery
avey \ā-vē\ see AVY
avia \ā-vē-ə\ Belgravia, Moldavia, Moravia • Scandinavia
avian \ā-vē-ən\ avian • Moravian • Scandinavian
avid \av-əd\ avid, gravid
avie \ā-vē\ see AVY
avil \av-əl\ see AVEL
avin \av-ən\ Avon, raven
aving \ā-viŋ\ caving, craving, paving, raving, saving, shaving • engraving, face-saving, flag-waving, lifesaving, time-saving • laborsaving
—*also* -ing *forms of verbs listed at* AVE²
avis \ā-vəs\ Davis, Mavis
avish¹ \ā-vish\ knavish, slavish
avish² \av-ish\ lavish, ravish
avity \av-ət-ē\ cavity, gravity • de-

pravity • antigravity, body cavity, zero gravity • center of gravity

avl \äv-əl\ see OVEL[1]

avo \äv-ō\ bravo • centavo • Rio Bravo

avon[1] \ā-vən\ see AVEN[1]

avon[2] \a-vən\ see AVIN

avor \ā-vər\ see AVER[2]

avored \ā-vərd\ favored, flavored • ill-favored
—*also* -ed *forms of verbs listed at* AVER[2]

avory \āv-rē\ see AVERY

avus \ā-vəs\ see AVIS

avvy \av-ē\ navvy, savvy

avy \ā-vē\ Davy, gravy, navy, slavey, wavy

aw[1] \o\ aw, awe, caw, claw, craw, draw, flaw, gnaw, haw, jaw, la, law, maw, pa, paw, pshaw, Ra, rah, raw, saw, shah, slaw, spa, squaw, straw, thaw, yaw • band saw, bedstraw, blue law, bucksaw, buzz saw, bylaw, chain saw, Choctaw, coleslaw, Corn Law, Danelaw, declaw, dewclaw, Esau, forepaw, geegaw, grandma, grandpa, guffaw, hacksaw, handsaw, hee-haw, hurrah, in-law, jackdaw, jigsaw, last straw, leash law, lockjaw, macaw, Moose Jaw, Nassau, outdraw, outlaw, pasha, pawpaw, rickshaw, ripsaw, scofflaw, scrimshaw, seesaw, southpaw, Utah, Warsaw, whipsaw, withdraw • Arkansas, Chickasaw, Chippewa, civil law, common-law, court of law, crosscut saw, foofaraw, higher law, homestead law, in the raw, keyhole saw, Kiowa, lemon law, mackinaw, Murphy's Law, Omaha, Ottawa, oversaw, panama, private law, public law, roman law, Saginaw, son-in-law, tragic flaw, Wichita, williwaw • brotherin-law, circular saw, criminal law,

daughter-in-law, father-in-law, mother-in-law, sister-in-law, stick in one's craw, unwritten law

aw[2] \äv\ see OLVE[2]

aw[3] \of\ see OFF[2]

aw[4] \äf\ see OFF[1]

awa[1] \ä-wə\ Chihuahua, Tarawa • Okinawa, Tokugawa

awa[2] \ä-və\ see AVA[1]

awar \aur\ see OWER[2]

awber[1] \äb-ər\ see OBBER

awber[2] \ob-ər\ see AUBER

awd \od\ see AUD[1]

awddle \äd-ᵊl\ see ODDLE

awdry \o-drē\ Audrey, tawdry

awdy \od-ē\ bawdy, gaudy

awe \o\ see AW[1]

awed \od\ see AUD[1]

aweless \o-ləs\ see AWLESS

awer \or\ see OR[1]

awers \orz\ see OORS

awful \o-fəl\ awful, lawful, offal • unlawful

awfully \of-ə-lē\ awfully, lawfully • unlawfully

awing \oiŋ\ cloying, drawing • line drawing
—*also* -ing *forms of verbs listed at* AW[1]

awk \ok\ see ALK

awker \o-kər\ see ALKER

awkish \o-kish\ hawkish, mawkish

awky \o-kē\ see ALKIE

awl \ol\ see ALL[1]

awler \o-lər\ see ALLER[1]

awless \o-ləs\ flawless, lawless

awling \o-liŋ\ see ALLING

awly \o-lē\ brawly, crawly, dolly, drawly, Raleigh, scrawly, squally • Bengali

awm \om\ see AUM[1]

awn[1] \än\ see ON[1]

awn[2] \on\ see ON[3]

awner[1] \on-ər\ fawner, goner

awner[2] \än-ər\ see ONOR[1]

awney \o-nē\ see AWNY[1]

awning \än-iŋ\ see ONING[1]

awny[1] \ȯ-nē\ brawny, scrawny, tawny • mulligatawny

awny[2] \än-ē\ see ANI[1]

awrence \ȯr-ən(t)s\ Florence, Lawrence, warrants • abhorrence, Saint Lawrence

awry \ȯr-ē\ see ORY

aws \ȯz\ see AUSE[1]

awse \ȯz\ see AUSE[1]

awy \ȯi\ see OY

awyer \ȯ-yər\ lawyer, sawyer • trial lawyer • criminal lawyer

ax[1] \äks\ see OX

ax[2] \aks\ ax, fax, flax, lax, max, Max, sax, tax, wax • Ajax, anthrax, beeswax, borax, broadax, climax, earwax, Fairfax, IMAX, meat-ax, pickax, poll tax, pretax, relax, sales tax, surtax, syntax, thorax • aftertax, ball of wax, battle-ax, Halifax, hidden tax, income tax, overtax, sealing wax, to the max, Turtle Wax • anticlimax

—also -s, -'s, and -s' forms of nouns and -s forms of verbs listed at ACK[2]

axant \ak-sənt\ see ACCENT

axen \ak-sən\ see AXON

axi \ak-sē\ see AXY

axon \ak-sən\ flaxen, Jackson, Saxon, waxen • Anglo-Saxon

axy \ak-sē\ maxi, taxi, waxy • air taxi • water taxi

ay[1] \ā\ a, ae, bay, bray, clay, day, eh, Faye, fey, flay, fray, gay, gray, hay, hey, Hue, j, jay, Jay, k, Kay, lay, lei, may, May, nay, née, neigh, pay, play, pray, prey, quay, Rae, ray, Ray, re, say, slay, sleigh, spay, splay, spray, stay, stray, sway, they, tray, way, weigh, whey, yea • airplay, airway, aisleway, all-day, allay, archway, array, ashtray, assay, astray, at bay, away, aweigh, ballet, base pay, belay, beltway, beret, betray, bikeway, birthday, Biscay, Bizet, blasé, Bombay, bouquet, breezeway, Broadway, buffet, byway, café, Cape May, Cartier, Cathay, causeway, chalet, child's play, cliché, convey, Coos Bay, crawlway, crochet, croquet, DA, daresay, D-day, death ray, decay, deejay, defray, delay, dismay, display, DJ, doomsday, doorway, dossier, downplay, driveway, duvet, Earl Grey, entrée, essay, fair play, fairway, field day, filet, fillet, fishway, Flag Day, flight pay, flyway, foray, forte, foul play, foyer, frappé, freeway, Friday, Galway, gangway, Gaspé, gateway, give way, gourmet, Green Bay, gunplay, hair spray, halfway, hallway, harm's way, hatchway, headway, hearsay, heyday, highway, hold sway, hooray, horseplay, in play, inlay, Jolliet, leeway, Lord's day, maguey, mainstay, make hay, Malay, Manet, Marseilles, match play, May Day, Mayday, melee, midday, midway, Midway, Millay, mislay, misplay, Monday, Monet, moray, noonday, Norway, no way, obey, OK, olé, one-way, osprey, outlay, outplay, outstay, outweigh, PA, parfait, parkway, parlay, parquet, partway, passé, pathway, payday, pearl gray, Pele, per se, Pompeii, portray, prepay, puree, purvey, raceway, Rahway, railway, relay, Rene, Renee, repay, replay, risqué, roadway, Roget, role-play, runway, sachet, saint's day, sashay, sauté, screenplay, seaway, Shark Bay, shar-pei, shipway, sick bay, sick day, sick pay, slideway, soiree, someday, soufflé, speedway, spillway, squeeze play, stairway, Steinway, stingray, straightway, stroke play, subway, Sunday, survey, swordplay, Taipei, tea tray, three-way, thruway, Thursday, today, tollway, touché, toupee, trackway, Tuesday, Twelfth Day, two-way, valet, V-day, veejay, walkway, waylay, Wednesday, weekday, wordplay, workday, X ray • Agnus Dei, A-OK, alleyway, All Fools' Day, All Saints' Day, All Souls' Day, all the way, antigay, anyway, appliqué, Arbor Day, attaché, back away, Baffin Bay, bang away, Bastille Day, beta ray, bird of prey, Biscayne Bay, blow away, Boxing Day, breakaway, break away, Bristol Bay, Buzzards Bay, by the way, cabaret, cableway, Cam Ranh Bay, canapé, Cape Cod Bay, caraway, carriageway, Cartier, castaway, cathode ray, china clay, Chippewa, cog railway, consommé, cosmic ray, croupier, cutaway, day-to-day, déclassé, devotee, Dingle Bay, disarray, disobey, divorcé, divorcée, DNA, dollar day, double play, dress-down day, eagle ray, ember day, émigré, Empire Day, entranceway, entryway, everyday, exposé, expressway, fall away, Faraday, faraway, Fathers Day, feet of clay, fiancé, fiancée, fire away, foldaway, gal Friday, gamma ray, getaway, girl Friday, giveaway, give away, Glacier Bay, Groundhog Day, Guy Fawkes Day, hell to pay, Hemingway, hideaway, hit the hay, holiday, holy day, Hudson Bay, Hugh Capet, Humboldt Bay, in a way, interplay, IRA, Joliet, judgment day, keep-away, Labor Day, layaway, lay away, lingerie, macramé, Mandalay, manta ray, matinee, meet halfway, MIA, Milky Way, Monterrey, Mother's Day, motorway, multiday, mystery play, negligee, New Year's Day, New York Bay, night and day, off Broadway, Ojibwa, on the way, out of play, overlay, overpay, overplay, overstay, overweigh, Paraguay, passageway, pass away, passion play, pepper spray, photoplay, play-by-play, plug-and-play, power play, present-day, protégé, Prudhoe Bay, pull away, put away, Rabelais, rainy-day, reconvey, repartee, résumé, ricochet, right away, right-of-way, RNA, runaway, run away, salt away, San Jose, Santa Fe, São Tomé, Saturday, severance pay, sock away, square away, stowaway, straightaway, street railway, Table Bay, takeaway, taxiway, thataway, throwaway, throw away, Thunder Bay, triple play, turn away, Turtle Bay, underlay, underpay, underway, Uruguay, vertebra, waterway, Whitsunday, workaday, working day, Zuider Zee • Appian Way, April Fool's Day, Armistice Day, Ascension Day, Australia Day, Bay of Biscay, Botany Bay, carry away, Chesapeake Bay, Columbus Day, communiqué, corps de ballet, Delaware Bay, devil to pay, Dominion Day, Election Day, electric ray, far and away, fiddle away, Frobisher Bay, Giant's Causeway, High Holiday, instant replay, Jamaica Bay, Korea Bay, medley relay, Midsummer Day, miracle play, Montego Bay, Morgan le Fay, off-off-Broadway, out-of-the-way, papier-mâché, Patriots' Day, photo-essay, preholiday, Presidents' Day, Rogation Day, Saginaw Bay, Saint Patrick's Day, superhighway, Thanksgiving Day, Valentine's

Day, Veterans Day • Independence Day, Memorial Day, morality play • cinema verité

ay[2] \ē\ see EE[1]

ay[3] \ī\ see Y[1]

aya[1] \ī-ə\ see IAH[1]

aya[2] \ä-ə\ see AIA[1]

ayable \ā-ə-bəl\ payable, playable, sayable • displayable, unplayable, unsayable

ayah \ī-ə\ see IAH[1]

ayal \āl\ see AIL

ayan[1] \ā-ən\ crayon • Chilean, Malayan, Pompeian • Galilean, Himalayan

ayan[2] \ī-ən\ see ION[1]

aybe[1] \ā-bē\ see ABY

aybe[2] \eb-ē\ see EBBY

ayday \ā-dā\ Mayday, May Day

aye[1] \ā\ see AY[1]

aye[2] \ī\ see Y[1]

ayed \ād\ see ADE[1]

ayer \ā-ər\ layer, mayor, payer, player, prayer, slayer, sprayer, stayer • ballplayer, betrayer, bricklayer, cardplayer, conveyor, doomsayer, manslayer, naysayer, purveyor, soothsayer, surveyor, taxpayer
—*also* -er *forms of adjectives listed at* AY[1]

ayered \erd\ see AIRED

ayest \ā-əst\ mayest, sayest • essayist
—*also* -est *forms of adjectives listed at* AY[1]

ayin[1] \ī-ən\ see ION[1]

ayin[2] \īn\ see INE[1]

aying \ā-iŋ\ fraying, playing, saying • bricklaying, doomsaying, longplaying, nay-saying, soothsaying, surveying, taxpaying
—*also* -ing *forms of verbs listed at* AY[1]

ayish \ā-ish\ clayish, grayish

ayist \ā-əst\ see AYEST

ayle \āl\ see AIL

ayless \ā-ləs\ rayless, talus, wayless • aurora australis

ayling \ā-liŋ\ see AILING

aylor \ā-lər\ see AILER

ayman \ā-mən\ see AMEN[1]

ayment \ā-mənt\ claimant, payment, raiment • co-payment, down payment, nonpayment, prepayment, stop payment

ayne \ān\ see ANE[1]

ayness \ā-nəs\ grayness, heinous, Janus • Uranus • everydayness

ayo[1] \ā-ō\ see EO[1]

ayo[2] \ī-ō\ see IO[1]

ayon \ā-ən\ see AYAN[1]

ayor \ā-ər\ see AYER

ayou[1] \ī-ə\ see IAH[1]

ayou[2] \ī-ō\ see IO[1]

ayr \er\ see ARE[4]

ays[1] \ez\ fez, Fez, prez, says • Chávez, Cortés, Inez, Suez, unsays • Mayagüez

ays[2] \āz\ see AZE[1]

aysia \ā-zhə\ see ASIA

ay-so \ā-sō\ see ESO

ayyid[1] \ī-əd\ see YAD

ayyid[2] \ēd-ē\ see EEDY

az[1] \az\ see AZZ

az[2] \äz\ see OISE[1]

az[3] \äts\ see OTS

aza[1] \äz-ə\ Gaza, plaza • piazza

aza[2] \az-ə\ plaza • piazza

aze[1] \āz\ blaze, braise, chaise, craze, days, daze, faze, gaze, glaze, graze, haze, laze, maize, Mays, maze, phase, phrase, praise, raise, raze, vase, ways • ablaze, amaze, appraise, crossways, dog days, edgeways, endways, leastways, lengthways, malaise, pj's, rephrase, Roget's, sideways, slantways, stargaze, weekdays • anyways, holidays, hollandaise, mayonnaise, multiphase, nowadays, out of phase, overgraze, overpraise, paraphrase • parting of the ways

—*also* -s, -'s, *and* -s' *forms of
nouns and* -s *forms of verbs listed
at* AY[1]

aze[2] \äz\ see OISE[1]

aze[3] \äz-ē\ see AZI[1]

azed \āzd\ unfazed
—*also* -ed *forms of verbs listed at*
AZE[1]

azen \āz-ᵊn\ see AZON

azer \ā-zər\ blazer, glazer, laser,
razor, Taser • appraiser, fund-
raiser, hair-raiser, hell-raiser,
stargazer, trailblazer • crystal-
gazer, curtain-raiser

azi[1] \äz-ē\ quasi, Swazi • Benghazi
• Anasazi, Ashkenazi, kamikaze

azi[2] \az-ē\ see AZZY

azi[3] \at-sē\ Nazi, patsy, Patsy • neo-
Nazi

azier \ā-zhər\ brazier, Frasier,
leisure, measure, pleasure, treasure

azing \ā-ziŋ\ see AISING

azon \āz-ᵊn\ blazon, brazen, raisin
• emblazon

azor \ā-zər\ see AZER

azquez \as-kəs\ see ASCUS

azy \ā-zē\ crazy, daisy, Daisy, hazy,
lazy, mazy • like crazy, stir-crazy
• Shasta daisy

azz \az\ as, has, jazz, razz • free
jazz, Hejaz, La Paz, pizzazz,
topaz, whereas • razzmatazz

azza[1] \az-ə\ see AZA[2]

azza[2] \äz-ə\ see AZA[1]

azza[3] \ät-sə\ see ATZO[1]

azzle \az-əl\ basil, Basil, dazzle,
frazzle • bedazzle, sweet basil
• razzle-dazzle

azzo \ät-sō\ matzo • palazzo • pa-
parazzo

azzy \az-ē\ jazzy, snazzy • pizzazzy
• Ashkenazi

E

e[1] \ā\ see AY[1]

e[2] \ē\ see EE[1]

é \ā\ see AY[1]

ea[1] \ā\ see AY[1]

ea[2] \ā-ə\ see AIA[1]

ea[3] \ē\ see EE[1]

ea[4] \ē-ə\ see IA[1]

eabee \ē-bē\ see EBE[1]

eace \ēs\ see IECE

eaceable \ē-sə-bəl\ see EASABLE[1]

each \ēch\ beach, beech, bleach,
breach, each, leach, leech, peach,
preach, reach, screech, speech,
teach • beseech, free speech, im-
peach, Long Beach, outreach, Palm
Beach, unteach • copper beech,
Myrtle Beach, Newport Beach,

overreach, part of speech, practice-
teach • Daytona Beach, figure of
speech, Huntington Beach, Miami
Beach, Omaha Beach, Redondo
Beach, Virginia Beach

eachable \ē-chə-bəl\ bleachable,
reachable, teachable • impeach-
able, unreachable, unteachable
• unimpeachable

eacher \ē-chər\ bleacher, creature,
feature, preacher, reacher,
screecher, teacher • schoolteacher
• double feature, overreacher,
practice teacher, student teacher

eaching \ē-chiŋ\ see EECHING

eachy \ē-chē\ beachy, chichi, Nietz-
sche, peachy, preachy, screechy

eacly \ē-klē\ see EEKLY

eacon \ē-kən\ beacon, deacon, sleeken, weaken • archdeacon, Mohican, subdeacon • Nuyorican, radar beacon • radio beacon

ead[1] \ed\ bed, bled, bread, bred, dead, dread, ed, Ed, fed, fled, Fred, head, Jed, lead, led, med, Ned, pled, read, red, Red, said, shed, shred, sled, sped, spread, stead, Ted, thread, tread, wed • abed, ahead, airhead, baldhead, beachhead, bedspread, bedstead, behead, biped, blackhead, blockhead, bloodred, bloodshed, bobsled, bonehead, brain-dead, break bread, brown bread, bulkhead, bullhead, coed, corn bread, cornfed, cowshed, crossbred, daybed, deadhead, death's-head, deathbed, dogsled, drop-dead, egghead, embed, farmstead, fathead, flatbed, forehead, French bread, fry bread, gearhead, godhead, highbred, hogshead, homebred, homestead, hotbed, hothead, illbred, inbred, instead, jarhead, knock dead, lowbred, lunkhead, masthead, meathead, misled, misread, moped, outsped, outspread, phys ed, pinhead, point spread, premed, purebred, quick bread, redhead, red lead, retread, roadbed, roadstead, saphead, scarehead, screw thread, seabed, seedbed, sheepshead, shortbread, sickbed, skinhead, sorehead, spearhead, spoon bread, streambed, subhead, sweetbread, toolshed, towhead, trailhead, unbred, undead, unread, unsaid, unthread, warhead, well-bred, well-read, white-bread, whitehead, white lead, widespread, wingspread, woodshed • aforesaid, arrowhead, bubblehead, chowderhead, chucklehead, copperhead, Diamond Head, dunderhead, featherbed, featherhead, fiddlehead, figurehead, fountainhead, get ahead, gingerbread, go-ahead, hammerhead, head-to-head, infrared, interbred, knucklehead, letterhead, Lizard Head, loggerhead, Marblehead, metalhead, newlywed, overhead, overspread, pinniped, quadruped, riverbed, Samoyed, scratch one's head, showerhead, sleepyhead, slugabed, soda bread, standardbred, straight-ahead, talking head, thoroughbred, thunderhead, turn one's head, underbred, underfed, watershed • cylinder head, fireengine red, go to one's head, over one's head

ead[2] \ēd\ see EED

ead[3] \əd\ see UD[1]

eadable \ed-ə-bəl\ see EDIBLE

eaded \ed-əd\ bedded, headed • bareheaded, bullheaded, clearheaded, coolheaded, embedded, hardheaded, hotheaded, lightheaded, pigheaded, unleaded, wrongheaded • empty-headed, hydra-headed, levelheaded, muddleheaded

—also -ed *forms of verbs listed at* EAD[1]

eaden \ed-ᵊn\ deaden, leaden, redden • Armageddon

eader[1] \ēd-ər\ beader, bleeder, breeder, cedar, feeder, kneader, leader, pleader, reader, seeder, speeder, weeder • bandleader, cheerleader, floor leader, lay reader, lip-reader, loss leader, mind reader, nonreader, proofreader, ringleader, sight reader, stockbreeder • bottom-feeder

eader[2] \ed-ər\ cheddar, header, shredder, sledder, spreader, threader, treader • homesteader • doubleheader, triple-header

eadily \ed-ᵊl-ē\ headily, readily, steadily • unsteadily

eading[1] \ed-iŋ\ bedding, heading, Reading, sledding, wedding • bobsledding, farmsteading, subheading • featherbedding
—*also* -ing *forms of verbs listed at* EAD[1]

eading[2] \ed-ᵊn\ see EADEN

eading[3] \ēd-ᵊn\ see EDON

eading[4] \ēd-iŋ\ see EEDING[1]

eadle[1] \ed-ᵊl\ see EDAL[1]

eadle[2] \ēd-ᵊl\ see EEDLE

eadly \ed-lē\ see EDLEY

eady[1] \ed-ē\ Eddie, eddy, Freddie, heady, ready, steady, Teddy • already, go steady, unsteady • at the ready, rough-and-ready

eady[2] \ēd-ē\ see EEDY

eaf[1] \ef\ see EF[1]

eaf[2] \ēf\ see IEF[1]

eafy \ē-fē\ see EEFY

eag \ēg\ see IGUE

eagan \ā-gən\ see AGIN

eager \ē-gər\ eager, meager • beleaguer, big leaguer, bush leaguer, intriguer • Ivy Leaguer, Little Leaguer, major leaguer, overeager

eagh \ā\ see AY[1]

eagle \ē-gəl\ see EGAL

eague \ēg\ see IGUE

eaguer \ē-gər\ see EAGER

eah \ē-ə\ see IA[1]

eak[1] \ēk\ beak, bleak, cheek, chic, clique, creak, creek, Creek, eke, freak, geek, Greek, leak, leek, meek, peak, peek, pique, reek, seek, sheikh, shriek, Sikh, sleek, sneak, speak, squeak, streak, teak, tweak, weak, week, wreak • antique, batik, Belgique, bespeak, blue streak, boutique, Cloud Peak, critique, debeak, Grays Peak, grosbeak, hairstreak, midweek, misspeak, muzhik, mystique, nonpeak, oblique, offpeak, physique, Pikes Peak, pip-

squeak, technique, Tajik, unique, workweek • Battle Creek, Boundary Peak, Chesapeake, control freak, doublespeak, ecofreak, Granite Peak, hide-and-seek, Holy Week, Lassen Peak, Lenin Peak, Martinique, Mozambique, Passion Week, tongue-in-cheek, up the creek, Wheeler Peak, widow's peak • microtechnique, quarterback sneak, semi-antique • Communism Peak, opéra comique, turn the other cheek

eak[2] \āk\ see AKE[1]

eak[3] \ek\ see ECK

eakable \ā-kə-bəl\ see AKABLE

eake \ēk\ see EAK[1]

eaked[1] \ē-kəd\ peaked, streaked

eaked[2] \ēkt\ beaked, freaked, peaked, streaked
—*also* -ed *forms of verbs listed at* EAK[1]

eaken \ē-kən\ see EACON

eaker[1] \ē-kər\ beaker, leaker, phreaker, seeker, sneaker, speaker, squeaker • loudspeaker, self-seeker, sunseeker • keynote speaker
—*also* -er *forms of adjectives listed at* EAK[1]

eaker[2] \ā-kər\ see AKER[1]

eaking \ē-kiŋ\ freaking, phreaking, sneaking, speaking, streaking • heat-seeking, self-seeking • public speaking
—*also* -ing *forms of verbs listed at* EAK[1]

eakish \ē-kish\ cliquish, freakish, weakish

eakly \ē-klē\ see EEKLY

eaky \ē-kē\ cheeky, cliquey, creaky, freaky, geeky, leaky, sneaky, squeaky, streaky, tiki • boutiquey, dashiki

eal[1] \ē-əl\ laryngeal, marmoreal, pharyngeal

eal[2] \ēl\ creel, deal, eel, feel, heal,

heel, he'll, keel, kneel, meal, Neil, peal, peel, real, reel, seal, she'll, spiel, squeal, steal, steel, teal, veal, we'll, wheel, zeal • all-wheel, anneal, appeal, Bastille, big deal, big wheel, bonemeal, Camille, cam wheel, Castile, cartwheel, Cecile, chenille, cogwheel, conceal, congeal, cornmeal, done deal, eared seal, fifth wheel, fish meal, flywheel, for real, four-wheel, freewheel, fur seal, genteel, get real, good deal, great seal, handwheel, harp seal, ideal, Lucille, mill wheel, misdeal, mobile, Mobile, monk seal, mouthfeel, New Deal, newsreel, nosewheel, oatmeal, ordeal, piecemeal, pinwheel, prayer wheel, raw deal, repeal, reveal, schlemiel, spike heel, surreal, Tar Heel, unreal, unreel, unseal • bearded seal, bloodmobile, bookmobile, carbon steel, chamomile, cockatiel, color wheel, commonweal, conger eel, cut a deal, dishabille, down-at-heel, Ferris wheel, glockenspiel, goldenseal, Guayaquil, harbor seal, lamprey eel, leopard seal, megadeal, mercantile, moray eel, orange peel, package deal, paddle wheel, pedal steel, potter's wheel, reel-to-reel, skimobile, snob appeal, snowmobile, spinning reel, stainless steel, thunderpeal, waterwheel • automobile, electric eel, elephant seal, Solomon's seal, stiletto heel

eal³ \āl\ see AIL

eal⁴ \il\ see ILL

ealable \ē-lə-bəl\ peelable, reelable, stealable • appealable, concealable, resealable

ealand \ē-lənd\ see ELAND

eald \ēld\ see IELD

ealed \ēld\ see IELD

ealer \ē-lər\ dealer, feeler, healer, peeler, sealer • concealer, faith healer, four-wheeler, freewheeler, New Dealer, newsdealer, scene-stealer, side-wheeler, stern-wheeler, three-wheeler, two-wheeler, ward heeler • double-dealer, eighteen-wheeler, 18-wheeler, paddle wheeler, snowmobiler, wheeler-dealer

ealie \ē-lē\ see EELY

ealing \ē-liŋ\ see EELING

eally¹ \il-ē\ see ILLY

eally² \ē-lē\ see EELY

ealm \elm\ see ELM

ealot \el-ət\ see ELLATE

ealotry \el-ə-trē\ see ELOTRY

ealous \el-əs\ Ellis, jealous, trellis, zealous • Marcellus

ealousy \el-ə-sē\ see ELACY

ealth \elth\ health, stealth, wealth • bill of health, commonwealth, public health

ealthy \el-thē\ healthy, stealthy, wealthy • heart-healthy, unhealthy

ealty \ēl-tē\ fealty, realty

eam¹ \ēm\ beam, cream, crèeme, deem, dream, gleam, meme, Nîmes, ream, scheme, scream, seam, seem, steam, stream, team, teem, theme • agleam, airstream, bireme, blaspheme, bloodstream, centime, coal seam, cold cream, crossbeam, daydream, downstream, dream team, esteem, extreme, Gulf Stream, high beam, hornbeam, I beam, ice cream, inseam, jet stream, low beam, mainstream, midstream, millstream, moonbeam, pipe dream, redeem, regime, rhyme scheme, slipstream, sour cream, sunbeam, supreme, tag team, trireme, upstream • academe, balance beam, blow off steam, double-team, head of steam, heavy cream, on the beam, Ponzi scheme, self-esteem • ancien régime, in the extreme, vanishing cream • American dream, Bavarian cream

eam² \im\ see IM¹

eaman \ē-mən\ see EMON¹

eamed¹ \emt\ see EMPT

eamed² \emd\ steamed
—*also* -ed *forms of verbs listed at* EAM¹

eamer \ē-mər\ creamer, dreamer, femur, lemur, reamer, screamer, steamer, streamer • blasphemer, daydreamer, redeemer

eaming \ē-miŋ\ see EEMING

eamish \ē-mish\ beamish, squeamish

eamless \ēm-ləs\ dreamless, seamless

eamon \ē-mən\ see EMON¹

eamster \ēm-stər\ seamster, teamster

eamy \ē-mē\ creamy, dreamy, gleamy, preemie, seamy, steamy

ean¹ \ē-ən\ eon, Ian, Leon, paean, peon • Aegean, Chilean, Crimean, Fijian, Judaean, Korean, plebeian • Caribbean, cyclopean, empyrean, European, Galilean, Herculean, Jacobean, Manichaean, Sisyphean, Tennessean • epicurean, Ponce de Leon, Pythagorean, un-European • Indo-European

ean² \ēn\ see INE³

ean³ \ȯn\ see ON³

ean⁴ \ä-ən\ see AYAN¹

eane \ēn\ see INE³

eaner \ē-nər\ cleaner, gleaner, screener, wiener • demeanor, dry cleaner, pipe cleaner • misdemeanor, submariner, trampoliner, vacuum cleaner
—*also* -er *forms of adjectives listed at* INE³

eanery \ēn-rē\ beanery, greenery, scenery • machinery

eanie \ē-nē\ see INI¹

eaning \ē-niŋ\ leaning, meaning, screening • dry cleaning, housecleaning, spring-cleaning, well-meaning • overweening
—*also* -ing *forms of verbs listed at* INE³

eanist \ē-nəst\ see INIST²

eanliness \en-lē-nəs\ see ENDLINESS

eanly¹ \ēn-lē\ cleanly, keenly, meanly, queenly • routinely

eanly² \en-lē\ see ENDLY

eanne \ēn\ see INE³

eanness \ēn-nəs\ cleanness, greenness, keenness, meanness • uncleanness

eannie \ē-nē\ see INI¹

eano \ē-nō\ see INO²

eanor \ē-nər\ see EANER

eanse \enz\ see ENS¹

eant \ent\ see ENT¹

eany \ē-nē\ see INI¹

eap \ēp\ see EEP

eapen \ē-pən\ see EEPEN

eaper \ē-pər\ see EEPER

eapie \ē-pē\ see EEPY

eapo \ē-pō\ see EPOT

ear¹ \er\ see ARE⁴

ear² \ir\ see EER²

earable¹ \er-ə-bəl\ bearable, shareable, spareable, tearable, terrible, wearable • unbearable, unwearable

earable² \ar-ə-bəl\ see ARABLE

earage \ir-ij\ see EERAGE

earance¹ \ir-əns\ see ERENCE¹

earance² \er-əns\ see ARENCE¹

earch \ərch\ see URCH

eard¹ \ird\ beard, eared, tiered, weird • bat-eared, crop-eared, dog-eared, graybeard, jug-eared, lop-eared, spade beard, whitebeard • chandeliered, engineered, multitiered • pre-engineered
—*also* -ed *forms of verbs listed at* EER²

eard² \ərd\ see IRD

eare \ir\ see EER²

earean \ir-ē-ən\ see ERIAN[1]
eared[1] \erd\ see AIRED
eared[2] \ird\ see EARD[1]
earer[1] \er-ər\ bearer, error, sharer, terror, wearer • cupbearer, pallbearer, seafarer, talebearer, torchbearer, wayfarer • standard-bearer, stretcher-bearer
—also -er forms of adjectives listed at ARE[4]
earer[2] \ir-ər\ mirror • sheepshearer • rearview mirror
—also -er forms of adjectives listed at EER[2]
earful \ir-fəl\ cheerful, earful, fearful, tearful
earies \ir-ēz\ see ERIES
earing[1] \ir-iŋ\ clearing, earring, gearing, searing • God-fearing, sheepshearing • engineering, hard-of-hearing, mountaineering, power steering • orienteering • bioengineering, social engineering
—also -ing forms of verbs listed at EER[2]
earing[2] \er-iŋ\ see ARING[1]
earish \er-ish\ see ARISH[1]
earl \ərl\ see IRL
earler \ər-lər\ see IRLER
earless \ir-ləs\ cheerless, fearless, peerless, tearless
earling \ər-lən\ see ERLIN
early[1] \ir-lē\ clearly, dearly, merely, nearly, queerly, sheerly, yearly • austerely, biyearly, severely, sincerely • cavalierly, insincerely, semiyearly
early[2] \ər-lē\ see URLY
earn \ərn\ see URN
earned \ərnd\ see URNED
earner \ər-nər\ see URNER
earnist \ər-nəst\ see ERNIST
earnt \ərnt\ burnt, learnt, weren't
earring \ir-iŋ\ see EARING[1]
earsal \ər-səl\ see ERSAL

earse \ərs\ see ERSE
earst \ərst\ see URST
eart \ärt\ see ART[1]
earted \ärt-əd\ parted • bighearted, coldhearted, departed, downhearted, fainthearted, goodhearted, greathearted, halfhearted, hard-hearted, kindhearted, largehearted, lighthearted, softhearted, stouthearted, truehearted, uncharted, warmhearted, wholehearted • brokenhearted, chickenhearted, openhearted, tenderhearted
—also -ed forms of verbs listed at ART[1]
earth[1] \ärth\ see ARTH
earth[2] \ərth\ see IRTH
eartha \ər-thə\ see ERTHA
earthy \ər-thē\ see ORTHY
eartily \ärt-ᵊl-ē\ see ARTILY
eartless \ärt-ləs\ see ARTLESS
earty \ärt-ē\ see ARTY[1]
eary \ir-ē\ aerie, beery, bleary, cheery, dreary, eerie, Erie, leery, Peary, query, teary, veery, weary • Fort Erie, Kashmiri, Lake Erie, Valkyrie, world-weary • hara-kiri
eas \ē-əs\ see EUS[1]
easable[1] \ē-sə-bəl\ leasable, peaceable
easable[2] \ē-zə-bəl\ see EASIBLE
easand \iz-ᵊn\ see ISON[2]
ease[1] \ēs\ see IECE
ease[2] \ēz\ see EZE
eased[1] \ēzd\ diseased, self-pleased
—also -ed forms of verbs listed at EZE
eased[2] \ēst\ see EAST[1]
easel \ē-zəl\ bezel, diesel, easel, teasel, weasel
easeless \ē-sləs\ ceaseless, creaseless, greaseless
easelly \ē-zlē\ see EASLY
easer[1] \ē-sər\ greaser, piecer
easer[2] \ē-zər\ Caesar, freezer, geezer, greaser, pleaser, squeezer,

teaser, tweezer • appeaser, brain-
teaser, crowd-pleaser

eash \ēsh\ see ICHE[2]

easible \ē-zə-bəl\ feasible, squeez-
able

easil \ē-zəl\ see EASEL

easily \ēz-lē\ see EASLY

easing[1] \ē-siŋ\ leasing • unceasing
—*also -ing forms of verbs listed at*
IECE

easing[2] \ē-ziŋ\ freezing, pleasing
• subfreezing
—*also -ing forms of verbs listed at*
EZE

easingly \ē-siŋ-lē\ decreasingly,
increasingly, unceasingly

easle \ē-zəl\ see EASEL

easly \ēz-ə-lē\ easily, measly,
weaselly

eason \ēz-ᵊn\ reason, season, treason • high treason, in season, off-
season, postseason, preseason,
with reason • age of reason,
diocesan, open season, out of
season, rhyme or reason, silly
season, within reason

easonable \ēz-nə-bəl\ reasonable,
seasonable, treasonable • unrea-
sonable, unseasonable

easoning \ēz-niŋ\ reasoning, sea-
soning • unreasoning

easor \ē-zər\ see EASER[2]

east[1] \ēst\ beast, east, East, feast,
fleeced, least, priest, yeast • arch-
priest, artiste, at least, batiste,
deceased, Far East, Near East,
northeast, southeast • baker's
yeast, hartebeest, Middle East,
north-northeast, pointillist, wilde-
beest
—*also -ed forms of verbs listed at*
IECE

east[2] \est\ see EST

easted \es-təd\ see ESTED

easter \ē-stər\ Easter, feaster,
keister • northeaster

eastly \ēst-lē\ beastly, priestly

easurable \ezh-rə-bəl\ pleasurable,
treasurable • immeasurable

easure[1] \ezh-ər\ leisure, measure,
pleasure, treasure • displeasure,
dry measure, square measure,
tape measure • countermeasure,
cubic measure, for good measure,
liquid measure

easure[2] \ā-zhər\ see AZIER

easurer \ezh-ər-ər\ measurer,
treasurer

easy[1] \ē-zē\ breezy, cheesy, easy,
greasy, queasy, sleazy, sneezy,
wheezy • breathe easy, go easy,
Parcheesi, speakeasy, uneasy,
Zambezi • free and easy, over
easy

easy[2] \ē-sē\ see EECY

eat[1] \ēt\ beat, beet, bleat, cheat,
cleat, Crete, deet, eat, feat, fleet,
greet, heat, meat, meet, mete,
neat, peat, Pete, pleat, seat, sheet,
skeet, sleet, street, suite, sweet,
teat, treat, tweet, wheat • aes-
thete, athlete, backbeat, backseat,
backstreet, bedsheet, box seat,
browbeat, buckwheat, car seat,
cheat sheet, cold feet, compete,
complete, conceit, concrete,
crabmeat, crib sheet, deadbeat,
dead heat, dead meat, deceit,
defeat, delete, deplete, discreet,
discrete, downbeat, drumbeat,
dutch treat, effete, elite, entreat,
esthete, excrete, gamete, ground-
sheet, hard wheat, heartbeat,
helpmeet, hoofbeat, hot seat, ice
sheet, ill-treat, jump seat, love
seat, Main Street, maltreat,
mesquite, mincemeat, mistreat,
offbeat, petite, preheat, rap sheet,
receipt, red heat, red meat, re-
heat, repeat, replete, retreat,
secrete, side street, soft wheat,
spreadsheet, swap meet, through
street, unseat, upbeat, Wall Street,
white heat • balance sheet, bitter-

sweet, booster seat, bucket seat, cellulite, cookie sheet, county seat, decathlete, drag one's feet, driver's seat, durum wheat, easy street, incomplete, indiscreet, lorikeet, make ends meet, Marguerite, meet and greet, miss a beat, nonathlete, obsolete, on one's feet, overeat, overheat, Paraclete, parakeet, pentathlete, prickly heat, rumble seat, saddle seat, scandal sheet, semisweet, shredded wheat, spirochete, to one's feet, triathlete, trick or treat, two-way street, window seat • beat a retreat, ejection seat, man in the street, radiant heat, take a back seat, vote with one's feet

eat² \āt\ see ATE¹

eat³ \et\ see ET¹

eat⁴ \it\ see IT¹

eatable \ēt-ə-bəl\ beatable, eatable, heatable, treatable • defeatable, repeatable, unbeatable

eated¹ \ēt-əd\ heated, pleated • conceited, deep-seated, repeated • overheated, superheated
—*also* -ed *forms of verbs listed at* EAT¹

eated² \et-əd\ see ETID

eated³ \it-əd\ see ITTED

eaten¹ \ēt-ᵊn\ eaten, beaten, Cretan, cretin, Eton, neaten, sweeten, wheaten • browbeaten, Grand Teton, moth-eaten, unbeaten, worm-eaten • overeaten, weatherbeaten

eaten² \āt-ᵊn\ see ATEN¹

eater¹ \ēt-ər\ beater, cheater, eater, greeter, heater, liter, meter, Peter, teeter, tweeter • ammeter, anteater, beefeater, Demeter, eggbeater, fire-eater, flowmeter, light meter, man-eater, ohmmeter, repeater, space heater, voltmeter, Wall Streeter, wattmeter, world-beater • altimeter, cen-

tiliter, centimeter, deciliter, decimeter, dekaliter, dekameter, hectoliter, lotus-eater, milliliter, millimeter, overeater, parking meter, postage meter, taximeter, trick-or-treater, water heater, water meter
—*also* -er *forms of adjectives listed at* EAT¹

eater² \et-ər\ see ETTER

eath¹ \ēth\ heath, Keith, sheath, wreath • beneath, bequeath • underneath

eath² \ēth\ see EATHE

eathe \ēth\ breathe, seethe, sheathe, teethe, wreathe • bequeath, unsheathe

eather¹ \eth-ər\ see ETHER¹

eather² \ē-thər\ see EITHER

eathery \eth-rē\ feathery, leathery

eathing \ē-thiŋ\ breathing, sheathing, teething • air-breathing, firebreathing
—*also* -ing *forms of verbs listed at* EATHE

eathless \eth-ləs\ breathless, deathless

eating \ēt-iŋ\ beating, eating, fleeting, greeting, meeting, seating, sheeting • breast-beating, camp meeting, drumbeating, fire-eating, man-eating, prayer meeting, space heating, town meeting
—*also* -ing *forms of verbs listed at* EAT¹

eatise \ēt-əs\ see ETUS

eatly¹ \āt-lē\ see ATELY¹

eatly² \ēt-lē\ see EETLY

eaton \ēt-ᵊn\ see EATEN¹

eats¹ \ēts\ Keats
—*also* -s, -'s, *and* -s' *forms of nouns and* -s *forms of verbs listed at* EAT¹

eats² \āts\ see ATES¹

eature \ē-chər\ see EACHER

eaty \ēt-ē\ meaty, peaty, sleety, sweetie, treaty, ziti • entreaty, graffiti, Tahiti • spermaceti

eau \ō\ see OW[1]

eaucracy \äk-rə-sē\ see OCRACY

eauteous \üt-ē-əs\ see UTEOUS

eautiful \üt-i-fəl\ see UTIFUL

eauty \üt-ē\ see OOTY[1]

eaux \ō\ see OW[1]

eavable \ē-və-bəl\ see EIVABLE

eaval \ē-vəl\ see IEVAL

eave[1] \ēv\ eve, Eve, grieve, heave, leave, peeve, sheave, sleeve, Steve, thieve, weave, we've • achieve, aggrieve, believe, bereave, conceive, deceive, frost heave, Maldive, motive, naive, perceive, pet peeve, receive, relieve, reprieve, retrieve, shirtsleeve, shore leave, sick leave, unweave • basket weave, disbelieve, Genevieve, interleave, interweave, makebelieve, misconceive, on one's sleeve, preconceive, Tel Aviv, up one's sleeve • overachieve, Saint Agnes' Eve, underachieve • absent without leave

eave[2] \iv\ see IVE[2]

eaved \ēvd\ leaved, sleeved • aggrieved, bereaved, broad-leaved, relieved

—*also* -ed *forms of verbs listed at* EAVE[1]

eavement \ēv-mənt\ see EVEMENT

eaven \ev-ən\ Devon, Evan, heaven, Kevin, leaven, seven • eleven, hog heaven • seventh heaven

eaver \ē-vər\ see IEVER

eaward \ē-wərd\ see EEWARD

eaze[1] \ēz\ see EZE

eaze[2] \āz\ see AZE[1]

eazo \ē-zō\ see IZO

eazy \ē-zē\ see EASY[1]

eb \eb\ deb, ebb, reb, web • celeb, cobweb, Horeb, subdeb, Zagreb • cause célèbre, Johnny Reb, spiderweb, World Wide Web

eba \ē-bə\ Reba, Sheba • amoeba, Beersheba

ebate \ab-ət\ see ABIT

ebb \eb\ see EB

ebbie \eb-ē\ see EBBY

ebble \eb-əl\ pebble, rebel, treble

ebby \eb-ē\ Debbie, webby • cobwebby

ebe[1] \ē-bē\ BB, freebie, Phoebe, Seabee

ebe[2] \ēb\ plebe • sahib

ebel \eb-əl\ see EBBLE

eber \ā-bər\ see ABOR

ebes \ēbz\ Thebes

—*also* -s, -'s, *and* -s' *forms of nouns listed at* EBE[2]

eble \eb-əl\ see EBBLE

ebo \ē-bō\ see IBO

ebral \ē-brəl\ cerebral, vertebral

ebs \eps\ see EPS

ebt \et\ see ET[1]

ebted \et-əd\ see ETID

ebtor \et-ər\ see ETTER

ec[1] \ek\ see ECK

ec[2] \ets\ see ETS

eca \ē-kə\ see IKA[1]

ecan \ek-ən\ see ECKON

ecca \ek-ə\ Decca, mecca, Mecca • Rebecca

eccable \ek-ə-bəl\ see ECKABLE

eccan \ek-ən\ see ECKON

ecce \ek-ē\ see ECKY

ecco \ek-ō\ see ECHO

ecency \ēs-ᵊn-sē\ decency, recency • indecency

ecent \ēs-ᵊnt\ decent, recent • indecent

ech[1] \ek\ see ECK

ech[2] \ək\ see UCK[1]

ech[3] \esh\ see ESH[1]

eche[1] \āsh\ crèche • Andhra Pradesh, Madhya Pradesh, Uttar Pradesh

eche[2] \esh\ see ESH[1]

eche[3] \ē-chē\ see EACHY

êche \esh\ see ESH[1]

èche \esh\ see ESH[1]

eched \echt\ see ETCHED

echie \ek-ē\ see ECKY

echin \ek-ən\ see ECKON
echo \ek-ō\ echo, gecko • art deco,
El Greco, reecho
echt \ekt\ see ECT
ecia \ē-shə\ see ESIA[1]
ecially \esh-lē\ see ESHLY
ecian \ē-shən\ see ETION[1]
ecibel \es-ə-bəl\ see ESSIBLE
ecie[1] \ē-sē\ see EECY
ecie[2] \ē-shē\ see ISHI
ecies \ē-sēz\ species, theses • pros-
theses, subspecies
ecil[1] \ē-səl\ Cecil, diesel
ecil[2] \es-əl\ see ESTLE[1]
ecile \es-əl\ see ESTLE[1]
eciman \es-mən\ see ESSMAN
ecious \ē-shəs\ specious • capricious, facetious, Lucretius
eck \ek\ beck, check, Czech, deck,
dreck, fleck, heck, Lech, neck,
pec, peck, sec, spec, speck, trek,
wreak, wreck • Aztec, bed check,
bedeck, Bishkek, blank check,
breakneck, bull neck, crew neck,
cross-check, exec, fact-check,
flight deck, flyspeck, gooseneck,
gut check, hatcheck, henpeck,
high tech, in check, kopeck, low-
tech, Lubeck, on deck, OPEC,
parsec, paycheck, poop deck,
Quebec, rain check, roughneck,
shipwreck, spell-check, spot-
check, Steinbeck, sundeck, tape
deck, Toltec, Uzbek, V-neck, vo-
tech • biotech, bottleneck,
cashier's check, Chiang Kai-shek,
countercheck, discotheque, dou-
ble-check, double-deck, hunt-
and-peck, leatherneck, neck and
neck, quarterdeck, rubber check,
rubberneck, turtleneck, weather
deck, Yucatec, Zapotec • breathe
down one's neck, cinematheque,
Melchizedek, mock turtleneck,
promenade deck, Toulouse-
Lautrec, traveler's check • reality
check

eckable \ek-ə-bəl\ checkable • im-
peccable
ecked \ekt\ see ECT
ecker \ek-ər\ checker, decker,
pecker, trekker, wrecker • fact-
checker, Quebecer, spell-checker,
three-decker, woodpecker • dou-
ble-decker, rubbernecker, triple-
decker
ecking \ek-iŋ\ necking
—*also* -ing *forms of verbs listed at*
ECK
ecklace \ek-ləs\ see ECKLESS
eckle \ek-əl\ freckle, heckle,
shekel, speckle
eckless \ek-ləs\ feckless, necklace,
reckless
ecko \ek-ō\ see ECHO
eckon \ek-ən\ beckon, reckon
• Aztecan, misreckon, Toltecan
• Yucatecan
ecks, eks see EX
ecky \ek-ē\ Becky, techie
econ \ek-ən\ see ECKON
econd \ek-ənd\ see ECUND
ecque \ek\ see ECK
ecs \eks\ see EX
ect \ekt\ Brecht, necked, sect,
specked • abject, affect, aspect,
bisect, bullnecked, collect, con-
nect, correct, cowl-necked, defect, deflect, deject, detect, direct,
dissect, Dordrecht, effect, eject,
elect, erect, expect, goosenecked,
infect, inflect, inject, insect, in-
spect, neglect, object, perfect,
project, prospect, protect, reflect,
reject, respect, roll-necked, select,
stiff-necked, subject, suspect,
transect, trisect, Utrecht, V-
necked • architect, birth defect,
circumspect, deselect, dialect,
disconnect, disinfect, disrespect,
double-decked, genuflect, incor-
rect, indirect, in effect, intellect,
interject, intersect, misdirect,
preselect, recollect, reconnect,

redirect, reelect, resurrect, retro-
spect, self-respect, side effect,
turtlenecked • aftereffect,
Doppler effect, idiolect, intercon-
nect, ripple effect • domino effect, landscape architect, placebo
effect • politically correct
—*also* -ed *forms of verbs listed at*
ECK

ectable \ek-tə-bəl\ collectible,
connectable, correctable, delec-
table, detectable, electable, ex-
pectable, injectable, perfectible,
respectable, selectable • unde-
tectable

ectacle \ek-ti-kəl\ see ECTICAL

ectal \ek-tᵊl\ see ECTILE

ectant \ek-tənt\ expectant • disin-
fectant

ectar \ek-tər\ see ECTOR

ected \ek-təd\ affected, collected,
connected, dejected, directed,
dissected • disaffected, discon-
nected, fuel-injected, self-selected,
unaffected, undirected, unex-
pected, unprotected, unselected
• inner-directed, interconnected,
other-directed
—*also* -ed *forms of verbs listed at*
ECT

ecter \ek-tər\ see ECTOR

ectible \ek-tə-bəl\ see ECTABLE

ectic \ek-tik\ hectic • eclectic
• anorectic, apoplectic, dialectic

ectical \ek-ti-kəl\ spectacle • di-
alectical

ectile \ek-tᵊl\ projectile • dialectal

ecting \ek-tiŋ\ affecting, respecting
• self-correcting, self-respecting
—*also* -ing *forms of verbs listed at*
ECT

ection \ek-shən\ flexion, section
• affection, collection, complex-
ion, confection, connection, con-
vection, correction, cross section,
C-section, defection, deflection,
dejection, detection, direction,

ejection, election, infection, in-
flection, injection, inspection,
midsection, objection, perfection,
projection, protection, reflection,
rejection, selection, subjection,
subsection, trisection • circum-
spection, conic section, disaffec-
tion, disinfection, fuel injection,
golden section, imperfection,
indirection, insurrection, interjec-
tion, intersection, introspection,
misdirection, predilection, recol-
lection, reconnection, redirection,
reelection, reinfection, resurrec-
tion, self-direction, self-protec-
tion, self-selection, stage
direction, vivisection • equal
protection, general election,
house of correction, interconnec-
tion • cesarean section

ectional \ek-shnəl\ sectional • cor-
rectional, cross-sectional, direc-
tional • omnidirectional,
unidirectional

ectionist \ek-shə-nəst\ perfection-
ist, projectionist, protectionist
• insurrectionist

ective \ek-tiv\ affective, collective,
connective, corrective, defective,
detective, directive, effective,
elective, invective, objective,
perspective, prospective, protec-
tive, reflective, respective, selec-
tive, subjective • cost-effective,
house detective, ineffective, intro-
spective, nonobjective, retrospec-
tive, self-reflective • private
detective

ectless \ek-ləs\ see ECKLESS

ectly \ekt-lē\ abjectly, correctly,
directly, erectly • circumspectly,
incorrectly, indirectly

ectomy \ek-tə-mē\ mastectomy,
vasectomy • appendectomy, hys-
terectomy, laryngectomy, tonsil-
lectomy

ector \ek-tər\ hector, Hector, lector, nectar, rector, sector, specter, vector • collector, connector, defector, detector, director, ejector, elector, erector, injector, inspector, objector, projector, prospector, protector, reflector, selector, subsector • lie detector, smoke detector, stage director • casting director, funeral director, program director, solar collector

ectoral \ek-trəl\ pectoral, spectral • electoral

ectorate \ek-tə-rət\ directorate, electorate, protectorate

ectory \ek-tə-rē\ rectory • directory, trajectory

ectral \ek-trəl\ see ECTORAL

ectrum \ek-trəm\ plectrum, spectrum • broad-spectrum

ectual \ek-chə-wəl\ effectual • ineffectual, intellectual • anti-intellectual

ectually \ek-chə-lē\ effectually • ineffectually, intellectually

ectural¹ \ek-chə-rəl\ conjectural • architectural

ectural² \ek-shrəl\ conjectural • architectural

ecture \ek-chər\ lecture • conjecture • architecture

ecular \ek-yə-lər\ secular • molecular

ecund \ek-ənd\ fecund, second • split-second • microsecond, millisecond, nanosecond
—*also* -ed *forms of verbs listed at* ECKON

ed \ed\ see EAD¹

e'd \ēd\ see EED

eda¹ \ēd-ə\ Frieda, Leda • Alameda

eda² \ād-ə\ see ADA²

edal¹ \ed-°l\ medal, meddle, pedal, peddle • Air Medal, backpedal, soft-pedal • service medal

edal² \ēd-°l\ see EEDLE

edance \ēd-°ns\ see EDENCE

edar¹ \ed-ər\ see EADER²

edar² \ēd-ər\ see EADER¹

edator \ed-ət-ər\ see EDITOR

edd \ed\ see EAD¹

eddar \ed-ər\ see EADER²

edded \ed-əd\ see EADED

edden \ed-°n\ see EADEN

edder \ed-ər\ see EADER²

eddie \ed-ē\ see EADY¹

edding \ed-iŋ\ see EADING¹

eddle \ed-°l\ see EDAL¹

eddler \ed-lər\ meddler, peddler • intermeddler

eddon \ed-°n\ see EADEN

eddy \ed-ē\ see EADY¹

ede¹ \ād\ see ADE¹

ede² \ēd\ see EED

ede³ \ā-dā\ see AYDAY

edel \ād-°l\ see ADLE

eden \ēd-°n\ Eden, Sweden • Garden of Eden

edence \ēd-°ns\ credence • impedance, precedence

edent \ēd-°nt\ needn't • decedent, precedent • antecedent

eder¹ \ād-ər\ see ADER

eder² \ēd-ər\ see EADER¹

edge \ej\ dredge, edge, fledge, hedge, ledge, pledge, sedge, sledge, veg, wedge • allege, gilt-edge, knife-edge, on edge, straightedge • cutting edge, flying wedge, leading edge, trailing edge

edged \ejd\ edged, wedged • alleged, full-fledged, gilt-edged, hard-edged, rough-edged, unfledged • double-edged
—*also* -ed *forms of verbs listed at* EDGE

edger \ej-ər\ dredger, hedger, ledger, pledger

edgie \ej-ē\ see EDGY

edgy \ej-ē\ edgy, Reggie, veggie, wedgie

edi \ād-ē\ see ADY

edia \ēd-ē-ə\ media • mixed media • multimedia • encyclopedia

edian \ēd-ē-ən\ median • come-
dian, tragedian
ediant \ēd-ē-ənt\ see EDIENT
edible \ed-ə-bəl\ credible, edible,
spreadable • incredible, inedible
edic \ēd-ik\ comedic • orthopedic
• encyclopedic
edience \ēd-ē-əns\ expedience,
obedience • disobedience
—*also* -s, -'s, *and* -s' *forms of
nouns listed at* EDIENT
edient \ēd-ē-ənt\ expedient, ingre-
dient, obedient • disobedient,
inexpedient
ediment \ed-ə-mənt\ pediment,
sediment • impediment
edin \ēd-ᵊn\ see EDEN
eding \ēd-iŋ\ see EEDING¹
edious \ē-jəs\ see EGIS
edit \ed-ət\ credit, edit • accredit,
discredit • copyedit, line of credit
editor \ed-ət-ər\ creditor, editor,
predator • chief editor, coeditor
• city editor, copy editor
edium \ēd-ē-əm\ medium, tedium
• mass medium
edlar \ed-lər\ see EDDLER
edley \ed-lē\ deadly, medley
edly \ed-lē\ see EDLEY
edo¹ \ēd-ō\ credo, speedo • aikido,
libido, Toledo, torpedo, tuxedo
edo² \ād-ō\ see ADO²
edo³ \ēd-ə\ see EDA¹
edo⁴ \e-dō\ Edo, meadow
edom \ēd-əm\ see EDUM
edon \ēd-ᵊn\ Eden • cotyledon
edouin \ed-wən\ see EDWIN
edulous \ej-ə-ləs\ credulous, sedu-
lous • incredulous
edum \ēd-əm\ Edam, freedom
• Medal of Freedom
edure \ē-jər\ besieger, procedure
edwin \ed-wən\ Edwin • bedouin
ee¹ \ē\ b, be, bee, Brie, c, cay, cee,
Cree, d, Dee, e, fee, flea, flee,
free, g, gee, glee, he, key, knee,
lea, lee, Lee, Leigh, me, mi, p,

pea, pee, plea, quay, re, sea, see,
she, si, ski, spree, t, tea, tee, the,
thee, three, ti, tree, v, vee, we,
wee, whee, ye, z, zee • agree, at
sea, bailee, banshee, bee tree,
Belgae, big tree, Black Sea,
bootee, break free, bungee, Capri,
carefree, CB, CD, Chablis, chick-
pea, chili, cowpea, curie, Curie,
Dead Sea, debris, decree, deep-
sea, degree, draftee, Dundee,
emcee, ennui, esprit, flame tree,
foresee, for free, germfree,
goatee, grandee, grand prix,
grantee, greens fee, green tea,
he/she, high tea, home free, hot
key, Humvee, IV, Jaycee, jayvee,
KP, latchkey, look-see, low-key,
LP, lychee, Marie, marquee, MC,
métis, ming tree, must-see,
Nancy, North Sea, OD, off-key,
Parsi, passkey, Pawnee, payee,
PC, peewee, pewee, PG, puree, qt,
rani, Red Sea, Ross Sea, rupee,
RV, scot-free, settee, shade tree,
Shawnee, s/he, shift key, shoe
tree, sightsee, signee, sirree,
smoke tree, snap pea, snow pea,
spondee, squeegee, standee, state
tree, strophe, suttee, TB, tepee,
testee, 3-D, to-be, toll-free, to sea,
trainee, trochee, trustee, turnkey,
tutee, Tutsi, TV, White Sea,
whoopee, would-be, Yangtze
• abductee, absentee, addressee,
adoptee, advisee, amputee,
apogee, appointee, Aral Sea,
assignee, attendee, awardee,
Beaufort Sea, Bering Sea, bour-
geoisie, bumblebee, camphor tree,
Cherokee, chickadee,
chimpanzee, China Sea, Christmas tree, coati, conferee, cop a
plea, Coral Sea, counselee, cru-
elty-free, DDT, Debussy, depor-
tee, detainee, devotee, disagree,
divorcé, divorcée, dungaree, duty-

free, employee, enlistee, enrollee, escapee, ESP, evictee, family tree, fancy-free, fantasy, filigree, franchisee, fricassee, function key, Galilee, Gemini, Greenland Sea, guarantee, Hawaii, HIV, Holy See, honeybee, honoree, housemaid's knee, inductee, Inland Sea, invitee, Irish Sea, jamboree, Java Sea, Joshua tree, jubilee, Judas tree, killer bee, LCD, LED, licensee, LSD, maître d', Malay Sea, master key, Medici, Model T, nominee, oversea, oversee, parolee, pedigree, peppertree, pharisee, planer tree, potpourri, referee, refugee, repartee, retiree, Rosemarie, rubber tree, Sadducee, Salton Sea, selectee, shivaree, spelling bee, Tappan Zee, Tennessee, third degree, TNT, to a tee, transferee, tulip tree, undersea, user fee, VIP, vis-à-vis, wannabe, warrantee, Wounded Knee • advanced degree, Aegean Sea, Amundsen Sea, carpenter bee, Caspian Sea, Celebes Sea, East China Sea, evacuee, fortunately, Galilei, interviewee, Labrador Sea, omega-3, Sargasso Sea, Sault Sainte Marie, Simon Legree, skeleton key, South China Sea, to a degree, umbrella tree • Adriatic Sea, Africanized bee, Arabian Sea, bark up the wrong tree, Caribbean Sea, Ionian Sea, Sea of Galilee • Tweedledum and Tweedledee

ee² \ā\ see AY[1]

ée \ā\ see AY[1]

eeable \ē-ə-bəl\ seeable, skiable • agreeable, foreseeable • disagreeable, unforeseeable

eebie \ē-bē\ see EBE[1]

eece \ēs\ see IECE

eeced \ēst\ see EAST[1]

eech \ēch\ see EACH

eecher \ē-chər\ see EACHER

eeches \ich-əz\ see ITCHES

eeching \ē-chiŋ\ screeching, teaching • far-reaching • practice teaching, student teaching
—also -ing *forms of verbs listed at* EACH

eechy \ē-chē\ see EACHY

eecy \ē-sē\ fleecy, greasy • Tbilisi, AC/DC

eed \ēd\ bead, bleed, breed, cede, creed, deed, feed, greed, he'd, heed, keyed, knead, kneed, lead, mead, need, plead, read, reed, Reed, Reid, screed, seed, she'd, speed, steed, Swede, treed, tweed, Tweed, we'd, weed • accede, airspeed, bindweed, birdseed, blueweed, breast-feed, cheerlead, chickweed, concede, crossbreed, duckweed, exceed, fireweed, flaxseed, force-feed, Godspeed, ground speed, gulfweed, halfbreed, hand-feed, hawkweed, hayseed, high-speed, horseweed, impede, inbreed, indeed, ironweed, knapweed, knotweed, Lake Mead, linseed, lip-read, milkweed, misdeed, mislead, misread, moonseed, nosebleed, oilseed, pigweed, pinweed, pokeweed, pondweed, precede, proceed, proofread, ragweed, rapeseed, recede, reseed, rockweed, seaweed, secede, Siegfried, sight-read, smartweed, sneezeweed, speed-read, spoonfeed, stall-feed, stampede, stinkweed, succeed, ten-speed, warp speed, weak-kneed, witchweed, wormseed • aniseed, beggarweed, bottle-feed, bugleweed, centipede, chicken feed, cottonseed, crazyweed, double reed, Ganymede, go to seed, interbreed, intercede, jewelweed, jimsonweed, locoweed, millipede, Nicene Creed, overfeed, pedi-

greed, poppy seed, Port Said,
pumpkinseed, Runnymede, super-
sede, thimbleweed, title deed,
tumbleweed, underfeed, up to
speed, waterweed • Apostles'
Creed, canary seed, caraway seed
—*also* -ed *forms of verbs listed at*
EE[1]

eedal \ēd-ᵊl\ see EEDLE

eeder \ēd-ər\ see EADER[1]

eedful \ēd-fəl\ heedful, needful

eeding[1] \ēd-iŋ\ bleeding, breeding,
leading, reading • inbreeding,
lipreading, preceding, proceeding
• care and feeding
—*also* -ing *forms of verbs listed at*
EED

eeding[2] \ēd-ᵊn\ see EDON

eedle \ēd-ᵊl\ needle, wheedle
• darning needle

eedless \ēd-ləs\ heedless, needless,
seedless

eedn't \ēd-ᵊnt\ see EDENT

eedo \ēd-ō\ see EDO[1]

eedom \ēd-əm\ see EDUM

eeds \ēdz\ Leeds, needs • love
beads, prayer beads, proceeds
• special needs, worry beads
—*also* -s, -'s, *and* -s' *forms of nouns
and* -s *forms of verbs listed at* EED

eedy \ēd-ē\ beady, greedy, needy,
reedy, seedy, speedy, tweedy,
weedy

eef \ēf\ see IEF[1]

eefe \ēf\ see IEF[1]

eefy \ē-fē\ beefy, leafy

eegee \ē-jē\ see IJI

eeing \ē-iŋ\ being, seeing, skiing
• farseeing, sightseeing, well-being
• waterskiing
—*also* -ing *forms of verbs listed at*
EE[1]

eek[1] \ik\ see ICK

eek[2] \ēk\ see EAK[1]

eeked \ēkt\ see EAKED[2]

eeken \ē-kən\ see EACON

eeker \ē-kər\ see EAKER[1]

eekie \ē-kē\ see EAKY

eeking \ē-kiŋ\ see EAKING

eekly \ē-klē\ bleakly, meekly,
sleekly, weakly, weekly, treacly
• biweekly, midweekly,
newsweekly

eeky \ē-kē\ see EAKY

eel \ēl\ see EAL[2]

eelable \ē-lə-bəl\ see EALABLE

eele \ēl\ see EAL[2]

eeled \ēld\ see IELD

eeler \ē-lər\ see EALER

eeley \ē-lē\ see EELY

eelie \ē-lē\ see EELY

eeling \ē-liŋ\ ceiling, dealing, feel-
ing, peeling • appealing, Darjeel-
ing, faith healing, freewheeling,
glass ceiling, revealing, self-seal-
ing, unfeeling • double-dealing,
hit the ceiling, snowmobiling,
unappealing
—*also* -ing *forms of verbs listed at*
EAL[2]

eely \ē-lē\ eely, freely, mealy,
really, steelie, steely, stele,
wheelie • Swahili • Isle of Ely,
touchy-feely

eem \ēm\ see EAM[1]

eeman \ē-mən\ see EMON[1]

eemer \ē-mər\ see EAMER

eemie \ē-mē\ see EAMY

eeming \ē-miŋ\ scheming, scream-
ing, seeming, streaming
—*also* -ing *forms of verbs listed at*
EAM[1]

eemly \ēm-lē\ seemly • extremely,
supremely, unseemly

een[1] \in\ see IN[3]

een[2] \ēn\ see INE[3]

e'en \ēn\ see INE[3]

eena \ē-nə\ see INA[2]

eene \ēn\ see INE[3]

eener \ē-nər\ see EANER

eenery \ēn-rē\ see EANERY

eening \ē-niŋ\ see EANING

eenly \ēn-lē\ see EANLY[1]

eenness \ēn-nəs\ see EANNESS

eens \ēnz\ Queens, teens • by all means, by no means, Grenadines, New Orleans, Philippines, refried beans, smithereens, ways and means

eenwich \in-ich\ see INACH

eeny \ē-nē\ see INI[1]

eep \ēp\ beep, bleep, cheap, cheep, creep, deep, heap, Jeep, keep, leap, peep, reap, seep, sheep, sleep, steep, sweep, veep, weep • asleep, barkeep, black sheep, bopeep, dirt cheap, housekeep, knee-deep, scrap heap, skin-deep, upkeep, upsweep • bighorn sheep, chimney sweep, mountain sheep, on the cheap, overleap, oversleep, quantum leap • Louis Philippe

eepage \ē-pij\ creepage, seepage

eepen \ē-pən\ cheapen, deepen, steepen

eepence \əp-əns\ see UPPANCE

eeper \ē-pər\ beeper, creeper, Dnieper, keeper, leaper, peeper, reaper, sleeper, sweeper, weeper • barkeeper, beekeeper, bookkeeper, doorkeeper, gamekeeper, gatekeeper, goalkeeper, grim reaper, groundskeeper, housekeeper, innkeeper, minesweeper, peacekeeper, scorekeeper, shopkeeper, spring peeper, storekeeper, timekeeper, zookeeper • chimney sweeper
—*also* -er *forms of adjectives listed at* EEP

eepie \ē-pē\ see EEPY

eeping \ē-piŋ\ creeping, keeping, weeping • beekeeping, bookkeeping, gatekeeping, housekeeping, minesweeping, peacekeeping, safekeeping, timekeeping
—*also* -ing *forms of verbs listed at* EEP

eeple \ē-pəl\ see EOPLE

eepy \ē-pē\ cheapie, creepy, seepy, sleepy, tepee, weepy

eer[1] \ē-ər\ seer, skier, we're • sightseer • overseer, water-skier

eer[2] \ir\ beer, bier, blear, cheer, clear, dear, deer, ear, fear, gear, hear, here, jeer, Lear, leer, mere, near, peer, pier, Pierre, queer, rear, sear, seer, shear, sheer, smear, sneer, spear, sphere, steer, tear, tier, veer, weir, we're, year • adhere, all clear, ampere, appear, austere, besmear, brassiere, Bronx cheer, by ear, Cape Fear, career, cashier, cashmere, Cheshire, clavier, cohere, dog-ear, endear, footgear, frontier, headgear, inhere, Kashmir, killdeer, leap year, light-year, man-year, midyear, mishear, monsieur, mule deer, musk deer, nadir, New Year, off year, premier, premiere, red deer, rehear, reindeer, revere, Revere, roe deer, root beer, severe, Shakespeare, Shropshire, sincere, steer clear, Tangier, tapir, tin ear, veneer, Vermeer, vizier, wind shear, worm gear, Yorkshire, Zaire • atmosphere, auctioneer, balladeer, bandolier, belvedere, biosphere, black-tailed deer, bombardier, boutonniere, brigadier, buccaneer, budgeteer, cannoneer, canyoneer, cavalier, chandelier, chanticleer, chocolatier, commandeer, crystal clear, disappear, domineer, ecosphere, engineer, fallow deer, financier, fiscal year, gadgeteer, gazetteer, ginger beer, Gloucestershire, gondolier, grenadier, Guinevere, hemisphere, Herefordshire, Hertfordshire, Holy Year, inner ear, insincere, interfere, in the clear, Lancashire, landing gear, marketeer, middle ear, mountaineer, multiyear, musketeer, mutineer, outer ear, overhear, overseer, Oxfordshire, pamphleteer, persevere, pioneer, privateer, profiteer, puppeteer, racketeer, rocketeer, sloganeer, sonneteer, souvenir, Staffordshire, steering gear, stratosphere, summiteer, swimmer's ear, troposphere, vintage year, Vladimir, volunteer, Warwickshire, white-tailed deer, Worcestershire, yesteryear • black marketeer, charioteer, conventioneer, electioneer, ionosphere, Nottinghamshire, orienteer • academic year, bioengineer, cauliflower ear, civil engineer, Jammu and Kashmir

e'er \er\ see ARE[4]

eerage \ir-ij\ peerage, steerage

eered \ird\ see EARD[1]

eerer \ir-ər\ see EARER[2]

eeress \ir-əs\ see EROUS

eerful \ir-fəl\ see EARFUL

eerie \ir-ē\ see EARY

eering \ir-iŋ\ see EARING[1]

eerist \ir-əst\ see ERIST[1]

eerless \ir-ləs\ see EARLESS

eerly \ir-lē\ see EARLY[1]

eersman \irz-mən\ steersman • frontiersman

eerut \ir-ət\ see IRIT

eery \ir-ē\ see EARY

ees \ēz\ see EZE

eese \ēz\ see EZE

eesh \ēsh\ see ICHE[2]

eesi \ē-zē\ see EASY[1]

eesia \ē-zhə\ see ESIA[2]

eest[1] \āst\ see ACED

eest[2] \ēst\ see EAST[1]

eesy \ē-zē\ see EASY[1]

eet \ēt\ see EAT[1]

eetah \ēt-ə\ see ITA

eete \āt-ē\ see ATY

eeten \ēt-ᵊn\ see EATEN[1]

eeter \ēt-ər\ see EATER[1]

eethe \ēth\ see EATHE

eether \ē-thər\ see EITHER

eething \ē-thiŋ\ see EATHING

eetie \ēt-ē\ see EATY

eeting \ēt-iŋ\ see EATING

eetle \ēt-ᵊl\ see ETAL[1]

eetly \ēt-lē\ fleetly, neatly, sweetly • completely, concretely, discreetly • bittersweetly, incompletely, indiscreetly

eety \ēt-ē\ see EATY

ee-um \ē-əm\ see EUM[1]

eeve \ēv\ see EAVE[1]

eeved \ēvd\ see EAVED

eevil \ē-vəl\ see IEVAL

eevish \ē-vish\ peevish, thievish

eeward \ē-wərd\ leeward, seaward

eewee \ē-wē\ kiwi, peewee, pewee

eewit \ü-ət\ see UET

eez \ēz\ see EZE

eezable \ē-zə-bəl\ see EASIBLE

eeze \ēz\ see EZE

eezer \ē-zər\ see EASER[2]

eezing \ē-ziŋ\ see EASING[2]

eezy \ē-zē\ see EASY[1]

ef[1] \ef\ chef, clef, deaf, ef, f, ref • bass clef, Brezhnev, C clef, Kiev, stone-deaf, tone-deaf • emf, Gorbachev, treble clef, UNICEF • Prokofiev

ef[2] \ā\ see AY[1]

ef[3] \ēf\ see IEF[1]

efanie \ef-ə-nē\ see EPHONY

efany \ef-ə-nē\ see EPHONY

eferable \ef-rə-bəl\ preferable, referable

eference \ef-rəns\ deference, preference, reference • cross-reference • frame of reference

eferent \ef-rənt\ deferent, referent

eff \ef\ see EF[1]

effer \ef-ər\ see EPHOR

eficence \ef-ə-səns\ beneficence, maleficence

eft \eft\ cleft, deft, eft, heft, left, theft • bereft, grand theft, stage left • ultraleft • identity theft

efty \ef-tē\ hefty, lefty

eg[1] \āg\ Craig, plague, vague • The Hague • bubonic plague

eg² \eg\ beg, Craig, egg, Greg, keg, leg, peg, reg • bootleg, bowleg, foreleg, JPEG, MPEG, nutmeg, peg leg, renege • break a leg, powder keg, pull one's leg, Winnipeg • mumblety-peg

eg³ \ej\ see EDGE

ega¹ \eg-ə\ mega • omega • Lake Onega, rutabaga

ega² \ä-gə\ see AGA²

ega³ \ē-gə\ see IGA

egal \ē-gəl\ beagle, eagle, legal, regal • bald eagle, illegal, sea eagle, spread-eagle • golden eagle

egan \ē-gən\ Megan, vegan • Mohegan, Monhegan, Waukegan

ege¹ \ezh\ cortege, Liège

ege² \eg\ see EG²

ege³ \ej\ see EDGE

ege⁴ \ēg\ see IGUE

ege⁵ \ig\ see IG

eged \ejd\ see EDGED

egel \āgəl\ see AGEL

eger \ej-ər\ see EDGER

egg \eg\ see EG²

eggar \eg-ər\ see EGGER

eggary \eg-ə-rē\ beggary, Gregory

egger \eg-ər\ beggar • bootlegger • thousand-legger, Winnipegger

eggie \ej-ē\ see EDGY

eggs \egz\ see EGS

eggy \eg-ē\ leggy, Peggy, plaguey • Carnegie

egia \ē-jə\ Ouija • paraplegia, quadriplegia

egian \ē-jən\ see EGION

egic \ē-jik\ strategic • paraplegic, quadriplegic

egie \eg-ē\ see EGGY

egion \ē-jən\ legion, region • collegian, Norwegian, subregion

egious \ē-jəs\ see EGIS

egis \ē-jəs\ aegis, Regis, tedious • egregious

egm \em\ see EM¹

egn \ān\ see ANE¹

egnant \eg-nənt\ pregnant, regnant

egnly \ān-lē\ see AINLY

ego¹ \ē-gō\ ego • amigo • alter ego, impetigo

ego² \ā-gō\ see AGO²

egory \eg-ə-rē\ see EGGARY

egs \egz\ yellowlegs • daddy longlegs

—*also* -s, -'s, *and* -s' *forms of nouns and* -s *forms of verbs listed at* EG²

eh¹ \ā\ see AY¹

eh² \a\ see AH³

ehen \ān\ see ANE¹

ehner \ā-nər\ see AINER

ei¹ \ā\ see AY¹

ei² \ī\ see Y¹

eia¹ \ē-ə\ see IA¹

eia² \ī-ə\ see IAH¹

eial \ē-əl\ see EAL¹

eian¹ \ē-ən\ see EAN¹

eian² \ā-ən\ see AYAN¹

eiche \āsh\ see ECHE¹

eickel \ī-kəl\ see YCLE¹

eid¹ \āt\ see ATE¹

eid² \īt\ see ITE¹

eid³ \ēd\ see EED

eidel¹ \ād-əl\ see ADLE

eidel² \īd-ºl\ see IDAL

eidi \īd-ē\ see IDAY

eidon \īd-ºn\ see IDEN

eier \īr\ see IRE¹

eifer \ef-ər\ see EPHOR

eige \āzh\ beige • Mount Neige

eiger \ī-gər\ see IGER

eigh¹ \ā\ see AY¹

eigh² \ē\ see EE¹

eighbor \ā-bər\ see ABOR

eight¹ \āt\ see ATE¹

eight² \īt\ see ITE¹

eighter \āt-ər\ see ATOR

eightless \āt-ləs\ see ATELESS

eights \īts\ see IGHTS

eighty \āt-ē\ see ATY

eign \ān\ see ANE¹

eigner \ā-nər\ see AINER

eii \ā\ see AY¹

eiian \ā-ən\ see AYAN¹

eiji \ā-jē\ see AGY
eik \ēk\ see EAK[1]
eikh \ēk\ see EAK[1]
eil[1] \āl\ see AIL
eil[2] \el\ see EL[1]
eil[3] \ēl\ see EAL[2]
eil[4] \īl\ see ILE[1]
eila \ē-lə\ see ELA[1]
eiled \āld\ see AILED
eiler \ī-lər\ see ILAR
eiling[1] \ā-liŋ\ see AILING
eiling[2] \ē-liŋ\ see EELING
eill \ēl\ see EAL[2]
eilles[1] \ā\ see AY[1]
eilles[2] \ālz\ see ALES[1]
eilly \ā-lē\ see AILY
eim[1] \ām\ see AME[1]
eim[2] \īm\ see IME[1]
eimer \ī-mər\ see IMER[1]
eims[1] \ä[n]s\ see ANCE[1]
eims[2] \ēmz\ Rheims
  —also -s, -'s, and -s' forms of
  nouns and -s forms of verbs listed
  at EAM[1]
ein[1] \ān\ see ANE[1]
ein[2] \ē-ən\ see EAN[1]
ein[3] \ēn\ see INE[3]
ein[4] \īn\ see INE[1]
eine[1] \ān\ see ANE[1]
eine[2] \ēn\ see INE[3]
eine[3] \ī-nə\ see INA[1]
eine[4] \en\ see EN[1]
eined \ānd\ see AINED
einer[1] \ā-nər\ see AINER
einer[2] \ē-nər\ see EANER
eing \ē-iŋ\ see EEING
einie \ī-nē\ see INY[1]
eining \ā-niŋ\ see AINING
einous \ā-nəs\ see AYNESS
eins \ānz\ see AINS
eint \ānt\ see AINT
einte \ant\ see ANT[5]
einy \ā-nē\ see AINY
eipt \ēt\ see EAT[1]
eir \er\ see ARE[4]
eira \ir-ə\ see ERA[2]
eird \ird\ see EARD[1]

eiress \ar-əs\ see ARIS[2]
eiric \ī-rik\ see YRIC
eiro \er-ō\ see ERO[2]
eirs \erz\ see AIRS
eis[1] \ās\ see ACE[1]
eis[2] \ē-əs\ see EUS[1]
eis[3] \īs\ see ICE[1]
eisant \ēs-[ə]nt\ see ECENT
eise \ēz\ see EZE
eisel \ī-zəl\ see ISAL[2]
eisen \īz-[ə]n\ see IZEN[1]
eiser \ī-zər\ see IZER
eisha[1] \ā-shə\ see ACIA
eisha[2] \ē-shə\ see ESIA[1]
eisin \ēz-[ə]n\ see EASON
eiss \īs\ see ICE[1]
eissen \īs-[ə]n\ see ISON[1]
eist[1] \ā-əst\ see AYEST
eist[2] \īst\ see IST[1]
eister[1] \ī-stər\ keister, shyster
  • spinmeister • concertmeister
eister[2] \ē-stər\ see EASTER
eisure \ē-zhər\ see EIZURE
eit[1] \ē-ət\ fiat • albeit
eit[2] \it\ see IT[1]
eit[3] \ēt\ see EAT[1]
eit[4] \īt\ see ITE[1]
eited \ēt-əd\ see EATED[1]
eiter[1] \it-ər\ see ITTER
eiter[2] \ī-tər\ see ITER[1]
eith \ēth\ see EATH[1]
either \ē-thər\ breather, either,
  neither • fire-breather
eitus \īt-əs\ see ITIS
eity \ē-ət-ē\ deity • spontaneity
  • homogeneity, simultaneity
eivable \ē-və-bəl\ achievable, be-
  lievable, conceivable, perceivable,
  receivable, retrievable • incon-
  ceivable, irretrievable, unbeliev-
  able
eive \ēv\ see EAVE[1]
eiver \ē-vər\ see IEVER
eix \āsh\ see ECHE[1]
eize[1] \āz\ see AZE[1]
eize[2] \ēz\ see EZE
eizure \ē-zhər\ leisure, seizure

eji \ej-ē\ see EDGY
ejo \ā-ō\ see EO¹
ek \ek\ see ECK
eka¹ \ek-ə\ see ECCA
eka² \ē-kə\ see IKA¹
ekah \ek-ə\ see ECCA
eke \ēk\ see EAK¹
ekel \ek-əl\ see ECKLE
ekh \ek\ see ECK
eki \ek-ē\ see ECKY
ekker \ek-ər\ see ECKER
ekoe \ē-kō\ see ICOT
el¹ \el\ bell, Bell, belle, cell, dell, dwell, el, Elle, fell, gel, hell, jell, knell, l, quell, sell, shell, smell, spell, swell, tell, they'll, well, yell • Adele, band shell, barbell, befell, bluebell, bombshell, Boswell, cartel, Chanel, clamshell, compel, Cornell, corral, cowbell, Cromwell, Danielle, dispel, doorbell, dry cell, dumbbell, eggshell, Estelle, excel, expel, farewell, fat cell, foretell, fuel cell, gazelle, germ cell, Giselle, groundswell, half shell, handbell, hard sell, hotel, impel, inkwell, lapel, Maxwell, Michelle, misspell, Moselle, motel, nerve cell, Nobel, noel, nutshell, oil well, Orwell, outsell, pastel, pell-mell, pixel, propel, rappel, Ravel, rebel, repel, respell, retell, Roswell, scalpel, seashell, sequel, Seychelles, sleigh bell, soft sell, soft-shell, stairwell, star shell, stem cell, tooth shell, unwell, wind-bell • Annabelle, Appenzell, asphodel, bagatelle, Cape Farewell, caramel, caravel, carousel, chanterelle, chaparral, citadel, clientele, cockleshell, Cozumel, decibel, diving bell, fare-thee-well, Isabel, Jezebel, killer cell, kiss-and-tell, ne'er-do-well, New Rochelle, nonpareil, oversell, parallel, personnel, Philomel, pimpernel, Raphael, rebel yell, red blood cell, Sanctus bell, San Rafael, São Miguel, show-and-tell, sickle cell, solar cell, tortoiseshell, undersell, white blood cell, William Tell, zinfandel • Aix-la-Chapelle, artesian well, au naturel, crème caramel, mademoiselle, maître d'hôtel, matériel, Mont-Saint-Michel • antipersonnel • AWOL

el² \āl\ see AIL
ela¹ \ē-lə\ chela, Leila, Sheila • tequila • Philomela
ela² \ā-lə\ see ALA³
ela³ \el-ə\ see ELLA
elable \el-ə-bəl\ see ELLABLE
elacy \el-ə-sē\ jealousy, prelacy
elagh \ā-lē\ see AILY
elah \ē-lə\ see ELA¹
eland \ē-lənd\ eland, Zeeland • New Zealand
elanie \el-ə-nē\ see ELONY
elar \ē-lər\ see EALER
elate \el-ət\ see ELLATE
elatin \el-ət-ᵊn\ see ELETON
elba \el-bə\ Elba, Elbe, Melba
elbe \el-bə\ see ELBA
elbert \el-bərt\ Delbert, Elbert • Mount Elbert
elch \elch\ belch, squelch, welch
eld¹ \eld\ geld, held, meld, shelled, weld • beheld, handheld, hardshelled, upheld, withheld • jet-propelled, self-propelled • unparalleled
—*also* -ed *forms of verbs listed at* EL¹
eld² \elt\ see ELT
elder \el-dər\ elder, welder
eldt \elt\ see ELT
ele¹ \ā-lē\ see AILY
ele² \el\ see EL¹
ele³ \el-ē\ see ELLY
ele⁴ \ē-lē\ see EELY
eled¹ \eld\ see ELD¹
eled² \ēld\ see IELD
elen \el-ən\ see ELON

80

eleon \ēl-yən\ see ELIAN[2]

eleton \el-ət-³n\ gelatin, skeleton

eleus \ē-lē-əs\ see ELIOUS

elf \elf\ elf, pelf, self, shelf • book-shelf, herself, himself, itself, my-self, oneself, ourself, top-shelf, thyself, yourself • mantelshelf, off-the-shelf, Ross Ice Shelf • do-it-yourself • continental shelf

elfish \el-fish\ elfish, selfish • un-selfish

elhi \el-ē\ see ELLY

eli \el-ē\ see ELLY

elia[1] \ēl-yə\ Delia, Lelia, Sheila • Amelia, camellia, Camellia, Cecilia, Cornelia, Karelia, lobelia, Ophelia • psychedelia

elia[2] \il-ē-ə\ see ILIA[1]

elian[1] \ē-lē-ən\ Pelion • Mendelian

elian[2] \ēl-yən\ Aurelian, chameleon, Mendelian, parhelion • perihelion • Aristotelian, Mephistophelian

elian[3] \el-ē-ən\ see ELLIAN

elible \el-ə-bəl\ see ELLABLE

elic \el-ik\ relic • angelic, smart aleck • archangelic, philatelic, psychedelic

elion[1] \el-ē-ən\ see ELLIAN

elion[2] \ēl-yən\ see ELIAN[2]

elion[3] \ēl-ē-ən\ see ELIAN[1]

elios \ē-lē-əs\ see ELIOUS

elious \ē-lē-əs\ Helios • Cornelius

elish \el-ish\ see ELLISH

elist \el-əst\ cellist, trellised • No-belist, pastelist

elius \ē-lē-əs\ see ELIOUS

elix \ē-liks\ Felix, helix • double helix

elk[1] \elk\ elk, whelk

elk[2] \ilk\ see ILK

ell \el\ see EL[1]

e'll \ēl\ see EAL[2]

ella \el-ə\ Della, Ella, fella, fellah, Stella • Estella, Gisela, Luella, Marcella, Mandela, novella, patella, rubella, umbrella, vanilla • a cappella, Cinderella, citronella, Isabella, mozzarella, salmonella, sarsaparilla, tarantella

ellable \el-ə-bəl\ sellable • com-pellable, indelible

ellah \el-ə\ see ELLA

ellan \el-ən\ see ELON

ellant \el-ənt\ appellant, flagellant, propellant, repellent • water-repellent

ellar \el-ər\ see ELLER

ellas \el-əs\ see EALOUS

ellate \el-ət\ pellet, prelate, zealot • appellate

elle[1] \el\ see EL[1]

elle[2] \el-ə\ see ELLA

ellean \el-ē-ən\ see ELLIAN

elled \eld\ see ELD[1]

ellen \el-ən\ see ELON

ellent \el-ənt\ see ELLANT

eller \el-ər\ cellar, dweller, seller, sheller, speller, stellar, teller, yeller • best seller, bookseller, foreteller, propeller, tale-teller • fortune-teller, interstellar, Rockefeller, storyteller

elles[1] \el\ see EL[1]

elles[2] \elz\ see ELLS

ellet \el-ət\ see ELLATE

elley \el-ē\ see ELLY

elli \el-ē\ see ELLY

ellia \ēl-yə\ see ELIA[1]

ellian \el-ē-ən\ Orwellian • Machi-avellian

ellie \el-ē\ see ELLY

elline \el-ən\ see ELON

elling \el-iŋ\ dwelling, selling, spelling, swelling, telling • best-selling, bookselling, cliff-dwelling, compelling, lake dwelling, mis-spelling, tale-telling, upwelling • fortune-telling, self-propelling, storytelling
—*also* -ing *forms of verbs listed at* EL[1]

ellington \el-iŋ-tən\ Ellington, Wellington • beef Wellington

ellion \el-yən\ hellion • rebellion
ellis \el-əs\ see EALOUS
ellised \el-əst\ see ELIST
ellish \el-ish\ hellish, relish • embellish
ellist \el-əst\ see ELIST
ello \el-ō\ bellow, cello, fellow, Jell-O, mellow, yellow • bedfellow, bordello, Longfellow, marshmallow, Odd Fellow, Othello, playfellow, schoolfellow • Pirandello • Robin Goodfellow, violoncello
ell-o \el-ō\ see ELLO
ellous \el-əs\ see EALOUS
ellow¹ \el-ə\ see ELLA
ellow² \el-ō\ see ELLO
ells \elz\ Seychelles • Dardanelles —*also* -s, -'s, *and* -s' *forms of nouns and* -s *forms of verbs listed at* EL¹
ellum \el-əm\ vellum • clitellum, flagellum, postbellum • antebellum, cerebellum
ellus \el-əs\ see EALOUS
elly \el-ē\ belly, Delhi, deli, jelly, Kelly, Nellie, Shelley, smelly, telly • New Delhi, pork belly, potbelly, sowbelly • Botticelli, Delhi belly, nervous Nellie, royal jelly, underbelly, vermicelli • Machiavelli
ellyn \el-ən\ see ELON
elm \elm\ elm, helm, realm • overwhelm
elma \el-mə\ Selma, Velma
elmar \el-mər\ see ELMER
elmer \el-mər\ Delmar, Elmer
elmet \el-mət\ helmet, Helmut • crash helmet, pith helmet
elmut \el-mət\ see ELMET
elo \ē-lō\ see ILO²
elon \el-ən\ Ellen, felon, Helen, melon • Magellan, muskmelon • watermelon • Strait of Magellan
elony \el-ə-nē\ felony, Melanie
elop \el-əp\ develop, envelop • overdevelop

elos \ā-ləs\ see AYLESS
elot \el-ət\ see ELLATE
elotry \el-ə-trē\ helotry, zealotry
elp \elp\ help, kelp, whelp, yelp • self-help
elsea \el-sē\ see ELSIE
elsie \el-sē\ Chelsea, Elsie
elt \elt\ belt, Celt, dealt, dwelt, felt, melt, pelt, smelt, spelt, svelte, veld, welt • black belt, Frostbelt, greenbelt, heartfelt, lap belt, rust belt, seat belt, snowbelt, snowmelt, Sunbelt, web belt • Bible Belt, cartridge belt, Roosevelt, safety belt, shoulder belt • asteroid belt, below the belt
elte \elt\ see ELT
elted \el-təd\ belted, melted, pelted
elter \el-tər\ shelter, smelter, swelter, welter • tax shelter • helter-skelter
eltered \el-tərd\ tax-sheltered —*also* -ed *forms of verbs listed at* ELTER
elting \el-tiŋ\ belting, felting, melting —*also* -ing *forms of verbs listed at* ELT
elve \elv\ delve, shelve, twelve
elves \elvz\ elves • ourselves, themselves, yourselves —*also* -s, -'s, *and* -s' *forms of nouns and* -s *forms of verbs listed at* ELVE
elvin \el-vən\ Elvin, Kelvin, Melvin
elvyn \el-vən\ see ELVIN
ely \ē-lē\ see EELY
em¹ \em\ Clem, crème, em, gem, hem, m, phlegm, REM, stem, them • ahem, AM, brain stem, condemn, FM, item, mayhem, modem, poem, problem, pro tem • ABM, Bethlehem, diadem, stratagem • ad hominem, cable modem, carpe diem, crème de la crème, ICBM • collector's item, post meridiem

em² \əm\ see UM¹

ema \ē-mə\ Lima • eczema, edema • emphysema, Hiroshima, Iwo Jima

emacist \em-ə-səst\ see EMICIST

eman¹ \em-ən\ see EMON²

eman² \ē-mən\ see EMON¹

emane \em-ə-nē\ see EMONY

ember \em-bər\ ember, member • December, dismember, nonmember, November, remember, September • charter member

emble \em-bəl\ tremble • assemble, dissemble, resemble • disassemble

embler \em-blər\ temblor • assembler, dissembler

emblor \em-blər\ see EMBLER

embly \em-blē\ trembly • assembly • disassembly, subassembly

eme¹ \em\ see EM¹

eme² \ēm\ see EAM¹

emely \ēm-lē\ see EEMLY

emen¹ \ē-mən\ see EMON¹

emen² \em-ən\ see EMON²

emen³ \ā-mən\ see AMEN¹

emer \ē-mər\ see EAMER

emery \em-rē\ emery, Emory, memory

emi \em-ē\ see EMMY

emia \ē-mē-ə\ anemia, bohemia, Bohemia, leukemia, toxemia, uremia • academia

emic¹ \ē-mik\ anemic, uremic • emphysemic

emic² \em-ik\ endemic, pandemic, polemic, systemic, totemic • academic, epidemic

emical \em-i-kəl\ chemical • alchemical, polemical • biochemical, petrochemical

emicist \em-ə-səst\ polemicist, supremacist • white supremacist

eming \em-iŋ\ Fleming, lemming —also -ing forms of verbs listed at EM¹

eminge \em-iŋ\ see EMING

emini \em-ə-nē\ see EMONY

eminy \em-ə-nē\ see EMONY

emis \ē-məs\ see EMUS

emish \em-ish\ blemish, Flemish

emlin \em-lən\ gremlin, Kremlin

emma \em-ə\ Emma • dilemma

emme \em\ see EM¹

emmer \em-ər\ hemmer, tremor

emming \em-iŋ\ see EMING

emmy \em-ē\ Emmy, phlegmy, semi, stemmy

emn \em\ see EM¹

emner \em-ər\ see EMMER

emnity \em-nət-ē\ indemnity, solemnity

emo \em-ō\ demo, memo

emon¹ \ē-mən\ demon, freeman, seaman • Lake Leman, Philemon

emon² \em-ən\ Bremen, lemon, Yemen

emone \em-ə-nē\ see EMONY

emony \em-ə-nē\ Gemini, lemony • anemone, Gethsemane, hegemony

emor \em-ər\ see EMMER

emory \em-rē\ see EMERY

emous \ē-məs\ see EMUS

emp \emp\ hemp, temp

emplar \em-plər\ exemplar, Knight Templar

emps \äⁿ\ see ANT¹

empt \emt\ dreamt, tempt • attempt, contempt, exempt, preempt, undreamed, unkempt • tax-exempt

emption \em-shən\ exemption, preemption, redemption

emptive \em-tiv\ preemptive, redemptive

emur \ē-mər\ see EAMER

emus \ē-məs\ Remus • in extremis, Polyphemus

emy \ē-mē\ see EAMY

en¹ \en\ Ben, den, en, glen, Glen, Gwen, hen, Ken, Len, men, n, pen, Penn, Seine, Sten, ten, then, when, wren, yen, Zen • again, amen, Ardennes, Big Ben, bull pen, Cayenne, Cheyenne, Estienne, game hen, hang ten, light pen, marsh hen, moorhen, peahen, pigpen, Phnom Penh, playpen, RN • Adrienne, bornagain, cactus wren, five-and-ten, fountain pen, guinea hen, lion's den, LPN, mother hen, Sun Yatsen, water hen • carcinogen, comedienne, equestrienne, time and again • again and again

en² \ēn\ see INE³

en³ \aⁿ\ see IN⁴

en⁴ \ən\ see UN¹

en⁵ \äⁿ\ see ANT¹

ena¹ \ā-nə\ see ANA²

ena² \ē-nə\ see INA²

enable \en-ə-bəl\ tenable • amenable, untenable

enace \en-əs\ see ENIS

enae \e-nē\ see INI¹

enal \ēn-ᵊl\ penal, renal, venal • adrenal, vaccinal

enant \en-ənt\ pennant, tenant • lieutenant, subtenant • sublieutenant

enary \en-ə-rē\ hennery, plenary • centenary, millenary • bicentenary

enas \ē-nəs\ see ENUS¹

enate \en-ət\ see ENNET

enator \en-ət-ər\ see ENITOR

ençal \en-səl\ see ENCIL

ence¹ \ens\ see ENSE

ence² \äⁿs\ see ANCE¹

ence³ \äns\ see ANCE²

encel \en-səl\ see ENCIL

enceless \en-sləs\ see ENSELESS

encer \en-sər\ see ENSOR

ench \ench\ bench, clench, drench, French, mensch, quench, stench, trench, wench, wrench • entrench, pipe wrench, retrench, unclench, workbench • Allen wrench, monkey wrench, socket wrench • Mariana Trench

enchant \en-chənt\ see ENTIENT

encher \en-chər\ see ENTURE

enchman \ench-mən\ Frenchman, henchman

encia \en-chə\ see ENTIA

encil \en-səl\ pencil, stencil, tensile • grease pencil, lead pencil, prehensile, utensil • eyebrow pencil

end \end\ bend, blend, end, fend, friend, lend, mend, rend, send, spend, tend, trend, vend, wend • amend, append, ascend, attend, bartend, befriend, Big Bend, bookend, boyfriend, commend, contend, dead end, dead-end, defend, depend, descend, distend, downtrend, emend, expend, extend, front-end, girlfriend, godsend, high-end, impend, intend, Land's End, loose end, low-end, misspend, no end, offend, on end, outspend, portend, pretend, rearend, resend, South Bend, split end, stipend, suspend, tag end, tail end, tight end, transcend, unbend, upend, uptrend, weekend, year-end • apprehend, bitter end, business end, comprehend, condescend, dividend, in the end, on the mend, overspend, recommend • at one's wit's end, hyperextend, misapprehend, overextend, stock dividend, superintend • go off the deep end —*also* -ed *forms of verbs listed at* EN¹

enda \en-də\ Brenda, Glenda • agenda • hacienda • hidden agenda

endable \en-də-bəl\ lendable, mendable, spendable • commendable, defendable, dependable, expendable, extendable, unbendable • recommendable, undependable

endal \en-dᵊl\ Grendel, Kendall, Mendel, Wendell

endall \en-dᵊl\ see ENDAL

endance \en-dəns\ see ENDENCE
endancy \en-dən-sē\ see ENDENCY
endant \en-dənt\ see ENDENT
ende¹ \end\ see END
ende² \en-dē\ see ENDI
ended \en-dəd\ ended, splendid
• extended, intended, pretended,
unfriended • open-ended
—*also* -ed *forms of verbs listed at*
END
endel \en-dᵊl\ see ENDAL
endell \en-dᵊl\ see ENDAL
endence \en-dəns\ ascendance,
attendance, dependence, tran-
scendence • independence, Independence
—*also* -s, -'s, *and* -s' *forms of
nouns listed at* ENDENT
endency \en-dən-sē\ tendency
• ascendancy, dependency • code-
pendency
endent \en-dənt\ pendant • ascen-
dant, attendant, defendant, de-
pendent, descendant, intendant,
transcendent • codependent,
independent • overdependent,
superintendent
ender \en-dər\ bender, blender,
fender, gender, lender, render,
sender, slender, spender, splen-
dor, tender, vendor • bartender,
commender, contender, defender,
engender, extender, fork-tender,
goaltender, hellbender, offender,
pretender, surrender, suspender,
transgender, weekender • money-
lender
endi \en-dē\ trendy, Wendy
• modus vivendi
endible \en-də-bəl\ see ENDABLE
endid \en-dəd\ see ENDED
ending \en-diŋ\ ending, pending,
sending • ascending, attending,
fence-mending, goaltending,
heartrending, mind-bending,
nerve ending, unbending, unend-
ing • condescending, gender-

bending • uncomprehending
—*also* -ing *forms of verbs listed at*
END
endless \end-ləs\ endless, friend-
less
endliness \en-lē-nəs\ cleanliness,
friendliness • uncleanliness, un-
friendliness
endly \en-lē\ friendly • uncleanly,
unfriendly • user-friendly
endo \en-dō\ kendo • crescendo
• innuendo
endor \en-dər\ see ENDER
endous \en-dəs\ horrendous, stu-
pendous, tremendous
ends \enz\ see ENS¹
endum \en-dəm\ addendum • ref-
erendum
endy \en-dē\ see ENDI
ene¹ \en\ see EN¹
ene² \en-ē\ see ENNY
ene³ \ē-nē\ see INI¹
ene⁴ \ēn\ see INE³
ene⁵ \ān\ see ANE¹
enel \en-ᵊl\ see ENNEL
ener \ē-nər\ see EANER
enery¹ \en-ə-rē\ see ENARY
enery² \ēn-rē\ see EANERY
enet \en-ət\ see ENNET
eng¹ \aŋ\ see ANG²
eng² \əŋ\ see UNG¹
enge \enj\ avenge, revenge, Stone-
henge
ength¹ \eŋth\ length, strength
• arm's-length, at length, floor-
length, full-length, half-length,
wavelength • industrial-strength
ength² \enth\ see ENTH
engthen \eŋ-thən\ lengthen,
strengthen
enh \en\ see EN¹
enia¹ \ē-nē-ə\ Armenia, Slovenia
• schizophrenia
enia² \ē-nyə\ Armenia, Eugenia,
gardenia
enial \ē-nē-əl\ genial, menial, ve-
nial • congenial

enian \ē-nē-ən\ Armenian, Athenian, Cyrenian, Slovenian, Turkmenian

enic¹ \ēn-ik\ scenic • hygienic

enic² \en-ik\ arsenic, Edenic, Hellenic, hygienic • allergenic, calisthenic, cryogenic, hygienic, photogenic, schizophrenic, telegenic • carcinogenic • hallucinogenic, hypoallergenic

enice \en-əs\ see ENIS

enics \en-iks\ calisthenics, cryogenics
—*also* -s, -'s, *and* -s' *forms of nouns listed at* ENIC²

enie¹ \en-ē\ see ENNY

enie² \ē-nē\ see INI¹

enience \ē-nyəns\ lenience • convenience • inconvenience

enient \ēn-yənt\ lenient • convenient • inconvenient

enim \en-əm\ see ENOM

enin \en-ən\ see ENNON

enis \en-əs\ Dennis, genus, menace, tennis, Venice • lawn tennis • table tennis

enison¹ \en-ə-sən\ Tennyson, venison

enison² \en-ə-zən\ denizen, venison

enitor \en-ət-ər\ senator • progenitor

enity \en-ət-ē\ see ENTITY

enizen \en-ə-zən\ see ENISON²

enn \en\ see EN¹

enna \en-ə\ Glenna, henna • antenna, sienna, Vienna • whip antenna

ennae \en-ē\ see ENNY

ennant \en-ənt\ see ENANT

enne¹ \en\ see EN¹

enne² \en-ē\ see ENNY

enne³ \an\ see AN⁵

ennec \en-ik\ see ENIC²

enned \end\ see END

ennel \en-ᵊl\ fennel, kennel

ennery \en-ə-rē\ see ENARY

ennes \en\ see EN¹

ennet \en-ət\ senate, tenet

ennett \en-ət\ see ENNET

enney \en-ē\ see ENNY

enni \en-ē\ see ENNY

ennial \en-ē-əl\ biennial, centennial, decennial, millennial, perennial, quadrennial, triennial • bicentennial

ennig \en-ik\ see ENIC²

ennin \en-ən\ see ENNON

ennis \en-əs\ see ENIS

ennit \en-ət\ see ENNET

ennium \en-ē-əm\ biennium, millennium

ennon \en-ən\ Lenin, Lennon • antivenin

enny \en-ē\ any, benny, Benny, Denny, genie, Jenny, Kenny, many, penny, Penny • antennae, halfpenny, sixpenny, so many, tenpenny, threepenny, twopenny • spinning jenny

ennyson \en-ə-sən\ see ENISON¹

eno \ā-nō\ see ANO²

enom \en-əm\ denim, venom

enon \en-ən\ see ENNON

enous \ē-nəs\ see ENUS¹

ens¹ \enz\ cleanse, lens • amends, hand lens, weekends, zoom lens • odds and ends • Homo sapiens
—*also* -s, -'s, *and* -s' *forms of nouns and* -s *forms of verbs listed at* EN¹

ens² \ens\ see ENSE

ensable \en-sə-bəl\ see ENSIBLE

ensal \en-səl\ see ENCIL

ensary \ens-rē\ see ENSORY

ensch \ench\ see ENCH

ense \ens\ dense, fence, hence, pence, sense, tense, thence, whence • commence, condense, defense, dispense, expense, horse sense, immense, incense, intense, nonsense, offense, past tense, pretense, sequence, sixpence, sixth sense, suspense, twopence • common sense, confidence,

consequence, diffidence, evidence, frankincense, no-nonsense, present tense, providence, Providence, recompense, residence, self-defense, zone defense • coincidence, inconsequence, nonresidence, self-confidence
—also -s, -'s, *and* -s' *forms of nouns listed at* ENT[1]

enseful \ens-fəl\ senseful • suspenseful

enseless \en-sləs\ fenceless, senseless • defenseless, offenseless

enser \en-sər\ see ENSOR

ensian \en-chən\ see ENSION

ensible \en-sə-bəl\ sensible • defensible, dispensable, extensible, insensible, ostensible • commonsensible, comprehensible, indefensible, indispensable, reprehensible • incomprehensible

ensil \en-səl\ see ENCIL

ensile \en-səl\ see ENCIL

ension \en-shən\ mention, pension, tension • abstention, ascension, attention, contention, convention, declension, detention, dimension, dissension, extension, high-tension, indention, intention, invention, pretension, prevention, retention, suspension • apprehension, circumvention, comprehension, condescension, contravention, fourth dimension, hypertension, hypotension, inattention, reinvention, third dimension • hyperextension, incomprehension, misapprehension, nonintervention, overextension • Geneva convention, honorable mention

ensional \ench-nəl\ conventional, dimensional, intentional • four-dimensional, one-dimensional, three-dimensional, two-dimensional, unconventional, unintentional

ensis \en-səs\ see ENSUS

ensity \en-sət-ē\ density • immensity, intensity, propensity

ensive \en-siv\ pensive • defensive, expensive, extensive, intensive, offensive • apprehensive, comprehensive, inexpensive, inoffensive • counteroffensive, labor-intensive

ensor \en-sər\ censor, fencer, sensor, Spencer, tensor • condenser, dispenser, extensor, sequencer
—also -er *forms of adjectives listed at* ENSE

ensory \ens-rē\ sensory • dispensary • extrasensory, multisensory

ensual[1] \en-chəl\ see ENTIAL

ensual[2] \ench-wəl\ see ENTUAL[1]

ensure \en-chər\ see ENTURE

ensus \en-səs\ census • consensus • amanuensis

ent[1] \ent\ bent, Brent, cent, dent, gent, Ghent, Kent, lent, Lent, meant, pent, rent, scent, sent, spent, tent, Trent, vent, went • absent, accent, Advent, ascent, assent, augment, cement, comment, consent, content, convent, descent, dissent, event, extent, ferment, foment, fragment, frequent, hell-bent, indent, intent, invent, lament, low-rent, outspent, percent, pigment, portent, present, prevent, pup tent, relent, repent, resent, segment, Tashkent, torment, well-meant • accident, argument, circumvent, compartment, complement, compliment, confident, diffident, discontent, document, evident, heaven-sent, implement, incident, instrument, malcontent, nonevent, ornament, orient, president, provident, regiment, reinvent, represent, resident, sediment, Stoke-on-Trent, subsequent, supplement, underwent • age of consent, disorient, experiment, glove compartment, misrepresent, nonresident, oxygen tent, portland cement, rubber cement, self-confident, self-evident, vice president • in any event, media event

ent² \änt\ see ANT²

ent³ \äⁿ\ see ANT¹

enta \ent-ə\ magenta, placenta, polenta

entable \ent-ə-bəl\ rentable • lamentable, presentable, preventable • documentable, representable

entacle \ent-i-kəl\ see ENTICAL

entage \ent-ij\ tentage • percentage

ental \ent-ᵊl\ dental, gentle, lentil, mental, rental • judgmental, parental • accidental, apartmental, compartmental, continental, departmental, detrimental, elemental, fundamental, governmental, grandparental, incidental, incremental, instrumental, monumental, nonjudgmental, occidental, oriental, ornamental, regimental, sacramental, sentimental, supplemental, temperamental, transcendental • coincidental, developmental, environmental, experimental, transcontinental • intercontinental, interdepartmental

entalist \ent-ᵊl-əst\ fundamentalist, instrumentalist, orientalist, sentimentalist, transcendentalist • environmentalist

entance \ent-ᵊns\ see ENTENCE

entary \en-trē\ entry, gentry, sentry • reentry, subentry • alimentary, complementary, complimentary, documentary, elementary, mockumentary, parliamentary, port of entry, sedimentary, supplementary • uncomplimentary

entative \ent-ət-iv\ tentative • preventative • argumentative, representative

ente¹ \ent-ē\ see ENTY

ente² \änt\ see ANT²

ented \ent-əd\ contented, demented, lamented, segmented • discontented, malcontented, oriented, self-contented • unprecedented • overrepresented, underrepresented
—*also* -ed *forms of verbs listed at* ENT¹

enten \ent-ᵊn\ dentin, Lenten, Quentin, Trenton

entence \ent-ᵊns\ sentence • death sentence, repentance

enter \ent-ər\ center, enter, mentor, renter • dissenter, frequenter, inventor, nerve center, presenter, reenter, tormentor • epicenter, front and center, shopping center, trauma center • experimenter

entered \en-tərd\ centered • self-centered
—*also* -ed *forms of verbs listed at* ENTER

enterie \en-trē\ see ENTARY

entful \ent-fəl\ eventful, resentful • uneventful

enth \enth\ nth, strength, tenth • crème de menthe • industrial-strength

enthe \enth\ see ENTH

enti \ent-ē\ see ENTY

entia \en-shə\ dementia, Valencia • in absentia

ential \en-shəl\ consensual, credential, essential, eventual, potential, prudential, sequential, tangential, torrential • confidential, consequential, deferential, differential, existential, exponential, inessential, influential, nonessential, penitential, pestilential, preferential, presidential, providential, quintessential, residential, reverential, unessential • inconsequential, vice presidential

entian \en-shən\ see ENSION

entiary \ensh-rē\ century • penitentiary • plenipotentiary

entical \ent-i-kəl\ tentacle • identi-
cal

entice \ent-əs\ see ENTOUS

enticle \ent-i-kəl\ see ENTICAL

entient \en-chənt\ penchant, sen-
tient, trenchant

entil \ent-ᵊl\ see ENTAL

entin \ent-ᵊn\ see ENTEN

enting \ent-iŋ\ dissenting • unre-
lenting
—*also* -ing *forms of verbs listed at*
ENT[1]

ention \en-shən\ see ENSION

entional \ensh- nəl\ see ENSIONAL

entioned \en-shənd\ mentioned
• aforementioned, well-inten-
tioned

entious \en-chəs\ contentious,
licentious, pretentious, senten-
tious, tendentious • conscientious,
unpretentious

entis \ent-əs\ see ENTOUS

entity \en-ət-ē\ entity • amenity,
identity, nonentity, obscenity,
serenity

entive \ent-iv\ attentive, incentive,
inventive, preventive, retentive
• inattentive

entle \ent-ᵊl\ see ENTAL

entment \ent-mənt\ contentment,
resentment • discontentment

ento \en-tō\ lento • memento,
pimiento, Sorrento • Sacramento
• divertimento, risorgimento
• pronunciamento

enton \ent-ᵊn\ see ENTEN

entor \ent-ər\ see ENTER

entous \ent-əs\ apprentice, mo-
mentous, portentous • compos
mentis • non compos mentis

entry \en-trē\ see ENTARY

ents \ents\ two cents • at all events,
dollars-and-cents
—*also* -s, -'s, *and* -s' *forms of nouns
and* -s *forms of verbs listed at* ENT[1]

entual[1] \en-shə-wəl\ sensual • ac-
centual, consensual, eventual

entual[2] \en-chəl\ see ENTIAL

enture \en-chər\ censure, denture,
quencher, venture • adventure,
backbencher, debenture, inden-
ture • misadventure

entury \ench-rē\ see ENTIARY

enty \ent-ē\ plenty, twenty
• aplenty • horn of plenty, twenty-
twenty

enuis \en-yə-wəs\ see ENUOUS

enum \en-əm\ see ENOM

enuous \en-yə-wəs\ strenuous,
tenuous • ingenuous • disingenu-
ous

enus[1] \ē-nəs\ genus, venous, Venus
• Maecenas • intravenous

enus[2] \en-əs\ see ENIS

eny \ā-nē\ see AINY

enys \en-əs\ see ENIS

enza \en-zə\ cadenza, credenza
• influenza

eo[1] \ā-ō\ kayo, mayo • cacao,
rodeo • Galileo, San Mateo
• Montevideo

eo[2] \ē-ō\ see IO[2]

eoff[1] \ef\ see EF[1]

eoff[2] \ēf\ see IEF[1]

eoffor \ef-ər\ see EPHOR

eoman \ō-mən\ see OMAN

eon[1] \ē-ən\ see EAN[1]

eon[2] \ē-än\ eon, Freon, neon, prion

eopard \ep-ərd\ leopard, peppered,
shepherd • snow leopard • German shepherd

eopardess \ep-ərd-əs\ leopardess,
shepherdess

eople \ē-pəl\ people, steeple
• craftspeople, laypeople, sales-
people, townspeople, tradespeople
• businesspeople, little people
• beautiful people

eorem \ir-əm\ see ERUM

eorge \órj\ see ORGE

eorist \ir-əst\ see ERIST[1]

eoul \ōl\ see OLE[1]

eous \ē-əs\ see EUS[1]

ep \ep\ pep, prep, rep, schlepp, step, steppe, strep, yep • doorstep, footstep, goose-step, half step, instep, in step, lockstep, misstep, sidestep, twelve-step, whole step • in lockstep, out of step, overstep, step-by-step

eparable \ep-rə-bəl\ reparable, separable • inseparable, irreparable

epard \ep-ərd\ see EOPARD

epe \āp\ see APE[1]

epee \ē-pē\ see EEPY

eper \ep-ər\ see EPPER

eperous \ep-rəs\ leprous • obstreperous

eph \ef\ see EF[1]

ephen \ē-vən\ see EVEN

epherd \ep-ərd\ see EOPARD

epherdess \ep-ərd-əs\ see EOPARDESS

ephone \ef-ə-nē\ see EPHONY

ephony \ef-ə-nē\ Stephanie • Persephone, telephony

ephor \ef-ər\ heifer, zephyr

epht \eft\ see EFT

ephyr \ef-ər\ see EPHOR

epid \ep-əd\ tepid • intrepid

epo \ēp-ō\ see EPOT

epot \ēp-ō\ depot • el cheapo

epp \ep\ see EP

eppe \ep\ see EP

epped \ept\ see EPT

epper \ep-ər\ leper, pepper • bell pepper, green pepper, hot pepper, red pepper, sidestepper, sweet pepper • chili pepper

eppy \ep-ē\ peppy, preppy

eprous \ep-rəs\ see EPEROUS

eps \eps\ biceps, forceps, triceps • quadriceps
—*also* -s, -'s, *and* -s' *forms of nouns and* -s *forms of verbs listed at* EP

ept \ept\ crept, kept, slept, stepped, swept, wept • accept, adept, backswept, concept, except, inept, precept, upswept, windswept • intercept, overslept
—*also* -ed *forms of verbs listed at* EP

eptable \ep-tə-bəl\ see EPTIBLE

eptacle \ep-ti-kəl\ skeptical • receptacle

eptible \ep-tə-bəl\ acceptable, perceptible, susceptible • imperceptible, unacceptable

eptic \ep-tik\ peptic, septic, skeptic • dyspeptic • antiseptic, epileptic, narcoleptic

eptical \ep-ti-kəl\ see EPTACLE

eption \ep-shən\ conception, deception, exception, inception, perception, reception • interception, misconception, preconception, take exception

epy \ep-ē\ see EPPY

epys \ēps\ for keeps
—*also* -s, -'s, *and* -s' *forms of nouns and* -s *forms of verbs listed at* EEP

equal \ē-kwəl\ equal, sequel • coequal, unequal

eque \ek\ see ECK

equel \ē-kwəl\ see EQUAL

equer \ek-ər\ see ECKER

er[1] \ā\ see AY[1]

er[2] \er\ see ARE[4]

er[3] \ər\ see EUR[1]

er[4] \ir\ see EER[2]

era[1] \er-ə\ Berra, era, Hera, Sarah • mascara, Rivera, Sahara, sierra, tiara • aloe vera, Common Era, habanera, riviera, Riviera, Santa Clara • Islamic Era, Spanish Sahara, Western Sahara

era[2] \ir-ə\ era, Hera, lira, Vera • chimera, Madeira, mbira • Common Era • Islamic Era

erah \ir-ə\ see ERA[2]

eral[1] \ir-əl\ Cyril, feral, virile

eral[2] \er-əl\ see ERIL

eral[3] \ər-əl\ see ERRAL

erald \er-əld\ Gerald, Harold, herald

eraph \er-əf\ see ERIF

eratin \er-ət-ᵊn\ keratin, Sheraton • Samaritan

erative \er-ət-iv\ see ARATIVE[1]

eraton \er-ət-ᵊn\ see ERATIN

erb \ərb\ blurb, curb, herb, Serb, verb • adverb, disturb, exurb, perturb, proverb, reverb, suburb, superb

erbal \ər-bəl\ burble, gerbil, herbal, verbal • nonverbal

erbally \ər-bə-lē\ verbally • hyperbole, nonverbally

erber \ər-bər\ see URBER

erbia \ər-bē-ə\ see URBIA

erbil \ər-bəl\ see ERBAL

erbole \ər-bə-lē\ see ERBALLY

erby \ər-bē\ derby, herby, Kirby • Roller Derby • demolition derby

erce \ərs\ see ERSE

ercery \ərs-rē\ see URSARY

erch \ərch\ see URCH

ercial \ər-shəl\ Herschel • commercial • controversial, infomercial, uncommercial

ercian \ər-shən\ see ERTIAN

ercible \ər-sə-bəl\ see ERSIBLE

ercion \ər-zhən\ see ERSION[1]

ercive \ər-siv\ see ERSIVE

ercular \ər-kyə-lər\ see IRCULAR

ercy \ər-sē\ Circe, mercy, Percy • controversy

erd \ərd\ see IRD

erde[1] \erd\ see AIRED

erde[2] \ərd\ see IRD

erde[3] \ərd-ē\ see URDY

erder \ərd-ər\ birder, girder, herder, murder • sheepherder

erdi \ər-dē\ see URDY

erding \ərd-iŋ\ wording • sheepherding
—also -ing *forms of verbs listed at* IRD

erdure \ər-jər\ see ERGER

ere[1] \er\ see ARE[4]

ere[2] \er-ē\ see ARY[1]

ere[3] \ir\ see EER[2]

ere[4] \ir-ē\ see EARY

ere[5] \ər\ see EUR[1]

e're \ē-ər\ see EER[1]

ère \er\ see ARE[4]

ereal \ir-ē-əl\ see ERIAL

ereid \ir-ē-əd\ see ERIOD

erek \erik\ see ERIC[1]

erely \ir-lē\ see EARLY[1]

erence[1] \ir-əns\ clearance • adherence, appearance, coherence • disappearance, incoherence, interference, perseverance • run interference

erence[2] \ər-əns\ see URRENCE

erence[3] \er-əns\ see ARENCE[1]

erent \er-ənt\ see ARENT[1]

eren't[1] \ərnt\ see EARNT

eren't[2] \ər-ənt\ see URRENT

ereo \er-ē-ō\ see ARIO

ereous \ir-ē-əs\ see ERIOUS

erer \ir-ər\ see EARER[2]

eres[1] \erz\ see AIRS

eres[2] \ir-ēz\ see ERIES

eres[3] \ərs\ see ERS[1]

ereth \er-ət\ see ERIT

ereus \ir-ē-əs\ see ERIOUS

erf \ərf\ see URF

erge \ərj\ see URGE

ergence \ər-jəns\ convergence, divergence, emergence, resurgence
—also -s, -'s, *and* -s' *forms of nouns listed at* URGENT

ergency \ər-jən-sē\ urgency • emergency, insurgency • counterinsurgency

ergent \ər-jənt\ see URGENT

ergeon \ər-jin\ see URGEON

erger \ər-jər\ merger, perjure, verdure

ergic \ər-jik\ allergic • dramaturgic

ergne[1] \ərn\ see URN

ergne[2] \ern\ see ERN[1]

ergy \ər-jē\ see URGY

eri[1] \er-ē\ see ARY[1]

eri² \ir-ē\ see EARY
eria¹ \ir-ē-ə\ Syria • Algeria, Assyria, bacteria, criteria, diphtheria, Elyria, Iberia, Illyria, Liberia, Nigeria, Siberia, wisteria • cafeteria
eria² \er-ē-ə\ see ARIA
erial \ir-ē-əl\ aerial, cereal, serial • arterial, bacterial, ethereal, funereal, imperial, material, venereal • immaterial, magisterial, managerial, ministerial, raw material • antibacterial
erian¹ \ir-ē-ən\ Algerian, Assyrian, Chaucerian, criterion, Faulknerian, Hitlerian, Iberian, Liberian, Nigerian, Shakespearean, Siberian, Sumerian, valerian, Wagnerian • Presbyterian
erian² \er-ē-ən\ see ARIAN¹
eric¹ \er-ik\ cleric, Derek, derrick, Eric • generic, Homeric, numeric • atmospheric, esoteric, hemispheric, stratospheric • alphanumeric, ionospheric
eric² \ir-ik\ lyric, Pyrrhic, spheric • satiric, vampiric • atmospheric, hemispheric, panegyric, stratospheric
erica \er-i-kə\ Erica • America • North America, South America • Central America, Latin America, Middle America
erical¹ \er-i-kəl\ clerical, spherical • hysterical, numerical • anticlerical
erical² \ir-i-kəl\ lyrical, miracle, spherical • empirical • hemispherical
erich \erik\ see ERIC¹
erics \er-iks\ hysterics
—*also* -s, -'s, *and* -s' *forms of nouns listed at* ERIC¹
eried \ir-ē-əd\ see ERIOD
eries \ir-ēz\ Ceres, queries, series • in series, World Series • miniseries

—*also* -s, -'s, *and* -s' *forms of nouns listed at* EARY
erif \er-əf\ seraph, sheriff
eriff \er-əf\ see ERIF
erik \erik\ see ERIC¹
erika \er-i-kə\ see ERICA
eril \er-əl\ beryl, Beryl, Cheryl, Errol, feral, peril, Sheryl, sterile • imperil
erile \er-əl\ see ERIL
erilous \er-ə-ləs\ perilous, querulous
erin \er-ən\ see ARON¹
ering \ar-iŋ\ see ARING¹
eriod \ir-ē-əd\ myriad, period • grace period
erion \ir-ē-ən\ see ERIAN¹
erior \ir-ē-ər\ anterior, exterior, inferior, interior, posterior, superior, ulterior • Lake Superior
—*also* -er *forms of adjectives listed at* EARY
eriot \er-ē-ət\ see ARIAT¹
erious \ir-ē-əs\ serious, Sirius • delirious, imperious, mysterious, Tiberius • deleterious
eris¹ \ir-əs\ see EROUS
eris² \er-əs\ see ERROUS
erist¹ \ir-əst\ theorist
—*also* -est *forms of adjectives listed at* EER²
erist² \er-əst\ see ARIST
erit \er-ət\ ferret, merit • demerit, inherit • disinherit
eritable \er-ət-ə-bəl\ veritable • inheritable
eritor \er-ət-ər\ ferreter • inheritor
erity \er-ət-ē\ rarity, verity • asperity, austerity, dexterity, posterity, prosperity, severity, sincerity, temerity • insincerity
erium \ir-ē-əm\ Miriam • bacterium, delirium
erius¹ \er-ē-əs\ see ARIOUS
erius² \ir-ē-əs\ see ERIOUS
erjure \ər-jər\ see ERGER
erjury \ərj-rē\ perjury, surgery

• tree surgery • microsurgery, neurosurgery, plastic surgery, psychosurgery

erk \ərk\ see ORK[1]

erker \ər-kər\ see ORKER[1]

erkin \ər-kən\ see IRKIN

erking \ər-kiŋ\ see ORKING

erky \ər-kē\ jerky, murky, perky, smirky, turkey, Turkey • talk turkey • Albuquerque, herky-jerky

erle \ərl\ see IRL

erlie \er-lē\ see AIRLY

erlin \ər-lən\ merlin, Merlin, yearling

erling \ər-liŋ\ see URLING

erlon \ər-lən\ see ERLIN

erlyn \ər-lən\ see ERLIN

erm \ərm\ see ORM[1]

erma \ər-mə\ dharma, Irma • terra firma

ermal \ər-məl\ dermal, thermal • epidermal

erman \ər-mən\ ermine, German, Herman, merman, sermon, Sherman, vermin • determine, Mount Hermon • predetermine

ermanent \ərm-nənt\ permanent • determinant, impermanent • semipermanent

ermann \ər-mən\ see ERMAN

erment \ər-mənt\ deferment, interment, preferment • disinterment

ermi \ər-mē\ see ERMY

ermic \ər-mik\ karmic • geothermic, hypodermic, taxidermic

ermin \ər-mən\ see ERMAN

erminal \ərm-nəl\ germinal, terminal

erminant \ərm-nənt\ see ERMANENT

ermine \ər-mən\ see ERMAN

ermined \ər-mənd\ ermined • determined • self-determined • overdetermined

erminous \ər-mə-nəs\ terminus, verminous

erminus \ər-mə-nəs\ see ERMINOUS

ermis \ər-məs\ dermis, thermos • epidermis

ermit \ər-mət\ hermit, Kermit

ermon \ər-mən\ see ERMAN

ermos \ər-məs\ see ERMIS

ermy \ər-mē\ germy, squirmy, wormy • taxidermy

ern[1] \ern\ bairn, cairn

ern[2] \ərn\ see URN

erna \ər-nə\ Myrna, Verna

ernal \ərn-ᵊl\ colonel, journal, kernel, vernal • eternal, external, fraternal, infernal, internal, maternal, nocturnal, paternal

erne[1] \ern\ see ERN[1]

erne[2] \ərn\ see URN

erned \ərnd\ see URNED

ernel \ərn-ᵊl\ see ERNAL

erner \ər-nər\ see URNER

ernes[1] \ern\ see ERN[1]

ernes[2] \ərn\ see URN

ernest \ər-nəst\ see ERNIST

ernia \ər-ne-ə\ hernia • Hibernia

ernian \ər-nē-ən\ Hibernian, Saturnian

ernible \ər-nə-bəl\ see URNABLE

ernie \ər-nē\ see OURNEY[1]

ernion \ər-nē-ən\ see ERNIAN

ernist \ər-nəst\ earnest, Ernest • internist

ernity \ər-nət-ē\ eternity, fraternity, maternity, modernity, paternity

ernment \ərn-mənt\ adjournment, discernment, internment

erny \ər-nē\ see OURNEY[1]

ero[1] \ē-rō\ gyro, hero, Nero, zero • ground zero, subzero • superhero

ero[2] \er-ō\ pharaoh, taro, tarot • bolero, sombrero, torero, vaquero • caballero, pistolero • Rio de Janeiro

ero[3] \ir-ō\ gyro, hero, zero • ground zero, subzero

erold \er-əld\ see ERALD

eron \er-ən\ see ARON[1]

erous \ir-əs\ cirrus, Eris, peeress, Pyrrhus, seeress

erp \ərp\ see URP

erpe \ər-pē\ see IRPY

erque \ər-kē\ see ERKY

err[1] \er\ see ARE[4]

err[2] \ər\ see EUR[1]

erra \er-ə\ see ERA[1]

errace \er-əs\ see ERROUS

erral \ər-əl\ squirrel • conferral, deferral, referral, transferal

errance \er-əns\ see ARENCE[1]

errand \er-ənd\ errand, gerund

errant \er-ənt\ see ARENT[1]

erre \er\ see ARE[4]

errell \er-əl\ see ERIL

errence[1] \ər-əns\ see URRENCE

errence[2] \er-əns\ see ARENCE[1]

erret \er-ət\ see ERIT

erreter \er-ət-ər\ see ERITOR

erria \er-ē-ə\ see ARIA

errible \er-ə-bəl\ see EARABLE[1]

erric \er-ik\ see ERIC[1]

errick \er-ik\ see ERIC[1]

errie \er-ē\ see ARY[1]

erried \er-ēd\ berried, serried, varied
—*also* -ed *forms of verbs listed at* ARY[1]

errier \er-ē-ər\ terrier • bull terrier, fox terrier, Welsh terrier
—*also* -er *forms of adjectives listed at* ARY[1]

errill \er-əl\ see ERIL

errily \er-ə-lē\ see ARILY

erring[1] \ar-iŋ\ see ARING[1]

erring[2] \ər-iŋ\ see URRING

erris \er-əs\ see ERROUS

errol \er-əl\ see ERIL

errold \er-əld\ see ERALD

erron \er-ən\ see ARON[1]

error \er-ər\ see EARER[1]

errous \er-əs\ Eris, terrace • millionairess

errule \er-əl\ see ERIL

erry \er-ē\ see ARY[1]

ers[1] \ərz\ hers • somewheres
—*also* -s, -'s, *and* -s' *forms of nouns and* -s *forms of verbs listed at* EUR[1]

ers[2] \ā\ see AY[1]

ersable \ər-sə-bəl\ see ERSIBLE

ersal \ər-səl\ dispersal, rehearsal, reversal, traversal • dress rehearsal, universal

ersary \ərs-rē\ see URSARY

erse \ərs\ curse, hearse, nurse, purse, terse, verse, worse • adverse, averse, coerce, commerce, converse, Converse, disburse, disperse, diverse, free verse, immerse, inverse, Nez Percé, obverse, perverse, rehearse, reverse, scrub nurse, submerse, transverse, traverse, wet nurse • e-commerce, in reverse, intersperse, nonsense verse, reimburse, universe • chapter and verse, practical nurse, registered nurse, visiting nurse • chamber of commerce

ersed \ərst\ see URST

ersey \ər-zē\ jersey, Jersey, Mersey • New Jersey

erschel \ər-shəl\ see ERCIAL

ershel \ər-shəl\ see ERCIAL

ersial \ər-shəl\ see ERCIAL

ersian \ər-zhən\ see ERSION[1]

ersible \ər-sə-bəl\ conversable, immersible, reversible, submersible • irreversible

ersion[1] \ər-zhən\ Persian, version • aversion, coercion, conversion, dispersion, diversion, excursion, immersion, incursion, inversion, perversion, reversion, submersion, subversion • extroversion, introversion, King James Version, reconversion

ersion[2] \ər-shən\ see ERTIAN

ersive \ər-siv\ cursive • coercive, discursive, subversive

erson \ərs-ᵊn\ person, worsen

• chairperson, craftsperson, first person, in person, layperson, MacPherson, newsperson, salesperson, spokesperson, third person • anchorperson, businessperson, second person, weatherperson

erst \ərst\ see URST

ersy \ər-sē\ see ERCY

ert¹ \ərt\ Bert, blurt, curt, Curt, dirt, flirt, hurt, pert, shirt, skirt, spurt, squirt • advert, alert, assert, avert, concert, convert, covert, desert, dessert, divert, dress shirt, exert, expert, frankfurt, hair shirt, hoopskirt, inert, insert, invert, nightshirt, overt, pay dirt, pervert, revert, Schubert, seagirt, sea squirt, stuffed shirt, subvert, sweatshirt, T-shirt • disconcert, extrovert, in concert, inexpert, introvert, miniskirt, overskirt, polo shirt, reconvert, red alert, undershirt, underskirt • Hawaiian shirt

ert² \er\ see ARE⁴

ert³ \at\ see AT⁵

erta \ərt-ə\ Gerta • Alberta, Roberta

ertain \ərt-ᵊn\ Burton, certain, curtain • for certain, uncertain

erted \ərt-əd\ concerted, perverted, T-shirted • extroverted, miniskirted, undershirted
—*also* -ed *forms of verbs listed at* ERT¹

erter \ərt-ər\ curter, squirter • converter, deserter, frankfurter, Frankfurter

erth \ərth\ see IRTH

ertha \ər-thə\ Bertha, Eartha

ertial \ər-shəl\ see ERCIAL

ertian \ər-shən\ assertion, Cistercian, desertion, exertion, insertion • self-assertion

ertile \ərt-ᵊl\ fertile, hurtle, myrtle, Myrtle, turtle • crape myrtle, infertile, sea turtle, turn turtle, wax myrtle • snapping turtle

erting \ərt-iŋ\ shirting, skirting • disconcerting
—*also* -ing *forms of verbs listed at* ERT¹

ertion \ər-shən\ see ERTIAN

ertive \ərt-iv\ furtive • assertive • self-assertive, unassertive

erton \ərt-n\ see ERTAIN

ertor \ərt-ər\ see ERTER

erts \ərts\ hertz • gigahertz, kilohertz, megahertz
—*also* -s, -'s, *and* -s' *forms of nouns and* -s *forms of verbs listed at* ERT¹

erty \ər-tē\ see IRTY

ertz \ərts\ see ERTS

erule \er-əl\ see ERIL

erulous \er-ə-ləs\ see ERILOUS

erum \ir-əm\ theorem, serum • blood serum, truth serum

erund \er-ənd\ see ERRAND

erunt \er-ənt\ see ARENT¹

erval \ər-vəl\ see ERVIL

ervancy \ər-vən-sē\ see ERVENCY

ervant \ər-vənt\ fervent, servant • bond servant, maidservant, manservant, observant • civil servant, inobservant, public servant

ervative \ər-vət-iv\ conservative, preservative • ultraconservative

erve \ərv\ curve, MIRV, nerve, serve, swerve, verve • conserve, deserve, hors d'oeuvre, observe, preserve, reserve, self-serve, sine curve, unnerve • facial nerve, in reserve, learning curve, optic nerve, spinal nerve, vagus nerve • cranial nerve, sciatic nerve

erved \ərvd\ nerved • deserved, reserved • unreserved
—*also* -ed *forms of verbs listed at* ERVE

ervency \ər-vən-sē\ fervency • conservancy

ervent \ər-vənt\ see ERVANT

erver \ər-vər\ fervor, server • conserver, observer, timeserver • altar server, life preserver

ervice \ər-vəs\ nervous, service • curb service, disservice, fullservice, lip service, room service, self-service, wire service • civil service, divine service, foreign service, public service, secret service, social service

ervil \ər-vəl\ chervil, servile

ervile \ər-vəl\ see ERVIL

erving \ər-viŋ\ Erving, Irving, serving • deserving, self-serving, timeserving, unswerving
—*also* -ing *forms of verbs listed at* ERVE

ervor \ər-vər\ see ERVER

ervous \ər-vəs\ see ERVICE

ervy \ər-vē\ see URVY

erwick \er-ik\ see ERIC[1]

erwin \ər-wən\ Irwin, Sherwin

ery[1] \er-ē\ see ARY[1]

ery[2] \ir-ē\ see EARY

eryl \er-əl\ see ERIL

es[1] \ā\ see AY[1]

es[2] \ās\ see ACE[1]

es[3] \āz\ see AZE[1]

es[4] \es\ see ESS

es[5] \ēz\ see EZE

e's \ēz\ see EZE

esa \ā-sə\ mesa • Theresa

esage \es-ij\ see ESSAGE

esan[1] \āz-ᵊn\ see AZON

esan[2] \ēz-ᵊn\ see EASON

esant \ez-ᵊnt\ peasant, pheasant, pleasant, present • at present, unpleasant, omnipresent

esce \es\ see ESS

escence \es-ᵊns\ essence • excrescence, florescence, fluorescence, pubescence, quintessence, senescence • acquiescence, adolescence, convalescence, effervescence, efflorescence, evanescence, incandescence, iridescence, luminescence, obsolescence, phosphorescence
—*also* -s, -'s, *and* -s' *forms of nouns listed at* ESCENT

escent \es-ᵊnt\ crescent • depressant, fluorescent, incessant, pubescent, quiescent, senescent, suppressant • acquiescent, adolescent, convalescent, effervescent, efflorescent, evanescent, Fertile Crescent, incandescent, iridescent, luminescent, obsolescent, phosphorescent • antidepressant, preadolescent

escible \es-ə-bəl\ see ESSIBLE

escive \es-iv\ see ESSIVE

esco \es-kō\ fresco • alfresco, UNESCO • Ionesco

escue \es-kyü\ fescue, rescue

ese[1] \ēs\ see IECE

ese[2] \ēz\ see EZE

ese[3] \ā-sē\ see ACY

eseus \ē-sē-əs\ Theseus • Tiresias

esh[1] \esh\ crèche, flesh, fresh, mesh, thresh • afresh, enmesh, gooseflesh, refresh • Bangladesh, Gilgamesh, intermesh, in the flesh, Marrakech, press the flesh • Uttar Pradesh

esh[2] \āsh\ see ECHE[1]

esh[3] \ash\ see ASH[3]

eshed \esht\ fleshed, meshed
—*also* -ed *forms of verbs listed at* ESH[1]

eshen \esh-ən\ see ESSION

esher \esh-ər\ see ESSURE

eshly \esh-lē\ fleshly, freshly, specially • especially

esi[1] \ā-zē\ see AZY

esi[2] \ā-sē\ see ACY

esia[1] \ē-shə\ Letitia, Lucretia, Phoenicia

esia[2] \ē-zhə\ amnesia, Rhodesia, Silesia, Tunisia • analgesia, anesthesia, Indonesia, kinesthesia, Melanesia, Micronesia, Polynesia, synesthesia • milk of magnesia

esian[1] \ē-zhən\ lesion • adhesion, Cartesian, cohesion, Rhodesian • Indonesian, Melanesian, Micronesian, Polynesian • Peloponnesian

esian[2] \ē-shən\ see ETION[1]

esias \ē-sē-əs\ see ESEUS

esidency \ez-əd-ən-sē\ presidency, residency • vice presidency

esident \ez-əd-ənt\ president, resident • nonresident, vice president

esion \ē-zhən\ see ESIAN[1]

esis \ē-səs\ Croesus, thesis • prosthesis • Dionysus, exegesis • Peloponnesus, telekinesis • amniocentesis

esium \ē-zē-əm\ see EZIUM

esk \esk\ see ESQUE

esley \es-lē\ see ESSLY

eslie \es-lē\ see ESSLY

esne \ēn\ see INE[3]

eso \ā-sō\ peso, say-so

espite \es-pət\ see ESPOT

espot \es-pət\ despot, respite

esque \esk\ desk • burlesque, grotesque • arabesque, copydesk, gigantesque, picaresque, picturesque, statuesque

ess \es\ bless, chess, dress, ess, fess, guess, less, mess, press, s, stress, tress, yes • abscess, access, address, assess, bench-press, caress, clothespress, compress, confess, cross-dress, depress, destress, digress, distress, drill press, duress, excess, express, finesse, full-dress, headdress, housedress, impress, largess, Loch Ness, much less, nightdress, no less, obsess, oppress, outguess, possess, princess, process, profess, progress, recess, regress, repress, shirtdress, SS, success, sundress, suppress, transgress, undress, unless, winepress • ABS, acquiesce, baroness, bitter cress, coa-

lesce, convalesce, crown princess, decompress, deliquesce, dispossess, effervesce, evanesce, full-court press, granny dress, in-process, less and less, letterpress, minidress, more or less, nonetheless, overdress, politesse, repossess, reprocess, retrogress, second-guess, SOS, underdress, watercress, word process • keynote address, nevertheless, random-access • limited-access

essa \es-ə\ see ESSE[3]

essable \es-ə-bəl\ see ESSIBLE

essage \es-ij\ message, presage

essamine \es-mən\ see ESSMAN

essan \es-ᵊn\ see ESSEN

essant \es-ᵊnt\ see ESCENT

esse[1] \es\ see ESS

esse[2] \es-ē\ see ESSY

esse[3] \es-ə\ Hesse • Odessa, Vanessa

essed \est\ see EST

essedly \es-əd-lē\ blessedly • confessedly, professedly

essel \es-əl\ see ESTLE[1]

essen \es-ᵊn\ Essen, lessen, lesson • object lesson • delicatessen

essence \es-ᵊns\ see ESCENCE

esser \es-ər\ see ESSOR

essex \es-iks\ Essex, Wessex

essful \es-fəl\ stressful • distressful, successful • unsuccessful

essian \esh-ən\ see ESSION

essible \es-ə-bəl\ decibel, guessable • accessible, assessable, compressible, expressible • inaccessible, inexpressible, irrepressible

essie \es-ē\ see ESSY

essile \es-əl\ see ESTLE[1]

ession \esh-ən\ freshen, session • accession, aggression, bull session, compression, concession, confession, depression, digression, discretion, expression, impression, jam session, obsession, oppression, possession, procession, profession, progression, recession, regression, repression, secession, skull session, succession, suppression, transgression • decompression, indiscretion, intercession, misimpression, nonaggression, repossession, self-confession, self-expression

essional \esh-nəl\ congressional, obsessional, processional, professional, recessional • unprofessional

essionist \esh-nəst\ expressionist, impressionist, secessionist

essity \es-tē\ see ESTY

essive \es-iv\ aggressive, depressive, digressive, excessive, expressive, impressive, obsessive, oppressive, possessive, progressive, successive, transgressive • inexpressive, unexpressive • manic-depressive, passive-aggressive

essly \es-lē\ Leslie, Wesley • expressly

essman \es-mən\ chessman, pressman • specimen

essment \es-mənt\ see ESTMENT

esson \es-ᵊn\ see ESSEN

essor \es-ər\ dresser, lesser, stressor • addresser, aggressor, assessor, compressor, confessor, cross-dresser, hairdresser, oppressor, processor, professor, successor, transgressor • food processor, predecessor, word processor

essure \esh-ər\ fresher, pressure • blood pressure, high-pressure, low-pressure, refresher • acupressure

essy \es-ē\ Bessie, dressy, Jesse, Jessie, messy

est \est\ best, breast, Brest, chest, crest, guest, jest, lest, nest, pest, quest, rest, test, vest, west, West, wrest, zest • abreast, abscessed, armrest, arrest, at best, at rest, attest, backrest, bed rest, behest, bequest, blood test, Celeste, compressed, conquest, contest, crow's nest, depressed, detest, digest, distressed, divest, field-test, flight-test, footrest, gabfest, hard-pressed, headrest, high-test, hope chest, houseguest, incest, infest, ingest, inquest, interest, invest, Key West, lovefest, love nest, low-test, Midwest, molest, northwest, pretest, professed, protest, repressed, request, road test, scratch test, screen test, sea chest, skin test, slugfest, southwest, stress test, suggest, unblessed, undressed, unrest, unstressed, war chest, Wild West • acid test, anapest, Bucharest, Budapest, decongest, disinvest, empty-nest, false arrest, hornet's nest, house arrest, manifest, north-northwest, placement test, predigest, reinvest, second-best, self-addressed, self-confessed, self-interest, self-possessed, sweatervest, true-false test, vision quest • aptitude test, beauty contest, compound interest, feather one's nest, robin redbreast, simple interest, under arrest, vested interest • citizen's arrest

—*also* -ed *forms of verbs listed at* ESS

esta \es-tə\ Vesta • celesta, fiesta, siesta

estable \es-tə-bəl\ see ESTIBLE

estae \es-tē\ see ESTY

estan \es-tən\ see ESTINE

estant \es-tənt\ contestant, protestant • decongestant

este \est\ see EST

ested \es-təd\ crested, tested, vested • time-tested • barrel-chested, double-breasted, hairy-chested, single-breasted

—also -ed *forms of verbs listed at* EST

ester \es-tər\ Chester, Esther, fester, Hester, jester, Leicester, Lester, nester, pester, quester, tester • ancestor, arrester, investor, Manchester, molester, northwester, Rochester, semester, sequester, southwester, sou'wester, Sylvester, trimester, Winchester • empty nester, polyester

esti \es-tē\ see ESTY

estible \es-tə-bəl\ testable • comestible, detestable, digestible, suggestible • incontestable, indigestible

estic \es-tik\ domestic, majestic • anapestic

estimate \es-tə-mət\ estimate, guesstimate • underestimate

estine \es-tən\ destine • clandestine, intestine, predestine • large intestine, small intestine

esting \es-tiŋ\ resting • arresting • interesting
—also -ing *forms of verbs listed at* EST

estion \es-chən\ question • congestion, cross-question, digestion, ingestion, self-question, suggestion • call in question, decongestion, essay question, indigestion, pop the question • autosuggestion

estive \es-tiv\ festive, restive • congestive, digestive, suggestive • decongestive

estle¹ \es-əl\ Cecil, nestle, pestle, trestle, vessel, wrestle • blood vessel • Indian-wrestle

estle² \as-əl\ see ASSEL²

estle³ \əs-əl\ see USTLE

estment \es-mənt\ vestment • assessment, divestment, investment • reinvestment

esto \es-tō\ pesto, presto • Modesto • manifesto

eston \es-tən\ see ESTINE

estor \es-tər\ see ESTER

estra \es-trə\ orchestra • Clytemnestra

estral \es-trəl\ kestrel • ancestral, orchestral

estrel \es-trəl\ see ESTRAL

estrian \es-trē-ən\ equestrian, pedestrian

estry \es-trē\ vestry • ancestry

esty \es-tē\ chesty, pesty, testy, zesty • necessity

esus \ē-səs\ see ESIS

et¹ \et\ bet, Bret, Chet, debt, fête, fret, get, jet, let, Lett, met, net, pet, set, sweat, Tet, threat, vet, wet, whet, yet • abet, all wet, Annette, asset, Babette, baguette, banquette, barrette, beget, beset, briquette, brochette, brunet, cadet, cassette, Claudette, Colette, coquette, cornet, corvette, croquette, dinette, dip net, diskette, dragnet, duet, egret, fan-jet, fishnet, forget, gazette, Georgette, Gillette, gillnet, gill net, handset, headset, ink-jet, inlet, inset, Jeanette, jet set, Juliet, kismet, layette, life net, Lynette, Marquette, mind-set, moonset, motet, Nanette, nerve net, nonet, octet, offset, onset, outlet, outset, pipette, preset, quartet, quintet, ramjet, regret, reset, rocket, rosette, roulette, septet, sestet, sextet, soubrette, spinet, sublet, subset, sunset, tea set, thickset, Tibet, toilette, typeset, upset, vignette, well-set, Yvette • alphabet, Antoinette, avocet, bassinet, bayonet, Bernadette, calumet, castanet, cigarette, clarinet, coronet, crepe suzette, epaulet, epithet, Ethernet, etiquette, featurette, flannelette, heavyset, Joliet, Juliet, kitchenette, Lafayette, launderette,

leatherette, luncheonette, majorette, marmoset, martinet,
minaret, minuet, netiquette, nov-
elette, Olivet, parapet, pirouette,
safety net, silhouette, sobriquet,
soviet, space cadet, statuette,
suffragette, superjet, teacher's
pet, towelette, triple threat, ush-
erette, vinaigrette • bachelorette,
drum majorette, marionette,
microcassette, mosquito net,
Russian roulette, snowy egret
• audiocassette, Marie Antoinette,
videocassette

et² \ā\ see AY¹

et³ \āt\ see ATE¹

et⁴ \es\ see ESS

eta¹ \āt-ə\ see ATA²

eta² \et-ə\ see ETTA

eta³ \ēt-ə\ see ITA

etable¹ \et-ə-bəl\ see ETTABLE

etable² \ēt-ə-bəl\ see EATABLE

etal¹ \ēt-ᵊl\ beetle, fetal

etal² \et-ᵊl\ see ETTLE

etan¹ \et-ᵊn\ Breton, threaten
• Cape Breton, Tibetan

etan² \ēt-ᵊn\ see EATEN¹

etch \ech\ catch, etch, fetch, ketch,
kvetch, retch, sketch, stretch,
vetch, wretch • backstretch,
homestretch, outstretch

etched \echt\ teched • far-fetched
—also -ed forms of verbs listed at
ETCH

etcher \ech-ər\ etcher, catcher,
fetcher, Fletcher, lecher,
sketcher, stretcher • cowcatcher,
dogcatcher, dream catcher, eye-
catcher, flycatcher

etching \ech-iŋ\ etching, fetching
—also -ing forms of verbs listed at
ETCH

etchy \ech-ē\ sketchy, stretchy,
tetchy

ete¹ \āt\ see ATE¹

ete² \et\ see ET¹

ete³ \ēt\ see EAT¹

ete⁴ \āt-ē\ see ATY

ête \āt\ see ATE¹

eted \ād\ see ADE¹

etel \ēt-ᵊl\ see ETAL¹

etely \ēt-lē\ see EETLY

eteor \ēt-ē-ər\ meteor
—also -er forms of adjectives listed
at EATY

eter \ēt-ər\ see EATER¹

etera \e-trə\ see ETRA

etes \ēt-əs\ see ETUS

eth¹ \eth\ Beth, breath, breadth,
death, saith, Seth • black death,
brain death, crib death, hand-
breadth, hairbreadth, Macbeth
• baby's breath, hold one's breath,
in one breath, kiss of death, life-
and-death, living death, morning
breath, out of breath, shibboleth,
sudden death, waste one's breath
• Elizabeth, under one's breath

eth² \ās\ see ACE¹

eth³ \āt\ see ATE¹

eth⁴ \et\ see ET¹

etha \ē-thə\ Aretha, Ibiza

ethane \e-thān\ ethane, methane

ether¹ \eth-ər\ feather, heather,
Heather, leather, nether, tether,
weather, whether • bellwether,
buff leather, fair-weather, glove
leather, kid leather, pinfeather,
shoe-leather, together, untether
• altogether, get-together, hang
together, hell-for-leather, knock
together, patent leather, pull
together, put together, saddle
leather, tar and feather, throw
together • under the weather

ether² \əth-ər\ see OTHER¹

ethyl \eth-əl\ Bethel, Ethel, ethyl,
methyl

eti¹ \ēt-ē\ see EATY

eti² \āt-ē\ see ATY

etia \ē-shə\ see ESIA¹

etian \ē-shən\ see ETION¹

etic \et-ik\ aesthetic, ascetic, athletic, balletic, bathetic, cosmetic,

eidetic, frenetic, gametic, genetic,
hermetic, kinetic, magnetic,
pathetic, phonetic, poetic,
prophetic, prosthetic, synthetic
• alphabetic, anesthetic, apathetic,
arithmetic, copacetic, cybernetic,
diabetic, dietetic, diuretic, empa-
thetic, energetic, sympathetic,
synesthetic • apologetic, geomag-
netic, hyperkinetic, peripatetic,
telekinetic, unsympathetic • elec-
tromagnetic, general anesthetic,
unapologetic • onomatopoetic

etical \et-i-kəl\ heretical, poeti-
cal • antithetical, arithmetical,
hypothetical, parenthetical, theo-
retical

etics \et-iks\ aesthetics, athletics,
genetics, kinetics, phonetics,
poetics, prosthetics • cybernetics,
dietetics
—*also* -s, -'s, *and* -s' *forms of
nouns listed at* ETIC

etid \et-əd\ fetid, fretted, sweated
• indebted
—*also* -ed *forms of verbs listed at*
ET[1]

etin \ēt-ᵊn\ *see* EATEN[1]

etion[1] \ē-shən\ Grecian • accretion,
completion, deletion, depletion,
excretion, Helvetian, Phoenician,
secretion, Tahitian, Venetian
• Diocletian, Melanesian, Polynesian

etion[2] \esh-ən\ *see* ESSION

etious \ē-shəs\ *see* ECIOUS

etis \ēt-əs\ *see* ETUS

etist \et-əst\ cornetist, librettist
• clarinetist

etius \ē-shəs\ *see* ECIOUS

etl[1] \āt-ᵊl\ *see* ATAL

etl[2] \et-ᵊl\ *see* ETTLE

etland \et-lənd\ Shetland, wetland

eto[1] \āt-ō\ *see* ATO[2]

eto[2] \ēt-ō\ *see* ITO[1]

eton \ēt-ᵊn\ *see* EATEN[1]

etor[1] \et-ər\ *see* ETTER

etor[2] \ēt-ər\ *see* EATER[1]

etous \ēt-əs\ *see* ETUS

etra \e-trə\ Petra, tetra • etcetera

etric \e-trik\ metric • obstetric,
symmetric • asymmetric, baro-
metric, diametric, geometric,
isometric

etrical \e-tri-kəl\ metrical • obstet-
rical, symmetrical • asymmetrical,
diametrical, geometrical, unsym-
metrical

etrics \e-triks\ metrics, obstetrics
• isometrics

ets \ets\ let's
—*also* -s, -'s, *and* -s' *forms of nouns
and* -s *forms of verbs listed at* ET[1]

ett \et\ *see* ET[1]

etta \et-ə\ Etta, feta, Greta
• biretta, bruschetta, Loretta,
poinsettia, Rosetta, vendetta
• Henrietta, Marietta, operetta

ettable \et-ə-bəl\ forgettable, re-
grettable • unforgettable

ette \et\ *see* ET[1]

etter \et-ər\ better, bettor, debtor,
fetter, letter, setter, sweater
• abettor, air letter, bed wetter,
begetter, block letter, bonesetter,
chain letter, dead letter, fan letter, four-letter, go-getter, jet-
setter, Ledbetter, newsletter,
pacesetter, pinsetter, red-letter,
trendsetter, typesetter, unfetter
• English setter, go one better,
Irish setter, open letter, scarlet
letter

ettered \et-ərd\ lettered • unfet-
tered, unlettered

ettes \ets\ *see* ETS

ettia \et-ə\ *see* ETTA

ettie \et-ē\ *see* ETTY[1]

ettier \it-ē-ər\ *see* ITTIER

ettiness \it-ē-nəs\ *see* ITTINESS

etting \et-iŋ\ netting, setting • bed-
wetting, bloodletting, jet-setting,
pacesetting, place setting, trend-
setting, typesetting

—*also* -ing *forms of verbs listed at*
ET[1]

ettish \et-ish\ fetish, Lettish, pet-
tish, wettish • coquettish

ettle \et-°l\ fettle, kettle, metal,
mettle, nettle, petal, settle, shtetl
• bimetal, nonmetal, teakettle,
unsettle • Popocatépetl

etto \et-ō\ ghetto • falsetto, palmetto, stiletto • saw palmetto,
Tintoretto

etty[1] \et-ē\ Betty, Getty, jetty,
Nettie, netty, petty, sweaty, yeti
• brown Betty, confetti, machete,
Rossetti, spaghetti • Donizetti,
Serengeti, spermaceti

etty[2] \it-ē\ see ITTY

etus \ēt-əs\ fetus, Thetis, treatise
• diabetes

etzsche \ē-chē\ see EACHY

euben \ü-bən\ Cuban, Reuben,
Steuben

euce \üs\ see USE[1]

eucey \ü-sē\ see UICY

euch \ük\ see UKE

eud[1] \üd\ see UDE[1]

eud[2] \oid\ see OID[1]

eudal \üd-°l\ see OODLE

eudist \üd-əst\ see UDIST[1]

eudo \üd-ō\ see UDO

eue \ü\ see EW[1]

euer \ü-ər\ see EWER[1]

euil \āl\ see AIL

euille \ē\ see EE[1]

euk \ük\ see UKE

eul[1] \əl\ see ULL[1]

eul[2] \ərl\ see IRL

eulah \ü-lə\ see ULA

eulean \ü-lē-ən\ see ULEAN

eum[1] \ē-əm\ lyceum, museum, no-
see-um, per diem • coliseum,
colosseum, mausoleum, wax
museum

eum[2] \ā-əm\ see AHUM

eum[3] \üm\ see OOM[1]

euma \ü-mə\ see UMA

eume \üm\ see OOM[1]

eumon \ü-mən\ see UMAN

eumy \ü-mē\ see OOMY

eunice \ü-nəs\ see EWNESS

eunuch \ü-nik\ see UNIC

eur[1] \ər\ blur, burr, Burr, cur, err,
fir, for, fur, her, myrrh, per, purr,
sir, slur, spur, stir, 'twere, were,
whir, your, you're • as per, astir,
aver, bestir, Big Sur, chauffeur,
coiffeur, concur, confer, danseur,
defer, demur, deter, hauteur,
him/her, his/her, incur, infer,
inter, jongleur, larkspur, liqueur,
masseur, occur, Pasteur, poseur,
prefer, recur, refer, sandbur,
sandspur, transfer, voyeur, white
fir • amateur, balsam fir, cockle-
bur, connoisseur, curvature, de
rigueur, disinter, Douglas fir,
Fraser fir, monseigneur, ra-
conteur, saboteur, underfur,
voyageur • carillonneur, entrepreneur, provocateur, restaurateur

eur[2] \ur\ see URE[1]

eure \ər\ see EUR[1]

eurish \ər-ish\ see OURISH

eurs \ərz\ see ERS[1]

eury \ur-ē\ see URY[1]

eus[1] \ē-əs\ Aeneas, Linnaeus • Judas Maccabaeus

eus[2] \üs\ see USE[1]

euse[1] \əz\ buzz, 'cause, does, fuzz,
'twas, was • abuzz, because, out-
does, undoes

euse[2] \üs\ see USE[1]

euse[3] \üz\ see USE[2]

eut \üt\ see UTE

euter \üt-ər\ see UTER

euth \üth\ see OOTH[2]

eutian \ü-shən\ see UTION

eutical \üt-i-kəl\ see UTICAL

eutist \üt-əst\ see UTIST

euton \üt-°n\ see UTAN

euve \əv\ see OVE[1]

euver \ü-vər\ see OVER[3]

eux \ü\ see EW[1]

ev[1] \ef\ see EF[1]

ev² \òf\ see OFF²

eva \ē-və\ see IVA²

eval \ē-vəl\ see IEVAL

evalent \ev-ə-lənt\ see EVOLENT

evan¹ \ē-vən\ see EVEN

evan² \ev-ən\ see EAVEN

eve¹ \ev\ rev • Kiev, Negev

eve² \ēv\ see EAVE¹

evel \ev-əl\ bevel, devil, level, Neville, revel • bedevil, daredevil, dishevel, dust devil, high-level, low-level, sea level, split-level • entry-level, on the level, water level

eveler \ev-lər\ leveler, reveler

evelly \ev-ə-lē\ heavily, reveille

evement \ēv-mənt\ achievement, bereavement • underachievement

even \ē-vən\ even, Stephen • break even, Genevan, get even, uneven

eventh \ev-ənth\ seventh • eleventh

ever¹ \ev-ər\ clever, ever, lever, never, sever, Trevor • endeavor, forever, however, whatever, whenever, wherever, whichever, whoever, whomever • whatsoever, whomsoever, whosoever

ever² \ē-vər\ see IEVER

everage \ev-rij\ beverage, leverage

everence \ev-rəns\ reverence, severance • irreverence

every \ev-rē\ every, reverie

evice \ev-əs\ crevice • Ben Nevis

evil \ē-vəl\ see IEVAL

eville \ev-əl\ see EVEL

evilry \ev-əl-rē\ devilry, revelry • daredevilry

evin \ev-ən\ see EAVEN

evious \ē-vē-əs\ devious, previous

evis¹ \ev-əs\ see EVICE

evis² \ē-vəs\ see EVUS

evity \ev-ət-ē\ brevity, levity • longevity

evocable \ev-ə-kə-bəl\ evocable, revocable • irrevocable

evolence \ev-ə-ləns\ prevalence • benevolence, malevolence

evolent \ev-ə-lənt\ prevalent • benevolent, malevolent

evor \ev-ər\ see EVER¹

evous \ē-vəs\ grievous • Saint Kitts-Nevis

evus \ē-vəs\ see EVOUS

evy \ev-ē\ bevy, heavy, levee, levy • top-heavy

ew¹ \ü\ blue, boo, brew, chew, clue, coo, coup, crew, cue, dew, do, Drew, due, ewe, few, flew, flu, flue, glue, gnu, goo, hew, hue, Hugh, Jew, knew, lieu, loo, Lou, mew, moo, new, ooh, pew, phew, pooh, q, queue, rue, screw, shoe, shoo, shrew, Sioux, skew, slew, slough, slue, spew, stew, strew, sue, Sue, threw, through, to, too, true, two, u, view, whew, who, woo, Wu, yew, you, zoo • accrue, achoo, adieu, ado, aircrew, anew, Anjou, askew, au jus, Baku, bamboo, bayou, bijou, boo-boo, brand-new, breakthrough, can-do, canoe, Cebu, construe, Corfu, corkscrew, coypu, cuckoo, curfew, debut, doo-doo, ensue, eschew, fondue, ground crew, gumshoe, guru, hairdo, hereto, Hindu, home brew, Honshu, horseshoe, how-to, HQ, Hutu, igloo, IQ, K2, kazoo, Khufu, kung fu, lean-to, long view, make-do, Matthew, me-too, mildew, milieu, miscue, muumuu, Nehru, one-two, on view, outdo, outgrew, Peru, preview, pursue, purview, ragout, redo, renew, review, revue, run-through, see-through, set-to, shampoo, sinew, skiddoo, snafu, snowshoe, subdue, taboo, tattoo, thank-you, thereto, thumbscrew, to-do, tree shrew, undo, undue, unglue, unscrew, untrue, venue, voodoo, wahoo, walk-through, whereto, who's who, withdrew, worldview, yahoo, yoo-hoo • avenue, baby blue, ballyhoo, barbecue, bird's-eye view, black-and-blue, Brunswick stew, buckaroo, bugaboo, caribou, cobalt blue, cockatoo, counterview, curlicue, derring-do, follow-through, hitherto, honeydew, Iguaçu, ingenue, interview, IOU, Irish stew, Jiangsu, kangaroo, Kathmandu, kinkajou, manitou, marabou, microbrew, midnight blue, Montague, Montesquieu, Mountain View, ormolu, overdo, overdue, overflew, overgrew, overshoe, overthrew, overview, parvenu, pay-per-view, PDQ, peacock blue, peekaboo, petting zoo, point of view, rendezvous, residue, retinue, revenue, Richelieu, Ryukyu, seppuku, sneak preview, switcheroo, talking-to, teleview, thitherto, Timbuktu, w, waterloo, well-to-do, what have you, whoop-de-do, Xanadu • bolt from the blue, Brian Boru, cardinal virtue, cornflower blue, didgeridoo, downy mildew, hullabaloo, in deep doo-doo, Kalamazoo, mulligan stew, Ouagadougou, out of the blue, Seattle Slew, Vanuatu, Wandering Jew

ew² \ō\ see OW[1]

ewable¹ \ō-ə-bəl\ see OWABLE[1]

ewable² \ü-ə-bəl\ see UABLE

ewal \ü-əl\ see UEL[1]

ewar \ü-ər\ see EWER[1]

eward¹ \ürd\ see URED[1]

eward² \ü-ərd\ Seward, steward • shop steward

ewd \üd\ see UDE[1]

ewdness \üd-nəs\ see UDINOUS

ewe¹ \ō\ see OW[1]

ewe² \ü\ see EW[1]

ewed \üd\ see UDE[1]

ewee \ē-wē\ see EEWEE

ewel \ü-əl\ see UEL[1]

eweled \üld\ see OOLED

ewell \ü-əl\ see UEL[1]

ewer¹ \ü-ər\ brewer, chewer, doer, ewer, fewer, sewer, skewer, viewer, you're • me-tooer, misdoer, reviewer, snowshoer, wrongdoer • barbecuer, evildoer, interviewer, microbrewer
—*also* -er *forms of adjectives listed at* EW[1]

ewer² \ür\ see URE[1]

ewer³ \ō-ər\ see OER[4]

ewerage \ür-ij\ see OORAGE[1]

ewery \ür-ē\ see URY[1]

ewey \ü-ē\ see EWY

ewie \ü-ē\ see EWY

ewing¹ \ō-iŋ\ see OING[1]

ewing² \ü-iŋ\ see OING[2]

ewish \ü-ish\ bluish, Jewish, newish, shrewish

ewl \ül\ see OOL[1]

ewless \ü-ləs\ clueless, crewless, dewless, shoeless, viewless

ewly \ü-lē\ see ULY

ewman \ü-mən\ see UMAN

ewn \ün\ see OON[1]

ewness \ü-nəs\ blueness, Eunice, newness, Tunis

ewpie \ü-pē\ see OOPY

ews \üz\ see USE[2]

ewsman \üz-mən\ bluesman, newsman

ewsy \ü-zē\ see OOZY

ewt \üt\ see UTE

ewter \üt-ər\ see UTER

ewton \üt-ᵊn\ see UTAN

ewy \ü-ē\ bluey, buoy, chewy, Dewey, dewy, gluey, gooey, hooey, Louie, Louis, newie, phooey, screwy • bell buoy, chop suey, life buoy, mildewy • ratatouille

ex \eks\ ex, flex, hex, sex, specs, vex, x • annex, apex, codex, complex, convex, cortex, duplex, funplex, ibex, index, Kleenex, latex, narthex, perplex, Pyrex,

reflex, Rx, spandex, telex, Tex-
Mex, triplex, unsex, vertex, vor-
tex • belowdecks, circumflex,
cross-index, gentle sex, haruspex,
intersex, Malcolm X, megaplex,
Middlesex, multiplex, Rolodex,
thumb index, unisex • cerebral
cortex, Oedipus complex
—*also* -s, -'s, *and* -s' *forms of
nouns and* -s *forms of verbs listed
at* ECK
exas \ek-səs\ see EXUS
exed \ekst\ see EXT
exia \ek-sē-ə\ dyslexia • anorexia
exion \ek-shən\ see ECTION
exis \ek-səs\ see EXUS
exity \ek-sət-ē\ complexity, con-
vexity, perplexity
ext \ekst\ next, sexed, text, vexed
• context, perplexed, pretext
• hypertext
—*also* -ed *forms of verbs listed at*
EX
extant \ek-stənt\ extant, sextant
exural \ek-shrəl\ see ECTURAL[2]
exus \ek-səs\ nexus, Texas • Alexis
• solar plexus
exy \ek-sē\ sexy • apoplexy
ey[1] \ā\ see AY[1]
ey[2] \ē\ see EE[1]
ey[3] \ī\ see Y[1]
eya[1] \ā-ə\ see AIA[1]
eya[2] \ē-ə\ see IA[1]
eyance \ā-əns\ abeyance, con-
veyance, surveillance
ey'd \ād\ see ADE[1]
eye \ī\ see Y[1]
eyed[1] \ēd\ see EED
eyed[2] \īd\ see IDE[1]
eyeless \ī-ləs\ see ILUS
eyelet \ī-lət\ see ILOT
eyen \īn\ see INE[1]
eyer \īr\ see IRE[1]
eyes \īz\ see IZE[1]
eying \ā-iŋ\ see AYING
ey'll[1] \āl\ see AIL
ey'll[2] \el\ see EL[1]

eyn \in\ see IN[1]
eynes \ānz\ see AINS
eyness \ā-nəs\ see AYNESS
eyor \ā-ər\ see AYER
eyre \er\ see ARE[4]
ey're \er\ see ARE[4]
eyrie \īr-ē\ see IRY
eys \ēz\ see EZE
eyser \ī-zər\ see IZER
eyte \ā-tē\ see ATY
ey've \āv\ see AVE[2]
ez[1] \ez\ see AYS[1]
ez[2] \ā\ see AY[1]
ez[3] \ās\ see ACE[1]
eza \ē-zə\ Giza, Lisa, Pisa, visa, Visa
eze \ēz\ breeze, cheese, ease,
freeze, frieze, he's, jeez, please,
seize, she's, sleaze, sneeze,
squeeze, tease, tweeze, wheeze
• Andes, appease, Aries, at ease,
Belize, big cheese, blue cheese,
Burmese, chemise, Chinese, deep-
freeze, Denise, disease, displease,
d.t.'s, Elise, Ganges, Hermes, jack
cheese, Kirghiz, Louise, Maltese,
marquise, Pisces, quick-freeze,
Ramses, reprise, sea breeze,
striptease, strong breeze, Swiss
cheese, Tabriz, trapeze, unease,
unfreeze, Xerxes • antifreeze,
Balinese, Bengalese, Bhutanese,
Brooklynese, Cantonese, Cervantes, Ceylonese, cheddar
cheese, Congolese, cottage cheese,
Damocles, diocese, Eloise, expertise, Hebrides, Heracles, Hercules,
ill at ease, Japanese, Javanese,
journalese, Lake Louise, legalese,
overseas, Pekingese, Pericles,
Pyrenees, shoot the breeze,
Siamese, Socrates, Sophocles, to
one's knees • antipodes, archdiocese, bona fides, computerese,
Diogenes, Dodecanese, Dutch elm
disease, eminence grise, Euripi-
des, Florida Keys, Great Pyrenees, Hippocrates, Indo-Chinese,

mad cow disease, Thucydides, Vietnamese • Aristophanes, foot-and-mouth disease, Legionnaires' disease, Lou Gehrig's disease, Mephistopheles, Parkinson's disease, sword of Damocles • Pillars of Hercules

—*also* -s, -'s, *and* -s' *forms of nouns and* -s *forms of verbs listed at* EE[1]

ezel \ē-zəl\ see EASEL

ezi \ē-zē\ see EASY[1]

ezium \ē-zē-əm\ cesium • magnesium, trapezium

I

i[1] \ē\ see EE[1]

i[2] \ī\ see Y[1]

i[3] \ā\ see AY[1]

ia[1] \ē-ə\ Gaea, Leah, Mia, rhea, Rhea, via • Crimea, idea, Judaea, Korea, mantilla, Maria, Medea, Nicaea, rupiah, sangria, Sophia, tortilla • bougainvillea, diarrhea, Eritrea, fantasia, Galatea, gonorrhea, Hialeah, Kampuchea, Nicosia, panacea, pizzeria, pyorrhea, Santeria, Tanzania • Andalusia, Ave Maria, Cassiopeia, Sacagawea • onomatopoeia

ia[2] \ī-ə\ see IAH[1]

ia[3] \ä\ see A[1]

iable[1] \ī-ə-bəl\ dryable, dyeable, flyable, friable, liable, pliable, viable • deniable, reliable • certifiable, classifiable, falsifiable, justifiable, quantifiable, undeniable, verifiable • identifiable

iable[2] \ē-ə-bəl\ see EEABLE

iacal \ī-ə-kəl\ maniacal, zodiacal • egomaniacal

iad \ī-əd\ see YAD

iah[1] \ī-ə\ Maya, via • Mariah, messiah, papaya, pariah, Thalia • Hezekiah, jambalaya, Jeremiah, Nehemiah, Obadiah, Zechariah, Zephaniah • Iphigenia

iah[2] \ē-ə\ see IA[1]

ial \īl\ see ILE[1]

ialer \ī-lər\ see ILAR

ially \ē-ə-lē\ see EALLY[1]

iam \ī-əm\ Priam • per diem • carpe diem

ian[1] \ē-ən\ see EAN[1]

ian[2] \ī-ən\ see ION[1]

iance \ī-əns\ science • alliance, appliance, compliance, defiance, nonscience, reliance • misalliance, noncompliance, self-reliance —*also* -s, -'s, *and* -s' *forms of nouns listed at* IANT

iant \ī-ənt\ Bryant, client, giant, pliant • compliant, defiant, reliant • self-reliant, sleeping giant, supergiant

iao \aü\ see OW[2]

iaour \aür\ see OWER[2]

iaper \ī-pər\ see IPER

iar \īr\ see IRE[1]

iary[1] \ī-ə-rē\ diary, fiery, friary, priory

iary[2] \īr-ē\ see IRY

ias[1] \ī-əs\ bias, dais, pious, Pius • Elias, Tobias

ias[2] \ē-əs\ see EUS[1]

ias[3] \äsh\ see ASH[1]

iasis \ī-ə-səs\ diocese • archdiocese, psoriasis • elephantiasis, schistosomiasis

iat[1] \ē-ət\ see EIT[1]

iat² \ī-ət\ see IET

iate \ī-ət\ see IET

iath¹ \ī-əth\ Wyeth • Goliath

iath² \ē-ə\ see IA¹

iatry \ī-ə-trē\ podiatry, psychiatry

iaus \aús\ see OUSE²

ib¹ \ib\ bib, crib, fib, glib, jib, nib, rib, sib, squib • ad-lib, corncrib, false rib, sahib • floating rib

ib² \ēb\ see EBE²

ib³ \ēv\ see EAVE¹

iba \ē-bə\ see EBA

ibable \ī-bə-bəl\ bribable • indescribable

ibal \ī-bəl\ bible, Bible, libel, scribal, tribal • family Bible

ibb \ib\ see IB¹

ibband \ib-ən\ see IBBON

ibbed \ibd\ rock-ribbed —also -ed forms of verbs listed at IB¹

ibber \ib-ər\ cribber, fibber, gibber, ribber

ibbet \ib-ət\ exhibit, inhibit, prohibit • flibbertigibbet

ibble \ib-əl\ dribble, kibble, nibble, quibble, scribble, sibyl, Sibyl • double dribble

ibbler \ib-lər\ dribbler, nibbler, quibbler, scribbler

ibbon \ib-ən\ gibbon, ribbon • blue ribbon

ibby \ib-ē\ Libby, ribby

ibe¹ \īb\ bribe, jibe, scribe, tribe, vibe • ascribe, describe, imbibe, inscribe, prescribe, proscribe, subscribe, transcribe • circumscribe, diatribe • oversubscribe

ibe² \ē-bē\ see EBE¹

ibel \ī-bəl\ see IBAL

iber \ī-bər\ briber, fiber, Khyber, Tiber • subscriber

ibi \ē-bē\ see EBE¹

ibia \i-bē-ə\ Libya, tibia • Namibia

ibin \ib-ən\ see IBBON

ibit \ib-ət\ see IBBET

ibitor \ib-ət-ər\ exhibitor, inhibitor

ible \ī-bəl\ see IBAL

iblet \ib-lət\ driblet, giblet

ibo \ē-bō\ gazebo, placebo

ibs \ibz\ dibs • short ribs, spareribs —also -s, -'s, and -s' forms of nouns and -s forms of verbs listed at IB¹

ibute¹ \ib-yət\ tribute • attribute, contribute, distribute • redistribute

ibute² \ib-ət\ see IBBET

ibutive \ib-yət-iv\ attributive, contributive, distributive

ibutor \ib-ət-ər\ see IBITOR

ibyl \ib-əl\ see IBBLE

ic¹ \ik\ see ICK

ic² \ēk\ see EAK¹

ica¹ \ī-kə\ mica, Micah, pica • Formica • balalaika

ica² \ē-kə\ see IKA¹

icable \ik-ə-bəl\ despicable, explicable, extricable • inexplicable, inextricable

icah \ī-kə\ see ICA¹

ical \ik-əl\ see ICKLE

ican \ē-kən\ see EACON

icar \ik-ər\ see ICKER¹

icative \ik-ət-iv\ applicative, indicative

iccative \ik-ət-iv\ see ICATIVE

ice¹ \īs\ Bryce, dice, ice, lice, mice, nice, price, rice, slice, spice, thrice, twice, vice, vise • advice, allspice, black ice, brown rice, concise, deice, device, dry ice, entice, excise, fried rice, list price, make nice, no dice, on ice, pack ice, precise, shelf ice, suffice, white rice, wild rice • asking price, break the ice, comma splice, imprecise, merchandise, on thin ice, overprice, paradise, roll the dice, sacrifice, Spanish rice, sticker price • basmati rice, self-sacrifice

ice² \ē-chä\ see ICHE¹

ice³ \ēs\ see IECE

ice⁴ \ī-sē\ see ICY

ice⁵ \īz\ see IZE¹
iceless \ī-sləs\ iceless, priceless, spiceless
icely \īs-lē\ see ISTLY
iceous \ish-əs\ see ICIOUS¹
icey \ī-sē\ see ICY
ich¹ \ich\ see ITCH
ich² \ik\ see ICK
ichael \ī-kəl\ see YCLE¹
iche¹ \ēsh\ leash, niche, quiche, sheesh • pastiche, unleash • nouveau riche
iche² \ish\ see ISH¹
iche³ \ich\ see ITCH
iche⁴ \ē-chē\ see EACHY
icher \ich-ər\ see ITCHER
iches \ich-əz\ see ITCHES
ichi¹ \ē-chē\ see EACHY
ichi² \ē-shē\ see ISHI
ichment \ich-mənt\ see ITCHMENT
ichore \ik-rē\ see ICKERY
ichu \ish-ü\ see ISSUE¹
icia¹ \ish-ə\ see ITIA¹
icia² \ēsh-ə\ see ESIA¹
icial \ish-əl\ initial, judicial, official • artificial, beneficial, prejudicial, sacrificial, superficial, unofficial
ician \ē-shən\ see ETION¹
icient \ish-ənt\ deficient, efficient, omniscient, proficient, sufficient • coefficient, cost-efficient, inefficient, insufficient, self-sufficient
icing¹ \ī-siŋ\ icing • gene-splicing • self-sacrificing
—*also* -ing *forms of verbs listed at* ICE¹
icing² \ī-ziŋ\ see IZING
icious¹ \ish-əs\ vicious • ambitious, auspicious, capricious, delicious, fictitious, judicious, malicious, Mauritius, nutritious, officious, pernicious, propitious, seditious, suspicious • avaricious, expeditious, inauspicious, injudicious, meretricious, Red Delicious, repetitious, superstitious, surreptitious
icious² \ē-shəs\ see ECIOUS

icipal \is-ə-bəl\ see ISSIBLE
icit \is-ət\ complicit, elicit, explicit, illicit, implicit, solicit
icitor \is-tər\ see ISTER
icitous \is-ət-əs\ duplicitous, felicitous, solicitous • infelicitous
icity¹ \is-ət-ē\ centricity, complicity, duplicity, ethnicity, felicity, publicity, simplicity, toxicity, triplicity • authenticity, domesticity, eccentricity, elasticity, electricity, infelicity, multiplicity, specificity • ethnocentricity, inauthenticity, inelasticity, periodicity
icity² \is-tē\ Christie, misty, twisty, wristy • Corpus Christi
ick \ik\ brick, chick, click, crick, creek, Dick, flick, hick, kick, lick, nick, Nick, pic, pick, prick, quick, rick, sic, sick, slick, stick, thick, tic, tick, trick, wick • airsick, broomstick, carsick, Chap Stick, chick flick, chopstick, cowlick, deer tick, dipstick, dog tick, drop-kick, drumstick, ear pick, firebrick, fish stick, free kick, frog kick, goal kick, handpick, hat trick, hayrick, heartsick, homesick, ice pick, joystick, lipstick, lovesick, matchstick, nightstick, nitpick, nonstick, nutpick, oil slick, peacenik, pinprick, placekick, rubric, salt lick, seasick, self-stick, sidekick, slapstick, toothpick, unstick, uptick, wood tick, yardstick • bailiwick, biopic, Bolshevik, bone to pick, call in sick, candlestick, cattle tick, cherry-pick, corner kick, Dominic, do the trick, doublequick, flutter kick, heretic, lunatic, meterstick, pogo stick, point-and-click, politic, Reykjavik, rhythm stick, scissors kick, walking stick • arithmetic, carrotand-stick, impolitic, penalty kick

icka \ē-kə\ see IKA[1]
icked \ikt\ see ICT[1]
ickel \ik-əl\ see ICKLE
icken \ik-ən\ chicken, quicken, sicken, stricken, thicken
• awestricken, spring chicken
• panic-stricken, prairie chicken, rubber-chicken • poverty-stricken
ickens \ik-ənz\ dickens, Dickens, pickings
—*also* -s, -'s, *and* -s' *forms of nouns and* -s *forms of verbs listed at* ICKEN
icker[1] \ik-ər\ bicker, clicker, dicker, flicker, kicker, liquor, nicker, picker, pricker, slicker, snicker, sticker, ticker, vicar, wicker • dropkicker, nitpicker, placekicker, ragpicker • bumper sticker, cherry picker, city slicker, politicker
—*also* -er *forms of adjectives listed at* ICK
icker[2] \ek-ər\ see ECKER
ickery \ik-rē\ chicory, flickery, hickory, trickery • Terpsichore
icket \ik-ət\ cricket, picket, spigot, thicket, ticket, wicket • big-ticket, hot ticket, meal ticket • season ticket
ickett \ik-ət\ see ICKET
ickety \ik-ət-ē\ rickety, thickety
• persnickety
ickey \ik-ē\ see ICKY
icki \ik-ē\ see ICKY
ickie \ik-ē\ see ICKY
icking \ik-iŋ\ flat-picking, high-sticking, nit-picking, rollicking
• cotton-picking, fingerpicking
—*also* -ing *forms of verbs listed at* ICK
ickings \ik-ənz\ see ICKENS
ickish \ik-ish\ sickish, thickish
ickit \ik-ət\ see ICKET
ickle \ik-əl\ fickle, nickel, pickle, prickle, sickle, tickle, trickle
• bicycle, dill pickle, icicle, obsta-cle, Popsicle, tricycle • pumper-nickel • hammer and sickle
ickler \ik-lər\ stickler, tickler • bi-cycler, particular
ickly \ik-lē\ prickly, quickly, sickly, slickly, thickly
ickness \ik-nəs\ quickness, sick-ness, slickness, thickness • air-sickness, car sickness, homesickness, lovesickness, sea-sickness • motion sickness, moun-tain sickness, sleeping sickness
icksy \ik-sē\ see IXIE
icky \ik-ē\ dickey, hickey, icky, Mickey, picky, quickie, sickie, sticky, tricky, Vicky • doohickey, slapsticky
icle \ik-əl\ see ICKLE
icly[1] \ik-lē\ see ICKLY
icly[2] \ē-klē\ see EEKLY
ico \ē-kō\ see ICOT
icory \ik-rē\ see ICKERY
icot \ē-kō\ tricot • Puerto Rico
ics \iks\ see IX[1]
ict[1] \ikt\ strict, ticked • addict, af-flict, conflict, constrict, convict, depict, district, edict, evict, inflict, lipsticked, predict, restrict, verdict
• Benedict, contradict, derelict, in-terdict, Lake District • eggs Bene-dict
—*also* -ed *forms of verbs listed at* ICK
ict[2] \īt\ see ITE[1]
ictable \īt-ə-bəl\ see ITABLE[1]
icted \ik-təd\ conflicted, restricted
—*also* -ed *forms of verbs listed at* ICT[1]
icter \ik-tər\ see ICTOR
ictim \ik-təm\ see ICTUM
iction \ik-shən\ diction, fiction, friction • addiction, affliction, constriction, conviction, depic-tion, eviction, infliction, nonfic-tion, prediction, restriction
• benediction, contradiction, crucifixion, dereliction, interdic-tion, jurisdiction, science fiction

ictional \ik-shnəl\ fictional • non-fictional • jurisdictional

ictive \ik-tiv\ fictive • addictive, afflictive, constrictive, predictive, restrictive, vindictive • nonrestrictive

ictment \īt-mənt\ see ITEMENT

ictor \ik-tər\ victor • constrictor, depicter, inflicter • boa constrictor

ictory \ik-tə-rē\ victory • contradictory, valedictory

ictual \it-ᵊl\ see ITTLE

ictum \ik-təm\ dictum, victim

icture \ik-chər\ picture, stricture • big picture • motion picture

icular¹ \ik-yə-lər\ curricular, funicular, particular, vehicular • in particular, perpendicular • extracurricular

icular² \ik-lər\ see ICKLER

iculate \ik-yə-lət\ articulate, particulate • inarticulate

iculous \ik-yə-ləs\ meticulous, ridiculous

icy \ī-sē\ dicey, icy, pricey, spicy

id¹ \id\ bid, did, grid, hid, id, kid, Kidd, lid, mid, quid, rid, skid, slid, squid • amid, backslid, El Cid, eyelid, forbid, grandkid, Madrid, nonskid, outdid, schoolkid, undid • arachnid, giant squid, katydid, pyramid, underbid • Valladolid

id² \ēd\ see EED

I'd \īd\ see IDE¹

ida¹ \ēd-ə\ see EDA¹

ida² \ī-də\ Haida, Ida • Oneida

idal \īd-ᵊl\ bridal, bridle, idle, idol, idyll, sidle, tidal • fratricidal, fungicidal, genocidal, germicidal, herbicidal, homicidal, pesticidal, suicidal

idance \īd-ᵊns\ guidance • misguidance

iday \īd-ē\ Friday, Heidi, tidy • girl Friday, Good Friday, man Friday, untidy • bona fide

idd \id\ see ID¹

idden \id-ᵊn\ bidden, hidden, ridden • bedridden, forbidden • overridden

idder \id-ər\ bidder, kidder • consider • reconsider

iddie \id-ē\ see IDDY

iddish \id-ish\ kiddish, Yiddish

iddity \id-ət-ē\ see IDITY

iddle \id-ᵊl\ fiddle, griddle, middle, piddle, riddle, twiddle • bass fiddle • play second fiddle

iddling \id-liŋ\ fiddling, middling, piddling

iddly \id-le\ diddly, piddly, Ridley

iddock \id-ik\ see IDIC

iddur \id-ər\ see IDDER

iddy \id-ē\ biddy, giddy, kiddie

ide¹ \īd\ bide, bride, chide, Clyde, eyed, fried, glide, guide, hide, I'd, pied, plied, pride, ride, side, slide, snide, stride, tide, tried, wide • abide, allied, applied, aside, astride, backside, backslide, beachside, bedside, beside, bestride, betide, blue-eyed, broadside, bromide, bug-eyed, clear-eyed, cockeyed, cold-eyed, collide, confide, courtside, cowhide, cross-eyed, curbside, decide, deride, divide, dockside, downside, downslide, dry-eyed, ebb tide, elide, field guide, fireside, flip side, flood tide, fluoride, four-eyed, free ride, freeze-dried, Girl Guide, graveside, hang glide, hawkeyed, hayride, high tide, hillside, horsehide, inside, in stride, joyride, lakeside, landslide, low tide, lynx-eyed, misguide, noontide, offside, onside, outride, outside, poolside, pop-eyed, preside, provide, rawhide, red tide, reside, ringside, riptide, roadside, seaside, sharp-eyed, shipside, snowslide, springtide, squint-eyed, stateside, statewide, storewide,

streamside, subside, tongue-tied, topside, untried, upside, vat-dyed, walleyed, wayside, wide-eyed, wild-eyed, worldwide, yuletide • alongside, bleary-eyed, bona fide, chicken-fried, Christmastide, citified, citywide, classified, coincide, countrified, countryside, countrywide, cut-and-dried, cyanide, dignified, dioxide, double-wide, eagle-eyed, Eastertide, eventide, far and wide, fratricide, fungicide, genocide, germicide, goggle-eyed, googly-eyed, harborside, herbicide, homicide, misty-eyed, monoxide, mountainside, nationwide, Naugahyde, on the side, open-eyed, override, Passiontide, pesticide, planetwide, qualified, rarefied, riverside, side by side, sissified, subdivide, suicide, underside, waterside, wintertide • by the wayside, dissatisfied, fit to be tied, formaldehyde, infanticide, insecticide, Jekyll and Hyde, preoccupied, self-satisfied • carbon dioxide, carbon monoxide, overqualified
—*also* -ed *forms of verbs listed at* Y[1]

ide[2] \ēd\ *see* EED

idean \id-ē-ən\ *see* IDIAN

ided \īd-əd\ sided • divided, lopsided, misguided, one-sided • many-sided
—*also* -ed *forms of verbs listed at* IDE[1]

iden \īd-ᵊn\ guidon, Haydn, Leiden, Sidon, widen • Poseidon

idence \īd-ᵊns\ *see* IDANCE

ident \īd-ᵊnt\ strident, trident

ideon \id-ē-ən\ *see* IDIAN

ideous \id-ē-əs\ *see* IDIOUS

ider[1] \īd-ər\ cider, glider, rider, snider, spider, wider • backslider, decider, divider, hang glider, insider, joyrider, lowrider, mis-guider, outrider, outsider, provider, sea spider, Top-Sider, wolf spider • paraglider, waterstrider

ider[2] \id-ər\ *see* IDDER

ides \īdz\ ides • besides
—*also* -s, -'s, *and* -s' *forms of nouns and* -s *forms of verbs listed at* IDE[1]

idge \ij\ bridge, fridge, midge, ridge • abridge, Blue Ridge, drawbridge, footbridge, Oak Ridge, truss bridge • biting midge, contract bridge, covered bridge • suspension bridge

idged \ijd\ unabridged
—*also* -ed *forms of verbs listed at* IDGE

idgen \ij-ən\ *see* YGIAN

idget \ij-ət\ Brigitte, digit, fidget, midget, widget • double-digit

idgin \ij-ən\ *see* YGIAN

idi \id-ē\ *see* IDDY

idia \i-dē-ə\ Lydia • Numidia

idian \id-ē-ən\ Gideon, Lydian, Midian • Floridian, meridian, obsidian, quotidian • prime meridian

idic \id-ik\ acidic, druidic, Hasidic

idical \id-i-kəl\ druidical, juridical • pyramidical

idiem \id-ē-əm\ idiom • iridium • post meridiem • ante meridiem

iding \īd-iŋ\ riding, siding, tiding • abiding, confiding, deciding, hang gliding, joyriding • law-abiding, paragliding
—*also* -ing *forms of verbs listed at* IDE[1]

idiom \id-ē-əm\ *see* IDIEM

idious \id-ē-əs\ hideous • fastidious, insidious, invidious, perfidious

idity \id-ət-ē\ acidity, aridity, avidity, cupidity, fluidity, frigidity, humidity, liquidity, lucidity, morbidity, rapidity, rigidity, solidity, stupidity, timidity, validity

idium \id-ē-əm\ see IDIEM
idle \īd-ᵊl\ see IDAL
idley \id-lē\ see IDDLY
idney \id-nē\ kidney, Sidney, Sydney
ido¹ \īd-ō\ Dido, fido • Hokkaido
ido² \ēd-ō\ see EDO¹
idol \īd-ᵊl\ see IDAL
ids¹ \idz\ rapids • Grand Rapids
　—also -s, -'s, and -s' forms of nouns and -s forms of verbs listed at ID¹
ids² \ēdz\ see EEDS
idst \idst\ didst, midst • amidst
idual¹ \ij-wəl\ residual • individual
idual² \ij-əl\ see IGIL
idy \īd-ē\ see IDAY
idyll \īd-ᵊl\ see IDAL
ie¹ \ā\ see AY¹
ie² \ē\ see EE¹
ie³ \ī\ see Y¹
iece \ēs\ cease, crease, fleece, grease, Greece, lease, Nice, niece, peace, piece • apiece, at peace, Bernice, Burmese, caprice, chemise, Chinese, Clarice, Cochise, crosspiece, decease, decrease, Denise, Dumfries, earpiece, Elise, eyepiece, Felice, grandniece, hairpiece, headpiece, increase, Maltese, Matisse, Maurice, mouthpiece, nosepiece, obese, one-piece, police, release, showpiece, sublease, Therese, timepiece, three-piece, two-piece, valise • altarpiece, Balinese, Bengalese, Brooklynese, Cantonese, centerpiece, Ceylonese, chimneypiece, Congolese, diocese, expertise, frontispiece, Gabonese, Golden Fleece, Guyanese, hold one's peace, Japanese, Javanese, journalese, kiss of peace, Lebanese, legalese, manganese, mantelpiece, masterpiece, Nepalese, of a piece, Pekingese, Portuguese, predecease, rerelease,

Siamese, timed-release, Viennese • archdiocese, bureaucratese, computerese, Indo-Chinese, officialese, Peloponnese, secret police, Vietnamese • conversation piece, justice of the peace
iecer \ē-sər\ see EASER¹
ied¹ \ēd\ see EED
ied² \ēt\ see EAT¹
ied³ \īd\ see IDE¹
ieda \ēd-ə\ see EDA¹
ief¹ \ēf\ beef, brief, chief, fief, grief, leaf, reef, sheaf, thief • bay leaf, belief, chipped beef, crew chief, debrief, fig leaf, fire chief, gold leaf, in brief, kerchief, loose-leaf, motif, relief, sneak thief, Tallchief • bas-relief, cloverleaf, come to grief, disbelief, handkerchief, misbelief, neckerchief, unbelief • barrier reef, comic relief • commander in chief, editor in chief, Great Barrier Reef
ief² \ēv\ see EAVE¹
iefly \ē-flē\ briefly, chiefly
ieg¹ \ēg\ see IGUE
ieg² \ig\ see IG
iege¹ \ēj\ siege • besiege, prestige
iege² \ēzh\ see IGE¹
ieger \ē-jər\ see EDURE
iek \ēk\ see EAK¹
iel \ēl\ see EAL²
iela \el-ə\ see ELLA
ield \ēld\ field, shield, wheeled, wield, yield • afield, airfield, coalfield, cornfield, force field, four-wheeled, Garfield, goldfield, heat shield, ice field, infield, left field, midfield, minefield, oil field, outfield, right field, snowfield, Springfield, unsealed, well-heeled, windshield • Bakersfield, battlefield, center field, landing field, Mount Mansfield, playing field, track-and-field
　—also -ed forms of verbs listed at EAL²

ielder \ēl-dər\ fielder, shielder
• infielder, left fielder, midfielder,
outfielder, right fielder • center
fielder
ields \ēldz\ elysian fields
—*also* -s, -'s, *and* -s' *forms of
nouns and* -s *forms of verbs listed
at* IELD
ieler \ē-lər\ see EALER
ieless \ī-ləs\ see ILUS
ieling \ē-liŋ\ see EELING
iem[1] \ē-əm\ see EUM[1]
iem[2] \ī-əm\ see IAM
ien \ēn\ see INE[3]
ience \ī-əns\ see IANCE
iend \end\ see END
iendless \en-ləs\ see ENDLESS
iendliness \en-lē-nəs\ see ENDLINESS
iendly \en-lē\ see ENDLY
iene \ēn\ see INE[3]
iener[1] \ē-nər\ see EANER
iener[2] \ē-nē\ see INI[1]
ienic \en-ik\ see ENIC[2]
ienics \en-iks\ see ENICS
ienie \ē-nē\ see INI[1]
ienist \ē-nəst\ see INIST[2]
iennes \en\ see EN[1]
ient \ī-ənt\ see IANT
ieper \ē-pər\ see EEPER
ier[1] \ir\ see EER[2]
ier[2] \ē-ər\ see EER[1]
ier[3] \īr\ see IRE[1]
ierate \ir-ət\ see IRIT
ierce \irs\ fierce, pierce
iere[1] \er\ see ARE[4]
iere[2] \ir\ see EER[2]
iered \ird\ see EARD[1]
ieria \ir-ē-ə\ see ERIA[1]
ierial \ir-ē-əl\ see ERIAL
ierian \ir-ē-ən\ see ERIAN[1]
ierly \ir-lē\ see EARLY[1]
ierre[1] \ir\ see EER[2]
ierre[2] \er\ see ARE[4]
iers \irz\ Sears • Algiers
—*also* -s, -'s, *and* -s' *forms of
nouns and* -s *forms of verbs listed
at* EER[2]

iersman \irz-mən\ see EERSMAN
iery \ī-ə-rē\ see IARY[1]
ies[1] \ēz\ see EZE
ies[2] \ē\ see EE[1]
ies[3] \ēs\ see IECE
iesel[1] \ē-zəl\ see EASEL
iesel[2] \ē-səl\ see ECIL[1]
iesian \ē-zhən\ see ESIAN[1]
iesis \ī-ə-səs\ see IASIS
iest \ēst\ see EAST[1]
iester \ē-stər\ see EASTER
iestley \ēst-lē\ see EASTLY
iestly \ēst-lē\ see EASTLY
iet \ī-ət\ diet, fiat, quiet, riot • dis-
quiet, race riot, run riot, unquiet
ietal \ī-ət-ᵊl\ parietal, societal,
varietal
ieter \ī-ət-ər\ dieter, rioter • propri-
etor
ietor \ī-ət-ər\ see IETER
iety \ī-ət-ē\ piety • anxiety, impiety,
propriety, sobriety, society, variety • impropriety, notoriety • garden variety, honor society, secret
society
ietzsche \ē-chē\ see EACHY
ieu \ü\ see EW[1]
ieur \ir\ see EER[2]
iev \ef\ see EF[1]
ievable \ē-və-bəl\ see EIVABLE
ieval \ē-vəl\ evil, weevil • boll
weevil, coeval, medieval,
primeval, retrieval, upheaval
ieve[1] \iv\ see IVE[2]
ieve[2] \ēv\ see EAVE[1]
ieved \ēvd\ see EAVED
ievement \ēv-mənt\ see EVEMENT
iever \ē-vər\ beaver, cleaver, fever,
weaver • achiever, believer, con-
ceiver, deceiver, orb weaver,
receiver, reliever, retriever, trans-
ceiver • cantilever, disbeliever,
eager beaver, true believer, unbe-
liever, wide receiver • golden
retriever, overachiever, under-
achiever
ievish \ē-vish\ see EEVISH

ievous \ē-vəs\ see EVOUS

ieze \ēz\ see EZE

if¹ \if\ see IFF

if² \ēf\ see IEF¹

ife¹ \īf\ fife, Fife, knife, life, rife, strife, wife • good life, half-life, housewife, jackknife, lowlife, midlife, nightlife, penknife, real-life, shelf life, steak knife, still life, true-life, wildlife • afterlife, bowie knife, Duncan Phyfe, fact of life, get a life, nurse-midwife, palette knife, paring knife, pocketknife, putty knife, Yellowknife • utility knife

ife² \ēf\ see IEF¹

ifeless \ī-fləs\ lifeless, strifeless, wifeless

ifer \ī-fər\ see IPHER

iferous \if-ər-əs\ coniferous, pestiferous, splendiferous, vociferous • odoriferous

iff \if\ biff, cliff, diff, glyph, if, jiff, miff, riff, skiff, sniff, stiff, tiff, whiff • midriff, what-if • hieroglyph

iffany \if-ə-nē\ see IPHONY

iffe \if\ see IFF

iffed \ift\ see IFT

iffey \if-ē\ see IFFY

iffish \if-ish\ sniffish, stiffish

iffle \if-əl\ riffle, sniffle, Wiffle

iffness \if-nəs\ stiffness, swiftness

iffy \if-ē\ iffy, jiffy, Liffey, sniffy, spiffy

ific \if-ik\ horrific, pacific, Pacific, prolific, specific, terrific • beatific, hieroglyphic, honorific, scientific, soporific, South Pacific

ifle \ī-fəl\ rifle, stifle, trifle • air rifle, a trifle, squirrel rifle • assault rifle, Enfield rifle, M1 rifle, Springfield rifle

ifling \ī-fliŋ\ rifling, stifling, trifling

ift \ift\ drift, gift, lift, rift, shift, shrift, sift, swift, Swift, thrift • adrift, airlift, chairlift, down-shift, face-lift, forklift, gearshift, makeshift, shape-shift, shoplift, ski lift, snowdrift, spendthrift, spindrift, split shift, stick shift, swing shift, uplift, upshift • chimney swift, graveyard shift • continental drift
—*also* -ed *forms of verbs listed at* IFF

ifter \if-tər\ drifter, sifter • scene-shifter, shape-shifter, shoplifter, weight lifter

ifth \ith\ see ITH²

iftness \if-nəs\ see IFFNESS

ifty \if-tē\ drifty, fifty, nifty, shifty, thrifty • fifty-fifty, LD₅₀

ig \ig\ big, brig, cig, dig, fig, gig, Grieg, jig, pig, prig, rig, sprig, swig, twig, Whig, wig, zig • bigwig, Danzig, earwig, Leipzig, renege, shindig • guinea pig, hit it big, jury-rig, whirligig, WYSIWYG • potbellied pig, thingamajig

iga \ē-gə\ Antigua, omega

igamous \ig-ə-məs\ bigamous • polygamous

igamy \ig-ə-mē\ bigamy • polygamy

igate \ig-ət\ see IGOT¹

ige¹ \ēzh\ siege • prestige

ige² \ēj\ see IEGE¹

igel \ij-əl\ see IGIL

igenous \ij-ə-nəs\ see IGINOUS

igeon \ij-ən\ see YGIAN

iger \ī-gər\ tiger • Bengal tiger, paper tiger • saber-toothed tiger • Siberian tiger, Tasmanian tiger

igerent \ij-rənt\ belligerent, refrigerant

iggard \ig-ərd\ triggered
—*also* -ed *forms of verbs listed at* IGGER

igged \igd\ twigged • jerry-rigged
—*also* -ed *forms of verbs listed at* IG

igger \ig-ər\ chigger, jigger, rigor, snigger, trigger, vigor • ditchdigger, gold digger, hair trigger, outrigger • pull the trigger

iggered \ig-ərd\ see IGGARD

iggie \ig-ē\ see IGGY

iggish \ig-ish\ biggish, piggish, priggish

iggle \ig-əl\ giggle, jiggle, squiggle, wiggle, wriggle

iggler \ig-lər\ giggler, wiggler, wriggler

iggy \ig-ē\ biggie, piggy, twiggy

igh \ī\ see Y[1]

ighed \īd\ see IDE[1]

ighland \ī-lənd\ highland, island, Thailand • Long Island, Rhode Island, Wake Island • Christmas Island, Coney Island, Devil's Island, Easter Island, Ellis Island, Staten Island • Prince Edward Island, Vancouver Island

ighlander \ī-lən-dər\ highlander, islander

ighlands \ī-lənz\ Highlands • Aran Islands, Cayman Islands, Channel Islands, Falkland Islands, Gilbert Islands, Leeward Islands, Marshall Islands, Thousand Islands, Virgin Islands, Windward Islands • Aegean Islands, Aleutian Islands, Canary Islands, Hawaiian Islands, Philippine Islands
—*also* -s, -'s, *and* -s' *forms of nouns listed at* IGHLAND

ighly \ī-lē\ see YLY

ighness \ī-nəs\ see INUS[1]

ight \īt\ see ITE[1]

ightable \īt-ə-bəl\ see ITABLE[1]

ighted \īt-əd\ blighted, sighted • benighted, clear-sighted, farsighted, foresighted, nearsighted, shortsighted, united
—*also* -ed *forms of verbs listed at* ITE[1]

ighten \īt-ᵊn\ brighten, chitin, frighten, heighten, lighten, tighten, titan, Titan, triton, whiten • enlighten

ightener \īt-nər\ brightener, lightener, tightener, whitener

ightening \īt-niŋ\ see IGHTNING

ighter \īt-ər\ see ITER[1]

ightful \īt-fəl\ frightful, rightful, spiteful • delightful, insightful

ightie \īt-ē\ see ITE[2]

ighting \īt-iŋ\ see ITING

ightless \īt-ləs\ flightless, lightless, nightless, sightless

ightly \īt-lē\ brightly, knightly, lightly, nightly, rightly, slightly, sprightly, tightly • contritely, finitely, forthrightly, politely, unsightly, uprightly • impolitely

ightment \īt-mənt\ see ITEMENT

ightning \īt-niŋ\ lightning, tightening • ball lightning, belt-tightening, heat lightning, sheet lightning
—*also* -ing *forms of verbs listed at* IGHTEN

ighton \īt-ən\ see IGHTEN

ights \īts\ lights, nights, tights • by rights, footlights, houselights, last rites, states' rights, weeknights • bill of rights, civil rights, Golan Heights, human rights, northern lights, Shaker Heights, southern lights • animal rights
—*also* -s, -'s, *and* -s' *forms of nouns and* -s *forms of verbs listed at* ITE[1]

ighty \īt-ē\ see ITE[2]

igian \ij-ən\ see YGIAN

igid \ij-əd\ Brigid, frigid, rigid

igil \ij-əl\ vigil • residual

iginous \ij-ə-nəs\ indigenous, vertiginous

igion \ij-ən\ see YGIAN

igious \ij-əs\ litigious, prestigious, prodigious, religious • irreligious

igit \ij-ət\ see IDGET

igitte \ij-ət\ see IDGET

igm[1] \im\ see IM[1]

igm[2] \īm\ see IME[1]

igma \ig-mə\ sigma, stigma • enigma

igment \ig-mənt\ figment, pigment
ign \īn\ see INE[1]
ignant \ig-nənt\ indignant, malignant
igned \īnd\ see IND[1]
igner \ī-nər\ see INER[1]
igning \ī-niŋ\ see INING
ignity \ig-nət-ē\ dignity • indignity
ignly \īn-lē\ see INELY[1]
ignment \īn-mənt\ alignment, assignment, confinement, refinement • realignment
ignon \in-yən\ see INION
igo \ē-gō\ see EGO[1]
igoe \ē-gō\ see EGO[1]
igor \ig-ər\ see IGGER
igorous \ig-rəs\ rigorous, vigorous
igot[1] \ig-ət\ bigot, frigate, spigot
igot[2] \ik-ət\ see ICKET
igour \ig-ər\ see IGGER
igue \ēg\ Grieg, league • big-league, blitzkrieg, bush-league, colleague, fatigue, intrigue • Ivy League, Little League, major-league, minor-league • battle fatigue, combat fatigue
iguer \ē-gər\ see EAGER
iguous \ig-yə-wəs\ ambiguous, contiguous • unambiguous
igured \ig-ərd\ see IGGARD
ii \ī\ see Y[1]
iing \ē-iŋ\ see EEING
ija \ē-jə\ see EGIA
iji \ē-jē\ Fiji, squeegee
ijia \ē-jə\ see EGIA
ijl \īl\ see ILE[1]
ijn \īn\ see INE[1]
ik[1] \ik\ see ICK
ik[2] \ēk\ see EAK[1]
ika[1] \ē-kə\ paprika, Topeka • Costa Rica, Dominica, Frederica, Tanganyika
ika[2] \ī-kə\ see ICA[1]
ike[1] \ī-kē\ crikey, Nike, Psyche, spiky
ike[2] \īk\ bike, dike, hike, like, mike, Mike, pike, psych, shrike, spike, strike, trike, tyke • alike, boatlike, childlike, Christlike, dirt bike, dislike, dreamlike, feel like, fishlike, flu-like, godlike, grasslike, hitchhike, Klondike, lifelike, rocklike, springlike, suchlike, trail bike, trancelike, turnpike, unlike, vicelike, warlike, wavelike, winglike • and the like, businesslike, down the pike, hunger strike, ladylike, leatherlike, look-alike, machinelike, minibike, motorbike, mountain bike, northern pike, open mike, soundalike, sportsmanlike, statesmanlike, take a hike, workmanlike • exercise bike, sympathy strike, unsportsmanlike
iked \īkt\ spiked
—*also* -ed *forms of verbs listed at* IKE[2]
iker \ī-kər\ biker, hiker, striker • hitchhiker • hunger striker, minibiker, mountain biker
ikey \ī-kē\ see IKE[1]
ikh \ēk\ see EAK[1]
iki[1] \ik-ē\ see ICKY
iki[2] \ē-kē\ see EAKY
iking \ī-kiŋ\ liking, striking, Viking
—*also* -ing *forms of verbs listed at* IKE[2]
ikker \ik-ər\ see ICKER[1]
iky \ī-kē\ see IKE[1]
il[1] \il\ see ILL
il[2] \ēl\ see EAL[2]
ila[1] \il-ə\ see ILLA[2]
ila[2] \ē-lə\ see ELA[1]
ilae \ī-le\ see YLY
ilage \ī-lij\ mileage, silage
ilar \ī-lər\ dialer, filer, miler, smiler, styler, tiler, Tyler • compiler, rottweiler, stockpiler
ilate \ī-lət\ see ILOT
ilbert \il-bərt\ filbert, Gilbert
ilch[1] \ilk\ see ILK
ilch[2] \ilch\ filch, zilch
ild[1] \īld\ child, mild, piled, wild,

Wilde • brainchild, godchild,
grandchild, hog-wild, Rothschild,
schoolchild, self-styled, stepchild,
with child • flower child, latchkey
child, poster child, self-exiled
—*also* -ed *forms of verbs listed at*
ILE[1]

ild² \il\ *see* ILL
ild³ \ilt\ *see* ILT
ild⁴ \ild\ *see* ILLED
ilde \īld\ *see* ILD[1]
ilder¹ \il-dər\ builder • bewilder,
boatbuilder, Mound Builder,
shipbuilder • bodybuilder
ilder² \īl-dər\ Wilder
—*also* -er *forms of adjectives listed
at* ILD[1]

ilding \il-diŋ\ building, gilding
• boatbuilding, outbuilding, ship-
building • bodybuilding
—*also* -ing *forms of verbs listed at*
ILLED

ildish \īl-dish\ childish, wildish
ildly \īld-lē\ mildly, wildly
ile¹ \īl\ aisle, bile, dial, file, guile,
I'll, isle, Kyle, Lyle, mile, Nile,
pile, rile, smile, style, tile, trial,
vial, vile, viol, while • agile, air
mile, argyle, awhile, bass viol,
beguile, Blue Nile, compile, de-
file, denial, docile, erstwhile,
exile, febrile, field trial, fragile,
freestyle, futile, gentile, hairstyle,
high style, hostile, lifestyle, mean-
while, mistrial, mobile, nail file,
nubile, on file, profile, puerile,
quartile, redial, reptile, retrial,
revile, sandpile, senile, servile,
stockpile, sundial, tactile, tensile,
textile, time trial, turnstile, un-
pile, virile, woodpile, worthwhile
• chamomile, crocodile, domicile,
family style, in denial, infantile,
insectile, juvenile, low-profile,
mercantile, percentile, prehensile,
projectile, rank and file, recon-
cile, self-denial, single file, statute

mile, versatile • audiophile, circular file, Indian file, once in a
while • cafeteria-style
ile² \il\ *see* ILL
ile³ \ē-lē\ *see* EELY
ile⁴ \ēl\ *see* EAL²
ile⁵ \il-ē\ *see* ILLY
ilead \il-ē-əd\ *see* ILIAD
ileage \ī-lij\ *see* ILAGE
ileal \il-ē-əl\ *see* ILIAL
iler¹ \ē-lər\ *see* EALER
iler² \ī-lər\ *see* ILAR
iles \īlz\ Giles, Miles • British Isles,
Western Isles
—*also* -s, -'s, *and* -s' *forms of
nouns and* -s *forms of verbs listed
at* ILE[1]
iley \ī-lē\ *see* YLY
ili¹ \il-ē\ *see* ILLY
ili² \ē-lē\ *see* EELY
ilia¹ \il-ē-ə\ Celia, cilia • Cecilia
• hemophilia • memorabilia
ilia² \il-yə\ Brasília • bougainvillea
• memorabilia
ilia³ \ēl-yə\ *see* ELIA[1]
iliad \il-ē-əd\ Gilead, Iliad • balm
of Gilead
ilial \il-ē-əl\ filial • familial
ilian¹ \il-ē-ən\ Gillian, Ilian, Lillian
• reptilian • crocodilian
ilian² \il-yən\ *see* ILLION
ilias \il-ē-əs\ *see* ILIOUS[1]
ilic \il-ik\ acrylic, Cyrillic, dactylic,
idyllic
ilience \il-yəns\ *see* ILLIANCE
iliency \il-yən-sē\ *see* ILLIANCY
ilient \il-yənt\ brilliant • resilient
iling¹ \ī-liŋ\ filing, piling, styling,
tiling • hairstyling
—*also* -ing *forms of verbs listed at*
ILE[1]
iling² \ē-liŋ\ *see* EELING
ilion¹ \il-yən\ *see* ILLION
ilion² \il-ē-ən\ *see* ILIAN[1]
ilious¹ \il-ē-əs\ punctilious • supercilious
ilious² \il-yəs\ bilious • supercilious

ility \il-ət-ē\ ability, agility, civility, debility, docility, facility, fertility, fragility, futility, gentility, hostility, humility, mobility, nobility, senility, stability, sterility, tranquility, utility, virility • affability, capability, countability, credibility, culpability, disability, durability, fallibility, feasibility, flexibility, gullibility, imbecility, immobility, inability, incivility, infertility, instability, legibility, liability, likability, livability, plausibility, portability, possibility, probability, readability, sensibility, sociability, suitability, tunability, usability, versatility, viability, visibility, volatility • acceptability, accessibility, accountability, adaptability, advisability, affordability, applicability, attainability, availability, believability, compatibility, deniability, dependability, desirability, electability, eligibility, excitability, illegibility, impossibility, improbability, incapability, infallibility, inflexibility, invisibility, manageability, marketability, measurability, navigability, predictability, profitability, public utility, reliability, respectability, responsibility, susceptibility, sustainability, upward mobility, variability, vulnerability

ilk \ilk\ bilk, ilk, milk, silk • corn silk, ice milk, skim milk • buttermilk, condensed milk, malted milk • cry over spilled milk

ilky \il-kē\ milky, silky

ill \il\ bill, Bill, chill, dill, drill, fill, frill, gill, grill, grille, hill, ill, Jill, kill, krill, mill, nil, Phil, pill, quill, rill, shrill, sill, skill, spill, still, swill, thrill, til, till, trill, twill, will, Will • anthill, at will, backfill, bluegill, Brazil, Catskill, Churchill, crossbill, de Mille, distill, doorsill, downhill, duckbill, dullsville, dunghill, fire drill, foothill, freewill, free will, fulfill, goodwill, gristmill, handbill, hornbill, Huntsville, ill will, instill, Knoxville, landfill, Melville, mixed grill, molehill, Nashville, pep pill, playbill, refill, roadkill, sawmill, Schuylkill, Seville, spoonbill, standstill, stock-still, storksbill, treadmill, true bill, twin bill, twist drill, unreal, until, uphill, vaudeville, waxbill, windchill, windmill • Brazzaville, Bunker Hill, Chapel Hill, chlorophyll, daffodil, de Tocqueville, double bill, espadrille, Evansville, fiberfill, fill the bill, fit to kill, if you will, Jacksonville, living will, Louisville, overfill, overkill, pepper mill, poison pill, puppy mill, rototill, San Juan Hill, sleeping pill, sugar pill, windowsill, whippoor-will • Buffalo Bill, Capitol Hill, over-the-hill, run-of-the-mill

I'll \īl\ see ILE[1]

illa[1] \ē-yə\ mantilla, tortilla • quesadilla

illa[2] \il-ə\ villa, Willa • Anguilla, Attila, Camilla, cedilla, chinchilla, flotilla, gorilla, guerrilla, manila, mantilla, Priscilla, scintilla, vanilla • sarsaparilla

illa[3] \ē-ə\ see IA[1]

illa[4] \ēl-yə\ see ELIA[1]

illa[5] \ē-lə\ see ELA[1]

illable \il-ə-bəl\ billable, drillable, fillable, spillable, syllable, tillable • refillable, trisyllable • monosyllable, polysyllable

illage \il-ij\ pillage, spillage, tillage, village • global village, Greenwich Village • Potemkin village

illah \il-ə\ see ILLA[2]

illain \il-ən\ see ILLON

illar \il-ər\ see ILLER

illate

illate \il-ət\ see ILLET

ille¹ \il\ see ILL

ille² \ē\ see EE¹

ille³ \ēl\ see EAL²

illea \il-yə\ see ILIA²

illed \ild\ build, gild, gilled, guild, skilled, willed • gold-filled, rebuild, tendriled, unskilled • overbuild, semiskilled
—*also* -ed *forms of verbs listed at* ILL

illedness \il-nəs\ see ILLNESS

illein \il-ən\ see ILLON

iller \il-ər\ chiller, filler, killer, miller, pillar, thriller, tiller • distiller, painkiller, time killer • caterpillar, lady-killer, Rototiller, techno-thriller
—*also* -er *forms of adjectives listed at* ILL

illery \il-rē\ pillory • artillery, distillery • field artillery

illes \il-ēz\ see ILLIES

illet \il-ət\ millet, skillet • distillate

illful \il-fəl\ skillful, willful • unskillful

illi¹ \il-ē\ see ILLY

illi² \ē-lē\ see EELY

illian¹ \il-ē-ən\ see ILIAN¹

illian² \il-yən\ see ILLION

illiance \il-yəns\ brilliance • resilience

illiancy \il-yən-sē\ brilliancy • resiliency

illiant \il-yənt\ see ILIENT

illick \il-ik\ see ILIC

illie \il-ē\ see ILLY

illies \il-ēz\ willies • Achilles, Antilles • Greater Antilles, Lesser Antilles
—*also* -s, -'s, *and* -s' *forms of nouns listed at* ILLY

illin \il-ən\ see ILLON

illing \il-iŋ\ billing, drilling, filling, killing, milling, shilling, willing • bone-chilling, fulfilling, painkilling, spine-chilling, top

billing, unwilling • mercy killing, self-fulfilling
—*also* -ing *forms of verbs listed at* ILL

illion \il-yən\ billion, Lillian, million, trillion, zillion • Brazilian, Castilian, civilian, cotillion, gazillion, pavilion, quadrillion, reptilian, Sicilian, vaudevillian, vermilion • crocodilian, Maximilian

illis \il-əs\ see ILLUS

illness \il-nəs\ illness, shrillness, stillness

illo¹ \il-ō\ billow, pillow, willow • Amarillo, armadillo, cigarillo, peccadillo

illo² \ē-ō\ see IO²

illon \il-ən\ Dylan, villain • penicillin

illory \il-rē\ see ILLERY

illous \il-əs\ see ILLUS

illow¹ \il-ə\ see ILLA²

illow² \il-ō\ see ILLO¹

illowy \il-ə-wē\ billowy, pillowy, willowy

ills \ilz\ Black Hills, no-frills • Alban Hills, Berkshire Hills, Chiltern Hills, Cotswold Hills, Malvern Hills, Naga Hills • Beverly Hills, Cheviot Hills, Grampian Hills
—*also* -s, -'s, *and* -s' *forms of nouns and* -s *forms of verbs listed at* ILL

illus \il-əs\ Phyllis, Willis • bacillus • amaryllis

illy \il-ē\ Billie, billy, Chile, chili, chilly, dilly, filly, frilly, hilly, Lillie, lily, Lily, Millie, really, shrilly, silly, Tilly, Willie • daylily, hillbilly • rockabilly, willy-nilly

iln¹ \il\ see ILL

iln² \iln\ kiln, Milne

ilne \iln\ see ILN²

ilo¹ \ī-lō\ Milo, phyllo, silo

ilo² \ē-lō\ kilo, phyllo

ilom \ī-ləm\ see ILUM
iloquist \il-ə-kwəst\ soliloquist, ventriloquist
iloquy \il-ə-kwē\ soliloquy, ventriloquy
ilot \ī-lət\ eyelet, islet, Pilate, pilot • bush pilot, copilot, test pilot • autopilot, Pontius Pilate • automatic pilot
ilt \ilt\ built, gilt, guilt, hilt, jilt, kilt, lilt, quilt, silt, stilt, tilt, wilt • atilt, Brunhild, full tilt, homebuilt, rebuilt, unbuilt • crazy-quilt, custom-built, jerry-built, patchwork quilt, to the hilt, Vanderbilt
ilter \il-tər\ filter, kilter, quilter • off-kilter • color filter
ilth \ilth\ filth, tilth
iltie \il-tē\ see ILTY
ilton \ilt-ᵊn\ Hilton, Milton
ilty \il-tē\ guilty, silty
ilum \ī-ləm\ phylum, xylem • asylum, subphylum
ilus \ī-ləs\ eyeless, stylus, tieless
ily¹ \ī-lē\ see YLY
ily² \il-ē\ see ILLY
im¹ \im\ brim, dim, grim, Grimm, gym, him, hymn, Jim, Kim, limb, prim, rim, scrim, skim, slim, swim, Tim, trim, vim, whim • forelimb, prelim, Purim, Sikkim • acronym, antonym, pseudonym, seraphim, synonym • Pacific Rim
im² \ēm\ see EAM¹
I'm \īm\ see IME¹
ima \ē-mə\ see EMA
image \im-ij\ image, scrimmage • self-image • father image, graven image, mirror image, spitting image, line of scrimmage
iman \ē-mən\ see EMON¹
imate \ī-mət\ climate, primate • acclimate
imb¹ \im\ see IM¹
imb² \īm\ see IME¹
imbal \im-bəl\ see IMBLE
imbale \im-bəl\ see IMBLE

imbed \imd\ brimmed, limbed, rimmed
 —also -ed *forms of verbs listed at* IM¹
imber¹ \im-bər\ limber, timber
imber² \ī-mər\ see IMER¹
imble \im-bəl\ cymbal, nimble, symbol, thimble • peace symbol
imbo \im-bō\ bimbo, limbo • akimbo
imbre \am-bər\ see AMBAR²
ime¹ \īm\ chime, climb, clime, crime, dime, grime, I'm, lime, mime, prime, rhyme, slime, thyme, time • all-time, bedtime, big time, big-time, buy time, call time, daytime, downtime, enzyme, full-time, halftime, hate crime, in time, key lime, lead time, lifetime, longtime, lunchtime, make time, Mannheim, mark time, mealtime, meantime, nighttime, noontime, old-time, onetime, on time, part-time, pastime, peacetime, playtime, prime time, quicklime, quick time, ragtime, real time, rock climb, schooltime, seedtime, showtime, small-time, sometime, Sondheim, space-time, springtime, sublime, teatime, two-time, war crime, wartime, wind chime • Anaheim, anytime, borrowed time, central time, Christmastime, dinnertime, double-time, eastern time, Father Time, harvesttime, local time, maritime, mountain time, nursery rhyme, on a dime, overtime, pantomime, paradigm, running time, standard time, summertime, take one's time, wintertime • Alaska time, Atlantic time, at the same time, from time to time, Greenwich mean time, Pacific time, nickel-and-dime • daylight saving time, geologic time

ime² \ēm\ see EAM¹

imeless \īm-ləs\ crimeless, timeless

imely \īm-lē\ timely • sublimely, untimely

imen \ī-mən\ hymen, Hymen, Simon

imeon \im-ē-ən\ see IMIAN

imer¹ \ī-mər\ climber, primer, rhymer, timer • big-timer, egg timer, full-timer, old-timer, part-timer, small-timer • Oppenheimer, wisenheimer

imer² \im-ər\ see IMMER

imes \ēm\ see EAM¹

imeter \im-ət-ər\ scimitar • altimeter, perimeter

imian \im-ē-ən\ Simeon, simian • Endymion

imic \im-ik\ see YMIC

imicry \im-i-krē\ gimmickry, mimicry

imile \im-ə-lē\ simile, swimmily • facsimile

iminal \im-ən-ᵊl\ criminal • subliminal, war criminal

imitable \im-ət-ə-bəl\ illimitable, inimitable

imitar \im-ət-ər\ see IMETER

imiter \im-ət-ər\ see IMETER

imits \im-its\ Nimitz • off-limits

imity \im-ət-ē\ proximity, sublimity • anonymity, equanimity, magnanimity, unanimity

imitz \im-its\ see IMITS

imm \im\ see IM¹

immage \im-ij\ see IMAGE

imme \i-mē\ see IMMY

immed \imd\ see IMBED

immer \im-ər\ dimmer, glimmer, grimmer, primer, shimmer, simmer, skimmer, slimmer, swimmer

immick \im-ik\ see YMIC

immickry \im-i-krē\ see IMICRY

immily \im-ə-lē\ see IMILE

immy \im-ē\ gimme, jimmy, shimmy

imn \im\ see IM¹

imner \im-ər\ see IMMER

imon \ī-mən\ see IMEN

imp \imp\ blimp, chimp, crimp, imp, limp, primp, scrimp, shrimp, skimp, wimp • brine shrimp, rock shrimp • Colonel Blimp, fairy shrimp, tiger shrimp

impe \imp\ see IMP

imper \im-pər\ shrimper, simper, whimper

imple \im-pəl\ dimple, pimple, simple

imply \im-plē\ limply, pimply, simply

impy \im-pē\ shrimpy, skimpy, wimpy

imsy \im-zē\ flimsy, whimsy

imy \ī-mē\ grimy, limey, limy, slimy, stymie • old-timey

in¹ \in\ been, bin, chin, din, fin, Finn, gin, grin, Gwyn, in, inn, kin, Lynn, pin, shin, sin, skin, spin, thin, tin, twin, win, yin • again, akin, backspin, bearskin, begin, Benin, Berlin, blow in, Boleyn, break-in, bring in, buckskin, build in, built-in, butt in, calfskin, call in, call-in, cash in, cave-in, chagrin, check in, check-in, chime in, chip in, close in, clothespin, come in, coonskin, Corinne, crankpin, cut in, deerskin, dig in, doeskin, do in, drive-in, drop in, fade-in, fall in, fill in, fill-in, give in, goatskin, go in, hairpin, hang in, has-been, herein, horn in, kick in, kidskin, kingpin, lambskin, lay in, lead-in, linchpin, live-in, lived-in, log in, love-in, moleskin, move in, munchkin, ninepin, no-win, oilskin, phone-in, pigskin, pitch in, plug-in, plugged-in, pull in, pushpin, put in, rub in, ruin, sealskin, send in, set in, sharkskin, sheepskin, shoo-in, shut-in, sign in, sit-in, sleep in, sleep-in, sloe gin, snakeskin, sock in, stand in, stand-in, step in, stickpin, suck in, swear in, swim fin, tail fin, tailspin, take in, tenpin, therein, throw in, tie-in, tiepin, tip-in, Tonkin, topspin, trade in, trade-in, tune in, tunedin, Turin, turn in, unpin, walk-in, wear thin, weigh in, wherein, wineskin, win-win, within, work in, write-in, Yeltsin • bobby pin, born-again, candlepin, come again, cotter pin, cotton gin, deadly sin, firing pin, Ho Chi Minh, listen in, listener-in, Lohengrin, loony bin, mandolin, mortal sin, motor inn, next of kin, onionskin, paper-thin, pelvic fin, rolling pin, safety pin, set foot in, thick and thin, violin • Gulf of Tonkin, Holiday Inn, original sin, pectoral fin, rub one's nose in, Siamese twin, under one's skin • again and again • on-again off-again

in² \ēn\ see INE³

in³ \an\ see AN⁵

in⁴ \aⁿ\ Chopin, dauphin, Gauguin, Louvain, Rodin • Claude Lorrain, Saint-Germain

in⁵ \ən\ see UN¹

ina¹ \ī-nə\ china, China, Dinah, Ina, mynah • angina, bone china, Regina, stone china • Carolina, Indochina, kamaaina • North Carolina, South Carolina

ina² \ē-nə\ Lena, Nina, Tina • arena, Athena, Christina, czarina, Edwina, farina, Georgina, hyena, Kristina, marina, Marina, Medina, Messina, novena, patina, Regina, Rowena, subpoena • Angelina, Argentina, ballerina, Carolina, Catalina, concertina, Filipina, Katerina, ocarina, Pasadena, semolina, signorina, Wilhelmina • Herzegovina, Pallas Athena, Strait of Messina

inach \in-ich\ Greenwich, spinach

inah¹ \ē-nə\ see INA²

inah² \ī-nə\ see INA¹

inal¹ \īn-ᵊl\ final, spinal, vinyl • doctrinal • quarterfinal, semifinal

inal² \ēn-ᵊl\ see ENAL

inally \īn-ᵊl-ē\ finally, spinally

inas¹ \ī-nəs\ see INUS¹

inas² \ē-nəs\ see ENUS¹

inative \in-ət-iv\ see INITIVE

inc \iŋk\ see INK

inca \iŋ-kə\ Dinka, Inca

incal \iŋ-kəl\ see INKLE

incan \iŋ-kən\ Incan, Lincoln

ince¹ \ins\ blintz, chintz, mince, prince, quince, rinse, since, wince • convince, crown prince, evince, shin splints • Port-au-Prince —also -s, -'s, and -s' forms of nouns and -s forms of verbs listed at INT

ince² \ans\ see ANCE³

incely \in-slē\ princely, tinselly

incer \in-chər\ see INCHER

inch \inch\ cinch, clinch, finch, flinch, grinch, inch, lynch, pinch, winch • bullfinch, chaffinch, goldfinch • every inch, inch by inch, purple finch

incher \in-chər\ clincher, pincer • penny-pincher • Doberman pinscher

inching \in-chiŋ\ unflinching • penny-pinching —also -ing forms of verbs listed at INCH

incible \in-sə-bəl\ principal, principle • invincible

incing \in-siŋ\ ginseng • convincing • unconvincing —also -ing forms of verbs listed at INCE¹

incipal \in-sə-bəl\ see INCIBLE

inciple \in-sə-bəl\ see INCIBLE

inck \iŋk\ see INK

incky \iŋ-kē\ see INKY

incoln \iŋ-kən\ see INCAN

inct \iŋt\ linked • distinct, extinct, instinct, precinct, succinct • indistinct • killer instinct

inction \iŋ-shən\ distinction, extinction • contradistinction

ind¹ \īnd\ bind, blind, find, grind, hind, kind, mind, rind, spined, wind • behind, confined, fly blind, inclined, mankind, refined, remind, rewind, sand-blind, snow-blind, spellbind, streamlined, unbind, unkind, unwind • ax to grind, bear in mind, blow one's mind, bring to mind, color-blind, fall behind, frame of mind, humankind, in a bind, mastermind, never mind, nonaligned, put in mind, unaligned, undersigned, well-defined, womankind • back of one's mind, piece of one's mind, presence of mind, venetian blind

—*also* -ed *forms of verbs listed at* INE¹

ind² \ind\ finned, skinned, wind • crosswind, downwind, headwind, rescind, tailwind, thick-skinned, thin-skinned, upwind, whirlwind, woodwind • in the wind, solar wind, spiny-finned • twist in the wind

—*also* -ed *forms of verbs listed at* IN¹

ind³ \int\ see INT

inda \in-də\ Linda • Lucinda, Melinda

indar \in-dər\ see INDER²

inded¹ \īn-dəd\ minded • broadminded, fair-minded, high-minded, like-minded, small-minded, snow-blinded, strong-minded, tough-minded, weak-minded • absentminded, bloody-minded, civic-minded, evil-minded, feebleminded, narrow-minded, open-minded, simpleminded, single-minded

—*also* -ed *forms of verbs listed at* IND¹

inded² \in-dəd\ long-winded, short-winded

—*also* -ed *forms of verbs listed at* IND²

inder¹ \īn-dər\ binder, finder, grinder • bookbinder, fact finder, faultfinder, pathfinder, range finder, reminder, ring binder, sidewinder, spellbinder, stemwinder, viewfinder, organ-grinder

—*also* -er *forms of adjectives listed at* IND¹

inder² \in-dər\ cinder, hinder, Pindar, tinder

indhi \in-dē\ see INDY

indi \in-dē\ see INDY

indie \in-dē\ see INDY

inding \īn-diŋ\ binding, finding, winding • bookbinding, fact-finding, faultfinding, self-winding, spellbinding

—*also* -ing *forms of verbs listed at* IND¹

indlass \in-ləs\ see INLESS

indle \in-dᵊl\ dwindle, kindle, spindle, swindle

indless \īn-ləs\ mindless, spineless

indling \ind-liŋ\ dwindling, kindling

indly¹ \in-lē\ see INLY

indly² \īn-lē\ see INELY¹

indness \īn-nəs\ blindness, fineness, kindness • night blindness, snow blindness, unkindness • color blindness, loving-kindness

indowed \in-dəd\ see INDED²

indy \in-dē\ Cindy, Hindi, indie, windy

ine¹ \īn\ brine, dine, fine, kine, line, mine, nine, pine, Rhine, rind, shine, shrine, sign, spine, stein, swine, thine, tine, twine, vine, whine, wine • A-line, airline, align, alpine, assign, at sign, baseline, beeline, benign, Bernstein, bloodline, blush wine, bovine, bowline, breadline, bustline, byline, call sign, canine, carbine, chow line, clothesline, cloud nine, coastline, combine, condign, confine, consign, cosign, cosine, dateline, deadline, decline, define, design, divine, earthshine, Einstein, enshrine, ensign, entwine, equine, feline, foul line, fräulein, frontline, front line, goal line, gold mine, grapevine, guideline, hairline, hard-line, hard pine, headline, hemline, high sign, Holstein, hotline, incline, in-line, Irvine, jawline, landline, land mine, lifeline, main line, malign, midline, moonshine, neckline, offline, old-line, online, opine, outline, outshine, Pauline, peace sign, pipeline, pitch pine, plumb line, plus sign, porcine, pound sign, punch line, quinine, recline, red pine, refine, resign, Rhine wine, ridgeline, roofline, saline, Scotch pine, scrub pine, shoreline, sideline, skyline, snow line, straight-line, streamline, strip mine, strychnine, sunshine, supine, time-line, times sign, towline, trapline, tree line, truckline, trunk line, turbine, untwine, ursine, V sign, waistline, white pine, white wine, woodbine, yard line • alkaline, Angeline, Apennine, aquiline, asinine, auld lang syne, balloon vine, battle line, borderline, bottom-line, Byzantine, calamine, Calvin Klein, Caroline, centerline, claymore mine, columbine, concubine, conga line, Constantine, contour line, coralline, countermine, countersign, credit line, crystalline, disincline, draw the line, equal sign, finish line, firing line, Florentine, Frankenstein, gas turbine, genuine, intertwine, iodine, knotty pine, leonine, Levantine, Liechtenstein, lodgepole pine, longleaf pine, minus sign, monkeyshine, mugho pine, on deadline, on the line, Palestine, party line, picket line, porcupine, realign, redefine, redesign, riverine, Rubenstein, saturnine, second-line, serpentine, shortleaf pine, sibylline, subalpine, sparkling wine, steam turbine, story line, table wine, timberline, toe the line, turpentine, underline, undermine, valentine, waterline, wind turbine, worry line • assembly line, elephantine, Evangeline, fall into line, Frankfurt am Main, graphic design, labyrinthine, lateral line, loblolly pine, Maginot Line, poverty line, production line, receiving line, Rembrandt van Rijn, ship of the line, sweetheart neckline, top-of-the-line • Mason-Dixon line

ine² \ēn\ bean, clean, dean, e'en, gene, Gene, glean, green, jean, Jean, Jeanne, keen, lean, lien, mean, mien, preen, queen, scene, screen, seen, sheen, spleen, teen, tween, wean • Aileen, Arlene, baleen, Benin, benzene, benzine, Bernstein, between, black bean, bovine, broad bean, caffeine, canteen, carbine, careen, Carlene, Cathleen, Charlene, chlorine, chorine, Christine, Claudine, codeine, colleen, Colleen, convene, Coreen, cuisine, Darlene, demean, dentine, Doreen, dryclean, eighteen, Eileen, Eugene, e-zine, fanzine, fifteen, fluorine, fourteen, Francine, gamine, gangrene, glassine, Helene, Hellene, Hermine, Holstein, houseclean, hygiene, Ilene, Irene, Jacqueline, Jeannine, Jolene, Justine, Kathleen, Kristine, lateen, latrine, Lorene, Lublin, machine, marine, Marlene, Maureen, Maxine, morphine, mung bean, Nadine, Nicene, nineteen, Noreen, obscene, offscreen, on-screen, Pauline, praline, preteen, pristine, protein, Racine, ravine, red bean, routine, saline, saltine, sardine, sateen, serene, Sharlene, siren, Sistine, sixteen, Slovene, snap bean, soybean, string bean, strychnine, subteen, sunscreen, thirteen, Tolkien, tureen, umpteen, unclean, unseen, vaccine, wax bean, white bean, windscreen • Aberdeen, almandine, amandine, Angeline, Argentine, Augustine, Balanchine, barkentine, Bernadine, brigantine, brilliantine, Byzantine, carotene, clandestine, columbine, Constantine, contravene, crystalline, Dramamine, drum machine, endocrine, Ernestine, evergreen, fava bean, figurine, Florentine, gabardine, gasoline, Geraldine, go-between, golden mean, guillotine, Halloween, Imogene, in-between, intervene, jelly bean, Josephine, jumping bean, kerosene, kidney bean, lethal gene, Levantine, libertine, lima bean, limousine, M16, magazine, make the scene, mezzanine, navy bean, Nazarene, nectarine, nicotine, overseen, Philistine, pinto bean, riverine, quarantine, saccharine, San Joaquin, San Martín, serpentine, seventeen, slot machine, submarine, subroutine, tambourine, tangerine, time machine, trampoline, Vaseline, velveteen, wintergreen, wolverine • acetylene, amphetamine, aquamarine, Benedictine, elephantine, Evangeline, flying machine, gar-

banzo bean, heart-lung machine, internecine, labyrinthine, merchant marine, milling machine, mujahideen, nouvelle cuisine, pinball machine, rowing machine, simple machine, threshing machine, ultramarine, vanilla bean, vending machine, voting machine, washing machine • answering machine, antihistamine, arithmetic mean, Mary Magdalene, NC-17 • oleomargarine

ine[3] \in-ē\ see INNY

ine[4] \ē-nē\ see INI[1]

ine[5] \ən\ see UN[1]

inea \in-ē\ see INNY

ined \īnd\ see IND[1]

inee \ī-nē\ see INY[1]

ineless \īn-ləs\ see INDLESS

inely[1] \īn-lē\ blindly, finely, kindly • divinely, unkindly

inely[2] \ēn-lē\ see EANLY[1]

inement \īn-mənt\ see IGNMENT

ineness \īn-nəs\ see INDNESS

iner[1] \ī-nər\ diner, finer, liner, miner, minor, shiner, Shriner, signer, whiner • airliner, cosigner, designer, eyeliner, hard-liner, headliner, jetliner, moonshiner, one-liner, recliner, refiner • Asia Minor, forty-niner • graphic designer

iner[2] \ē-nər\ see EANER

inery[1] \īn-rē\ finery, vinery, winery • refinery

inery[2] \ēn-rē\ see EANERY

ines[1] \ēn\ see INE[3]

ines[2] \ēnz\ see EENS

ines[3] \īnz\ Apennines • between the lines
   —*also* -s, -'s, *and* -s' *forms of nouns and* -s *forms of verbs listed at* INE[1]

inest \ī-nəst\ see INIST[1]

inet \in-ət\ see INNET

inew \in-yü\ see INUE

ing \iŋ\ bring, cling, ding, fling,

king, King, Ming, ping, ring, sing, sling, spring, sting, string, swing, thing, wing, wring, zing • backswing, bedspring, Beijing, bite-wing, bowstring, bullring, downswing, drawstring, earring, first-string, growth ring, hamstring, handspring, heartstring, hot spring, lacewing, latchstring, left-wing, mainspring, Nanjing, offspring, plaything, redwing, right-wing, shoestring, unstring, upswing, waxwing, wellspring, wingding • à la king, anything, apron string, ding-a-ling, everything, fairy ring, Highland fling, innerspring, on the wing, second-string, signet ring, teething ring, underwing • buffalo wing, cedar waxwing, if anything, under one's wing

inge \inj\ binge, cringe, fringe, hinge, singe, tinge, twinge • butt hinge, impinge, infringe, syringe, unhinge • lunatic fringe

inged \ind\ pinged, ringed, stringed, winged

ingement \inj-mənt\ impingement, infringement

ingency \in-jən-sē\ stringency • contingency

ingent \in-jənt\ stringent • astringent, contingent

inger[1] \iŋ-ər\ bringer, ringer, singer, stinger, stringer, swinger, wringer, zinger • Beijinger, first-stringer, folksinger, gunslinger, humdinger, left-winger, mudslinger, right-winger, torch singer

inger[2] \iŋ-gər\ finger, linger • forefinger, ring finger • index finger, ladyfinger, little finger, middle finger

inger[3] \in-jər\ ginger, Ginger, injure, singer, swinger • infringer

ingery \inj-rē\ gingery, injury

inghy \iŋ-ē\ see INGY[1]

inging \iŋ-iŋ\ ringing, springing, stringing, swinging • folksinging, free-swinging, gunslinging, hand-wringing, mudslinging, upbringing

—*also* -ing *forms of verbs listed at* ING

ingit \iŋ-kət\ see INKET

ingle \iŋ-gəl\ jingle, mingle, shingle, single, tingle • Kriss Kringle • intermingle

ingli \iŋ-glē\ see INGLY

ingly \iŋ-glē\ jingly, singly, tingly, Zwingli

ingo \iŋ-gō\ bingo, dingo, gringo, jingo, lingo • flamingo, Mandingo • Santo Domingo

ings \iŋz\ Hot Springs, Palm Springs, pull strings, purse strings, see things • Coral Springs, in the wings • Colorado Springs, Saratoga Springs

—*also* -s, -'s, *and* -s' *forms of nouns and* -s *forms of verbs listed at* ING

ingue \aŋ\ see ANG[2]

ingy[1] \iŋ-ē\ clingy, dinghy, springy, stringy, zingy

ingy[2] \in-jē\ dingy, mingy, stingy

inh \in\ see IN[1]

ini[1] \ē-nē\ beanie, genie, greeny, Jeannie, meanie, sheeny, teeny, weenie, weeny, wienie • Bernini, bikini, Bikini, Cyrene, Eugenie, Houdini, linguine, Mancini, martini, Mycenae, Puccini, Rossini, tahini, tankini, zucchini • fettuccine, Mussolini, Paganini, scaloppine, spaghettini, string bikini, teeny-weeny, tetrazzini, tortellini, Toscanini

ini[2] \in-ē\ see INNY

inia \in-ē-ə\ zinnia • gloxinia, Lavinia, Sardinia, Virginia • Abyssinia, West Virginia

inian[1] \in-ē-ən\ Darwinian, Sardinian, Virginian • Abyssinian, Ar-

gentinian, Augustinian, Carolin-
ian, Carthaginian, Palestinian

inian[2] \in-yən\ see INION

inic \in-ik\ clinic, cynic • rabbinic

inical \in-i-kəl\ clinical, cynical,
pinnacle

ining \ī-niŋ\ lining, mining, shining
• declining, designing, inclining
• interlining, silver lining
—*also* -ing *forms of verbs listed at*
INE[1]

inion \in-yən\ minion, pinion,
piñon • dominion, Justinian,
opinion, Sardinian • Abyssinian

inis \ī-nəs\ see INUS[1]

inish \in-ish\ finish, Finnish, thin-
nish • diminish, refinish • photo
finish

inist[1] \ī-nəst\ dynast, finest

inist[2] \ē-nəst\ hygienist, machinist
• trampolinist • dental hygienist

initive \in-ət-iv\ definitive, infinitive • split infinitive

inity \in-ət-ē\ trinity, Trinity
• affinity, divinity, infinity, salin-
ity, sanguinity, vicinity, virginity
• femininity, masculinity

inium \in-ē-əm\ delphinium • con-
dominium

injure \in-jər\ see INGER[3]

injury \inj-rē\ see INGERY

ink \iŋk\ blink, brink, chink, clink,
dink, drink, fink, gink, ink, kink,
link, mink, pink, plink, rink,
shrink, sink, skink, slink, stink,
sync, think, wink, zinc • cuff link,
eyeblink, groupthink, hoodwink,
hot link, lip-synch, outthink,
preshrink, rat fink, red ink, re-
think, soft drink, uplink
• bobolink, countersink, double-
think, hyperlink, interlink, in the
pink, kitchen-sink, missing link,
on the blink, rinky-dink, salmon
pink, shocking pink

inka \iŋ-kə\ see INCA

inkable \iŋ-kə-bəl\ drinkable,

shrinkable, sinkable, thinkable
• undrinkable, unsinkable, un-
thinkable

inkage \iŋ-kij\ linkage, shrinkage

inke \iŋ-kē\ see INKY

inked \iŋt\ see INCT

inker \iŋ-kər\ clinker, drinker,
sinker, stinker, thinker, tinker
• freethinker, headshrinker, hood-
winker, nondrinker • hook line
and sinker

inket \iŋ-kət\ Tlingit, trinket

inkey \iŋ-kē\ see INKY

inkgo \iŋ-kō\ see INKO

inki \iŋ-kē\ see INKY

inkie \iŋ-kē\ see INKY

inking \iŋ-kiŋ\ freethinking, un-
blinking, unthinking • wishful
thinking
—*also* -ing *forms of verbs listed at*
INK

inkle \iŋ-kəl\ crinkle, sprinkle,
tinkle, twinkle, wrinkle • periwin-
kle, Rip van Winkle

inkling \iŋ-kliŋ\ inkling, sprinkling,
twinkling
—*also* -ing *forms of verbs listed at*
INKLE

inkly \iŋ-klē\ crinkly, tinkly,
twinkly, wrinkly

inko \iŋ-kō\ ginkgo, pinko

inks \iŋs\ see INX

inky \iŋ-kē\ dinky, inky, kinky,
pinkie, pinky, slinky, stinky
• Helsinki

inland \in-lənd\ Finland, inland

inless \in-ləs\ chinless, sinless,
skinless

inley \in-lē\ see INLY

inly \in-lē\ spindly, thinly • McKinley • Mount McKinley

inn \in\ see IN[1]

innacle \in-i-kəl\ see INICAL

inned \ind\ see IND[2]

inner \in-ər\ dinner, inner, pinner,
sinner, skinner, spinner, thinner,
winner • beginner, blood thinner,

breadwinner, prizewinner • TV
dinner

innet \in-ət\ linnet, minute, spinet

inney \in-ē\ see INNY

inni \ē-nē\ see INI[1]

innia \in-ē-ə\ see INIA

innic \in-ik\ see INIC

innie \in-ē\ see INNY

inning \in-iŋ\ inning, spinning,
winning • beginning, blood-
thinning, breadwinning, prize-
winning • underpinning
—*also* -ing *forms of verbs listed at*
IN[1]

innish \in-ish\ see INISH

innity \in-ət-ē\ see INITY

innow \in-ō\ minnow, winnow

inny \in-ē\ finny, Guinea, mini,
Minnie, ninny, Pliny, shinny,
skinny, tinny, whinny, Winnie
• New Guinea • Papua New
Guinea

ino[1] \ī-nō\ dino, rhino, wino • al-
bino

ino[2] \ē-nō\ beano, chino, vino
• bambino, casino, Latino,
merino, neutrino • cappuccino,
concertino, Filipino, maraschino,
palomino, San Marino • San
Bernardino

ino[3] \ē-nə\ see INA[2]

iñon \in-yən\ see INION

inor[1] \in-ər\ see INNER

inor[2] \ī-nər\ see INER[1]

inot \ē-nō\ see INO[2]

inous \ī-nəs\ see INUS[1]

inscher \in-chər\ see INCHER

inse \ins\ see INCE[1]

inselly \in-slē\ see INCELY

inseng \in-siŋ\ see INCING

insk \insk\ Minsk, Pinsk

insky \in-skē\ Nijinsky, Stravinsky

inster \in-stər\ minster, spinster
• Westminster

int \int\ Clint, dint, flint, Flint,
glint, hint, lint, mint, print, quint,
splint, sprint, squint, stint, tint

• blueprint, footprint, handprint,
hoofprint, imprint, in-print, large-
print, newsprint, reprint, skin-
flint, spearmint, thumbprint,
voiceprint, wind sprint • aquatint,
fingerprint, peppermint, wun-
derkind

intage \int-ij\ mintage, vintage
• nonvintage

intain \int-ᵊn\ see INTON

inter \int-ər\ hinter, Pinter, printer,
splinter, sprinter, winter • im-
printer, line printer, midwinter
• impact printer, laser printer,
overwinter, teleprinter

inth \inth\ plinth, synth • hyacinth,
labyrinth

inting \int-iŋ\ printing • imprinting,
unstinting
—*also* -ing *forms of verbs listed at*
INT

into[1] \in-tō\ pinto, Shinto

into[2] \in-tü\ back into, break into,
bump into, buy into, check into,
come into, get into, go into, look
into, plug into, rip into, run into,
tap into, tear into • enter into,
marry into

inton \int-ᵊn\ Clinton • badminton

ints \ins\ see INCE[1]

inty \int-ē\ flinty, linty, minty,
squinty • pepperminty

intz \ins\ see INCE[1]

inue \in-yü\ sinew • continue • dis-
continue

inuous \in-yə-wəs\ sinuous • con-
tinuous • discontinuous

inus[1] \ī-nəs\ dryness, highness,
Minos, minus, shyness, sinus,
slyness • Longinus • Antoninus,
plus or minus

inus[2] \ē-nəs\ see ENUS[1]

inute \in-ət\ see INNET

inx \iŋs\ Brink's, jinx, links, lynx,
minx, sphinx • hijinks, methinks
• tiddledywinks
—*also* -s, -'s, *and* -s' *forms of*

nouns and -s *forms of verbs listed at* INK

iny[1] \ī-nē\ briny, heinie, piny, shiny, spiny, tiny, viny, whiny, winy • sunshiny

iny[2] \in-ē\ see INNY

inya \ē-nyə\ see ENIA[2]

inyan \in-yən\ see INION

inyl \īn-ᵊl\ see INAL[1]

io[1] \ī-ō\ bayou, bio, Clio, Io • Ohio • Cinco de Mayo

io[2] \ē-ō\ brio, Clio, Leo, Rio, trio • Trujillo

iocese \ī-ə-səs\ see IASIS

ion[1] \ī-ən\ Brian, Bryan, ion, lion, Mayan, Ryan, scion, Zion • Orion • dandelion, Paraguayan, Uruguayan

ion[2] \ē-ən\ see EAN[1]

ion[3] \ē-än\ see EON[2]

ior \īr\ see IRE[1]

iory \ī-ə-rē\ see IARY[1]

iot \ī-ət\ see IET

ioter \ī-ət-ər\ see IETER

iouan \ü-ən\ see UAN

ious \ī-əs\ see IAS[1]

ioux \ü\ see EW[1]

ip \ip\ blip, chip, clip, dip, drip, flip, grip, grippe, gyp, hip, lip, nip, pip, quip, rip, scrip, ship, sip, skip, slip, snip, strip, tip, trip, whip, yip, zip • airship, airstrip, backflip, blue-chip, bullwhip, catnip, cleft lip, clerkship, corn chip, courtship, death grip, drag strip, ear clip, equip, felt-tip, field trip, filmstrip, flagship, foul tip, friendship, frostnip, guilt-trip, gunship, half-slip, handgrip, hardship, harelip, horsewhip, judgeship, jump ship, kinship, let rip, longship, lordship, nonslip, palship, pink slip, road trip, rose hip, round-trip, sales slip, sideslip, spaceship, starship, steamship, tall ship, township, transship, troopship, unzip, V-chip, warship • authorship, battleship, brinkmanship, censorship, chairmanship, comic strip, crack the whip, dealership, draftsmanship, ego trip, ego-trip, fellowship, filter tip, fingertip, gamesmanship, Gaza Strip, horsemanship, internship, ladyship, landing strip, leadership, marksmanship, membership, microchip, mother ship, motor ship, ownership, paper clip, partnership, penmanship, pistol grip, pistol-whip, power strip, readership, rocket ship, scholarship, seamanship, showmanship, skinny-dip, sponsorship, sportsmanship, statesmanship, stewardship, swordsmanship, underlip, viewership, weather strip, workmanship • apprenticeship, championship, citizenship, companionship, containership, dictatorship, factory ship, Freudian slip, good-fellowship, guardianship, median strip, Möbius strip, musicianship, one-upmanship, partisanship, postnasal drip, potato chip, receivership, rejection slip, relationship, run a tight ship, shoot from the hip, stiff upper lip • bipartisanship, nonpartisanship

ipal \ē-pəl\ see EOPLE

ipari \ip-rē\ see IPPERY

ipatus \ip-ət-əs\ see IPITOUS

ipe \īp\ gripe, hype, pipe, ripe, snipe, stripe, swipe, tripe, type, wipe • bagpipe, blood type, blowpipe, drainpipe, half-pipe, hornpipe, pitch pipe, panpipe, pinstripe, sideswipe, stovepipe, tailpipe, touch-type, unripe, windpipe • archetype, corncob pipe, guttersnipe, overripe, prototype, Teletype • daguerreotype, stereotype

iped \īpt\ striped • pin-striped

—*also* -ed *forms of verbs listed at* IPE

ipend \ī-pənd\ ripened, stipend

iper \ī-pər\ diaper, griper, hyper, piper, riper, sniper, viper, wiper • bagpiper, pied piper, pit viper, sandpiper • candy striper, pay the piper • stereotyper

ipety \ip-ət-ē\ snippety • serendipity

iph \if\ see IFF

iphany \if-ə-nē\ see IPHONY

ipher \ī-fər\ cipher, lifer • decipher, pro-lifer • right-to-lifer

iphon \ī-fən\ see YPHEN

iphony \if-ə-nē\ Tiffany • epiphany, polyphony

ipi \ē-pē\ see EEPY

ipid \ip-əd\ lipid • insipid

iping \ī-piŋ\ piping, striping • blood-typing
—*also* -ing *forms of verbs listed at* IPE

ipit \ip-ət\ see IPPET

ipitous \ip-ət-əs\ precipitous • serendipitous

ipity \ip-ət-ē\ see IPETY

iple[1] \ip-əl\ see IPPLE

iple[2] \ī-pəl\ see YPAL

ipless \ip-ləs\ dripless, lipless, zipless

ipling \ip-liŋ\ Kipling, stripling
—*also* -ing *forms of verbs listed at* IPPLE

ipment \ip-mənt\ shipment • equipment, transshipment

ipo \ēp-ō\ see EPOT

ipoli \ip-ə-lē\ see IPPILY

ippe[1] \ip\ see IP

ippe[2] \ip-ē\ see IPPY

ippe[3] \ēp\ see EEP

ipped \ipt\ see IPT

ippee \ip-ē\ see IPPY

ipper \ip-ər\ chipper, clipper, flipper, gripper, kipper, nipper, ripper, shipper, skipper, slipper, tipper, zipper • Big Dipper, day-tripper, horsewhipper, Yom Kippur • double-dipper, ego-tripper, lady's slipper, Little Dipper, skinny-dipper

ippery \ip-rē\ frippery, slippery

ippet \ip-ət\ snippet, whippet

ippety \ip-ət-ē\ see IPETY

ippi \ip-ē\ see IPPY

ippie \ip-ē\ see IPPY

ippily \ip-ə-lē\ Tripoli • Gallipoli

ipping \ip-iŋ\ clipping, ripping, shipping, whipping • double-dipping, skinny-dipping
—*also* -ing *forms of verbs listed at* IP

ipple \ip-əl\ cripple, ripple, stipple, tipple, triple • participle

ippur \ip-ər\ see IPPER

ippy \ip-ē\ dippy, drippy, hippie, hippy, lippy, nippy, Skippy, snippy, tippy, yippee, zippy • Xanthippe • Mississippi

ips \ips\ snips • eclipse, ellipse, midships • amidships, fish-and-chips • apocalypse, lunar eclipse, solar eclipse, total eclipse
—*also* -s, -'s, *and* -s' *forms of nouns and* -s *forms of verbs listed at* IP

ipse \ips\ see IPS

ipster \ip-stər\ hipster, tipster

ipsy \ip-sē\ see YPSY

ipt \ipt\ crypt, hipped, ripped, script • conscript, harelipped, postscript, tight-lipped, transcript, typescript • manuscript, nondescript, shooting script
—*also* -ed *forms of verbs listed at* IP

iptic \ip-tik\ see YPTIC

iption \ip-shən\ conniption, description, Egyptian, encryption, inscription, prescription, subscription, transcription • nonprescription

iptych \ip-tik\ see YPTIC

ique \ēk\ see EAK[1]

iquey \ē-kē\ see EAKY

iquish \ē-kish\ see EAKISH

iquitous \ik-wət-əs\ iniquitous, ubiquitous

iquity \ik-wət-ē\ antiquity, iniquity, ubiquity

iquor \ik-ər\ see ICKER[1]

ir[1] \ir\ see EER[2]

ir[2] \ər\ see EUR[1]

ira[1] \ir-ə\ see ERA[2]

ira[2] \ī-rə\ see YRA

iracle \ir-i-kəl\ see ERICAL[2]

irae \īr-ē\ see IRY

iral \ī-rəl\ spiral, viral

irant \ī-rənt\ tyrant • aspirant

irate \ir-ət\ see IRIT

irby \ər-bē\ see ERBY

irca \ər-kə\ see URKA

irce \ər-sē\ see ERCY

irch \ərch\ see URCH

irchen \ər-kən\ see IRKIN

ircon \ər-kən\ see IRKIN

ircular \ər-kyə-lər\ circular • tubercular • semicircular

ird \ərd\ bird, curd, furred, gird, heard, herd, nerd, third, word • absurd, bean curd, bellbird, blackbird, bluebird, buzzword, byword, Cape Verde, catbird, catchword, cowbird, cowherd, crossword, cussword, game bird, goatherd, good word, guide word, headword, jailbird, jaybird, kingbird, last word, lovebird, lyrebird, password, rainbird, redbird, reword, ricebird, seabird, Sigurd, shorebird, snakebird, snowbird, songbird, state bird, sunbird, surfbird, swearword, swineherd, textured, unheard, watchword, yardbird • afterword, bowerbird, butcher-bird, cedarbird, dickey bird, dirty word, early bird, fighting word, frigate bird, hummingbird, in a word, ladybird, mockingbird, ovenbird, overheard, tailorbird, thunderbird, undergird, wading bird, weaverbird, whirlybird, word for word
—*also* -ed *forms of verbs listed at* EUR[1]

irder \ərd-ər\ see ERDER

irdie \ərd-ē\ see URDY

irdle \ərd-ᵊl\ see URDLE

ire[1] \īr\ briar, choir, dire, drier, fire, flier, friar, fryer, hire, ire, liar, lyre, mire, prior, pyre, shire, sire, spire, squire, tire, Tyre, wire • acquire, admire, afire, aspire, attire, backfire, barbed wire, barbwire, blow-dryer, bonfire, brushfire, bushfire, campfire, catbrier, catch fire, cease-fire, conspire, cross fire, denier, desire, empire, Empire, entire, esquire, expire, for hire, fox fire, grandsire, greenbrier, gunfire, haywire, hellfire, high-wire, hot-wire, inquire, inspire, live wire, misfire, on fire, perspire, prior, quagmire, require, respire, retire, sapphire, satire, Shropshire, snow tire, spitfire, surefire, suspire, sweetbriar, tightwire, town crier, transpire, trip wire, umpire, vampire, wildfire • amplifier, ball of fire, balloon tire, beautifier, chicken wire, like wildfire, multiplier, pacifier, play with fire, qualifier, rapid-fire, razor wire, retrofire, signifier, simplifier, star sapphire, under fire • British Empire, down-to-the-wire, identifier, intensifier, under the wire, water saffire • concertina wire, iron in the fire • Holy Roman Empire
—*also* -er *forms of adjectives listed at* Y[1]

ire[2] \ir\ see EER[2]

ire[3] \īr-ē\ see IRY

ire[4] \ər\ see EUR[1]

ired \īrd\ fired, spired, tired, wired • hardwired, inspired, retired
—*also* -ed *forms of verbs listed at* IRE[1]

ireless \īr-ləs\ tireless, wireless
ireman \īr-mən\ fireman, wireman
irement \īr-mənt\ acquirement, environment, requirement, retirement
iren \ī-rən\ Byron, Myron, siren • environ
irge \ərj\ see URGE
irgin \ər-jən\ see URGEON
iri \ir-ē\ see EARY
iriam \ir-ē-əm\ see ERIUM
iric \ir-ik\ see ERIC[2]
irile \ir-əl\ see ERAL[1]
irin \ī-rən\ see IREN
irine \ī-rən\ see IREN
iring \īr-iŋ\ firing, wiring • inspiring, retiring
—*also* -ing *forms of verbs listed at* IRE[1]
irious \ir-ē-əs\ see ERIOUS
iris \ī-rəs\ see IRUS
irish \īr-ish\ Irish • vampirish
irit \ir-ət\ spirit • dispirit, free spirit • Holy Spirit
irium \ir-ē-əm\ see ERIUM
irius \ir-ē-əs\ see ERIOUS
irk \ərk\ see ORK[1]
irker \ər-kər\ see ORKER[1]
irkie \ər-kē\ see ERKY
irkin \ər-kən\ firkin, gherkin, jerkin, zircon
irky \ər-kē\ see ERKY
irl \ərl\ churl, curl, earl, Earl, furl, girl, hurl, Merle, pearl, Pearl, purl, squirrel, swirl, twirl, whirl • awhirl, ball girl, bat girl, cowgirl, home girl, pin curl, playgirl, salesgirl, schoolgirl, shopgirl, showgirl, spit curl, uncurl, unfurl • Camp Fire girl, chorus girl, cover girl, flower girl, pinup girl, poster girl, Valley girl • mother-of-pearl
irler \ər-lər\ curler, twirler
irley \ər-lē\ see URLY
irlie \ər-lē\ see URLY
irling \ər-liŋ\ see URLING

irlish \ər-lish\ see URLISH
irly \ər-lē\ see URLY
irm \ərm\ see ORM[1]
irma \ər-mə\ see ERMA
irmess \ər-məs\ see ERMIS
irmy \ər-mē\ see ERMY
irn \ərn\ see URN
iro[1] \ir-ō\ see ERO[3]
iro[2] \ē-rō\ see ERO[1]
iro[3] \ī-rō\ see YRO[1]
iron[1] \īrn\ iron • andiron, cast-iron, environ, flatiron, gridiron, pig iron, pump iron, steam iron, wrought iron • climbing iron, curling iron, shooting iron, waffle iron • soldering iron
iron[2] \ī-rən\ see IREN
ironment \īr-mənt\ see IREMENT
irp \ərp\ see URP
irpy \ər-pē\ chirpy • Euterpe
irque \ərk\ see ORK[1]
irr[1] \ir\ see EER[2]
irr[2] \ər\ see EUR[1]
irra \ir-ə\ see ERA[2]
irrah \ir-ə\ see ERA[2]
irrel[1] \ərl\ see IRL
irrel[2] \ər-əl\ see ERRAL
irrely \ər-lē\ see URLY
irrhous \ir-əs\ see EROUS
irring \ər-iŋ\ see URRING
irror \ir-ər\ see EARER[2]
irrup \ər-əp\ chirrup, stirrup, syrup • corn syrup, cough syrup • maple syrup
irrupy \ər-ə-pē\ chirrupy, syrupy
irrus \ir-əs\ see EROUS
irry \ər-ē\ see URRY
irs \irz\ see IERS
irse[1] \irs\ see IERCE
irse[2] \ərs\ see ERSE
irst \ərst\ see URST
irt \ərt\ see ERT[1]
irted \ərt-əd\ see ERTED
irter \ərt-ər\ see ERTER
irth \ərth\ berth, birth, dearth, earth, firth, girth, mirth, Perth, worth • childbirth, Farnsworth,

Fort Worth, give birth, on earth, rebirth, scorched-earth, self-worth, stillbirth, unearth, Wool-worth, Wordsworth • down-to-earth, pennyworth, Solway Firth, two cents' worth, virgin birth

irthless \ərth-ləs\ mirthless, worthless

irting \ərt-iŋ\ see ERTING

irtle \ərt-ᵊl\ see ERTILE

irtually \ərch-lē\ see URCHLY

irty \ərt-ē\ dirty, flirty, QWERTY, thirty

irus \ī-rəs\ Cyrus, iris, Iris, Skyros, virus • desirous, Osiris, papyrus • bearded iris, rhinovirus, rotavirus, West Nile virus

irv \ərv\ see ERVE

irving \ər-viŋ\ see ERVING

irwin \ər-wən\ see ERWIN

iry \īr-ē\ diary, eyrie, friary, miry, wiry • expiry, inquiry

is¹ \is\ see ISS

is² \iz\ see IZ¹

is³ \ē\ see EE¹

is⁴ \ēs\ see IECE

is⁵ \ish\ see ISH¹

i's \īz\ see IZE¹

isa \ē-zə\ see EZA

isable \ī-zə-bəl\ see IZABLE

isal¹ \ī-səl\ sisal • paradisal

isal² \ī-zəl\ Geisel, sisal • reprisal, revisal, surprisal • paradisal

isan \is-ᵊn\ see ISTEN

isbane \iz-bən\ see ISBON

isbon \iz-bən\ Brisbane, Lisbon

isc \isk\ see ISK

iscate \is-kət\ see ISKET

isce \is\ see ISS

iscean¹ \ī-sē-ən\ Piscean • Dionysian

iscean² \is-ē-ən\ see YSIAN¹

ische \ēsh\ see ICHE²

iscia \ish-ə\ see ITIA¹

iscible \is-ə-bəl\ see ISSIBLE

iscient \ish-ənt\ see ICIENT

isco \is-kō\ disco • Francisco • San Francisco

iscous \is-kəs\ see ISCUS

iscuit \is-kət\ see ISKET

iscus \is-kəs\ discus, viscous • hibiscus

ise¹ \ēs\ see IECE

ise² \ēz\ see EZE

ise³ \īs\ see ICE¹

ise⁴ \īz\ see IZE¹

ised¹ \ist\ see IST¹

ised² \īzd\ see IZED

isel \iz-əl\ see IZZLE

iseled \iz-əld\ see IZZLED

iseler \iz-lər\ see IZZLER

isement \īz-mənt\ chastisement, disguisement • advertisement, enfranchisement

iser \ī-zər\ see IZER

ish¹ \ish\ dish, fish, squish, swish, whish, wish • blindfish, blowfish, bluefish, bonefish, catfish, clownfish, codfish, cold fish, crawfish, crayfish, death wish, deep-dish, dogfish, finfish, flatfish, fly-fish, game fish, garfish, goldfish, goosefish, hagfish, hogfish, jewfish, kingfish, knish, lungfish, monkfish, moonfish, panfish, pipefish, redfish, rockfish, sailfish, sawfish, shellfish, side dish, spearfish, sport fish, starfish, sunfish, swordfish, toadfish, trash fish, whitefish • angelfish, anglerfish, bony fish, chafing dish, cuttlefish, flying fish, jellyfish, John Bullish, lionfish, needlefish, overfish, petri dish, pilot fish, puffer fish, silverfish • gefilte fish, kettle of fish, satellite dish, tropical fish, walking catfish

ish² \ēsh\ see ICHE²

isha \ish-ə\ see ITIA¹

isher \ish-ər\ fisher, fissure • kingfisher, well-wisher

ishi \ē-shē\ chichi • maharishi

ishing \ish-iŋ\ fly-fishing, sportfishing, well-wishing

—*also* -ing *forms of verbs listed at* ISH[1]

ishioner \ish-nər\ see ITIONER

ishna \ish-nə\ Krishna, Mishnah

ishnah \ish-nə\ see ISHNA

ishu \ish-ü\ see ISSUE[1]

ishy \ish-ē\ fishy, squishy, swishy

isi[1] \ē-zē\ see EASY[1]

isi[2] \ē-sē\ see EECY

isia \ē-zhə\ see ESIA[2]

isian[1] \izh-ən\ see ISION

isian[2] \ē-zhən\ see ESIAN[1]

isible \iz-ə-bəl\ risible, visible • divisible, invisible • indivisible

isin \i-zən\ see ISON[2]

ising \ī-ziŋ\ see IZING

ision \izh-ən\ fission, vision • collision, concision, decision, derision, division, elision, elysian, envision, incision, Parisian, precision, provision, revision, Tunisian • cell division, circumcision, Dionysian, double vision, field of vision, imprecision, indecision, long division, short division, split decision, subdivision, supervision, television, tunnel vision

isional \izh-nəl\ divisional, provisional

isis \ī-səs\ crisis, Isis • Dionysus, midlife crisis

isit \iz-ət\ visit • exquisite, revisit

isite \iz-ət\ see ISIT

isitor \iz-ət-ər\ visitor • inquisitor

isive \ī-siv\ decisive, derisive, divisive, incisive • indecisive

isk \isk\ bisque, brisk, disk, frisk, risk, whisk • fly whisk, hard disk, slipped disk • asterisk, basilisk, compact disc, floppy disk, laser disc, obelisk, optic disk • optical disk, videodisc

isket \is-kət\ biscuit, brisket

iskey \is-kē\ see ISKY

iskie \is-kē\ see ISKY

isky \is-kē\ frisky, risky, whiskey

island \ī-lənd\ see IGHLAND

islander \ī-lən-dər\ see IGHLANDER

islands \ī-lənz\ see IGHLANDS

isle \īl\ see ILE[1]

isles \īlz\ see ILES

islet \ī-lət\ see ILOT

isling \iz-liŋ\ brisling, quisling

isly \iz-lē\ see IZZLY

ism \iz-əm\ ism, prism, schism • abysm, ageism, autism, baptism, bossism, Buddhism, charism, cubism, czarism, dwarfism, fascism, Maoism, Marxism, Nazism, nudism, racism, sadism, sexism, snobbism, Taoism, theism, tourism, truism • activism, alarmism, altruism, anarchism, aneurysm, animism, aphorism, archaism, atheism, barbarism, botulism, Briticism, Calvinism, careerism, Castroism, cataclysm, catechism, chauvinism, classicism, communism, criticism, cynicism, Darwinism, defeatism, despotism, dogmatism, dualism, dynamism, egoism, egotism, elitism, escapism, euphemism, exorcism, extremism, fatalism, feminism, feudalism, fogyism, formalism, futurism, globalism, gnosticism, gradualism, heathenism, Hebraism, hedonism, Hellenism, heroism, Hinduism, Hitlerism, humanism, hypnotism, idealism, Islamism, jingoism, journalism, John Bullism, Judaism, legalism, Leninism, lyricism, magnetism, mannerism, masochism, mechanism, methodism, me-tooism, modernism, monarchism, moralism, Mormonism, mysticism, narcissism, nationalism, nepotism, nihilism, NIMBYism, nomadism, occultism, optimism, organism, ostracism, pacifism, paganism, pantheism, paroxysm, pessimism,

plagiarism, pointillism, populism,
pragmatism, Quakerism, realism,
rheumatism, satanism, Semitism,
Shakerism, Shamanism, Shinto-
ism, skepticism, socialism, sole-
cism, solipsism, Southernism,
spiritism, Stalinism, stoicism,
syllogism, symbolism, terrorism,
tribalism, unionism, urbanism,
vandalism, veganism, vocalism,
vulgarism, warlordism, witticism,
Zionism • absenteeism, abso-
lutism, Africanism, alcoholism,
anachronism, Anglicanism, antag-
onism, astigmatism, athleticism,
behaviorism, Big Brotherism,
bilingualism, cannibalism, capital-
ism, Catholicism, commercialism,
Confucianism, conservatism,
consumerism, creationism, eco-
tourism, empiricism, ethnocen-
trism, evangelism, exoticism,
expressionism, factionalism,
fanaticism, favoritism, federalism,
hooliganism, impressionism,
infantilism, Keynesianism, liberal-
ism, Lutheranism, McCarthyism,
mercantilism, metabolism, mili-
tarism, minimalism, monasticism,
monotheism, negativism, neo-
Nazism, opportunism, pacificism,
parallelism, paternalism, patriot-
ism, perfectionism, photo-realism,
postmodernism, primitivism,
progressivism, protectionism,
Protestantism, provincialism,
puritanism, radicalism, rational-
ism, regionalism, revisionism,
revivalism, romanticism, scholas-
ticism, sectionalism, secularism,
somnambulism, surrealism, ven-
triloquism • abolitionism, anti-
Semitism, colloquialism,
colonialism, hyperrealism, imperi-
alism, isolationism, materialism,
neoclassicism, orientalism, photo-
journalism, Postimpressionism,

professionalism, sensationalism,
spiritualism, traditionalism, tran-
scendentalism, universalism

ismal \iz-məl\ see YSMAL

isme[1] \īm\ see IME[1]

isme[2] \izᵊm\ see ISM

isom \iz-əm\ see ISM

ison[1] \īs-ᵊn\ bison, Meissen, Tyson
• streptomycin

ison[2] \iz-ᵊn\ prison, risen • arisen,
imprison

isor \ī-zər\ see IZER

isory \īz-rē\ advisory • supervisory

isp \isp\ crisp, lisp, wisp • will-o-
the-wisp

isper \is-pər\ crisper, lisper, whisper • stage whisper

ispy \is-pē\ crispy, wispy

isque \isk\ see ISK

iss \is\ bliss, Chris, dis, Dis, hiss,
kiss, miss, sis, Swiss, this • abyss,
amiss, can't-miss, dismiss, French
kiss, near miss, remiss • amber-
gris, hit-and-miss, hit-or-miss,
junior miss, reminisce

issa \is-ə\ abscissa, Larissa, Melissa

issable \is-ə-bəl\ see ISSIBLE

issal \is-əl\ see ISTLE

isse[1] \is\ see ISS

isse[2] \ēs\ see IECE

issed \ist\ see IST[2]

issel \is-əl\ see ISTLE

issible \is-ə-bəl\ kissable, miscible
• admissible, municipal, omissi-
ble, permissible, transmissible
• impermissible, inadmissible

issile \is-əl\ see ISTLE

ission[1] \ish-ən\ see ITION

ission[2] \izh-ən\ see ISION

issioner \ish-nər\ see ITIONER

issive \is-iv\ missive • derisive,
dismissive, permissive, submis-
sive, transmissive

issor \iz-ər\ scissor, whizzer

issue[1] \ish-ü\ issue, tissue • nonis-
sue, reissue, scar tissue, take issue
• Mogadishu

issue[2] \ish-ə\ see ITIA[1]

issure \ish-ər\ see ISHER

issus \is-əs\ missus, Mrs. • narcissus, Narcissus

issy \is-ē\ missy, prissy, sissy

ist[1] \īst\ Christ, heist • zeitgeist • Antichrist, poltergeist
—*also* -ed *forms of verbs listed at* ICE[1]

ist[2] \ist\ cyst, fist, gist, grist, list, Liszt, mist, schist, tryst, twist, whist, wrist • A-list, assist, blacklist, checklist, consist, desist, enlist, exist, hit list, insist, persist, playlist, resist, short list, subsist, untwist, wish list • coexist, exorcist • love-in-a-mist
—*also* -ed *forms of verbs listed at* ISS

ist[3] \ēst\ see EAST[1]

ista \ē-stə\ barista • fashionista, Sandinista • hasta la vista

istaed \is-təd\ see ISTED

istal \is-t°l\ Bristol, crystal, Crystal, pistil, pistol

istan \is-tən\ see ISTON

istance \is-təns\ see ISTENCE

istant \is-tənt\ see ISTENT

iste[1] \is-tē\ see ICITY[2]

iste[2] \ēst\ see EAST[1]

isted \is-təd\ closefisted, enlisted, hardfisted, limp-wristed, tightfisted, two-fisted, unlisted • ironfisted, unassisted
—*also* -ed *forms of verbs listed at* IST[2]

istel \is-t°l\ see IST[2]

isten \is-°n\ christen, glisten, listen

istence \is-təns\ distance • assistance, existence, insistence, longdistance, outdistance, persistence, resistance, subsistence • coexistence, go the distance, keep one's distance, nonexistence, shouting distance, striking distance • passive resistance, public assistance

istent \is-tənt\ distant • assistant, consistent, insistent, persistent, resistant • equidistant, inconsistent, nonexistent

ister \is-tər\ blister, glister, lister, Lister, mister, sister, twister • half sister, resister, resistor, solicitor, stepsister, tongue twister, transistor • water blister

istery \is-trē\ see ISTORY

isthmus \is-məs\ see ISTMAS

isti \is-tē\ see ICITY[2]

istic \is-tik\ mystic • artistic, autistic, ballistic, fascistic, holistic, linguistic, logistic, sadistic, simplistic, sophistic, statistic, stylistic • altruistic, anarchistic, animistic, aphoristic, atavistic, atheistic, egoistic, egotistic, euphemistic, fatalistic, futuristic, hedonistic, humanistic, idealistic, inartistic, jingoistic, journalistic, legalistic, masochistic, modernistic, moralistic, narcissistic, nationalistic, nihilistic, optimistic, pessimistic, realistic, unrealistic • anachronistic, antagonistic, cannibalistic, capitalistic, characteristic, impressionistic, militaristic, opportunistic, paternalistic, propagandistic • imperialistic, materialistic

istical \is-ti-kəl\ mystical • logistical, statistical • egotistical

istich \is-tik\ see ISTIC

istics \is-tiks\ ballistics, linguistics, statistics • vital statistics
—*also* -s, -'s, *and* -s' *forms of nouns listed at* ISTIC

istie \is-tē\ see ICITY[2]

istil \is-t°l\ see ISTAL

istin \is-tən\ see ISTON

istine \is-tən\ see ISTON

istle \is-əl\ bristle, gristle, missal, missile, thistle, whistle • bull thistle, cruise missile, dismissal, epistle, globe thistle, wolf whistle • blow the whistle, guided missile, wet one's whistle • ballistic missile

istler \is-lər\ whistler, Whistler

istly \is-lē\ bristly, gristly, thistly • sweet cicely

istmas \is-məs\ Christmas, isthmus

isto \is-tō\ Christo • Callisto

istol \is-t³l\ see ISTAL

iston \is-tən\ Kristin, piston, Tristan

istor \is-tər\ see ISTER

istory \is-trē\ history, mystery • life history, prehistory • ancient history, natural history, oral history

isty \is-tē\ see ICITY²

isus \ī-səs\ see ISIS

iszt \ist\ see IST²

it¹ \it\ bit, Brit, chit, fit, flit, git, grit, hit, it, kit, knit, lit, mitt, nit, pit, quit, sit, skit, slit, snit, spit, split, twit, whit, wit, writ, zit • a bit, acquit, admit, armpit, base hit, befit, bowsprit, Brigitte, catch it, close-knit, cockpit, commit, cool it, culprit, cut it, dimwit, dog it, emit, firelit, gaslit, get it, gill slit, half-wit, hard-hit, house-sit, legit, make it, mess kit, misfit, moonlit, mosh pit, nitwit, no-hit, obit, omit, outfit, outwit, owe it, permit, pinch-hit, press kit, pulpit, refit, remit, rough it, sandpit, Sanskrit, starlit, submit, sunlit, switch-hit, tar pit, tidbit, tightknit, to wit, transmit, twilit, twobit, unfit, watch it, well-knit, with-it • babysit, benefit, bit-by-bit, cable-knit, candlelit, come off it, counterfeit, double knit, get with it, hissy fit, holy writ, hypocrite, infield hit, megahit, out of it, put to it, recommit, retrofit, step on it • banana split, bully pulpit, extra-base hit, fringe benefit, lickety-split, overcommit, sacrifice hit • jack-in-the-pulpit

it² \ē\ see EE¹

it³ \ēt\ see EAT¹

ita \ēt-ə\ cheetah, Nita, pita, Rita • Anita, Bonita, bonito, fajita, gordita, Granita, Juanita, Lolita • senhorita, señorita • Bhagavad Gita

itable¹ \īt-ə-bəl\ citable, writable • excitable, ignitable, indictable • copyrightable, extraditable

itable² \it-ə-bəl\ see ITTABLE

itae \īt-ē\ see ITE²

itain \it-n\ see ITTEN

ital¹ \īt-³l\ title, vital • entitle, recital, requital, subtitle

ital² \it-³l\ see ITTLE

italist \īt-³l-əst\ titlist • recitalist

itan \īt-³n\ see IGHTEN

itany \it-³n-ē\ Brittany, litany

itch \ich\ ditch, glitch, hitch, itch, kitsch, niche, pitch, rich, snitch, stitch, such, switch, twitch, which, witch • backstitch, bewitch, Bowditch, chain stitch, clove hitch, cross-stitch, enrich, fast-pitch, half hitch, jock itch, last-ditch, purl stitch, slow-pitch, topstitch, unhitch, whipstitch, wild pitch • bait and switch, czarevitch, featherstitch, fever pitch, perfect pitch, timber hitch, toggle switch • absolute pitch

itcher \ich-ər\ pitcher, richer, snitcher, stitcher, switcher

itchery \ich-ə-rē\ witchery • obituary

itches \ich-əz\ britches, riches • in stitches • Dutchman's-breeches —*also* -s, -'s, *and* -s' *forms of nouns and* -s *forms of verbs listed at* ITCH

itchman \ich-mən\ pitchman, switchman

itchment \ich-mənt\ bewitchment, enrichment • self-enrichment

itchy \ich-ē\ glitchy, itchy, pitchy, twitchy, witchy

it'd \it-əd\ see ITTED

ite¹ \īt\ bight, bite, blight, bright, byte, cite, Dwight, fight, flight,

fright, height, kite, knight, light,
lite, might, mite, night, plight,
quite, right, rite, sight, site,
sleight, slight, smite, spite, sprite,
Sprite, tight, trite, white, Wright,
write • affright, airtight, Albright,
alight, all right, all-night, aright,
backbite, backlight, bauxite,
birthright, black light, bobwhite,
bombsight, box kite, bullfight,
calcite, campsite, catfight, cock-
fight, contrite, cordite, daylight,
delight, despite, dogfight, down-
right, dust mite, earthlight, excite,
eyesight, fanlight, finite, firefight,
firelight, first night, fistfight,
flashlight, fleabite, floodlight,
foresight, forthright, fortnight,
frostbite, gall mite, gaslight,
ghostwrite, graphite, green light,
gunfight, Gunite, half-light, hand-
write, headlight, highlight, hind-
sight, Hittite, homesite, hoplite,
ignite, in-flight, incite, indict,
insight, in sight, invite, klieg light,
lamplight, Levite, lignite, lime-
light, Lucite, Luddite, midnight,
moonlight, night-light, off-site,
off-white, on sight, on-site, out-
right, penlight, playwright, polite,
preflight, prizefight, pyrite,
quartzite, recite, red light, re-
quite, rewrite, searchlight, Semite,
Shiite, shipwright, sidelight, sit
tight, skintight, skylight, skywrite,
snakebite, snow-white, sound
bite, spaceflight, spotlight, stage
fright, starlight, stoplight, street-
light, sunlight, Sunnite, taillight,
termite, tonight, top-flight, torch-
light, Twelfth Night, twilight, twi-
night, typewrite, unite, upright,
uptight, Web site, weeknight,
wheelwright, zinc white • acolyte,
Ammonite, anchorite, anthracite,
antiwhite, apartheid, appetite,
Bakelite, bedlamite, bipartite,

black-and-white, bring to light,
Brooklynite, Canaanite, candle-
light, Carmelite, cellulite, chestnut blight, Chinese white,
copyright, disunite, divine right,
dolomite, dynamite, erudite,
expedite, extradite, Fahrenheit,
featherlight, fight-or-flight, fly-by-
night, gesundheit, gigabyte,
Hashemite, Hitlerite, Houstonite,
impolite, inner light, Isle of
Wight, Israelite, Jacobite, Jerseyite, kilobyte, leading light,
Leninite, leukocyte, lily-white,
line of sight, lymphocyte, mag-
netite, malachite, Masonite,
megabyte, Mennonite, Mr. Right,
Muscovite, neophyte, out-of-
sight, overbite, overflight,
overnight, oversight, parasite,
patent right, pilot light, plebiscite,
recondite, reunite, running light,
satellite, second sight, see the
light, serve one right, socialite,
speed of light, stalactite, stalag-
mite, Sydneyite, traffic light,
transvestite, tripartite, troglodyte,
ultralight, underwrite, urbanite,
water sprite, watertight • anti-
Semite, cosmopolite, electrolyte,
exurbanite, go fly a kite, her-
maphrodite, meteorite, Michigan-
ite, multipartite, New
Hampshirite, New Jerseyite, potato blight, property right, subur-
banite, sweetness and light,
Turkish delight, Wyomingite
• Great Australian Bight, Pre-
Raphaelite
ite² \īt-ē\ flighty, mighty, nightie
• almighty, Almighty • Aphrodite,
arborvitae, high and mighty
ite³ \it\ see IT¹
ite⁴ \ēt\ see EAT¹
ited \īt-əd\ see IGHTED
iteful \īt-fəl\ see IGHTFUL
itely \īt-lē\ see IGHTLY

item \īt-əm\ item • line-item • ad infinitum, collector's item

itement \īt-mənt\ excitement, incitement, indictment

iten \īt-ᵊn\ see IGHTEN

itener \īt-nər\ see IGHTENER

iteor \ēt-ē-ər\ see ETEOR

iter[1] \īt-ər\ biter, fighter, lighter, miter, writer • all-nighter, backbiter, bullfighter, dogfighter, firefighter, ghostwriter, gunfighter, highlighter, igniter, inciter, lamplighter, moonlighter, nail-biter, prizefighter, rewriter, screenwriter, scriptwriter, skywriter, songwriter, speechwriter, sportswriter, street fighter, typewriter • candlelighter, copywriter, fly-by-nighter, freedom fighter, underwriter
—*also* -er *forms of adjectives listed at* ITE[1]

iter[2] \it-ər\ see ITTER

iter[3] \ēt-ər\ see EATER[1]

iterally \it-ər-lē\ see ITTERLY

ites \īts\ see IGHTS

itey \īt-ē\ see ITE[2]

ith[1] \ith\ fifth, kith, myth, pith, smith, Smith, with • bear with, blacksmith, do with, forthwith, goldsmith, Goldsmith, go with, gunsmith, herewith, hold with, live with, locksmith, run with, tinsmith • be friends with, come out with, come up with, complete with, coppersmith, dispense with, fall in with, Granny Smith, have done with, make off with, megalith, monolith, put up with, reckon with, run off with, silversmith, take up with, walk off with • come to grips with, do away with, get away with, get even with, have to do with, make away with, run away with, wipe the floor with

ith[2] \ēt\ see EAT[1]

ith[3] \ēth\ see EATH[1]

ithe[1] \īth\ blithe, lithe, scythe, tithe, writhe

ithe[2] \ith\ see ITH[2]

ithe[3] \ith\ see ITH[1]

ither \ith-ər\ dither, hither, slither, thither, whither, wither, zither • come-hither

ithy \ith-ē\ pithy, smithy

iti \ēt-ē\ see EATY

itia[1] \ish-ə\ Alicia, Letitia, militia, Patricia, Phoenicia • Dionysia

itia[2] \ē-shə\ see ESIA[1]

itial \ish-əl\ see ICIAL

itian[1] \ish-ən\ see ITION

itian[2] \ē-shən\ see ETION[1]

itiate \ish-ət\ initiate, novitiate

itic \it-ik\ critic • arthritic, granitic, Semitic • analytic, catalytic, dynamitic, paralytic, parasitic, sybaritic • anti-Semitic, hermaphroditic

itical \it-i-kəl\ critical • political, uncritical • analytical • geopolitical

itid \it-əd\ see ITTED

itimati \is-məs\ see ISTMAS

itin \īt-ᵊn\ see IGHTEN

iting \īt-iŋ\ biting, lighting, writing • backbiting, bullfighting, cockfighting, exciting, handwriting, infighting, inviting, nail-biting, newswriting, playwriting, prizefighting, skywriting, songwriting, typewriting
—*also* -ing *forms of verbs listed at* ITE[1]

ition \ish-ən\ fission, mission, Titian • addition, admission, ambition, attrition, audition, beautician, clinician, cognition, commission, condition, contrition, dentition, edition, emission, fruition, ignition, logician, magician, mortician, munition, musician, nutrition, omission, optician, partition, patrician, perdition, permission, petition, Phoenician, physician, position, remission, rendition, sedition, submission, suspicion, tactician, technician, tradition, transition, transmission, tuition, volition • abolition, acoustician, acquisition, admonition, air-condition, ammunition, apparition, coalition, competition, composition, decommission, definition, demolition, deposition, dietitian, Dionysian, disposition, disquisition, electrician, erudition, exhibition, expedition, exposition, extradition, imposition, in addition, inhibition, inquisition, intermission, intuition, malnutrition, mathematician, obstetrician, on commission, opposition, politician, precondition, premonition, preposition, prohibition, proposition, recognition, recondition, repetition, requisition, rescue mission, rhetorician, statistician, superstition, supposition, transposition • decomposition, dental technician, family physician, fetal position, general admission, high-definition, indisposition, juxtaposition, lotus position, open admission, out of commission, pediatrician, pocket edition, redefinition, theoretician

itional \ish-nəl\ additional, conditional, nutritional, traditional, transitional • definitional, prepositional, unconditional

itioner \i-shə-nər\ commissioner, conditioner, parishioner, petitioner, practitioner • air conditioner, nurse-practitioner • family practitioner, general practitioner

itionist \i-shə-nəst\ nutritionist • abolitionist, demolitionist, exhibitionist, prohibitionist

itious \ish-əs\ see ICIOUS[1]

itis \īt-əs\ Titus • arthritis, bronchitis, bursitis, colitis, detritus, gastritis, mastitis, nephritis, neuritis, phlebitis, tinnitus • cellulitis, dermatitis, gingivitis, hepatitis, laryngitis, meningitis, sinusitis, tonsillitis, tendinitis • appendicitis, conjunctivitis, encephalitis, endocarditis, peritonitis

itish \it-ish\ British, skittish

itius \ish-əs\ see ICIOUS[1]

itle \īt-ᵊl\ see ITAL[1]

it'll \it-ᵊl\ see ITTLE

itness \it-nəs\ fitness, witness • eyewitness, unfitness • character witness, Jehovah's Witness

itney \it-nē\ jitney, Whitney • Mount Whitney

ito[1] \ēt-ō\ Quito, Tito, veto • bandito, bonito, burrito, graffito, mosquito • Akihito, Hirohito, incognito, pocket veto • line-item veto

ito[2] \ēt-ə\ see ITA

iton[1] \it-ᵊn\ see ITTEN

iton[2] \īt-ᵊn\ see IGHTEN

its \its\ blitz, ditz, fritz, Fritz, glitz, grits, its, it's, quits, Ritz, spitz • Auschwitz, Berlitz, kibitz, Saint Kitts • Clausewitz, Horowitz, Saint Moritz • hominy grits —*also* -s, -'s, *and* -s' *forms of nouns and* -s *forms of verbs listed at* IT[1]

it's \its\ see ITS

itsch \ich\ see ITCH

itschy \ich-ē\ see ITCHY

itsy \it-sē\ see ITZY

itt \it\ see IT[1]

ittable \it-ə-bəl\ habitable, hospitable, transmittable • inhospitable

ittal \it-ᵊl\ see ITTLE

ittance \it-ᵊns\ pittance • admittance, remittance

ittany \it-ᵊn-ē\ see ITANY

itte \it\ see IT[1]

itted \it-əd\ fitted, it'd, pitted
• committed, dim-witted, half-witted, quick-witted, sharp-witted, slow-witted, thick-witted, unfitted • uncommitted
—*also* -ed *forms of verbs listed at* IT¹

ittee \it-ē\ *see* ITTY

itten \it-ᵊn\ bitten, Britain, Briton, kitten, Lytton, mitten, smitten, written • flea-bitten, Great Britain, hard-bitten, rewritten, unwritten

ittence \it-ᵊns\ *see* ITTANCE

itter \it-ər\ bitter, critter, fitter, flitter, fritter, glitter, hitter, litter, quitter, sitter, skitter, titter, twitter • aglitter, atwitter, embitter, emitter, fence-sitter, hairsplitter, house sitter, no-hitter, outfitter, pinch hitter, pipe fitter, rail-splitter, switch-hitter, transmitter • babysitter, counterfeiter, heavy hitter • neurotransmitter

itterer \it-ər-ər\ fritterer, litterer

itterly \it-ər-lē\ bitterly, literally

ittery \it-ə-rē\ glittery, jittery, skittery, twittery

ittie \it-ē\ *see* ITTY

ittier \it-ē-ər\ Whittier
—*also*-er *forms of adjectives listed at* ITTY

ittiness \it-ē-nəs\ grittiness, prettiness, wittiness

itting¹ \it-iŋ\ fitting, knitting, pitting, sitting, splitting, witting • befitting, earsplitting, fence-sitting, formfitting, hairsplitting, hard-hitting, house-sitting, pipe fitting, sidesplitting, unfitting, unwitting • unremitting
—*also* -ing *forms of verbs listed at* IT¹

itting² \it-ᵊn\ *see* ITTEN

ittish \it-ish\ *see* ITISH

ittle \it-ᵊl\ brittle, it'll, little, spittle, victual, whittle • acquittal, a little,

belittle, committal, hospital, lickspittle, transmittal • Chicken Little, noncommittal • little by little

ittol \it-ᵊl\ *see* ITTLE

ittor \it-ər\ *see* ITTER

itts \its\ *see* ITS

itty \it-ē\ bitty, city, ditty, gritty, kitty, Kitty, pity, pretty, witty • committee, Dodge City, self-pity, Sioux City • Carson City, central city, Hello Kitty, holy city, itty-bitty, Kansas City, megacity, New York City, nitty-gritty, Quezon City, Rapid City, Salt Lake City, subcommittee • Atlantic City, Ho Chi Minh City, Long Island City, Mexico City, Panama City, Vatican City

itual \ich-ə-wəl\ ritual • habitual

ituary \ich-ə-rē\ *see* ITCHERY

itum \īt-əm\ *see* ITEM

itus \īt-əs\ *see* ITIS

ity¹ \it-ē\ *see* ITTY

ity² \īt-ē\ *see* ITE²

itz \its\ *see* ITS

itzi \it-sē\ *see* ITZY

itzy \it-sē\ bitsy, ditzy, glitzy, Mitzi, ritzy

iu \ü\ *see* EW¹

ius¹ \ē-əs\ *see* EUS¹

ius² \ī-əs\ *see* IAS¹

iv¹ \iv\ *see* IVE²

iv² \ēf\ *see* IEF²

iv³ \if\ *see* IFF

iv⁴ \ēv\ *see* EAVE¹

iva¹ \ī-və\ Godiva, saliva

iva² \ē-və\ diva, Eva, kiva, Neva, Shiva, viva • Geneva, yeshiva

ivable¹ \ī-və-bəl\ drivable • derivable, survivable

ivable² \iv-ə-bəl\ livable • forgivable

ival \ī-vəl\ rival • archival, archrival, arrival, revival, survival • adjectival

ivalent \iv-ə-lənt\ ambivalent, equivalent

ivan \iv-ən\ see IVEN
ivance \ī-vəns\ connivance, contrivance
ive[1] \īv\ chive, Clive, dive, drive, five, hive, I've, jive, live, strive, thrive • alive, archive, arrive, beehive, connive, contrive, crash-dive, deprive, derive, disk drive, endive, hard drive, high five, high-five, line drive, nosedive, revive, skin-dive, skydive, survive, swan dive, take five, test-drive • eat alive, forty-five, four-wheel drive, hyperdrive, overdrive, power-dive, scuba dive
ive[2] \iv\ give, live, sieve • forgive, outlive, relive
ive[3] \ēv\ see EAVE[1]
ivel \iv-əl\ civil, drivel, shrivel, snivel, swivel • uncivil
iven \iv-ən\ driven, given, riven, striven • forgiven
iver[1] \ī-vər\ diver, driver, fiver, striver • cabdriver, pile driver, screwdriver, skin diver, skydiver, slave driver, survivor
iver[2] \iv-ər\ flivver, giver, liver, quiver, river, shiver, sliver • alms-giver, caregiver, chopped liver, deliver, downriver, East River, Fall River, lawgiver, upriver • up the river • Indian River, sell down the river
ivers \ī-vərz\ divers
   —also -s, -'s, and -s' forms of nouns listed at IVER[1]
ivery \iv-rē\ livery, shivery • delivery • general delivery, special delivery
ives \īvz\ fives, hives, Ives
   —also -s, -'s, and -s' forms of nouns and -s forms of verbs listed at IVE[1]
ivet \iv-ət\ civet, divot, pivot, privet, rivet, trivet
ivi \iv-ē\ see IVVY
ivia \iv-ē-ə\ trivia • Bolivia, Olivia

ivial \iv-ē-əl\ trivial • convivial
ivid \iv-əd\ livid, vivid
ivil \iv-əl\ see IVEL
iving \iv-iŋ\ giving, living • alms-giving, caregiving, forgiving, free-living, life-giving, misgiving, thanksgiving • cost of living, unforgiving • assisted living, standard of living
   —also -ing forms of verbs listed at IVE[2]
ivion \iv-ē-ən\ Vivian • Bolivian, oblivion
ivious \iv-ē-əs\ lascivious, oblivious
ivir \iv-ər\ see IVER[2]
ivity \iv-ət-ē\ activity, captivity, festivity, nativity, passivity, proclivity • conductivity, connectivity, creativity, inactivity, inclusivity, negativity, objectivity, productivity, relativity, selectivity, sensitivity, subjectivity • hyperactivity, insensitivity, overactivity • radioactivity
ivol \iv-əl\ see IVEL
ivor \ī-vər\ see IVER[1]
ivorous \iv-rəs\ carnivorous, herbivorous, omnivorous • insectivorous
ivot \iv-ət\ see IVET
ivus \ē-vəs\ see EVOUS
ivver \iv-ər\ see IVER[2]
ivvy \iv-ē\ chivy, divvy, Livy, privy, skivvy
ivy \iv-ē\ see IVVY
iwi \ē-wē\ see EEWEE
ix[1] \iks\ fix, mix, nix, six, Styx • affix, deep-six, prefix, premix, prix fixe, prolix, suffix, trail mix, transfix • cicatrix, crucifix, intermix, politics • geopolitics
   —also -s, -'s, and -s' forms of nouns and -s forms of verbs listed at ICK
ix[2] \ē\ see EE[1]
ixe[1] \iks\ see IX[1]
ixe[2] \ēsh\ see ICHE[2]

ixed \ikst\ fixed, mixed, twixt
• betwixt, well-fixed
—*also* -ed *forms of verbs listed at* IX[1]
ixen \ik-sən\ Nixon • Mason-Dixon
ixer \ik-sər\ fixer, mixer • elixir
ixie \ik-sē\ Dixie, pixie, tricksy
ixion \ik-shən\ see ICTION
ixir \ik-sər\ see IXER
ixon \ik-sən\ see IXEN
ixt \ikst\ see IXED
ixture \iks-chər\ fixture, mixture
• intermixture
iya \ē-ə\ see IA[1]
iyeh \ē-ə\ see IA[1]
iz[1] \iz\ biz, fizz, frizz, his, is, Ms.,
quiz, 'tis, whiz, wiz • gee-whiz,
pop quiz, show biz
iz[2] \ēz\ see EZE
iza[1] \ē-zə\ see EZA
iza[2] \ē-thə\ see ETHA
izable \ī-zə-bəl\ sizable • advisable
• analyzable, inadvisable, localiz-
able, recognizable
izar \ī-zər\ see IZER
izard \iz-ərd\ blizzard, gizzard,
lizard, wizard
ize[1] \īz\ guise, prize, rise, size, wise
• advise, apprise, arise, baptize,
bite-size, capsize, chastise, clock-
wise, comprise, crabwise, cross-
wise, demise, despise, devise,
disguise, door prize, downsize,
edgewise, endwise, excise, fran-
chise, full-size, high-rise, incise,
king-size, leastwise, lengthwise,
life-size, likewise, low-rise, man-
size, mid-rise, midsize, moonrise,
outsize, pint-size, queen-size,
revise, slantwise, streetwise, styl-
ize, suffice, sunrise, surmise,
surprise, twin-size, unwise • ad-
vertise, aggrandize, agonize,
amortize, analyze, atomize, au-
thorize, balkanize, booby prize,
bowdlerize, brutalize, burglarize,
canonize, capsulize, caramelize,
catalyze, catechize, cauterize,
centralize, Christianize, circum-
cise, civilize, colonize, colorize,
compromise, concertize, criticize,
crystalize, customize, demonize,
deputize, digitize, dramatize,
empathize, emphasize, energize,
enterprise, equalize, eulogize,
exercise, exorcise, fantasize,
feminize, fertilize, finalize, for-
malize, galvanize, ghettoize, glam-
orize, globalize, harmonize,
humanize, hypnotize, idolize,
immunize, improvise, itemize,
jeopardize, legalize, lionize, liq-
uidize, localize, magnetize, maxi-
mize, mechanize, memorize,
merchandise, mesmerize, mini-
mize, mobilize, modernize, mois-
turize, monetize, moralize,
motorize, neutralize, Nobel Prize,
normalize, notarize, novelize,
optimize, organize, ostracize,
otherwise, oversize, oxidize, paradise, paralyze, pasteurize, patron-
ize, penalize, penny-wise,
personalize, plagiarize, pluralize,
pocket-size, polarize, pressurize,
privatize, publicize, pulverize,
rationalize, realize, recognize,
rhapsodize, robotize, sanitize,
satirize, scandalize, scrutinize,
sensitize, sermonize, slenderize,
socialize, solemnize, specialize,
stabilize, standardize, sterilize,
stigmatize, strategize, subsidize,
summarize, supervise, symbolize,
sympathize, synchronize, synthe-
size, systemize, tantalize, televise,
tenderize, terrorize, theorize,
tranquilize, traumatize, tyrannize,
unionize, urbanize, utilize, van-
dalize, vaporize, verbalize, victim-
ize, vocalize, vulcanize, vulgarize,
weather-wise, weatherize, west-
ernize, winterize, worldly-wise
• accessorize, acclimatize,

Africanize, alphabetize, anes-
thetize, antagonize, anticlockwise,
apologize, cannibalize, capitalize,
categorize, characterize, comput-
erize, contrariwise, counterclock-
wise, criminalize, cut down to
size, decentralize, de-emphasize,
deglamorize, dehumanize, demag-
netize, democratize, demoralize,
deodorize, depressurize, desensi-
tize, disenfranchise, economize,
epitomize, evangelize, familiarize,
fictionalize, floor exercise, free
enterprise, generalize, homoge-
nize, hospitalize, hypothesize,
idealize, immobilize, immortalize,
infantilize, internalize, italicize,
legitimize, liberalize, marginalize,
metabolize, metastasize, milita-
rize, monopolize, nationalize,
naturalize, philosophize, politi-
cize, popularize, prioritize, prose-
lytize, Pulitzer prize, regularize,
reorganize, revitalize, romanti-
cize, systematize, trivialize,
visualize • Americanize, com-
partmentalize, consolation prize,
decriminalize, departmentalize,
individualize, industrialize, inter-
nationalize, legitimatize, material-
ize, memorialize, miniaturize,
private enterprise, professionalize,
psychoanalyze, revolutionize,
sensationalize, underutilize, uni-
versalize • editorialize, intellectu-
alize
—*also* -s, -'s, *and* -s' *forms of
nouns and* -s *forms of verbs listed
at* Y[1]
ize² \ēz\ see EZE
ized \īzd\ sized • advised, king-
sized, outsized, pearlized, queen-
sized • ill-advised, organized,

Sanforized, unadvised, under-
sized, well-advised • elasticized
—*also* -ed *forms of verbs listed at*
IZE[1]
izen¹ \īz-ᵊn\ bison • horizon
izen² \iz-ᵊn\ see ISON²
izer \ī-zər\ Dreiser, geyser, kaiser,
miser, riser, visor • adviser, divi-
sor, incisor • advertiser, appetizer,
atomizer, compromiser, ener-
gizer, equalizer, exerciser, fertil-
izer, improviser, modernizer,
moisturizer, moralizer, organizer,
pollenizer, pressurizer, stabilizer,
sterilizer, supervisor, sympathizer,
synthesizer, tenderizer, tranquil-
izer, vaporizer • popularizer,
proselytizer
izing \ī-ziŋ\ rising, sizing • uprising
• advertising, agonizing, appetiz-
ing, enterprising, merchandising,
unsurprising • self-sacrificing,
unappetizing, uncompromising
—*also* -ing *forms of verbs listed at*
IZE[1]
izo \ē-zō\ sleazo • mestizo
izon \īz-ᵊn\ see IZEN¹
izy \it-sē\ see ITZY
izz \iz\ see IZ¹
izzard \iz-ərd\ see IZARD
izzen \iz-ᵊn\ see ISON²
izzer \iz-ər\ see ISSOR
izzical \iz-i-kəl\ see YSICAL
izzie \i-zē\ see IZZY
izzle \iz-əl\ chisel, drizzle, fizzle,
grizzle, sizzle • cold chisel
izzled \iz-əld\ chiseled, grizzled
—*also* -ed *forms of verbs listed at*
IZZLE
izzler \iz-lər\ chiseler, sizzler
izzly \iz-lē\ drizzly, grisly, grizzly
izzy \iz-ē\ busy, dizzy, fizzy, frizzy,
tizzy • tin lizzie

O

o¹ \ü\ see EW¹

o² \ō\ see OW¹

oa¹ \ō-ə\ boa, Goa, Noah, Shoah • aloha, Balboa, Samoa • Krakatoa, Mauna Loa, Mount Gilboa, Shenandoah

oa² \ō\ see OW¹

oable \ü-ə-bəl\ see UABLE

oach \ōch\ broach, brooch, coach, poach, roach • approach, cockroach, encroach, reproach, stagecoach

oachable \ō-chə-bəl\ coachable • approachable • irreproachable, unapproachable

oacher \ō-chər\ cloture, poacher

oad¹ \ōd\ see ODE

oad² \ȯd\ see AUD¹

oader \ōd-ər\ see ODER

oadie \ōd-ē\ see ODY²

oady \ōd-ē\ see ODY²

oaf \ōf\ loaf, oaf • meat loaf • sugarloaf

oafer \ō-fər\ see OFER

oagie \ō-gē\ see OGIE

oah \ō-ə\ see OA¹

oak \ōk\ see OKE¹

oaken \ō-kən\ see OKEN

oaker \ō-kər\ see OKER

oaky \ō-kē\ see OKY

oal \ōl\ see OLE¹

oalie \ō-lē\ see OLY¹

oam \ōm\ see OME¹

oamer \ō-mər\ see OMER¹

oaming \ō-miŋ\ gloaming • Wyoming
—also -ing forms of verbs listed at OME¹

oamy \ō-mē\ foamy, homey, loamy, show-me • Naomi, Salome

oan¹ \ō-ən\ Owen, roan • Minoan, Samoan • Idahoan, protozoan • strawberry roan

oan² \ōn\ see ONE¹

oaner \ō-nər\ see ONER¹

oaning \ō-niŋ\ see ONING²

oap \ōp\ see OPE

oaper \ō-pər\ see OPER

oapy \ō-pē\ see OPI

oar \ȯr\ see OR¹

oard \ȯrd\ board, bored, chord, cord, floored, ford, Ford, gourd, hoard, horde, lord, Lord, oared, sword, toward, ward, Ward • aboard, accord, afford, award, backboard, baseboard, billboard, blackboard, breadboard, broadsword, cardboard, chalkboard, chessboard, clapboard, clipboard, concord, dart board, dashboard, discord, draft board, fjord, floorboard, headboard, inboard, keyboard, kickboard, landlord, lapboard, nerve cord, onboard, on board, outboard, pasteboard, Peg-Board, rearward, record, reward, scoreboard, shipboard, signboard, skateboard, slumlord, snowboard, soundboard, splashboard, springboard, surfboard, switchboard, untoward, wallboard, warlord, washboard, whiteboard, whipcord • aboveboard, bottle gourd, bungee cord, centerboard, checkerboard, circuit board, clavichord, cutting board, diving board, drawing board, emery board, fiberboard, fingerboard, harpsichord, mortarboard, motherboard, overboard, overlord, paddleboard, plasterboard, room

and board, sandwich board, shuf-
fleboard, smorgasbord, sounding
board, spinal cord, tape-record,
teeterboard, untoward • across-
the-board, bulletin board, extension cord, go by the board,
ironing board, off-the-record, on-
the-record, out of one's gourd,
particleboard • Federal Reserve
Board, platinum record • Acad-
emy Award
   —also -ed *forms of verbs listed at*
OR[1]

oarder \órd-ər\ see ORDER

oarding \órd-iŋ\ see ORDING[1]

oared \órd\ see OARD

oarer \ór-ər\ see ORER

oaring \ór-iŋ\ see ORING

oarious \ór-ē-əs\ see ORIOUS

oarse \órs\ see ORSE[1]

oarsman \órz-mən\ oarsman • out-
doorsman

oart \órt\ see ORT[1]

oary \ór-ē\ see ORY

oast \ōst\ see OST[2]

oastal \ōs-t³l\ see OSTAL[1]

oaster \ō-stər\ coaster, poster,
roaster, toaster • four-poster
• roller-coaster, roller coaster

oat \ōt\ bloat, boat, coat, dote,
float, gloat, goat, moat, mote,
note, oat, quote, rote, smote,
throat, tote, vote, wrote • afloat,
airboat, banknote, catboat,
C-note, compote, connote, coyote, cutthroat, demote, denote,
devote, dovecote, dreamboat,
eighth note, emote, fireboat,
flatboat, footnote, frock coat,
grace note, greatcoat, gunboat,
half note, houseboat, housecoat,
iceboat, keynote, lab coat,
lifeboat, longboat, promote, rain-
coat, redcoat, remote, rewrote,
rowboat, sailboat, sauceboat,
scapegoat, seed coat, sheepcote,
showboat, sore throat, speedboat,

steamboat, straw vote, strep
throat, Sukkoth, surfboat, top-
coat, towboat, trench coat, tug-
boat, turncoat, U-boat, unquote,
wainscot, whaleboat, whole note
• anecdote, antidote, assault boat,
billy goat, cashmere goat, cre-
osote, dead man's float, ferryboat,
flying boat, jolly boat, miss the
boat, motorboat, mountain goat,
nanny goat, overcoat, paddleboat,
petticoat, polo coat, powerboat,
PT boat, quarter note, riverboat,
rock the boat, sixteenth note,
sticky note, sugarcoat, Terre
Haute, undercoat, yellowthroat
• Angora goat, in the same boat,
lump in one's throat, torpedo
boat, treasury note

oate \ō-ət\ see OET

oated \ōt-əd\ bloated, coated,
noted, throated • devoted
   —also -ed *forms of verbs listed at*
OAT

oaten \ōt-³n\ see OTON

oater \ōt-ər\ boater, motor, rotor,
voter • keynoter, promoter, show-
boater • outboard motor

oath \ōth\ see OWTH

oathe \ō<u>th</u>\ see OTHE

oathing \ō-<u>th</u>iĭ\ see OTHING

oating \ōt-iŋ\ coating, floating
• free-floating, iceboating, sail-
boating, speedboating, wainscoting • motorboating,
powerboating, undercoating,
   —also -ing *forms of verbs listed at*
OAT

oaty \ōt-ē\ see OTE[1]

oax \ōks\ coax, hoax
   —also -s, -'s, *and* -s' *forms of*
nouns and -s *forms of verbs listed*
at OKE[1]

ob[1] \äb\ blob, bob, Bob, cob, daub,
fob, glob, gob, job, knob, lob,
mob, nob, rob, Saab, slob, snob,
sob, squab, swab, throb • corn-

cob, day job, doorknob, heart-
throb, hobnob, kebab, macabre,
Punjab, snow job • shish kebab
• thingamabob
ob² \ōb\ see OBE¹
oba \ō-bə\ jojoba • Manitoba
• Lake Manitoba
obably \äb-lē\ see OBBLY
obal \ō-bəl\ see OBLE
obar \ō-bər\ see OBER
obber \äb-ər\ bobber, clobber,
robber, slobber • hobnobber
obbery \äb-rē\ robbery, slobbery,
snobbery • highway robbery
obbie \äb-ē\ see OBBY
obbin \äb-ən\ see OBIN
obble \äb-əl\ see ABBLE¹
obbler \äb-lər\ cobbler, gobbler
obbly \äb-lē\ probably, wobbly
obby \äb-ē\ Bobbie, Bobby,
globby, hobby, knobby, lobby,
slobby, snobby • kohlrabi, Pun-
jabi • Abu Dhabi, Hammurabi
obe¹ \ōb\ globe, Job, lobe, probe,
robe, strobe • bathrobe, disrobe,
earlobe, enrobe, lap robe, mi-
crobe, wardrobe • claustrophobe,
frontal lobe, optic lobe, techno-
phobe, xenophobe • computer-
phobe, election probe, temporal
lobe • occipital lobe
obe² \ō-bē\ see OBY
obeah \ō-bē-ə\ see OBIA
obee \ō-bē\ see OBY
ober \ō-bər\ sober • October
obi \ō-bē\ see OBY
obia \ō-bē-ə\ phobia • Zenobia
• acrophobia, agoraphobia, claus-
trophobia, hydrophobia, techno-
phobia, xenophobia
• arachnophobia, computerpho-
bia
obic \ō-bik\ phobic • aerobic
• acrophobic, anaerobic, claustro-
phobic, hydrophobic, technopho-
bic, xenophobic • agoraphobic,
arachnophobic, computerphobic

obile \ō-bəl\ see OBLE
obin \äb-ən\ bobbin, dobbin, robin,
Robin • round-robin, sea robin
obit \ō-bət\ obit, Tobit
oble \ō-bəl\ global, mobile, noble
• ennoble, Grenoble, ignoble,
immobile • upwardly mobile
obo \ō-bō\ hobo, oboe • bonobo
oboe \ō-bō\ see OBO
obol \äb-əl\ see ABBLE¹
oboree \äb-ə-rē\ see OBBERY
obot \ō-bət\ see OBIT
obster \äb-stər\ lobster, mobster
• spiny lobster
oby \ō-bē\ Gobi, Kobe, Obie, Toby
• adobe, Nairobi • Okeechobee
obyn \äb-ən\ see OBIN
oc¹ \ōk\ see OKE¹
oc² \äk\ see OCK¹
oc³ \ȯk\ see ALK
oca \ō-kə\ coca, mocha • tapioca
ocal \ō-kəl\ focal, local, vocal,
yokel • bifocal
ocally \ō-kə-lē\ locally, vocally
occa \äk-ə\ see AKA¹
occer \äk-ər\ see OCKER
occie \äch-ē\ see OTCHY
occhi \ȯ-kē\ see ALKIE
occo \äk-ō\ socko, taco • morocco,
Morocco, sirocco
oce \ō-chē\ see OCHE¹
ocean \ō-shən\ see OTION
ocess \äs-əs\ process • colossus,
due process, proboscis, word
process
och¹ \äk\ see OCK¹
och² \ȯsh\ see ASH²
och³ \ȯk\ see ALK
ocha \ō-kə\ see OCA
ochal \äk-əl\ see OCKLE
oche¹ \ō-kē\ see OKY
oche² \ōch\ see OACH
oche³ \ȯsh\ see ASH²
ochee \ō-kē\ see OKY
ocher \ō-kər\ see OKER
ochi \ō-chē\ see OCHE¹
ochle \ək-əl\ see UCKLE

ochs \äks\ see OX

ociable \ō-shə-bəl\ sociable • negotiable, unsociable • renegotiable

ocile \äs-əl\ see OSSAL

ocious \ō-shəs\ atrocious, ferocious, precocious

ock[1] \äk\ Bach, bloc, block, clock, cock, crock, doc, dock, flock, frock, hock, Jacque, Jacques, jock, knock, loch, lock, moc, mock, pock, roc, rock, schlock, shock, smock, sock, Spock, stock, wok • ad hoc, air lock, amok, armlock, Bangkok, baroque, bedrock, burdock, crew sock, deadlock, debacle, defrock, dreadlock, dry dock, epoch, flintlock, forelock, foreshock, gridlock, Hancock, hard rock, haycock, headlock, hemlock, in stock, Iraq, jazz-rock, Kazakh, kapok, kneesock, Ladakh, livestock, o'clock, oarlock, padlock, peacock, picklock, punk rock, rimrock, roadblock, rootstock, rowlock, seed stock, shamrock, Sheetrock, shell shock, sherlock, shock jock, Sirach, slickrock, Slovak, soft rock, springbok, stopcock, sunblock, ticktock, time clock, time lock, unblock, uncock, van Gogh, warlock, wedlock, windsock, woodcock • acid rock, aftershock, alarm clock, antiknock, antilock, Antioch, Arawak, banjo clock, building block, butcher-block, chockablock, chopping block, cinder block, common stock, country rock, cuckoo clock, culture shock, hammerlock, hollyhock, interlock, John Hancock, laughingstock, Little Rock, manioc, mantlerock, Offenbach, on the block, out of stock, Plymouth Rock, poppycock, preferred stock, rolling stock, septic

shock, starting block, shuttle-cock, sticker shock, stumbling block, water clock, weathercock, writer's block • against the clock, around-the-clock, atomic clock, Czechoslovak, electroshock, grandfather clock, insulin shock, Mount Monadnock, out of wedlock, poison hemlock, run out the clock, turn back the clock, Vladivostok • chip off the old block

ock[2] \ȯk\ see ALK

ocke \äk\ see OCK[1]

ocked \äkt\ concoct, dreadlocked, half-cocked, landlocked, shellshocked
—*also* -ed *forms of verbs listed at* OCK[1]

ocker \äk-ər\ blocker, knocker, locker, mocker, rocker, shocker, soccer • alt-rocker, art-rocker, footlocker, punk rocker • knickerbocker • Davy Jones's locker

ockery \äk-rē\ crockery, mockery

ocket \äk-ət\ Crockett, docket, locket, pocket, rocket, socket, sprocket • air pocket, patch pocket, pickpocket, skyrocket, vest-pocket • cargo pocket, retrorocket

ockett \äk-ət\ see OCKET

ockey \äk-ē\ see OCKY

ockian \äk-ē-ən\ Hitchcockian, Slovakian • Czechoslovakian

ocking \äk-iŋ\ flocking, shocking, stocking • body stocking
—*also* -ing *forms of verbs listed at* OCK[1]

ockle \äk-əl\ debacle • streptococcal

ocko \äk-ō\ see OCCO

ocks \äks\ see OX

ocky \äk-ē\ blocky, cocky, hockey, jockey, rocky, schlocky, stocky • disc jockey, field hockey, ice hockey, Iraqi, street hockey • jabberwocky, Miyazaki, Nagasaki, sukiyaki, teriyaki

ocle \ō-kəl\ see OCAL

oco \ō-kō\ coco, cocoa, loco • rococo • crème de cacao, Orinoco

ocoa \ō-kō\ see OCO

ocracy \äk-rə-sē\ autocracy, bureaucracy, democracy, hypocrisy, mobocracy, plutocracy • aristocracy

ocre \ō-kər\ see OKER

ocrisy \äk-rə-sē\ see OCRACY

oct \äkt\ see OCKED

octor \äk-tər\ doctor, proctor • spin doctor, witch doctor • family doctor

ocular \äk-yə-lər\ jocular • binocular

ocus \ō-kəs\ crocus, focus, hocus • in focus, refocus, soft-focus • autumn crocus, hocus-pocus

ocused \ō-kəst\ see OCUST

ocust \ō-kəst\ locust • unfocused

od¹ \äd\ bod, clod, cod, Fahd, god, mod, nod, odd, plod, pod, prod, quad, rod, scrod, shod, sod, squad, trod, wad • Cape Cod, death squad, dry-shod, facade, fly rod, hot-rod, jihad, lingcod, Nimrod, ramrod, Riyadh, roughshod, seedpod, slipshod, sun god, synod, tightwad, tripod, unshod, vice squad • accolade, act of God, arthropod, cattle prod, demigod, dowsing rod, esplanade, firing squad, flying squad, gastropod, goldenrod, lightning rod, man of God, Novgorod, piston rod, promenade, son of God, spinning rod • cephalopod, connecting rod, divining rod, Holy Synod, Islamabad, Scheherazade, Upanishad

od² \ō\ see OW¹

od³ \ōd\ see ODE

od⁴ \u̇d\ see OOD¹

od⁵ \o̅d\ see AUD¹

o'd \üd\ see UDE¹

oda \ōd-ə\ coda, Rhoda, Skoda, soda • club soda, cream soda, pagoda • baking soda

odal \ōd-ᵊl\ modal, nodal, yodel

odden \äd-ᵊn\ Flodden, sodden, trodden • downtrodden, untrodden

odder \äd-ər\ dodder, fodder, odder, plodder, solder • flyrodder, hot-rodder • cannon fodder, Leningrader

oddery \äd-rē\ see AWDRY

oddess \äd-əs\ bodice, goddess • sun goddess • demigoddess

oddish \äd-ish\ cloddish, kaddish

oddle \äd-ᵊl\ coddle, model, swaddle, toddle, twaddle, waddle • remodel, role model • mollycoddle, supermodel

oddler \äd-lər\ coddler, modeler, toddler • mollycoddler

oddly \äd-lē\ see ODLY

oddy \äd-ē\ see ODY¹

ode \ōd\ bode, bowed, code, goad, load, lode, mode, node, ode, road, rode, strode, toad, toed • abode, anode, bar code, boatload, busload, byroad, carload, cartload, caseload, cathode, commode, corrode, crossroad, decode, diode, download, dress code, encode, erode, explode, forebode, freeload, geode, high road, horned toad, implode, inroad, lymph node, Morse code, offload, outmode, payload, planeload, railroad, shipload, side road, Silk Road, spring-load, squaretoed, trainload, truckload, twotoed, unload, upload, zip code • à la mode, Comstock Lode, down the road, electrode, episode, hit the road, mother lode, overrode, penal code, pigeon-toed, service road, wagonload • area code, genetic code, rule of the road • middle-of-the-road, Underground Railroad

—also -ed *forms of verbs listed at* OW[1]

odeine \ōd-ē-ən\ see ODIAN

odel \ōd-ᵊl\ see ODAL

odeler \äd-lər\ see ODDLER

odeon \ōd-ē-ən\ see ODIAN

oder \ōd-ər\ loader, Oder, odor • breechloader, freeloader, off-roader, railroader • middle-of-the-roader

oderate \äd-rət\ moderate • immoderate

odes \ōdz\ Rhodes
—also -s, -'s, *and* -s' *forms of nouns and* -s *forms of verbs listed at* ODE

odest \äd-əst\ modest, oddest • immodest

odeum \ōd-ē-əm\ see ODIUM

odge \äj\ see AGE[1]

odger \äj-ər\ codger, dodger, lodger, roger, Roger • Jolly Roger

odgy \äj-ē\ stodgy • demagogy

odian \ōd-ē-ən\ Cambodian, custodian, melodeon • nickelodeon

odic \äd-ik\ melodic, rhapsodic, spasmodic • episodic, periodic

odical \äd-i-kəl\ methodical • periodical

odice \äd-əs\ see ODDESS

odie \ō-dē\ see ODY[2]

odious \ōd-ē-əs\ odious • commodious, melodious

odity \äd-ət-ē\ oddity • commodity

odium \ōd-ē-əm\ podium, sodium

odius \ō-dē-əs\ see ODIOUS

odly \äd-lē\ godly, oddly • ungodly

odo \ōd-ō\ dodo • Quasimodo

odom \äd-əm\ shahdom, Sodom

odor \ōd-ər\ see ODER

odule \äj-ül\ module, lunar module, service module

ody[1] \äd-ē\ body, gaudy, Mahdi, shoddy, toddy • cell body, embody, homebody, nobody, somebody, wide-body • antibody, anybody, busybody, everybody, Irrawaddy, out-of-body, student body, underbody

ody[2] \ōd-ē\ Cody, Jodie, roadie, toady

odz \üj\ see UGE[1]

oe[1] \ō\ see OW[1]

oe[2] \ō-ē\ see OWY

oe[3] \ē\ see EE[1]

oea[1] \òi-ə\ see OIA

oea[2] \ē-ə\ see IA[1]

oeba \ē-bə\ see EBA

oebe \ē-bē\ see EBE[1]

oebel \ā-bəl\ see ABLE

oed \ōd\ see ODE

oehn \ən\ see UN[1]

oeia \ē-ə\ see IA[1]

oek \ùk\ see OOK[1]

oel \ō-əl\ Joel, Lowell, Noel • bestowal • protozoal

oeless[1] \ō-ləs\ see OLUS

oeless[2] \ü-ləs\ see EWLESS

oem \ōm\ see OME[1]

oeman \ō-mən\ see OMAN

oena \ē-nə\ see INA[2]

oentgen \en-chən\ see ENSION

oer[1] \òr\ see OR[1]

oer[2] \ü-ər\ see EWER[1]

oer[3] \ùr\ see URE[1]

oer[4] \ō-ər\ blower, grower, lower, mower, rower, slower, sower, thrower • beachgoer, churchgoer, fairgoer, flamethrower, filmgoer, glassblower, lawn mower, playgoer, snowblower, winegrower • concertgoer, moviegoer, operagoer, partygoer, whistle-blower • theatergoer

o'er \òr\ see OR[1]

oes[1] \əz\ see EUSE[1]

oes[2] \ōz\ see OSE[2]

oes[3] \üz\ see USE[2]

oesia \ē-shə\ see ESIA[1]

oesn't \əz-ᵊnt\ see ASN'T

oest \ü-əst\ see OOIST

oesus \ē-səs\ see ESIS

oet \ō-ət\ poet • inchoate, prose poet

oeuf \əf\ see UFF
oeur \ər\ see EUR[1]
oeuvre \ərv\ see ERVE
oey \ō-ē\ see OWY
of[1] \äv\ see OLVE[2]
of[2] \əv\ see OVE[1]
of[3] \ȯf\ see OFF[2]
ofar \ō-fər\ see OFER
ofer \ō-fər\ chauffeur, gopher, loafer, shofar • penny loafer
off[1] \äf\ coif, doff, prof, quaff, scoff • carafe, pilaf • Romanov
off[2] \ȯf\ cough, doff, off, scoff, trough • Azov, back off, beg off, blastoff, blow off, break off, bring off, brush-off, bug off, bump off, burn off, call off, cast-off, castoff, charge off, check off, Chekhov, cook-off, cutoff, cut off, drop-off, drop off, dust off, face-off, face off, falloff, far-off, fire off, first off, fob off, get off, give off, go off, goof-off, handoff, hand off, hands-off, haul off, head off, hold off, jump-off, kickoff, kick off, kill off, kiss-off, kiss off, knock-off, knock off, Khrushchev, laugh off, layoff, lay off, leadoff, lead off, leave off, liftoff, make off, nod off, palm off, pass off, payoff, pay off, peel off, pick off, play-off, pull off, push off, put off, reel off, rip-off, rip off, rub off, runoff, sawed-off, seal off, sell off, sell-off, send-off, set off, show-off, show off, shrug off, shut off, sign off, sound off, spin-off, standoff, stave off, swear off, takeoff, take off, teed off, tee off, tell off, throw off, tick off, tip-off, touch off, trade-off, turnoff, turn off, well-off, work off, write off • better-off, cooling-off, Gorbachev, hit it off, level off, Molotov, Nabokov, polish off, Pribilof, taper off • beat the pants off, beef Stroganoff, knock one's socks off, power take-off, Rachmaninoff • Mexican standoff, Rimsky-Korsakov

offal[1] \äf-əl\ see AFEL
offal[2] \ȯf-əl\ see AWFUL
offaly \ȯf-ə-lē\ see AWFULLY
offee \ȯ-fē\ coffee, toffee • Mr. Coffee
offer[1] \äf-ər\ coffer, offer, scoffer • counteroffer
offer[2] \ȯf-ər\ coffer, offer, scoffer • counteroffer
offin \ȯ-fən\ coffin, often, soften • every so often
offle \ȯ-fəl\ see AWFUL
oft[1] \ȯft\ croft, loft, oft, soft • aloft, choir loft, hayloft • Microsoft, semisoft, undercroft
    —*also* -ed *forms of verbs listed at* OFF[2]
oft[2] \äft\ see AFT[1]
often \ȯ-fən\ see OFFIN
ofty \ȯf-tē\ lofty, softy
og[1] \äg\ blog, bog, clog, cog, flog, fog, frog, grog, hog, jog, log, nog, Prague, slog, smog • agog, backlog, bullfrog, defog, eggnog, footslog, groundhog, hedgehog, ice fog, leapfrog, photog, prologue, road hog, sandhog, tree frog, unclog, warthog, whole hog, Yule log • analog, analogue, catalog, demagogue, dialogue, epilogue, leopard frog, monologue, pedagogue, pollywog, synagogue, travelogue, waterlog • card catalogue
og[2] \ȯg\ blog, bog, clog, dog, fog, frog, hog, jog, log, smog • backlog, bird dog, bulldog, bullfrog, corn dog, coydog, defog, groundhog, guide dog, gundog, hangdog, hedgehog, hotdog, ice fog, lapdog, leapfrog, prologue, road hog, sandhog, sheepdog, sled dog, top dog, tree frog, warthog, watchdog, whole-hog, wild dog, wolf

dog, Yule log • analog, analogue, attack dog, catalog, chili dog, dialogue, dog-eat-dog, epilogue, hearing dog, leopard frog, monologue, police dog, pollywog, prairie dog, shaggy-dog, travelogue, underdog, water dog, working dog • card catalog, Eskimo dog, Shetland sheepdog

og³ \ōg\ see OGUE¹

oga \ō-gə\ toga, yoga • Conestoga, hatha yoga

ogan \ō-gən\ shogun, slogan • Mount Logan

oge \üzh\ see UGE²

ogel \ō-gəl\ see OGLE¹

ogeny \äj-ə-nē\ progeny • misogyny

oger¹ \äj-ər\ see ODGER

oger² \òg-ər\ see OGGER²

ogey¹ \ō-gē\ see OGIE

ogey² \ùg-ē\ see OOGIE

oggan \äg-ən\ see OGGIN

oggar \äg-ər\ see OGGER¹

ogger¹ \äg-ər\ blogger, jogger, lager, logger • defogger • cataloger

ogger² \òg-ər\ auger, augur, jogger, logger • defogger, hotdogger • cataloger

oggin \äg-ən\ noggin • toboggan, Volkswagen • Copenhagen

oggle \äg-əl\ boggle, goggle, joggle, toggle • boondoggle • synagogal

oggy¹ \äg-ē\ boggy, foggy, groggy, smoggy, soggy

oggy² \òg-ē\ doggy, foggy, soggy

ogh¹ \ōg\ see OGUE¹

ogh² \ōk\ see OKE¹

ogh³ \äk\ see OCK¹

ogh⁴ \ō\ see OW¹

ogi \ō-gē\ see OGIE

ogian \ō-jən\ see OJAN

ogic \äj-ik\ logic • biologic, chronologic, demagogic, geologic, mythologic

ogical \äj-i-kəl\ logical • illogical

• astrological, biological, chronological, cosmological, ecological, geological, mythological, pathological, pedagogical, psychological, seismological, technological, theological, zoological • archaeological, dermatological, ideological, sociological

ogie \ō-gē\ bogey, bogie, dogie, fogy, hoagie, logy, stogie, yogi • pierogi

ogle¹ \ō-gəl\ Gogol, ogle

ogle² \äg-əl\ see OGGLE

ogna¹ \ō-nə\ see ONA¹

ogna² \ō-nē\ see ONY¹

ogna³ \ōn-yə\ see ONIA²

ogne \ōn\ see ONE¹

ogned \ōnd\ see ONED¹

ogo \ō-gō\ go-go, logo, Togo

ographer \äg-rə-fər\ biographer, cryptographer, discographer, photographer • choreographer, oceanographer, videographer • cinematographer

ography \äg-rə-fē\ biography, cryptography, discography, filmography, geography, photography, typography • bibliography, choreography, oceanography • autobiography, cinematography

ogress \ō-grəs\ ogress, progress

ogue¹ \ōg\ brogue, rogue, vogue, Vogue

ogue² \äg\ see OG¹

ogue³ \òg\ see OG²

oguish \ō-gish\ roguish, voguish

ogun \ō-gən\ see OGAN

ogyny \äj-ə-nē\ see OGENY

oh \ō\ see OW¹

oha \ō-ə\ see OA¹

ohl \ōl\ see OLE¹

ohm \ōm\ see OME¹

ohn \än\ see ON¹

ohns \änz\ see ONZE

ohn's \onz\ see ONZE

ohnson \än-sən\ Johnson • Wisconsin

ohr \ȯr\ see OR[1]

oi[1] \ä\ see A[1]

oi[2] \ȯi\ see OY

oia \ȯi-ə\ Goya, olla • sequoia, Sequoya • paranoia

oic \ō-ik\ stoic • echoic, heroic • Cenozoic, Mesozoic • Paleozoic

oice \ȯis\ choice, Joyce, voice • invoice, of choice, pro-choice, rejoice • with one voice • multiple-choice

oiced \ȯist\ see OIST

oicer \ȯi-sər\ pro-choicer, rejoicer

oid[1] \ȯid\ Floyd, Freud, void • android, avoid, deltoid, devoid, factoid, Negroid, ovoid, rhomboid, schizoid, steroid, tabloid, thyroid, typhoid • anthropoid, asteroid, celluloid, hemorrhoid, humanoid, Mongoloid, null and void, overjoyed, paranoid, planetoid, trapezoid, unalloyed, unemployed • underemployed
—also -ed *forms of verbs listed at* OY

oid[2] \ä\ see A[1]

oidal \ȯid-ᵊl\ adenoidal, asteroidal, trapezoidal

oie \ä\ see A[1]

oif \äf\ see OFF[1]

oign \ȯin\ see OIN[1]

oil \ȯil\ boil, broil, coil, foil, Hoyle, loyal, oil, roil, royal, soil, spoil, toil • airfoil, charbroil, coal oil, corn oil, despoil, disloyal, embroil, fish oil, fuel oil, gargoyle, hard-boil, palm oil, parboil, recoil, snake oil, subsoil, tinfoil, topsoil, trefoil, turmoil • baby oil, castor oil, desert soil, drying oil, holy oil, hydrofoil, linseed oil, London broil, mineral oil, neat's-foot oil, olive oil, peanut oil, prairie soil, quatrefoil, rapeseed oil, safflower oil, salad oil, soybean oil • canola oil, coconut oil, cod-liver oil, cottonseed oil, induction coil, sesame oil, vegetable oil • burn the midnight oil

oilage \ȯi-lij\ soilage, spoilage

oile[1] \äl\ see AL[1]

oile[2] \ȯil\ see OIL

oiled \ȯild\ oiled • hard-boiled, soft-boiled, uncoiled, well-oiled
—also -ed *forms of verbs listed at* OIL

oiler \ȯi-lər\ boiler, broiler, spoiler, toiler • potboiler, steam boiler • double boiler

oiling \ȯi-liŋ\ boiling, broiling
—also -ing *forms of verbs listed at* OIL

oilus \ȯi-ləs\ see OYLESS

oin[1] \ȯin\ coin, groin, join, loin • adjoin, Burgoyne, conjoin, Des Moines, enjoin, purloin, rejoin, sirloin • tenderloin

oin[2] \aⁿ\ see IN[4]

oine \än\ see ON[1]

oines \ȯin\ see OIN[1]

oing[1] \ō-iŋ\ Boeing, going, knowing, rowing, sewing, showing • churchgoing, foregoing, freeflowing, glassblowing, mindblowing, ongoing, outgoing, seagoing • concertgoing, easygoing, moviegoing, oceangoing, theatergoing, thoroughgoing, whistle-blowing • to-ing and fro-ing
—also -ing *forms of verbs listed at* OW[1]

oing[2] \ü-iŋ\ doing • undoing, wrongdoing • evildoing, nothing doing
—also -ing *forms of verbs listed at* EW[1]

oing[3] \ō-ən\ see OAN[1]

o-ing \ō-iŋ\ see OING[1]

oint[1] \ȯint\ joint, point • anoint, appoint, ballpoint, butt joint, checkpoint, clip joint, dew point, end point, flash point, grade point, gunpoint, hinge joint, hip

joint, juke joint, knifepoint, lap
joint, match point, midpoint, pen
point, pinpoint, standpoint, view-
point • at gunpoint, at knifepoint,
boiling point, breaking point,
brownie point, cardinal point,
case in point, counterpoint, disap-
point, focal point, freezing point,
knuckle joint, melting point,
miter joint, Montauk Point,
needlepoint, out of joint, point-to-
point, pressure point, sticking
point, talking point, to the point,
turning point, vantage point
• beside the point, decimal point,
percentage point, vanishing point

oint² \ant\ see ANT⁵

ointe \ant\ see ANT⁵

ointed \ȯint-əd\ jointed, pointed
• disjointed, loose-jointed • disap-
pointed, double-jointed, self-
appointed, well-appointed
—*also* -ed *forms of verbs listed at*
OINT¹

ointing \ȯin-tiŋ\ disappointing,
finger-pointing
—*also* -ing *forms of verbs listed at*
OINT¹

ointment \ȯint-mənt\ ointment
• anointment, appointment • dis-
appointment • fly in the ointment

oir¹ \īr\ see IRE¹

oir² \är\ see AR³

oir³ \ȯir\ see OYER

oir⁴ \ȯr\ see OR¹

oire¹ \är\ see AR³

oire² \ȯir\ see OYER

oire³ \ȯr\ see OR¹

ois¹ \ä\ see A¹

ois² \ȯi\ see OY

ois³ \ȯis\ see OICE

oise¹ \äz\ 'twas, vase, was • vichys-
soise
—*also* -s, -'s, *and* -s' *forms of nouns
and* -s *forms of verbs listed at* A¹

oise² \ȯiz\ noise, poise • turquoise,
white noise

—*also* -s, -'s, *and* -s' *forms of
nouns and* -s *forms of verbs listed
at* OY

oise³ \ȯi-zē\ see OISY

oist \ȯist\ foist, hoist, joist, moist,
voiced • unvoiced
—*also* -ed *forms of verbs listed at*
OICE

oister \ȯi-stər\ cloister, oyster,
roister • seed oyster

oisy \ȯi-zē\ Boise, noisy

oit¹ \ȯit\ adroit, Detroit, exploit

oit² \āt\ see ATE¹

oit³ \ō-ət\ see OET

oit⁴ \ä\ see A¹

oite \ät\ see OT¹

oiter \ȯit-ər\ goiter, loiter • De-
troiter • reconnoiter

oivre \äv\ see OLVE¹

oix¹ \ä\ see A¹

oix² \ȯi\ see OY

oiz \ȯis\ see OISE²

ojan \ō-jən\ Trojan • theologian

ok¹ \äk\ see OCK¹

ok² \ək\ see UCK¹

ok³ \ȯk\ see ALK

oka \ō-kə\ see OCA

oke¹ \ōk\ bloke, broke, choke,
cloak, coke, Coke, croak, folk,
joke, oak, poke, Polk, smoke,
soak, spoke, stoke, stroke, woke,
yoke, yolk • ad hoc, awoke, back-
stroke, baroque, breaststroke,
brushstroke, chain-smoke, con-
voke, cowpoke, downstroke,
evoke, heatstroke, in-joke, in-
voke, keystroke, kinfolk, kins-
folk, live oak, menfolk, pin oak,
presoak, provoke, red oak, re-
voke, scrub oak, sidestroke, slow-
poke, sunstroke, townsfolk,
upstroke, white oak • artichoke,
Bolingbroke, fisherfolk, go for
broke, masterstroke, okeydoke,
poison oak, Roanoke, thunder-
stroke, womenfolk

oke² \ō-kē\ see OKY

oke³ \ō\ see OW¹

oke⁴ \ŭk\ see OOK¹

okee \ō-kē\ see OKY

okel \ō-kəl\ see OCAL

oken \ō-kən\ broken, oaken, spoken, token, woken • awoken, betoken, heartbroken, housebroken, outspoken, plainspoken, soft-spoken, unbroken • by the same token

oker \ō-kər\ broker, croaker, joker, ocher, poker, smoker, stoker • chain-smoker, draw poker, pawnbroker, stockbroker, stud poker • mediocre, power broker, red-hot poker

okey \ō-kē\ see OKY

oki \ō-kē\ see OKY

oko \ō-kō\ see OCO

oky \ō-kē\ croaky, folkie, hokey, jokey, Loki, poky, smoky • Great Smoky • hokeypokey, karaoke • Okefenokee

ol¹ \ōl\ see OLE¹

ol² \äl\ see AL¹

ol³ \ȯl\ see ALL¹

ola \ō-lə\ cola, Lola • Angola, canola, Ebola, gondola, granola, Tortola, Victrola, viola, Viola • ayatollah, gladiola, Gorgonzola, Hispaniola, Osceola, Pensacola

olable \ō-lə-bəl\ see OLLABLE

olace \äl-əs\ see OLIS

olan \ō-lən\ see OLON

oland \ō-lənd\ see OWLAND

olar¹ \ō-lər\ see OLLER

olar² \äl-ər\ see OLLAR

olas \ō-ləs\ see OLUS

old¹ \ōld\ bold, bowled, cold, fold, gold, hold, mold, mould, old, scold, sold, soled, told • age-old, ahold, all told, behold, billfold, blindfold, blue mold, bread mold, choke hold, controlled, cuckold, eightfold, enfold, fivefold, fool's gold, foothold, foretold, fourfold, green mold, handhold, head cold,

household, ice-cold, knock cold, leaf mold, ninefold, on hold, potholed, scaffold, sheepfold, sixfold, slime mold, stone-cold, stronghold, take hold, tenfold, threefold, threshold, toehold, twofold, unfold, untold, uphold, withhold • centerfold, common cold, fingerhold, hundredfold, manifold, marigold, scissors hold, sevenfold, stranglehold, thousandfold, throttlehold • as good as gold, blow hot and cold, lo and behold, marsh marigold, out in the cold

—also -ed forms of verbs listed at OLE¹

old² \ȯld\ see ALD¹

oldan \ōl-dən\ see OLDEN

olden \ōl-dən\ golden, olden • beholden, embolden

older¹ \ōl-dər\ boulder, folder, holder, shoulder, smolder • beholder, bondholder, cardholder, householder, jobholder, landholder, leaseholder, penholder, placeholder, pot holder, shareholder, slaveholder, stockholder, toolholder • officeholder, titleholder

—also -er forms of adjectives listed at OLD¹

older² \äd-ər\ see ODDER

oldie \ōl-dē\ see OLDY

olding \ōl-diŋ\ folding, holding, molding, scolding • hand-holding, landholding, scaffolding, slaveholding

—also -ing forms of verbs listed at OLD¹

oldster \ōl-stər\ see OLSTER

oldt \ōlt\ see OLT¹

oldy \ōl-dē\ moldy, oldie • golden oldie

ole¹ \ōl\ bowl, coal, Cole, dole, droll, foal, goal, hole, knoll, mole, pole, Pole, poll, role, roll, scroll,

Seoul, shoal, sol, sole, soul, stole, stroll, toll, troll, vole, whole • airhole, armhole, atoll, bankroll, beanpole, bedroll, black hole, blowhole, bunghole, cajole, charcoal, console, control, creole, Creole, drumroll, egg roll, enroll, extol, eyehole, field goal, fishbowl, flagpole, foxhole, hard coal, half sole, hellhole, insole, keyhole, knothole, loophole, manhole, maypole, Mongol, Nicolle, North Pole, parole, patrol, payroll, peephole, pinhole, porthole, pothole, ridgepole, Sheol, ski pole, South Pole, spring roll, tadpole, unroll, washbowl, wormhole • buttonhole, camisole, casserole, coffee roll, cubbyhole, Dover sole, escarole, exit poll, finger hole, fumarole, honor roll, innersole, in the hole, Jackson Hole, jelly roll, kaiser roll, lemon sole, methanol, on the whole, oriole, ozone hole, pigeonhole, protocol, rabbit hole, rigmarole, rock and roll, Seminole, totem pole, water hole • ace in the hole, cholesterol, Costa del Sol, Haitian Creole, magnetic pole

ole² \ō-lē\ see OLY[1]

ole³ \ól\ see ALL[1]

olean \ō-lē-ən\ see OLIAN

oled \ōld\ see OLD[1]

oleful \ōl-fəl\ doleful, soulful

olely \ō-lē\ see OLY[1]

olemn \äl-əm\ see OLUMN

oleon \ō-lē-ən\ see OLIAN

oler¹ \ō-lər\ see OLLER

oler² \äl-ər\ see OLLAR

oless \ō-ləs\ see OLUS

oleum \ō-lē-əm\ see OLIUM

oley \ō-lē\ see OLY[1]

olf¹ \älf\ golf, Rolf • Adolph, Randolph, Rudolph, Lake Rudolf • miniature golf

olf² \əlf\ see ULF

olga \äl-gə\ Olga, Volga

oli \ō-lē\ see OLY[1]

olia \ō-lē-ə\ Mongolia • Anatolia, melancholia • Inner Mongolia, Outer Mongolia

olian \ō-lē-ən\ aeolian, Mongolian, napoleon, Napoleon, Tyrolean

olic \äl-ik\ colic, frolic, rollick • bucolic, symbolic, systolic • alcoholic, apostolic, chocoholic, diabolic, hyperbolic, melancholic, shopaholic, vitriolic, workaholic

olicking \ä-lik-iŋ\ frolicking, rollicking

olid \äl-əd\ solid, squalid, stolid • semisolid

olin¹ \äl-ən\ see OLLEN[5]

olin² \ō-lən\ see OLON

olis \äl-əs\ braless, solace, Wallace, Wallis • Cornwallis

olish \äl-ish\ polish • abolish, demolish • apple-polish, spit-and-polish

olity \äl-ət-ē\ see ALITY[1]

olium \ō-lē-əm\ linoleum, petroleum

olk¹ \elk\ see ELK[1]

olk² \ōk\ see OKE[1]

olk³ \əlk\ see ULK

olk⁴ \ók\ see ALK

olkie \ō-kē\ see OKY

olky \ō-kē\ see OKY

oll¹ \ōl\ see OLE[1]

oll² \ȧl\ see AL[1]

oll³ \ól\ see ALL[1]

olla¹ \äl-ə\ see ALA[2]

olla² \ȯi-ə\ see OIA

ollable \ō-lə-bəl\ controllable • inconsolable, uncontrollable

ollack \äl-ək\ see OLOCH

ollah¹ \ō-lə\ see OLA

ollah² \äl-ə\ see ALA[2]

ollah³ \əl-ə\ see ULLAH

ollar \äl-ər\ collar, dollar, holler, Mahler, scholar, squalor • bluecollar, dog collar, flea collar, halfdollar, sand dollar, shawl collar,

top dollar, white-collar • Eurodol-
lar, petrodollar • clerical collar

ollard \äl-ərd\ collard, collared,
hollered

olled \ōld\ see OLD[1]

ollee \ō-lē\ see OLY[1]

ollege \äl-ij\ see OWLEDGE

ollen[1] \ō-lən\ see OLON

ollen[2] \əl-ə\ see ULLAH

ollen[3] \əl-ən\ see ULLEN

ollen[4] \ò-lən\ see ALLEN

ollen[5] \äl-ən\ Colin, pollen

oller \ō-lər\ bowler, molar, polar,
poller, roller, solar, stroller
• bankroller, comptroller, con-
troller, high roller, logroller,
steamroller • rock and roller

ollet \äl-ət\ wallet • whatchama-
callit

ollett \äl-ət\ see OLLET

olley \äl-ē\ see OLLY[1]

ollick \äl-ik\ see OLIC

ollicking \ä-lik-iŋ\ see OLICKING

ollie \äl-ē\ see OLLY[1]

ollin \äl-ən\ see OLLEN[5]

olling \ō-liŋ\ bowling • high-
rolling, logrolling • exit polling
—*also* -ing *forms of verbs listed at*
OLE[1]

ollis \äl-əs\ see OLIS

ollity \äl-ət-ē\ see ALITY[1]

ollo \äl-ō\ see OLLOW[1]

ollop \äl-əp\ dollop, polyp, scallop,
trollop, wallop • bay scallop, sea
scallop

ollow[1] \äl-ō\ follow, hollow, swallow, wallow • Apollo, barn swallow, cliff swallow, tree swallow

ollow[2] \äl-ə\ see ALA[2]

ollower \äl-ə-wər\ follower, wal-
lower • camp follower

ollster \ōl-stər\ see OLSTER

olly[1] \äl-ē\ Bali, Cali, collie, Dalí,
dolly, folly, golly, Halle, holly,
jolly, Mali, Molly, Ollie, Polly,
Raleigh, trolley, volley • Denali,
finale, Kigali, Nepali, Somali,

Svengali, tamale • melancholy,
Mexicali

olly[2] \ò-lē\ see AWLY

olm \ōm\ see OME[1]

olman \ōl-mən\ dolmen • patrol-
man

olmen \ōl-mən\ see OLMAN

olmes \ōmz\ Holmes
—*also* -s, -'s, *and* -s' *forms of
nouns and* -s *forms of verbs listed
at* OME[1]

olo \ō-lō\ bolo, polo, solo • Marco
Polo, water polo

oloch \äl-ək\ Moloch, rowlock

ologist \äl-ə-jəst\ biologist, ecolo-
gist, gemologist, geologist,
mythologist, neurologist, oncolo-
gist, psychologist, seismologist,
zoologist • anthropologist, ar-
chaeologist, cardiologist, climatol-
ogist, cosmetologist,
dermatologist, Egyptologist, ento-
mologist, immunologist, musicol-
ogist, ophthalmologist,
ornithologist

ology \äl-ə-jē\ anthology, apology,
astrology, biology, chronology,
cosmology, doxology, ecology,
geology, mythology, pathology,
psychology, seismology, technol-
ogy, theology, zoology • anthro-
pology, archaeology, cardiology,
climatology, cosmetology, crimi-
nology, dermatology, Egyptology,
etymology, genealogy, ideology,
immunology, methodology, mineralogy, musicology, numerology,
ophthalmology, ornithology,
pharmacology, physiology, Scien-
tology, sociology, terminology
• microbiology, nanotechnology,
paleontology

olon \ō-lən\ bowline, Colin, colon,
Nolan, stolen, swollen • semi-
colon

olonel \ərn-ᵊl\ see ERNAL

olonist \äl-ə-nəst\ colonist, Stalinist

olor¹ \ō-lər\ see OLLER
olor² \äl-ər\ see OLLAR
olored \əl-ərd\ colored, dullard • tricolored
olp \ōp\ see OPE
olph \älf\ see OLF¹
olster \ōl-stər\ bolster, holster, oldster, pollster • upholster
olt¹ \ōlt\ bolt, colt, dolt, jolt, molt, volt • dead bolt, revolt, spring bolt, unbolt • thunderbolt
olt² \ȯlt\ see ALT
olta \äl-tə\ see ALTA
oltish \ōl-tish\ coltish, doltish
oluble \äl-yə-bəl\ soluble, voluble • insoluble • indissoluble
olumn \äl-əm\ column, slalom, solemn • fifth column • giant slalom, spinal column, steering column
olus \ō-ləs\ snowless, toeless • gladiolus
olve¹ \älv\ salve, solve • absolve, devolve, dissolve, evolve, involve, resolve, revolve
olve² \äv\ of, salve, Slav, suave • Gustav, thereof, whereof • Stanislav, unheard-of, well-thought-of, Yugoslav
oly¹ \ō-lē\ goalie, holy, lowly, mole, slowly, solely • cannoli, frijole, unholy • guacamole, ravioli, roly-poly
oly² \äl-ē\ see OLLY¹
olyp \äl-əp\ see OLLOP
om¹ \äm\ balm, bomb, calm, from, Guam, mom, palm, prom, psalm, qualm, tom • A-bomb, aplomb, ashram, becalm, bee balm, buzz bomb, car bomb, dive-bomb, dot-com, embalm, firebomb, grande dame, H-bomb, imam, Islam, napalm, noncom, phenom, pogrom, pom-pom, salaam, sit-com, stink bomb, therefrom, time bomb, tom-tom, wigwam • atom bomb, cardamom, CD-ROM,

cherry bomb, cluster bomb, diatom, intercom, lemon balm, letter bomb, neutron bomb, Peeping Tom, royal palm, sago palm, soccer mom, supermom, telecom, Uncle Tom, Vietnam • atomic bomb, coconut palm, Dar es Salaam, hydrogen bomb, Omar Khayyám
om² \ōm\ see OME¹
om³ \üm\ see OOM¹
om⁴ \əm\ see UM¹
om⁵ \ùm\ see UM²
om⁶ \ȯm\ see AUM¹
oma \ō-mə\ chroma, coma, Roma • aroma, diploma, glaucoma, lymphoma, Tacoma • carcinoma, melanoma, Oklahoma
omac \ō-mik\ see OMIC²
omace \äm-əs\ see OMISE
omaly \äm-ə-lē\ homily • anomaly
oman \ō-mən\ bowman, foeman, omen, Roman, showman, snowman, yeoman
omany \äm-ə-nē\ see OMINY
omas \äm-əs\ see OMISE
omb¹ \ōm\ see OME¹
omb² \üm\ see OOM¹
omb³ \äm\ see OM¹
omb⁴ \əm\ see UM¹
omba \äm-bə\ see AMBA
ombe¹ \ōm\ see OME¹
ombe² \üm\ see OOM¹
ombe³ \äm\ see OM¹
ombed \ümd\ see OOMED
omber¹ \äm-ər\ bomber • dive-bomber, embalmer
omber² \ō-mər\ see OMER¹
ombic \ō-mik\ see OMIC²
ombie \äm-bē\ zombie • Abercrombie
ombing \ō-miŋ\ see OAMING
ombo¹ \äm-bō\ combo, mambo
ombo² \əm-bō\ see UMBO
ombre \äm-bər\ see OMBER²
ome¹ \ōm\ chrome, comb, dome, foam, gnome, home, loam, ohm,

poem, roam, Rome, tome • at-
home, beachcomb, bring home,
Cape Nome, down-home,
genome, hot comb, Jerome, rest
home, rhizome, shalom, Stock-
holm, syndrome • catacomb,
chromosome, close to home,
Down syndrome, fine-tooth
comb, foster home, funeral home,
honeycomb, metronome, mobile
home, monochrome, motor
home, nursing home, onion
dome, polychrome, Reye's syndrome, soldiers' home, stay-at-
home, Styrofoam • detention
home, Mercurochrome, X chromosome, Y chromosome

ome² \ō-mē\ see OAMY

ome³ \əm\ see UM¹

omely \əm-lē\ see UMBLY²

omen \ō-mən\ see OMAN

omenal \äm-ən-ᵊl\ see OMINAL

omene \äm-ə-nē\ see OMINY

omer¹ \ō-mər\ homer, Homer,
roamer • beachcomber, mis-
nomer

omer² \əm-ər\ see UMMER

omery \əm-ə-rē\ see UMMERY

omet \äm-ət\ comet, grommet,
vomit

ometer \äm-ət-ər\ barometer,
chronometer, kilometer, microm-
eter, odometer, pedometer,
speedometer, tachometer, ther-
mometer

ometry \äm-ə-trē\ geometry, op-
tometry • plane geometry,
trigonometry

omey \ō-mē\ see OAMY

omi \ō-mē\ see OAMY

omic¹ \äm-ik\ comic • atomic,
Islamic • anatomic, diatomic,
economic, ergonomic, gastro-
nomic, metronomic, subatomic,
tragicomic

omic² \ō-mik\ gnomic • Potomac

omical \äm-i-kəl\ comical

• anatomical, astronomical, eco-
nomical

omics \äm-iks\ comics • economics, ergonomics • home economics

omily \äm-ə-lē\ see OMALY

ominal \äm-ən-ᵊl\ nominal • ab-
dominal, phenomenal

ominance \äm-nəns\ dominance,
prominence • predominance

ominant \äm-nənt\ dominant,
prominent • predominant

omine \äm-ə-nē\ see OMINY

ominence \äm-nəns\ see OMINANCE

ominent \äm-nənt\ see OMINANT

oming¹ \əm-iŋ\ coming, numbing,
plumbing • becoming, forthcom-
ing, have coming, homecoming,
incoming, mind-numbing, oncom-
ing, shortcoming, upcoming
• Second Coming, unbecoming,
up-and-coming
—*also* -ing *forms of verbs listed at*
UM¹

oming² \ō-miŋ\ see OAMING

omini \äm-ə-nē\ see OMINY

ominy \äm-ə-nē\ hominy
• ignominy • anno Domini

omise \äm-əs\ pomace, promise,
Thomas • Saint Thomas • breach
of promise, doubting Thomas
• lick and a promise

omit \äm-ət\ see OMET

omma \äm-ə\ see AMA²

ommel¹ \äm-əl\ pommel, Rommel

ommel² \əm-əl\ pommel, pummel
• Beau Brummell

ommet \äm-ət\ see OMET

ommie \äm-ē\ see AMI¹

ommon \äm-ən\ Brahman, common, shaman • in common • Tu-
tankhamen

ommy¹ \äm-ē\ see AMI¹

ommy² \əm-ē\ see UMMY

omo \ō-mō\ Como, promo • major-
domo

omon \ō-mən\ see OMAN

omp¹ \ämp\ champ, chomp, clomp,

pomp, romp, stamp, stomp,
swamp, tramp, tromp, whomp
omp² \əmp\ see UMP
ompass \əm-pəs\ compass, rumpus
• encompass
omper \äm-pər\ romper, stamper,
stomper
ompey \äm-pē\ see OMPY
ompt \au̇nt\ see OUNT²
ompy \äm-pē\ Pompey, swampy
on¹ \än\ ban, Bonn, con, dawn,
don, Don, drawn, faun, fawn,
gone, John, Jon, khan, on, pawn,
prawn, Ron, spawn, swan, wan,
yawn, yon, yuan • aeon, add-on,
Amman, anon, Anton, argon,
Argonne, Aswan, Avon, bank on,
baton, big on, bonbon, boron,
bouillon, bring on, build on,
bygone, caisson, call on, catch on,
Ceylon, chevron, chew on, chif-
fon, chignon, clip-on, come-on,
cordon, coupon, crampon,
crayon, crouton, Dacron, dead-
on, Dear John, doggone, dog-
goned, Don Juan, eon, far-gone,
foregone, Freon, futon, Gibran,
Golan, go on, hand on, hands-on,
hang on, head-on, high on, hit on,
hogan, hold on, Hunan, icon,
Inchon, ion, Ivan, jargon, keen
on, krypton, Leon, let on, lock
on, log on, look on, Luzon, Milan, moron, neon, neuron, neutron, Nippon, nylon, odds-on,
Oman, Orlon, pecan, peon, pho-
ton, pick on, piton, plankton,
pompon, proton, Pusan, put-on,
pylon, python, Qur'an, radon, rag
on, rayon, right-on, Saint John,
Saipan, salon, San Juan, shaman,
sign on, sit on, slip-on, snap-on,
solon, spot on, stand on, stuck on,
sweet on, Szechwan, Taiwan, take
on, Teflon, Tehran, toucan, Tristan, try on, Tucson, turned-on,
turn on, upon, wait on, walk-on,
wonton, work on, Yukon,
Yvonne, zircon • Abidjan, aileron,
amazon, Amazon, and so on,
Aragon, autobahn, Avalon, Baby-
lon, Barbizon, bear down on, beat
up on, biathlon, call upon, caril-
lon, carry-on, carry on, check up
on, come upon, cyclotron, decathlon, early on, echelon, elec-
tron, epsilon, fall back on,
Fuji-san, Genghis Khan, go back
on, going on, goings-on, Grand
Teton, hanger-on, helicon, hexa-
gon, hold out on, Kazakhstan,
Kublai Khan, Kyrgyzstan, Lake
Huron, lay eyes on, Lebanon,
leprechaun, lexicon, liaison, load
up on, make good on, marathon,
marzipan, mastodon, miss out on,
myrmidon, octagon, off and on,
omicron, Oregon, Pakistan, pan-
theon, paragon, Parmesan,
Parthenon, pentagon, pentathlon,
Phaethon, pick up on, polygon,
put-upon, Ramadan, ride herd on,
Rubicon, run low on, set eyes on,
set foot on, silicon, sneak up on,
talkathon, Teheran, telethon,
triathlon, undergone, upsilon,
walkathon, walk out on, whereupon, woebegone • Agamemnon,
automaton, Azerbaijan,
Bellerophon, emoticon, get a
move on, keep an eye on, oxy-
moron, phenomenon, pteran-
odon, Saskatchewan, set one's
heart on, set one's sights on, sine
qua non, t'ai chi ch'uan, take it
out on, turn one's back on, zoo-
plankton • a leg to stand on, put
one's finger on, throw cold water
on, ultramarathon
on² \ō̃\ fond, ton • baton, bouillon, Dijon, Gabon, Lyon, salon
• filet mignon
on³ \ȯn\ Bonn, brawn, dawn,
Dawn, drawn, faun, fawn, gone,

lawn, on, pawn, prawn, Sean,
spawn, Vaughn, won, yawn • add-
on, Argonne, begone, bygone,
clip-on, come-on, dead-on, doggone, far-gone, foregone, hands-
on, head-on, odds-on, put-on,
Quezon, run-on, slip-on, snap-on,
turned-on, turn-on, turn on,
upon, walk-on, whereon, with-
drawn • Ben-Gurion, carry-on,
goings-on, hanger-on, leprechaun,
put-upon, undergone, whereupon,
woebegone

on⁴ \ōn\ see ONE¹

on⁵ \ən\ see UN¹

ona¹ \ō-nə\ Jonah, Mona
• bologna, Bologna, corona, kimono, Leona, Pamplona, persona,
Pomona, Ramona, Verona • Ari-
zona, Barcelona, Desdemona

ona² \än-ə\ see ANA¹

oña \ōn-yə\ see ONIA²

onachal \än-i-kəl\ see ONICAL

onae \ō-nē\ see ONY¹

onah \ō-nə\ see ONA¹

onal \ōn-ᵊl\ tonal, zonal • hor-
monal

onald \än-ᵊld\ Donald, Ronald
• MacDonald

onant \ō-nənt\ see ONENT

onas \ō-nəs\ see ONUS²

onc \äŋk\ see ONK¹

once¹ \äns\ see ANCE²

once² \əns\ see UNCE

onch¹ \äŋk\ see ONK¹

onch² \änch\ see AUNCH¹

oncha \äŋ-kə\ see ANKA

oncho \än-chō\ honcho, poncho,
rancho

onco \äŋ-kō\ bronco, Franco

ond¹ \änd\ blond, bond, fond,
frond, pond, wand • abscond, ash-
blond, beyond, fishpond, gour-
mand, junk bond, millpond,
respond • bottle blond, corre-
spond, savings bond, vagabond,
Walden Pond • back of beyond,

slough of despond, strawberry
blond
—also -ed forms of verbs listed at ON¹

ond² \ōⁿ\ see ON²

ond³ \ȯnt\ see AUNT¹

onda \än-də\ Fonda, Honda,
Rhonda, Wanda • Golconda,
Rwanda, Uganda • anaconda

ondant \än-dənt\ see ONDENT

onday \ən-dē\ see UNDI

ondays \ən-dēz\ see UNDAYS

ondda \än-də\ see ONDA

onde \änd\ see OND¹

ondeau \än-dō\ see ONDO

ondent \än-dənt\ despondent,
respondent • correspondent

onder¹ \än-dər\ condor, maunder,
ponder, squander, wander, yon-
der • responder, transponder
—also -er forms of adjectives listed
at OND¹

onder² \ən-dər\ see UNDER

ondly \än-lē\ see ANLY

ondo \än-dō\ condo, rondo • glis-
sando • accelerando

ondor \än-dər\ see ONDER¹

ondrous \ən-drəs\ see UNDEROUS

one¹ \ōn\ blown, bone, clone,
cone, crone, drone, flown, groan,
grown, hone, Joan, known, loan,
lone, moan, mown, own, phone,
prone, Rhône, roan, Saône, scone,
sewn, shone, shown, sown, stone,
throne, thrown, tone, zone
• alone, atone, backbone, be-
moan, birthstone, bloodstone,
bluestone, breastbone, brimstone,
brownstone, calzone, Capone, cell
phone, cheekbone, cologne,
Cologne, colon, Colón, condone,
corn pone, curbstone, cyclone,
dethrone, dial tone, disown, drop
zone, earphone, earth tone, end
zone, enthrone, fieldstone, fire-
stone, flagstone, flyblown, full-
blown, gallstone, gemstone,
gravestone, grindstone, hailstone,

handblown, headphone, headstone, hearthstone, high-flown, hip bone, homegrown, hormone, ingrown, in stone, intone, jawbone, keystone, limestone, lodestone, long bone, milestone, millstone, moonstone, nose cone, outgrown, outshone, ozone, pay phone, pinecone, postpone, Ramon, rhinestone, sandstone, shinbone, Shoshone, snow cone, soapstone, strike zone, T-bone, tailbone, thighbone, time zone, tombstone, touchstone, touchtone, trombone, turnstone, twotone, Tyrone, unknown, war zone, well-known, whalebone, whetstone, windblown, wishbone • anklebone, Barbizon, baritone, buffer zone, Canal Zone, chaperon, cinder cone, cobblestone, collarbone, comfort zone, cornerstone, cortisone, crazy bone, cuttlebone, Dictaphone, free-fire zone, frigid zone, funny bone, gramophone, growth hormone, herringbone, hold one's own, icecream cone, kidney stone, knucklebone, leave alone, let alone, megaphone, microphone, minestrone, monotone, neutral zone, on one's own, overblown, overgrown, overthrown, overtone, Picturephone, provolone, saxophone, silicone, sousaphone, speakerphone, stand-alone, stepping-stone, telephone, temperate zone, torrid zone, traffic cone, twilight zone, undertone, vibraphone, xylophone, Yellowstone • accident-prone, Asunción, close to the bone, eau de cologne, fire-and-brimstone, radiophone, Rosetta stone, sine qua non, strawberry roan, testosterone, videophone • philosopher's stone, Ponce de León, Sierra Leone

one² \ō-nē\ see ONY¹

one³ \än\ see ON¹

one⁴ \ən\ see UN¹

one⁵ \ȯn\ see ON³

onean \ō-nē-ən\ see ONIAN¹

oned¹ \ōnd\ boned, toned • earthtoned, high-toned, pre-owned, rawboned, two-toned • cobblestoned
—also -ed forms of verbs listed at ONE¹

oned² \än\ see ON¹

onely \ōn-lē\ lonely, only • eyesonly

onement \ōn-mənt\ atonement, postponement • Day of Atonement

onent \ō-nənt\ component, exponent, opponent, proponent

oneous \ō-nē-əs\ see ONIOUS

oner¹ \ō-nər\ boner, cloner, donor, groaner, loaner, loner, owner, stoner • landowner, shipowner • telephoner

oner² \ȯn-ər\ see AWNER¹

onerous \än-ə-rəs\ onerous, sonorous

ones \ōnz\ Jones • bare-bones, Dow Jones • Davy Jones, lazybones, make no bones • skull and crossbones
—also -s, -'s, and -s' forms of nouns and -s forms of verbs listed at ONE¹

oney¹ \ō-nē\ see ONY¹

oney² \ən-ē\ see UNNY

oney³ \ü-nē\ see OONY

ong¹ \äŋ\ gong, prong, tong • Da Nang, Hong Kong, Mah-Jongg, Mekong, ping-pong, sarong • billabong, Pyongyang, Sturm und Drang, Vietcong

ong² \ȯŋ\ bong, gong, long, prong, song, strong, thong, throng, tong, wrong • along, Armstrong, belong, birdsong, chaise longue, daylong, ding-dong, dugong, fight

song, folk song, furlong,
Haiphong, headlong, headstrong,
Hong Kong, hour-long, lifelong,
livelong, Mekong, monthlong,
nightlong, oblong, part-song,
Ping-Pong, prolong, sarong, side-
long, singsong, so long, swan
song, theme song, torch song,
weeklong, work song, yearlong
• all along, before long, billabong,
come along, cradlesong, drinking
song, get along, go along, run
along, sing-along, siren song,
string along, summerlong, taga-
long, Vietcong

ong³ \əŋ\ see UNG¹

ong⁴ \u̇ng\ see UNG²

onga \äŋ-gə\ conga, Tonga
• chimichanga

onge \ənj\ see UNGE

onged \o̊ṅd\ pronged, wronged
• multipronged
—*also* -ed *forms of verbs listed at*
ONG²

onger¹ \əŋ-gər\ hunger, younger
• fearmonger, fishmonger, scare-
monger, warmonger • gossipmon-
ger, rumormonger,
scandalmonger

onger² \ən-jər\ see UNGER¹

ongery \əŋ-grē\ hungry • ironmon-
gery

ongful \o̊ṅ-fəl\ wrongful, songful

ongish \o̊ṅ-ish\ longish, strongish

ongo \äŋ-gō\ bongo, Congo • Belgian Congo, Pago Pago

ongous \əŋ-gəs\ see UNGOUS

ongue¹ \əŋ\ see UNG¹

ongue² \o̊ṅ\ see ONG²

ongy \ən-jē\ see UNGY

onhomous \än-ə-məs\ see ONYMOUS

oni \ō-nē\ see ONY¹

onia¹ \ō-nē-ə\ Estonia, Franconia,
Laconia, Slavonia, zirconia
• Amazonia, Babylonia, Caledonia, Catalonia, Macedonia, Patagonia • New Caledonia

onia² \ō-nyə\ doña, Sonia • ammo-
nia, begonia, Bologna, Estonia,
Franconia, Laconia, pneumonia,
Slavonia • Babylonia, Caledonia,
Catalonia, Macedonia, Patagonia
• double pneumonia, New Caledonia, walking pneumonia

onial \ō-nē-əl\ baronial, colonial
• ceremonial, Dutch Colonial,
matrimonial, testimonial

onian¹ \ō-nē-ən\ Bostonian, dra-
conian, Estonian, Houstonian,
Jacksonian, Miltonian, Newtonian, Wilsonian • Amazonian,
Arizonian, Babylonian, calypson-
ian, Catalonian, Ciceronian,
Emersonian, Hamiltonian, Jeffersonian, Macedonian, Oregonian,
Patagonian, Washingtonian

onian² \ō-nyən\ Bostonian, Eston-
ian, Franconian, Houstonian,
Miltonian, Newtonian, Nixonian,
Slavonian • Amazonian, Arizon-
ian, Babylonian, Ciceronian,
Emersonian, Jeffersonian, Mace-
donian, Oregonian, Patagonian,
Washingtonian

onic \än-ik\ chronic, conic, phonic,
sonic, tonic • bionic, bubonic,
cyclonic, demonic, harmonic,
iconic, Ionic, ironic, laconic,
Masonic, mnemonic, moronic,
planktonic, platonic, sardonic,
Slavonic, subsonic, symphonic,
tectonic, Teutonic • catatonic,
electronic, embryonic, histrionic,
Housatonic, philharmonic, poly-
phonic, quadraphonic, super-
sonic, ultrasonic • stereophonic

onica \än-i-kə\ Monica • harmonica, Veronica • electronica, glass
harmonica, Santa Monica, Thes-
salonica

onical \än-i-kəl\ chronicle, conical,
monocle • canonical

onicle \än-i-kəl\ see ONICAL

onics \än-iks\ onyx, phonics

• bionics, tectonics • electronics, plate tectonics
—*also* -s, -'s, *and* -s' *forms of nouns listed at* ONIC

onika \än-i-kə\ see ONICA

oning[1] \än-iŋ\ awning
—*also* -ing *forms of verbs listed at* ON[1]

oning[2] \ō-niŋ\ jawboning, landowning
—*also* -ing *forms of verbs listed at* ONE[1]

onion \ən-yən\ see UNION

onious \ō-nē-əs\ Antonius, erroneous, felonious, harmonious, Petronius, Polonius • acrimonious, ceremonious, parsimonious, sanctimonious • unceremonious

onis[1] \ō-nəs\ see ONUS[2]

onis[2] \än-əs\ see ONUS[1]

onish \än-ish\ admonish, astonish • leprechaunish

onishment \än-ish-mənt\ admonishment, astonishment

onium \ō-nē-əm\ euphonium, plutonium • pandemonium, Pandemonium

onius \ō-nē-əs\ see ONIOUS

onja \ō-nyə\ see ONIA[2]

onk[1] \äŋk\ bonk, bronc, conch, conk, honk, plonk, wonk, zonk • honky-tonk

onk[2] \əŋk\ see UNK

onkey[1] \äŋ-kē\ see ONKY

onkey[2] \əŋ-kē\ see UNKY

onky \äŋ-kē\ donkey, wonky, yanqui

onless \ən-ləs\ see UNLESS

only \ōn-lē\ see ONELY

onment \ōn-mənt\ see ONEMENT

onn[1] \än\ see ON[1]

onn[2] \ȯn\ see ON[3]

onna[1] \ȯn-ə\ Donna, fauna, sauna • prima donna

onna[2] \än-ə\ see ANA[1]

onne[1] \än\ see ON[1]

onne[2] \ən\ see UN[1]

onne[3] \ȯn\ see ON[3]

onner \än-ər\ see ONOR[1]

onnet \än-ət\ bonnet, sonnet • bluebonnet, sunbonnet, warbonnet • bee in one's bonnet

onnie \än-ē\ see ANI[1]

onnish \än-ish\ see ONISH

onnor \än-ər\ see ONOR[1]

onny[1] \än-ē\ see ANI[1]

onny[2] \ən-ē\ see UNNY

ono[1] \ō-nō\ kimono, pro bono

ono[2] \ō-nə\ see ONA[1]

ono[3] \än-ō\ see ANO[1]

onocle \än-i-kəl\ see ONICAL

onomist \än-ə-məst\ agronomist, economist • home economist

onomous \än-ə-məs\ see ONYMOUS

onomy \än-ə-mē\ agronomy, astronomy, autonomy, economy, gastronomy, taxonomy • Deuteronomy

onor[1] \än-ər\ goner, honor, yawner • dishonor, O'Connor • Afrikaner, maid of honor, marathoner, point of honor, weimaraner • Legion of Honor, matron of honor, Medal of Honor

onor[2] \ō-nər\ see ONER[1]

onorous \än-ə-rəs\ see ONEROUS

ons[1] \änz\ see ONZE

ons[2] \ō[m]\ see ON[2]

onsil \än-səl\ see ONSUL

onsin \än-sən\ see OHNSON

onson \än-sən\ see OHNSON

onsul \än-səl\ consul, tonsil • proconsul

ont[1] \ənt\ blunt, brunt, bunt, front, grunt, hunt, punt, runt, shunt, stunt, want • affront, beachfront, cold front, confront, forefront, home front, lakefront, manhunt, shorefront, storefront, up-front, warm front, witch hunt • battlefront, oceanfront, riverfront, waterfront • scavenger hunt

ont[2] \änt\ see ANT[2]

ont³ \ȯnt\ see AUNT¹

on't \ōnt\ don't, won't

ontal¹ \änt-ᵊl\ horizontal • periodontal

ontal² \ənt-ᵊl\ see UNTLE

ontas \änt-əs\ see ONTUS

onte¹ \änt-ē\ see ANTI¹

onte² \än-tā\ see ANTE¹

onted \ȯnt-əd\ vaunted, wonted • undaunted
—*also* -ed *forms of verbs listed at* AUNT¹

onter \ənt-ər\ see UNTER

onth \ənth\ month • billionth, millionth, trillionth, twelvemonth • gazillionth

ontil \änt-ᵊl\ see ONTAL¹

onto \än-tō\ see ANTO

ontra \än-trə\ contra, mantra

ontre \änt-ər\ see AUNTER¹

ontus \änt-əs\ Pontus • Pocahontas

onty \änt-ē\ see ANTI¹

onus¹ \än-əs\ Cronus, Faunus • Adonis

onus² \ō-nəs\ bonus, Cronus, Jonas, onus, slowness • Adonis

ony¹ \ō-nē\ bony, coney, crony, phony, pony, Sony, stony, Toni, Tony • baloney, bologna, cow pony, Giorgione, Marconi, Moroni, Shoshone, spumoni, tortoni • abalone, acrimony, alimony, ceremony, hegemony, macaroni, matrimony, minestrone, one-trick pony, patrimony, pepperoni, provolone, sanctimony, Shetland pony, testimony, zabaglione • phony-baloney • dramatis personae

ony² \än-ē\ see ANI¹

onya \ō-nyə\ see ONIA²

onymist \än-ə-məst\ see ONOMIST

onymous \än-ə-məs\ anonymous, autonomous, synonymous

onymy \än-ə-mē\ see ONOMY

onyon \ən-yən\ see UNION

onyx \än-iks\ see ONICS

onze \änz\ bronze • long johns, Saint John's • Afrikaans
—*also* -s, -'s, *and* -s' *forms of nouns and* -s *forms of verbs listed at* ON¹

oo¹ \ü\ see EW¹

oo² \ō\ see OW¹

oob \üb\ see UBE

oober \ü-bər\ see UBER

ooby \ü-bē\ booby, ruby, Ruby

ooch¹ \üch\ brooch, mooch, pooch, smooch

ooch² \ōch\ see OACH

oocher \ü-chər\ see UTURE

oochy \ü-chē\ smoochy • penuche, Vespucci

ood¹ \u̇d\ good, hood, should, stood, wood, would • basswood, boxwood, boyhood, brushwood, childhood, cordwood, corkwood, deadwood, dogwood, driftwood, falsehood, feel-good, firewood, for good, girlhood, greenwood, hardwood, heartwood, ironwood, knighthood, make good, manhood, Mount Hood, no-good, pinewood, plywood, priesthood, pulpwood, redwood, rosewood, sainthood, Sherwood, softwood, statehood, stinkwood, Talmud, Wedgwood, wifehood, withstood, wormwood • adulthood, bachelorhood, brotherhood, candlewood, cedarwood, cottonwood, fatherhood, Hollywood, knock on wood, likelihood, livelihood, maidenhood, motherhood, neighborhood, parenthood, Robin Hood, sandalwood, sisterhood, to the good, tulipwood, understood, widowhood, womanhood • blood brotherhood, grandparenthood, misunderstood, second childhood, unlikelihood

ood² \ōd\ see ODE

ood³ \üd\ see UDE¹

ood⁴ \əd\ see UD¹

ooded[1] \əd-əd\ blue-blooded, cold-blooded, full-blooded, half-blooded, hot-blooded, pure-blooded, red-blooded, star-studded, warm-blooded
—*also* -ed *forms of verbs listed at* UD[1]

ooded[2] \ud-əd\ hooded, wooded

ooder[1] \ud-ər\ *see* UDER

ooder[2] \əd-ər\ *see* UDDER

oodle \ud-əl\ doodle, feudal, noodle, poodle, strudel • caboodle, canoodle, toy poodle • Yankee-Doodle

oodoo \ud-ü\ doo-doo, hoodoo, kudu, voodoo • in deep doo-doo

oods \udz\ hoods • backwoods, dry goods, piece goods, white goods • bill of goods, piney woods • consumer goods, Lake of the Woods • deliver the goods
—*also* -s, -'s, *and* -s' forms of nouns listed at OOD[1]

oodsman \udz-mən\ woodsman • backwoodsman, ombudsman

oody[1] \ud-ē\ broody, Judy, moody, Rudy, Trudy

oody[2] \ud-ē\ goody, hoody, woody

oody[3] \əd-ē\ *see* UDDY[1]

ooer \ü-ər\ *see* EWER[1]

ooey \ü-ē\ *see* EWY

oof[1] \üf\ goof, hoof, poof, proof, roof, spoof, woof • aloof, bombproof, childproof, crushproof, fireproof, flameproof, foolproof, forehoof, germproof, greaseproof, heatproof, leakproof, lightproof, moonroof, pickproof, rainproof, reproof, rustproof, shockproof, soundproof, stainproof, sunroof, windproof • bulletproof, burglarproof, gable roof, gambrel roof, hit the roof, ovenproof, shatterproof, tamperproof, through the roof, waterproof, weatherproof • burden of proof, idiotproof

oof[2] \uf\ hoof, poof, roof, woof

• moon roof • cloven hoof, gable roof, gambrel roof, hit the roof, through the roof

oof[3] \ōf\ *see* OAF

oof[4] \üv\ *see* OVE[3]

oofer[1] \ü-fər\ roofer, twofer

oofer[2] \uf-ər\ hoofer, woofer

oofy \ü-fē\ goofy, Sufi

ooga \ü-gə\ *see* UGA

ooge \üj\ *see* UGE[1]

ooger \ug-ər\ *see* UGUR

oogie \ug-ē\ bogey, boogie • boogie-woogie

oo-goo \ü-gü\ *see* UGU

ooh \ü\ *see* EW[1]

ooi \ü-ē\ *see* EWY

ooist \ü-əst\ doest • tattooist, voodooist
—*also* -est *forms of adjectives listed at* EW[1]

ook[1] \uk\ book, brook, cook, Cook, crook, hook, look, nook, rook, shook, took • bankbook, checkbook, cookbook, e-book, forsook, fishhook, guidebook, handbook, hymnbook, Innsbruck, logbook, matchbook, mistook, Mount Cook, notebook, outlook, partook, phrase book, pothook, prayer book, schoolbook, scrapbook, sketchbook, songbook, stylebook, textbook, unhook, wordbook, workbook, yearbook • buttonhook, comic book, donnybrook, grappling hook, inglenook, off the hook, overlook, overtook, picture book, pocketbook, pocket book, pressure-cook, pruning hook, Sandy Hook, storybook, talking book, tenterhook, undertook • audiobook, coloring book, gobbledygook, ring off the hook, telephone book • by hook or by crook

ook[2] \ük\ *see* UKE

ooka \ü-kə\ yuca • bazooka, palooka

ooke \ùk\ see OOK[1]

ooker \ùk-ər\ booker, cooker, looker, snooker • good-looker, onlooker • pressure cooker

ookery \ùk-ə-rē\ cookery, rookery

ookie \ùk-ē\ bookie, cookie, hooky, rookie • fortune cookie

ooking \ùk-iŋ\ booking, cooking • good-looking • forward-looking, solid-looking
—also -ing *forms of verbs listed at* OOK[1]

ooklet \ùk-lət\ booklet, brooklet

ooks[1] \ùks\ deluxe
—also -s, -'s, *and* -s' *forms of nouns and* -s *forms of verbs listed at* UKE

ooks[2] \ùks\ Brooks, crux, looks • deluxe • on tenterhooks
—also -s, -'s, *and* -s' *forms of nouns and* -s *forms of verbs listed at* OOK[1]

ooky[1] \ü-kē\ kooky, spooky • bouzouki, Kabuki

ooky[2] \ùk-ē\ see OOKIE

ool[1] \ül\ cool, drool, fool, fuel, ghoul, mule, pool, rule, school, spool, stool, tool, you'll, yule • air-cool, B-school, carpool, church school, cesspool, day school, edge tool, footstool, gene pool, grade school, high school, homeschool, Kabul, misrule, Mosul, old school, prep school, preschool, refuel, retool, self-rule, step stool, synfuel, tide pool, toadstool, trade school, uncool, unspool, whirlpool • April fool, blow one's cool, boarding school, charter school, ducking stool, grammar school, Istanbul, Liverpool, machine tool, magnet school, middle school, minuscule, molecule, motor pool, nursery school, overrule, private school, public school, reform school, ridicule, summer school, Sunday school, training school, vestibule, wading pool • finishing school, junior high school, parochial school, primary school, senior high school • alternative school, secondary school

ool[2] \ùl\ see UL[1]

oola \ü-lə\ see ULA

oole \ül\ see OOL[1]

oolean \ü-lē-ən\ see ULEAN

ooled \üld\ bejeweled, unschooled
—also -ed *forms of verbs listed at* OOL[1]

ooler \ü-lər\ cooler, ruler • carpooler, grade-schooler, high schooler, homeschooler, preschooler, wine cooler • middle schooler, watercooler

oolie \ü-lē\ see ULY

oolish \ü-lish\ foolish, ghoulish, mulish

oolly[1] \ü-lē\ see ULY

oolly[2] \ùl-ē\ see ULLY[2]

oom[1] \üm\ bloom, boom, broom, doom, flume, fume, gloom, groom, loom, plume, room, spume, tomb, vroom, whom, womb, zoom • abloom, assume, backroom, ballroom, barroom, bathroom, bedroom, boardroom, bridegroom, chat room, checkroom, classroom, cloakroom, coatroom, consume, costume, courtroom, darkroom, entomb, exhume, greenroom, guardroom, headroom, heirloom, homeroom, Khartoum, legroom, legume, lunchroom, men's room, mushroom, perfume, playroom, poolroom, pressroom, presume, restroom, resume, schoolroom, showroom, sickroom, stateroom, stockroom, storeroom, sunroom, throne room, washroom, weight room, whisk broom, workroom • baby boom, banquet room, birthing room, elbow room, family room, ladies' room, living room, locker-room, nom de plume, powder room, rumpus room, sitting room, sonic boom, standing room, waiting room, women's room • lower the boom, master bedroom, recovery room • emergency room, recreation room

oom² \ùm\ see UM²

oomed \ümd\ plumed • well-groomed

—*also* -ed *forms of verbs listed at* OOM¹

oomer \ü-mər\ see UMER

oomily \ü-mə-lē\ doomily, gloomily

ooming¹ \ü-mən\ see UMAN

ooming² \ü-miŋ\ see UMING

oomy \ü-mē\ bloomy, boomy, doomy, gloomy, roomy • costumey

oon¹ \ün\ boon, Boone, coon, croon, dune, goon, hewn, June, loon, moon, noon, prune, rune, soon, spoon, swoon, strewn, tune • attune, baboon, balloon, bassoon, blue moon, buffoon, Calhoun, Cancún, cartoon, cocoon, commune, doubloon, dragoon, festoon, fine-tune, forenoon, full moon, half-moon, harpoon, high noon, immune, impugn, Kowloon, lagoon, lampoon, maroon, monsoon, Neptune, new moon, Pashtun, platoon, pontoon, raccoon, rough-hewn, saloon, soupspoon, teaspoon, tribune, tycoon, typhoon, Walloon • afternoon, Brigadoon, Cameroon, dessertspoon, greasy spoon, harvest moon, honeymoon, importune, macaroon, opportune, picayune, Saskatoon, silver spoon, tablespoon • contrabassoon, inopportune, over the moon, trial balloon

oon² \ōn\ see ONE¹

oona \ü-nə\ see UNA

oonal \ün-ᵊl\ see UNAL

oone \ün\ see OON¹

ooner \ü-nər\ crooner, lunar, schooner, tuner • harpooner • honeymooner, prairie schooner

oonery¹ \ün-rē\ buffoonery, lampoonery

oonery² \ü-nə-rē\ see UNARY

ooney \ü-nē\ see OONY

oonie \ü-nē\ see OONY

ooning \ü-niŋ\ ballooning, cartooning, cocooning

—*also* -ing *forms of verbs listed at* OON¹

oonish \ü-nish\ buffoonish, cartoonish

oonless \ün-ləs\ moonless, tuneless

oons \ünz\ afternoons, loony tunes

—*also* -s, -'s, *and* -s' *forms of nouns and* -s *forms of verbs listed at* OON¹

oony \ü-nē\ loony, Moonie, moony, puny, Zuni • cartoony

oop \üp\ coop, coupe, croup, droop, dupe, goop, group, hoop, loop, poop, scoop, sloop, snoop, soup, stoop, swoop, troop, troupe, whoop • age-group, blood group, duck soup, in-group, newsgroup, pea soup, playgroup, recoup, regroup, war whoop • alley-oop, Betty Boop, bird's-nest soup, for a loop, Guadeloupe, Hula Hoop, nincompoop, paratroop, pressure group, support group • alphabet soup, knock for a loop, mock turtle soup

o-op \üp\ see OOP

oopee \ü-pē\ see OOPY

ooper \ü-pər\ blooper, Cooper, looper, scooper, stupor, super, trooper, trouper • storm trooper • party pooper, paratrooper, pooper-scooper, super-duper

oops \ùps\ oops, whoops

oopy \ü-pē\ droopy, groupie, loopy, snoopy, Snoopy, soupy, whoopee

oor¹ \or\ see OR¹

oor² \ur\ see URE¹

oorage¹ \ur-ij\ moorage • sewerage

oorage² \or-ij\ see ORAGE²

oore¹ \or\ see OR¹

oore² \ur\ see URE¹

oored \ord\ see OARD

oorer \or-ər\ see ORER

oori \ur-ē\ see URY¹

ooring¹ \or-iŋ\ see ORING

ooring² \ur-iŋ\ see URING

oorish \ur-ish\ boorish, Moorish

oorly \ur-lē\ see URELY

oorman \or-mən\ see ORMAN

oors \orz\ drawers, yours • Azores, indoors, outdoors • out-of-doors
—*also* -s, -'s, *and* -s' *forms of nouns and* -s *forms of verbs listed at* OR¹

oorsman \orz-mən\ see OARSMAN

oort \ort\ see ORT¹

oosa \ü-sə\ see USA¹

oose¹ \üs\ see USE¹

oose² \üz\ see USE²

ooser¹ \ü-sər\ see UCER

ooser² \ü-zər\ see USER

oosey \ü-sē\ see UICY

oosh¹ \üsh\ see OUCHE

oosh² \ush\ see USH²

oost \üst\ boost, juiced, roost • self-induced
—*also* -ed *forms of verbs listed at* USE¹

oosy \ü-zē\ see OOZY

oot¹ \ut\ foot, put, root, soot • afoot, barefoot, bigfoot, Blackfoot, board foot, clubfoot, cube root, hard put, input, kaput, on foot, output, Rajput, shot put, square root, taproot, trench foot, uproot • arrowroot, athlete's foot, hand and foot, pussyfoot, tenderfoot, underfoot

oot² \üt\ see UTE

oot³ \ət\ see UT¹

ooted¹ \üt-əd\ booted, fruited, muted • deep-rooted, jackbooted, reputed
—*also* -ed *forms of verbs listed at* UTE

ooted² \ut-əd\ clubfooted, deep-rooted, flat-footed, fleet-footed, four-footed, heavy-footed, light-footed, slow-footed, surefooted, web-footed • cloven-footed
—*also* -ed *forms of verbs listed at* OOT¹

ooter¹ \ut-ər\ footer, putter • shot-putter • pussyfooter

ooter² \üt-ər\ see UTER

ooth¹ \üth\ smooth, soothe

ooth² \üth\ booth, Booth, Ruth, sleuth, tooth, truth, youth • bucktooth, dogtooth, Duluth, eyetooth, half-truth, in truth, milk tooth, sweet tooth, tollbooth, uncouth, untruth • baby tooth, snaggletooth, wisdom tooth • moment of truth, projection booth, telephone booth

oothe \üth\ see OOTH¹

oothed \ütht\ sleuthed, toothed • bucktoothed, gap-toothed • saber-toothed, snaggletoothed

oothless \üth-ləs\ see UTHLESS

ootie \üt-ē\ see OOTY¹

ooting¹ \ut-iŋ\ footing • off-putting, war footing
—*also* -ing *forms of verbs listed at* OOT¹

ooting² \üt-iŋ\ see UTING

ootle \üt-ᵊl\ see UTILE

ootless \üt-ləs\ fruitless, rootless

oots \üts\ grassroots, Vaduz
—*also* -s, -'s, *and* -s' *forms of nouns and* -s *forms of verbs listed at* UTE

ootsie \ut-sē\ footsie, tootsie

ooty¹ \üt-ē\ beauty, booty, cootie, cutie, duty, fruity, snooty, sooty • agouti, Djibouti • Funafuti, heavy-duty, tutti-frutti

ooty² \ət-ē\ see UTTY
oove \üv\ see OVE³
oover \ü-vər\ see OVER³
oovy \ü-vē\ groovy, movie • B movie
ooze \üz\ see USE²
oozer \ü-zər\ see USER
oozle \ü-zəl\ see USAL
oozy \ü-zē\ choosy, floozy, newsy, oozy, Susie, woozy • Jacuzzi
op¹ \äp\ bop, chop, clop, cop, crop, drop, flop, fop, glop, hop, lop, mop, plop, pop, prop, shop, slop, sop, stop, swap, top, whop • Aesop, airdrop, a pop, atop, backdrop, backstop, bakeshop, bebop, bellhop, benchtop, big top, blacktop, bookshop, cartop, cash crop, clip-clop, coin-op, cooktop, co-op, cough drop, desktop, dewdrop, doorstop, doo-wop, dry mop, dust mop, eavesdrop, field crop, flattop, flip-flop, gumdrop, hardtop, high-top, hilltop, hiphop, hockshop, housetop, laptop, name-drop, nonstop, one-stop, palmtop, pawnshop, pit stop, poptop, post-op, pre-op, ragtop, raindrop, rooftop, root crop, sharecrop, shortstop, snowdrop, sweatshop, sweetshop, tank top, teardrop, thrift shop, tip-top, treetop, truck stop, workshop • barbershop, beauty shop, belly flop, blow one's top, body shop, carrottop, channel-hop, coffee shop, countertop, cover crop, drag-and-drop, island-hop, lollipop, machine shop, mom-and-pop, mountaintop, photo op, set up shop, soda pop, tabletop, techno-pop, teenybop, turboprop, union shop, whistle-stop, windowshop • comparison shop
op² \ō\ see OW¹
opal \ō-pəl\ opal • Constantinople
ope \ōp\ cope, dope, grope, hope,

Hope, lope, mope, nope, ope, pope, Pope, rope, scope, slope, soap, taupe • downslope, elope, fly dope, jump rope, North Slope, skip rope, tightrope, towrope • antelope, cantaloupe, envelope, forlorn hope, gyroscope, horoscope, interlope, isotope, microscope, misanthrope, periscope, slippery slope, stethoscope, telescope • Cape of Good Hope, kaleidoscope, oscilloscope, pay envelope, stereoscope
opean \ō-pē-ən\ see OPIAN
opee \ō-pē\ see OPI
opence \əp-əns\ see UPPANCE
oper \ō-pər\ coper, soaper • eloper • interloper
opey \ō-pē\ see OPI
oph \ōf\ see OAF
ophe¹ \ō-fē\ see OPHY
ophe² \ōf\ see OFF²
opher \ō-fər\ see OFER
ophie \ō-fē\ see OPHY
ophir \ō-fər\ see OFER
ophy \ō-fē\ Sophie, strophe, trophy
opi \ō-pē\ dopey, Hopi, mopey, ropy, soapy
opia \ō-pē-ə\ myopia, utopia • cornucopia, Ethiopia
opian \ō-pē-ən\ Aesopian, utopian • Ethiopian
opic¹ \äp-ik\ topic, tropic • Aesopic, myopic, subtropic • gyroscopic, microscopic, misanthropic, philanthropic, semitropic, telescopic • kaleidoscopic, stereoscopic
opic² \ō-pik\ tropic • myopic • Ethiopic
opical \äp-i-kəl\ topical, tropical • subtropical
oplar \äp-lər\ see OPPLER
ople \ō-pəl\ see OPAL
opol \ō-pəl\ see OPAL
opolis \äp-ə-ləs\ acropolis, metropolis, necropolis • megalopolis

opoly \äp-ə-lē\ choppily, floppily, sloppily • monopoly, Monopoly, vox populi

opped \äpt\ see OPT

opper \äp-ər\ chopper, copper, dropper, hopper, proper, shopper, stopper, swapper, whopper • clodhopper, eavesdropper, eyedropper, eyepopper, grasshopper, heart-stopper, hip-hopper, improper, jaw-dropper, job-hopper, leafhopper, name-dropper, sharecropper, showstopper, woodchopper • teenybopper, window-shopper

oppily \äp-ə-lē\ see OPOLY

oppiness \äp-ē-nəs\ choppiness, sloppiness

opping \äp-iŋ\ hopping, sopping, topping, whopping • eye-popping, heart-stopping, jaw-dropping, job-hopping, name-dropping, outcropping, showstopping • channel-hopping
—*also* -ing *forms of verbs listed at* OP[1]

oppler \äp-lər\ Doppler, poplar

oppy \äp-ē\ choppy, copy, floppy, gloppy, poppy, sloppy, soppy • jalopy, serape • photocopy

ops \äps\ chops, copse, tops • Cheops, cyclops, Cyclops, eyedrops, Pelops • lick one's chops • from the housetops, triceratops
—*also* -s, -'s, *and* -s' *forms of nouns and* -s *forms of verbs listed at* OP[1]

opse \äps\ see OPS

opsy \äp-sē\ autopsy, biopsy

opt \äpt\ opt, topped • adopt, close-cropped, co-opt • carrot-topped
—*also* -ed *forms of verbs listed at* OP[1]

opter \äp-tər\ copter • adopter, helicopter

optic \äp-tik\ Coptic, optic • fiber-optic

option \äp-shən\ option • adoption

opuli \äp-ə-lē\ see OPOLY

opus \ō-pəs\ opus • Canopus, Mount Scopus • magnum opus

opy[1] \ō-pē\ see OPI

opy[2] \äp-ē\ see OPPY

oque[1] \ōk\ see OKE[1]

oque[2] \äk\ see OCK[1]

oque[3] \ōk\ see ALK

or[1] \ȯr\ boar, Boer, bore, chore, core, corps, door, drawer, floor, for, fore, four, gore, Gore, lore, Moore, more, nor, o'er, oar, or, ore, poor, pore, pour, roar, score, shore, snore, soar, sore, spoor, spore, store, swore, Thor, tor, tore, war, wore, yore, your, you're • abhor, adore, and/or, as for, ashore, backdoor, Bangor, bedsore, before, bookstore, box score, call for, candor, captor, centaur, chain store, closed-door, cold sore, condor, decor, deplore, dime-store, Dior, done for, donor, downpour, drugstore, Dutch door, encore, explore, eyesore, fall for, Fillmore, flexor, folklore, footsore, fourscore, French door, full-bore, galore, go for, ground floor, hard-core, ignore, implore, indoor, in for, in-store, Lahore, lakeshore, Lenore, look for, Luxor, memoir, mentor, Mysore, Nestor, next-door, offshore, onshore, outdoor, phosphor, rancor, rapport, raptor, Realtor, restore, savior, seafloor, seashore, sector, señor, sensor, Seymour, smooth-bore, s'more, sophomore, stand for, storm door, subfloor, Tagore, take for, temblor, tensor, therefore, threescore, Timor, top-drawer, trapdoor, uproar, vendor, what's more, wherefore, wild boar, woodlore • albacore, allosaur, alongshore, anymore, archosaur, at death's door, at one's door, Baltimore, Bangalore, bargain for, Barrymore, canker sore, carnivore, close the door, come in for, commodore, corridor, dinosaur, door-to-door, double door, Eastern shore, East Timor, Ecuador, either-or, Eleanor, elector, evermore, except for, forest floor, from the floor, furthermore, general store, go in for, guarantor, herbivore, heretofore, in line for, Labrador, man-of-war, matador, metaphor, meteor, Minotaur, more and more, Mount Rushmore, Mount Tabor, nevermore, omnivore, picador, pinafore, pompadour, predator, reservoir, saddle sore, Salvador, semaphore, Singapore, stand up for, stevedore, stick up for, struggle for, superstore, sycamore, take the floor, Theodore, to die for, troubadour, tug-of-war, two-by-four, uncalled-for, underscore • ambassador, conquistador, conservator, convenience store, Corregidor, department store, El Salvador, esprit de corps, foot in the door, forevermore, go to bat for, have it in for, insectivore, legislator, national seashore, revolving door, San Salvador, toreador, tyrannosaur • administrator, lobster thermidor, variety store

or² \ər\ see EUR¹

ora \ȯr-ə\ aura, Cora, Dora, flora, Flora, hora, Laura, Lora, Nora, Torah • Andorra, angora, aurora, fedora, Gomorrah, Lenora, menorah, Pandora, remora, señora, Sonora • Bora-Bora, Leonora, Simchas Torah

orable \ȯr-ə-bəl\ horrible, pourable, storable • adorable, deplorable, restorable

orace \ȯr-əs\ see AURUS

orage¹ \är-ij\ forage, porridge

orage² \ȯr-ij\ forage, porridge, storage • cold storage

orah \ȯr-ə\ see ORA

oral \ȯr-əl\ aural, choral, coral, floral, laurel, Laurel, moral, oral, quarrel • amoral, immoral, mayoral, monaural • electoral

oram \ȯr-əm\ see ORUM

orative \ȯr-ət-iv\ pejorative, restorative

oray \ə-rē\ see URRY

orb \ȯrb\ orb • absorb • reabsorb

orc \ȯrk\ see ORK²

orca \ȯr-ka\ orca • Majorca

orce \ȯrs\ see ORSE¹

orced \ȯrst\ see ORST¹

orceful \ȯrs-fəl\ see ORSEFUL

orcement \ȯr-smənt\ see ORSEMENT

orcer \ȯr-sər\ coarser, hoarser • enforcer

orch \ȯrch\ porch, scorch, torch • blowtorch, sunporch • sleeping porch

orcher \ȯr-chər\ scorcher, torture

orchid \ȯr-kəd\ forked, orchid

ord¹ \ȯrd\ see OARD

ord² \ərd\ see IRD

ord³ \ȯr\ see OR¹

ordan \ȯrd-ᵊn\ see ARDEN²

ordant \ȯrd-ᵊnt\ mordant • discordant

orde \ȯrd\ see OARD

orded \ȯrd-əd\ see ARDED²

ordent \ȯrd-ᵊnt\ see ORDANT

order \ȯrd-ər\ boarder, border, hoarder, order • back order, court order, disorder, gag order, in order, keyboarder, mail-order, on order, recorder, reorder, sailboarder, short-order, skateboarder, snowboarder, surfboarder, to order, transborder, word order • flight recorder, holy order, in short order, law-and-order, made-to-order, money order, mood disorder, pecking order, tape recorder, wire recorder • eating disorder, panic disorder, restraining order

ordered \órd-ərd\ bordered, ordered • disordered, well-ordered —*also* -ed *forms of verbs listed at* ORDER

orders \órd-ərz\ marching orders —*also* -s, -'s, *and* -s' *forms of nouns and* -s *forms of verbs listed at* ORDER

ordid \órd-əd\ see ARDED²

ording¹ \órd-iŋ\ hoarding • recording, rewarding, skateboarding • tape recording, weatherboarding —*also* -ing *forms of verbs listed at* OARD

ording² \ərd-iŋ\ see ERDING

ordion \órd-ē-ən\ accordion, Edwardian

ordon \órd-ᵊn\ see ARDEN²

ordure \ór-jər\ see ORGER

ordy \ərd-ē\ see URDY

ore¹ \ór-ē\ see ORY

ore² \ùr\ see URE¹

ore³ \ər-ə\ see OROUGH¹

ore⁴ \ór\ see OR¹

oreal \ór-ē-əl\ see ORIAL

orean \ór-ē-ən\ see ORIAN

oreas \ór-ē-əs\ see ORIOUS

ored \órd\ see OARD

orehead \ór-əd\ see ORRID

oreign¹ \är-ən\ see ARIN

oreign² \ór-ən\ see ORIN¹

oreigner \ór-ə-nər\ see ORONER

orem \ór-əm\ see ORUM

oreman \ór-mən\ see ORMAN

orence \ór-ən(t)s\ see AWRENCE

oreous \ór-ē-əs\ see ORIOUS

orer \ór-ər\ borer, corer, floorer, horror, poorer, pourer, scorer, snorer, sorer • adorer, corn borer, explorer • Sea Explorer

ores¹ \ór-əs\ see AURUS

ores² \órz\ see OORS

orest \ór-əst\ see ORIST

orester \ór-ə-stər\ see ORISTER

oreum \ór-ē-əm\ see ORIUM

oreward \ór-wərd\ see ORWARD

oreword \ór-wərd\ see ORWARD

orey \ór-ē\ see ORY

orf \órf\ see ORPH

org¹ \órg\ Borg, morgue • cyborg

org² \ór-ē\ see ORY

organ \ór-gən\ gorgon, Morgan, organ • hand organ, house organ, mouth organ, pipe organ, reed organ, sense organ • barrel organ

orge \órj\ forge, George, gorge • disgorge, engorge, Fort George, Lake George, Lloyd George • Royal Gorge • Olduvai Gorge

orger \ór-jər\ forger, ordure

orgi \ór-gē\ see ORGY

orgia \ór-jə\ Borgia, Georgia

orgon \ór-gən\ see ORGAN

orgue \órg\ see ORG¹

orgy \ór-gē\ corgi, porgy

ori \ór-ē\ see ORY

oria \ór-ē-ə\ Gloria • euphoria, Peoria, Pretoria, Victoria • Lake Victoria • phantasmagoria

orial \ór-ē-əl\ boreal, oriole • arboreal, armorial, authorial, corporeal, factorial, manorial, marmoreal, memorial, pictorial, sartorial, tutorial • curatorial, dictatorial, editorial, equatorial, immemorial, janitorial, professorial, senatorial, territorial • ambassadorial, conspiratorial, gubernatorial, prosecutorial, time immemorial

oriam \ór-ē-əm\ see ORIUM

orian \ór-ē-ən\ Dorian • Azorean, Gregorian, historian, praetorian, stentorian, Victorian • dinosaurian, Ecuadorean, Labradorean, Salvadorean, Singaporean • salutatorian, valedictorian

oric \ór-ik\ caloric, euphoric, folkloric, historic, phosphoric • metaphoric, meteoric,

noncaloric, prehistoric, sopho-
moric • phantasmagoric

orical \ȯr-i-kəl\ historical, rhetori-
cal • allegorical, categorical,
metaphorical, oratorical

orid \ȯr-əd\ see ORRID

oriel \ȯr-ē-əl\ see ORIAL

orin[1] \ȯr-ən\ chlorine, foreign,
Lauren, Orrin, warren, Warren
• Andorran

orin[2] \är-ən\ see ARIN

orine \ȯr-ən\ see ORIN[1]

oring \ȯr-iŋ\ boring, flooring,
roaring • outpouring, rip-roaring,
wood-boring
—also -ing *forms of verbs listed at*
OR[1]

öring \ər-iŋ\ see URRING

oriole \ȯr-ē-əl\ see ORIAL

orious \ȯr-ē-əs\ Boreas, glorious
• censorious, laborious, notori-
ous, uproarious, uxorious, vain-
glorious, victorious • meritorious

oris \ȯr-əs\ see AURUS

orish \u̇r-ish\ see OORISH

orist \ȯr-əst\ florist, forest, poorest,
sorest • Black Forest, deforest,
folklorist, reforest • Petrified
Forest

orister \ȯr-ə-stər\ chorister,
forester

ority \ȯr-ət-ē\ authority, majority,
minority, priority, seniority,
sonority, sorority • inferiority,
superiority

orium \ȯr-ē-əm\ emporium • audi-
torium, cafetorium, crematorium,
in memoriam, moratorium, sana-
torium

ork[1] \ərk\ clerk, Dirk, irk, jerk,
Kirk, lurk, murk, perk, quirk,
shirk, smirk, Turk, work • art-
work, at work, beadwork,
berserk, brickwork, brushwork,
casework, clockwork, Dunkirk,
earthwork, file clerk, firework,
footwork, framework, Grand

Turk, groundwork, guesswork,
handwork, homework, house-
work, ironwork, knee-jerk, leg-
work, lifework, make-work,
network, outwork, patchwork,
piecework, rework, roadwork,
salesclerk, schoolwork, Selkirk,
stonework, teamwork, town
clerk, waxwork, woodwork,
young Turk • Atatürk, basket-
work, bodywork, busywork,
cabinetwork, city clerk, clean-
and-jerk, handiwork, leather-
work, masterwork, metalwork,
needlework, out of work, over-
work, paperwork, piece of work,
shipping clerk, social work, soda
jerk, wickerwork

ork[2] \ȯrk\ cork, Cork, dork, fork,
pork, quark, stork, torque, York
• bulwark, Cape York, New York,
North York, pitchfork, salt pork,
uncork, wood stork

orked \ȯr-kəd\ see ORCHID

orker[1] \ər-kər\ lurker, shirker,
worker • caseworker,
dockworker, farmworker, field-
worker, ironworker, networker,
pieceworker, steelworker, tear-
jerker, woodworker
• autoworker, metalworker, social
worker, wonder-worker

orker[2] \ȯr-kər\ corker, porker
• New Yorker

orkie \ȯr-kē\ see ORKY

orking \ər-kiŋ\ hardworking, net-
working, tear-jerking, woodwork-
ing • metalworking,
wonder-working
—also -ing *forms of verbs listed at*
ORK[1]

orky \ȯr-kē\ dorky, Gorky, porky,
Yorkie

orl \ərl\ see IRL

orld \ərld\ world • dreamworld,
free world, New World, old-
world, Old World, real-world,

third world • afterworld, brave
new world, Disney World, in the
world, netherworld, otherworld,
underworld • for all the world,
man of the world, out of this
world • on top of the world
—*also* -ed *forms of verbs listed at*
IRL

orled \ərld\ see ORLD

orm[1] \ərm\ firm, germ, perm,
squirm, term, worm • affirm,
bookworm, budworm, confirm,
cutworm, deworm, earthworm,
flatworm, glowworm, heartworm,
hookworm, hornworm, inch-
worm, infirm, long-term,
midterm, pinworm, ringworm,
roundworm, short-term, silk-
worm, tapeworm, webworm
• pachyderm, reconfirm

orm[2] \òrm\ dorm, form, norm,
storm, swarm, warm • aswarm,
barnstorm, brainstorm, by storm,
conform, deform, dust storm,
firestorm, free-form, hailstorm,
ice storm, inform, landform, life-
form, lukewarm, perform, platform, preform, rainstorm,
re-form, reform, sandstorm,
snowstorm, transform, waveform,
windstorm • chloroform, cruci-
form, land reform, thunderstorm,
uniform • cuneiform, dress uniform, magnetic storm, quadratic
form

ormal \òr-məl\ formal, normal
• abnormal, informal, subnormal
• paranormal, semiformal

ormally \òr-mə-lē\ formally, for-
merly, normally, stormily • ab-
normally, informally
• paranormally

orman \òr-mən\ doorman, foreman, Foreman, Mormon, Nor-
man • longshoreman

ormant \òr-mənt\ dormant • in-
formant

ormative \òr-mət-iv\ formative,
normative • informative, transfor-
mative

orme \òrm\ see ORM[2]

ormed \òrmd\ deformed,
informed, malformed, unformed
• well-informed
—*also* -ed *forms of verbs listed at*
ORM[2]

ormer \òr-mər\ dormer, former,
warmer • barnstormer, bench-
warmer, brainstormer, heart-
warmer, informer, performer,
reformer, transformer

ormerly \òr-mə-lē\ see ORMALLY

ormily \òr-mə-lē\ see ORMALLY

orming \òr-miŋ\ brainstorming,
heartwarming, housewarming,
performing • habit-forming
—*also* -ing *forms of verbs listed at*
ORM[2]

ormity \òr-mət-ē\ conformity,
deformity, enormity • nonconfor-
mity, uniformity

ormless \òrm-ləs\ formless, gorm-
less

ormon \òr-mən\ see ORMAN

ormy \ər-mē\ see ERMY

orn[1] \òrn\ born, borne, corn, horn,
morn, mourn, scorn, shorn,
sworn, thorn, torn, warn, worn
• acorn, adorn, airborne, bighorn,
blackthorn, blue corn, boxthorn,
broomcorn, buckthorn, bullhorn,
Cape Horn, careworn, Dearborn,
dehorn, earthborn, field corn,
firethorn, firstborn, flint corn,
foghorn, forewarn, forlorn, free-
born, French horn, greenhorn,
hawthorn, Hawthorne, highborn,
inborn, longhorn, lovelorn, new-
born, outworn, popcorn, prong-
horn, ramshorn, reborn, saxhorn,
seaborne, shipborne, shoehorn,
shopworn, shorthorn, skyborne,
soilborne, stillborn, sweet corn,
tick-borne, timeworn, tinhorn,

tricorne, unborn, unworn, well-
born, well-worn, wind-borne
• barleycorn, Capricorn, English
horn, flügelhorn, foreign-born,
hunting horn, Matterhorn, pep-
percorn, powder horn, saddle
horn, unicorn, waterborne,
weatherworn • Indian corn, Little
Bighorn, Texas longhorn • to the
manner born, to the manor born

orn² \ərn\ see URN

ornament \ȯr-nə-mənt\ ornament,
tournament

orne \ȯrn\ see ORN¹

orned \ȯrnd\ horned, thorned
• unadorned
—also -ed forms of verbs listed at
ORN¹

orner \ȯr-nər\ corner, scorner,
Warner • kitty-corner

orney \ər-nē\ see OURNEY¹

ornful \ȯrn-fəl\ mournful, scornful

orning \ȯr-niŋ\ morning, mourning, warning
—also -ing forms of verbs listed at
ORN¹

ornment \ərn-mənt\ see ERNMENT

orny \ȯr-nē\ corny, thorny

oro \ər-ə\ see OROUGH¹

oroner \ȯr-ə-nər\ coroner, for-
eigner

orough¹ \ər-ə\ borough, burro,
burrow, furrow, ore, thorough
• Gainsborough, Greensboro
• Edinburgh, kookaburra

orough² \ər-ō\ see URROW¹

orous \ȯr-əs\ see AURUS

orp \ȯrp\ gorp, warp

orpe \ȯrp\ see ORP

orph \ȯrf\ dwarf, morph • Düssel-
dorf

orphan \ȯr-fən\ orphan • endor-
phin

orpheus \ȯr-fē-əs\ Morpheus,
Orpheus

orphin \ȯr-fən\ see ORPHAN

orpoise \ȯr-pəs\ see ORPUS

orps \ȯr\ see OR¹

orpsman \ȯr-mən\ see ORMAN

orpus \ȯr-pəs\ porpoise • habeas
corpus

orque \ȯrk\ see ORK²

orquer \ȯr-kər\ see ORKER²

orr \ȯr\ see OR¹

orra¹ \är-ə\ see ARA¹

orra² \ȯr-ə\ see ORA

orrah¹ \ȯr-ə\ see ORA

orrah² \är-ə\ see ARA¹

orran¹ \är-ən\ see ARIN

orran² \ȯr-ən\ see ORIN¹

orrence \ȯr-əns\ see AWRENCE

orrel \ȯr-əl\ see ORAL

orrent \ȯr-ənt\ torrent, warrant
• abhorrent, death warrant,
search warrant

orrer \ȯr-ər\ see ORER

orres \ȯr-əs\ see AURUS

orrest \ȯr-əst\ see ORIST

orrible \ȯr-ə-bəl\ see ORABLE

orrid \ȯr-əd\ florid, horrid, torrid

orridge¹ \är-ij\ see ORAGE¹

orridge² \ȯr-ij\ see ORAGE²

orrie¹ \är-ē\ see ARI¹

orrie² \ȯr-ē\ see ORY

orrier \ȯr-ē-ər\ see ARRIOR

orrin¹ \är-en\ see ARIN

orrin² \ȯr-ən\ see ORIN¹

orris¹ \är-əs\ Juárez, Maurice,
morris, Morris • Benares, Polaris

orris² \ȯr-əs\ see AURUS

orror \ȯr-ər\ see ORER

orrow¹ \är-ō\ borrow, morrow,
sorrow, taro • bizarro, Pizarro,
saguaro, tomorrow • Kilimanjaro

orrow² \är-ə\ see ARA¹

orry¹ \är-ē\ see ARI¹

orry² \ər-ē\ see URRY

ors \ȯrz\ see OORS

orsal \ȯr-səl\ see ORSEL

orse¹ \ȯrs\ coarse, course, force,
hoarse, horse, Morse, Norse,
source • clotheshorse, concourse,
crash course, dark horse, dead
horse, discourse, divorce, en-

dorse, enforce, golf course, gut course, high horse, iron horse, midcourse, of course, one-horse, packhorse, racecourse, racehorse, recourse, remorse, resource, sawhorse, sea horse, unhorse, warhorse, Whitehorse, workhorse • charley horse, Crazy Horse, harness horse, hobbyhorse, minicourse, pommel horse, quarter horse, reinforce, rocking horse, saddle horse, stalking horse, telecourse, tour de force, Trojan horse, vaulting horse, watercourse • collision course, matter of course, obstacle course, par for the course • Arabian horse

orse² \ərs\ see ERSE

orseful \òrs-fəl\ forceful • remorseful, resourceful

orsel \òr-səl\ dorsal, morsel

orseman \òr-smən\ horseman, Norseman

orsement \òr-smənt\ endorsement, enforcement • reinforcement

orsen \ərs-ᵊn\ see ERSON

orset \òr-sət\ corset, Dorset

orsion \òr-shən\ see ORTION

orst¹ \òrst\ forced
—also -ed forms of verbs listed at ORSE¹

orst² \ərst\ see URST

ort¹ \òrt\ court, fort, forte, port, quart, short, snort, sort, sport, thwart, tort, torte, wart • abort, airport, athwart, Bridgeport, carport, cavort, cohort, comport, consort, contort, deport, disport, distort, effort, escort, exhort, export, extort, fall short, for short, Gulfport, home port, in short, Newport, passport, presort, purport, report, re-sort, resort, retort, seaport, sell short, Shreveport, spaceport, spoilsport, support, transport • davenport, heliport,

hold the fort, life-support, non-support, of a sort, worrywart • pianoforte, the long and short

ort² \òr\ see OR¹

ort³ \ərt\ see ERT¹

ortage \òrt-ij\ portage, shortage • reportage

ortal \òrt-ᵊl\ chortle, mortal, portal • immortal

ortar \òrt-ər\ see ORTER

orte¹ \òrt\ see ORT¹

orte² \òrt-ē\ see ORTY

orted \òrt-əd\ assorted, purported • self-supported
—also -ed forms of verbs listed at ORT¹

orter \òrt-ər\ mortar, porter, Porter, quarter, shorter, sorter • exporter, headquarter, importer, reporter, supporter, transporter • brick-and-mortar • athletic supporter

orteur \òrt-ər\ see ORTER

orth¹ \òrth\ forth, fourth, north, North • bring forth, call forth, thenceforth • and so forth, back and forth, Firth of Forth

orth² \ərth\ see IRTH

orthless \ərth-ləs\ see IRTHLESS

orthy \ər-thē\ earthy, worthy • airworthy, blameworthy, crashworthy, newsworthy, noteworthy, praiseworthy, roadworthy, seaworthy, trustworthy, unworthy • creditworthy

ortie \òrt-ē\ see ORTY

orting \òrt-iŋ\ sporting • nonsporting • self-supporting
—also -ing forms of verbs listed at ORT¹

ortion \òr-shən\ portion, torsion • apportion, contortion, distortion, extortion, proportion • disproportion, in proportion, reapportion

ortionate \òr-shnət\ extortionate, proportionate • disproportionate

ortionist \ȯr-shnist\ contortionist, extortionist

ortis \ȯrt-əs\ mortise, tortoise • rigor mortis

ortise \ȯrt-əs\ see ORTIS

ortive \ȯrt-iv\ abortive, supportive

ortle \ȯrt-ᵊl\ see ORTAL

ortly \ȯrt-lē\ courtly, portly, shortly

ortment \ȯrt-mənt\ assortment, comportment, deportment

ortoise \ȯrt-əs\ see ORTIS

orts \ȯrts\ quartz, shorts, sports • boxer shorts, out of sorts, undershorts • Bermuda shorts, bicycle shorts
  —*also* -s, -'s, *and* -s' *forms of nouns and* -s *forms of verbs listed at* ORT¹

ortunate \ȯrch-nət\ fortunate • importunate, unfortunate

orture \ȯr-chər\ see ORCHER

orty \ȯrt-ē\ forty, shorty, sporty • pianoforte

orum \ȯr-əm\ forum, quorum • decorum • indecorum • sanctum sanctorum

orus \ȯr-əs\ see AURUS

orward \ȯr-wərd\ forward, foreword, shoreward • bring forward, fast-forward, flash forward, henceforward, look forward, put forward, set forward, straightforward, thenceforward

ory \ȯr-ē\ dory, glory, gory, Laurie, Lori, quarry, sorry, story, Tory • backstory, fish story, ghost story, Old Glory, short story, sob story • allegory, auditory, bedtime story, category, cover story, crematory, desultory, dilatory, dormitory, horror story, hunky-dory, inventory, Lake Maggiore, laudatory, lavatory, mandatory, migratory, Montessori, morning glory, offertory, oratory, predatory, prefatory, promissory, promon-

tory, purgatory, repertory, statutory, territory, transitory • accusatory, ambulatory, celebratory, compensatory, conservatory, dedicatory, defamatory, depository, derogatory, exculpatory, explanatory, exploratory, inflammatory, laboratory, masturbatory, obligatory, observatory, preparatory, reformatory, regulatory, repository, revelatory, respiratory • anticipatory, discriminatory, hallucinatory

orze \ȯrz\ see OORS

os¹ \äs\ boss, dross, floss, gloss, toss • Argos, chaos, cosmos, Delos, emboss, en masse, Eros, kudos, Lagos, Laos, Madras, Naxos, pathos, Patmos, Pharos, ringtoss • albatross, coup de grâce, demitasse, dental floss, gravitas, semigloss

os² \ō\ see OW¹

os³ \ōs\ see OSE¹

os⁴ \ȯs\ see OSS¹

osa \ō-sə\ Xhosa • Formosa, mimosa

osable \ō-zə-bəl\ disposable, opposable, reclosable

osal \ō-zəl\ Mosel • disposal, proposal

osch \äsh\ see ASH²

oschen \ō-shən\ see OTION

osco \äs-kō\ see OSCOE

oscoe \äs-kō\ Bosco, Roscoe • fiasco

ose¹ \ōs\ Bose, close, dose, gross • Carlos, cosmos, dextrose, engross, fructose, glucose, lactose, maltose, morose, pathos, sucrose, Sukkoth, up close, verbose • adios, bellicose, cellulose, comatose, diagnose, grandiose, Helios, lachrymose, megadose, overdose, varicose • metamorphose

ose² \ōz\ chose, close, clothes, doze, froze, hose, nose, pose,

prose, rose, Rose • Ambrose, arose, bedclothes, bulldoze, compose, depose, dextrose, disclose, dispose, dog rose, enclose, expose, foreclose, fructose, glucose, impose, Mount Rose, nightclothes, oppose, plainclothes, primrose, propose, pug nose, repose, rockrose, suppose, transpose, tuberose • Berlioz, cabbage rose, cellulose, China rose, Christmas rose, damask rose, decompose, diagnose, indispose, interpose, juxtapose, on the nose, panty hose, predispose, presuppose, shovelnose, swaddling clothes, thumb one's nose, underclothes • evening primrose, follow one's nose, look down one's nose, metamorphose, overexpose, pay through the nose, superimpose, under one's nose
—*also* -s, -'s, *and* -s' *forms of nouns and* -s *forms of verbs listed at* OW[1]

ose[3] \üz\ *see* USE[2]

osed \ōzd\ closed • composed, exposed, hard-nosed, opposed, pug-nosed, supposed • indisposed, shovel-nosed, well-disposed
—*also* -ed *forms of verbs listed at* OSE[2]

osee \ō-zē\ *see* OSY

osel \ō-zəl\ *see* OSAL

osen \ōz-³n\ chosen, frozen • deep-frozen, quick-frozen

oser[1] \ō-zər\ brownnoser, bulldozer, composer, disposer

oser[2] \ü-zər\ *see* USER

oset \äz-ət\ *see* OSIT

osey \ō-zē\ *see* OSY

osh[1] \ȯsh\ *see* ASH[2]

osh[2] \ōsh\ *see* OCHE[2]

oshed[1] \äsht\ galoshed
—*also* -ed *forms of verbs listed at* ASH[1]

oshed[2] \ȯsht\ *see* ASHED[1]

oshen \ō-shən\ *see* OTION

osher \äsh-ər\ *see* ASHER[1]

osible \ō-zə-bəl\ *see* OSABLE

osier \ō-zhər\ *see* OSURE

osily \ō-zə-lē\ cozily, nosily, rosily

osing \ō-ziŋ\ closing • disclosing, imposing, self-closing, supposing
—*also* -ing *forms of verbs listed at* OSE[2]

osion \ō-zhən\ corrosion, erosion, explosion, implosion

osis \ō-səs\ cirrhosis, hypnosis, meiosis, mitosis, neurosis, osmosis, prognosis, psychosis, sclerosis • diagnosis, halitosis, symbiosis • cystic fibrosis, tuberculosis • mononucleosis

osit \äz-ət\ closet, posit • composite, deposit

osite \äz-ət\ *see* OSIT

osius \ō-shəs\ *see* OCIOUS

osive \ō-siv\ corrosive, explosive, implosive, purposive • high explosive

osk \äsk\ mosque • kiosk

oso[1] \ō-sō\ mafioso, virtuoso • concerto grosso

oso[2] \ü-sō\ *see* USOE

osophy \äs-ə-fē\ philosophy, theosophy

osque \äsk\ *see* OSK

oss[1] \ȯs\ boss, cross, floss, gloss, loss, moss, Ross, sauce, toss • across, Blue Cross, brown sauce, club moss, crisscross, emboss, Greek cross, lacrosse, pathos, peat moss, Red Cross, ringtoss, tau cross, uncross, white sauce • albatross, applesauce, at a loss, béarnaise sauce, Celtic cross, chili sauce, come across, dental floss, double-cross, get across, hoisin sauce, Iceland moss, Irish moss, Latin cross, Maltese cross, Mornay sauce, motocross, Navy Cross, Northern Cross, papal cross, reindeer moss, run across, semigloss, Southern Cross, Spanish moss, tartar sauce, underboss • pectoral cross, sign of the cross, Worcestershire sauce • stations of the cross

oss² \ōs\ see OSE¹

oss³ \äs\ see OS¹

ossa \äs-ə\ see ASA¹

ossal \äs-əl\ docile, fossil, jostle, tassel, wassail • apostle, colossal

osse¹ \äs\ see OS¹

osse² \äs-ē\ see OSSY¹

osse³ \ós\ see OSS¹

ossed \óst\ see OST³

osser \ó-sər\ Chaucer, saucer • double-crosser, flying saucer

ossil \äs-əl\ see OSSAL

ossity \äs-ət-ē\ atrocity, ferocity, monstrosity, pomposity, precocity, velocity, verbosity, viscosity • animosity, curiosity, generosity, grandiosity, reciprocity, virtuosity • religiosity

ossly \ós-lē\ costly, crossly

osso \ō-sō\ see OSO¹

ossos \äs-əs\ see OCESS

ossum \äs-əm\ blossom, possum • opossum, play possum

ossus \äs-əs\ see OCESS

ossy¹ \äs-ē\ Aussie, bossy, glossy, posse, quasi

ossy² \ó-sē\ Aussie, bossy, mossy

ost¹ \äst\ accost • Pentecost
—*also* -ed *forms of verbs listed at* OS¹

ost² \ōst\ boast, coast, ghost, host, most, post, roast, toast • almost, at most, bedpost, compost, doorpost, endmost, foremost, French toast, gatepost, goalpost, Gold Coast, lamppost, milepost, pot roast, rearmost, rib roast, seacoast, signpost, Slave Coast, topmost, utmost • at the most, Barbary Coast, bottommost, coast-to-coast, command post, easternmost, Holy Ghost, inner-

most, Ivory Coast, melba toast, northernmost, outermost, parcel post, southernmost, trading post, uppermost, uttermost, whipping post • from coast to coast, give up the ghost, Mosquito Coast, Washington Post
—*also* -ed *forms of verbs listed at* OSE¹

ost³ \óst\ cost, frost, lost • accost, defrost, exhaust, hoarfrost, Jack Frost, star-crossed • holocaust, Pentecost, permafrost,
—*also* -ed *forms of verbs listed at* OSS¹

ost⁴ \əst\ see UST¹

ostal¹ \ōs-t³l\ coastal, postal • bicoastal

ostal² \äs-t³l\ see OSTEL

oste \ōst\ see OST²

ostel \äs-t³l\ hostile • youth hostel • Pentecostal

oster¹ \äs-tər\ foster, Foster, roster • impostor • paternoster

oster² \ós-tər\ foster, Foster, roster

oster³ \ō-stər\ see OASTER

ostic \äs-tik\ acrostic, agnostic • diagnostic

ostile \äs-t³l\ see OSTEL

ostle \äs-əl\ see OSSAL

ostly¹ \ōst-lē\ ghostly, mostly

ostly² \ós-lē\ see OSSLY

oston \ós-tən\ Austen, Austin, Boston

ostor \äs-tər\ see OSTER¹

ostrum \äs-trəm\ nostrum, rostrum

osure \ō-zhər\ closure, crosier • composure, disclosure, enclosure, exposure, foreclosure • time exposure • overexposure, underexposure

osy \ō-zē\ cozy, dozy, mosey, nosy, posy, prosy, rosy • ring-around-the-rosy

osz \ósh\ see ASH²

oszcz \ósh\ see ASH²

ot¹ \ät\ blot, bot, clot, cot, dot, got,

hot, jot, knot, lot, Lot, naught,
not, plot, pot, rot, Scot, Scott,
shot, slot, sot, spot, squat, swat,
tot, trot, watt, Watt, what, yacht
• Alcott, allot, a lot, a shot, big
shot, blind spot, bloodshot, boy-
cott, buckshot, cannot, cheap
shot, crackpot, despot, dogtrot,
dovecote, dry rot, dunk shot,
earshot, feedlot, fiat, forgot, foul
shot, fox-trot, gunshot, have-not,
hotshot, jackpot, jump shot,
kumquat, long shot, mascot, mug
shot, Pequot, Pol Pot, potshot,
Rabat, red-hot, reef knot, robot,
root rot, Sadat, sandlot, sexpot,
Shabbat, shallot, sheepcote, slap
shot, slingshot, slipknot, snapshot,
soft spot, somewhat, square knot,
stinkpot, stockpot, subplot,
sunspot, sweet spot, teapot, tin-
pot, upshot, wainscot, whatnot,
white-hot, woodlot • aeronaut,
apricot, aquanaut, argonaut,
astronaut, booster shot, Camelot,
caveat, chamber pot, chimney
pot, coffeepot, cosmonaut, coun-
terplot, diddley-squat, flowerpot,
granny knot, hit the spot, Hotten-
tot, Huguenot, juggernaut, kilo-
watt, Lancelot, like a shot, like as
not, lobster pot, megawatt, melting pot, microdot, monocot,
ocelot, on the spot, parking lot,
patriot, Penobscot, piping hot,
polka dot, scattershot, tie the
knot, touch-me-not, Windsor
knot • as like as not, by a long
shot, compatriot, forget-me-not,
Gordian knot, hit the jackpot,
penalty shot, stevedore knot,
whether or not • all over the lot
• Johnny-on-the-spot
ot² \ō\ see OW¹
ot³ \ōt\ see OAT
ot⁴ \ȯt\ see OUGHT¹
ôt \ō\ see OW¹

ota \ōt-ə\ quota • Carlota, Dakota,
iota, Lakota, Toyota • Minnesota,
North Dakota, Sarasota, South
Dakota
otable \ōt-ə-bəl\ notable, potable,
quotable
otal \ōt-ᵊl\ total • subtotal, sum
total • anecdotal
otany \ät-ᵊn-ē\ botany, cottony
• monotony
otary \ōt-ə-rē\ coterie, rotary
otas \ō-təs\ see OTUS
otch \äch\ blotch, botch, crotch,
notch, scotch, Scotch, splotch,
swatch, watch • bird-watch,
deathwatch, hopscotch,
Sasquatch, stopwatch, top-notch,
wristwatch • butterscotch
otchman \äch-mən\ Scotchman,
watchman
otchy \äch-ē\ blotchy, boccie,
splotchy • hibachi, Karachi • Lib-
erace, mariachi
ote¹ \ōt-ē\ throaty • coyote, peyote
• Don Quixote
ote² \ōt\ see OAT
ote³ \ät\ see OT¹
oted \ōt-əd\ see OATED
oten \ōt-ᵊn\ see OTON
oter \ōt-ər\ see OATER
oterie \ōt-ə-rē\ see OTARY
oth¹ \ȯth\ broth, cloth, froth,
moth, sloth, swath • breechcloth,
clothes moth, dishcloth, face-
cloth, ground cloth, ground sloth,
hawk moth, loincloth, oilcloth,
sailcloth, scotch broth, silk moth,
sphinx moth, washcloth • gypsy
moth, luna moth, Ostrogoth,
tablecloth, three-toed sloth, tiger
moth, two-toed sloth
oth² \äth\ Goth, sloth, swath • Ostrogoth, Visigoth
oth³ \ōs\ see OSE¹
oth⁴ \ōt\ see OAT
oth⁵ \ōth\ see OWTH
othe \ōt͟h\ clothe, loathe • unclothe

other[1] \əth̠-ər\ brother, mother, other, rather, smother • another, big brother, blood brother, den mother, each other, godmother, grandmother, half brother, queen mother, stepbrother, stepmother • fairy godmother

other[2] \äth̠-ər\ see ATHER[1]

otherly \əth̠-ər-lē\ brotherly, motherly, southerly • grandmotherly

othes \ōz\ see OSE[2]

othing \ō-thiŋ\ clothing, loathing • betrothing, unclothing • underclothing • wolf in sheep's clothing

otho \ō-tō\ see OTO

oti[1] \ōt-ē\ see OTE[1]

oti[2] \ȯt-ē\ see AUGHTY[1]

otiable \ō-shə-bəl\ see OCIABLE

otic \ät-ik\ aquatic, chaotic, despotic, erotic, exotic, hypnotic, narcotic, neurotic, psychotic, quixotic, robotic • idiotic, patriotic, symbiotic • antibiotic

otice \ōt-əs\ see OTUS

otics \ät-iks\ robotics • aeronautics, astronautics
—*also* -s, -'s, *and* -s' *forms of nouns listed at* OTIC

otid \ät-əd\ see OTTED

otile \ōt-ºl\ see OTAL

oting[1] \ōt-iŋ\ see OATING

oting[2] \ät-iŋ\ see OTTING

otinous \ät-ºn-əs\ see OTONOUS

otion \ō-shən\ Goshen, lotion, motion, notion, ocean, potion • commotion, demotion, devotion, emotion, Laotian, promotion, slow-motion • Arctic Ocean, locomotion, Nova Scotian, set in motion, Southern Ocean • Antarctic Ocean, Atlantic Ocean, Indian Ocean, Pacific Ocean

otional \ō-shnəl\ devotional, emotional, promotional • unemotional

otis \ōt-əs\ see OTUS

otive \ōt-iv\ motive, votive • emotive • automotive, locomotive

otl \ät-ºl\ see OTTLE

otle \ät-ºl\ see OTTLE

otley \ät-lē\ see OTLY

otly \ät-lē\ hotly, motley

oto \ō-tō\ photo • de Soto, in toto, Kyoto, Lesotho • telephoto, Yamamoto

otomy \ät-ə-mē\ dichotomy, lobotomy

oton \ōt-ºn\ oaten • Lofoten, verboten

otonous \ät-ºn-əs\ rottenness • monotonous

otor \ōt-ər\ see OATER

otory \ōt-ə-rē\ see OTARY

ots \äts\ Graz, lots, Scots • age spots, ersatz • call the shots • connect-the-dots, hit the high spots
—*also* -s, -'s, *and* -s' *forms of nouns and* -s *forms of verbs listed at* OT[1]

otsman \ät-smən\ Scotsman, yachtsman

ott \ät\ see OT[1]

otta \ät-ə\ see ATA[1]

ottage \ät-ij\ cottage, wattage

ottal \ät-ºl\ see OTTLE

otte[1] \ät\ see OT[1]

otte[2] \ȯt\ see OUGHT[1]

otted \ät-əd\ knotted, potted, spotted • besotted, unspotted • polka-dotted
—*also* -ed *forms of verbs listed at* OT[1]

otten \ät-ºn\ cotton, gotten, rotten • au gratin, forgotten, ill-gotten • misbegotten, sauerbraten

ottenness \ät-ºn-əs\ see OTONOUS

otter \ät-ər\ blotter, daughter, hotter, otter, plotter, potter, Potter, Qatar, rotter, spotter, squatter, swatter, Tatar, totter, trotter, water • backwater, bathwater, boycotter, breakwater, Clearwater, deepwater, dishwater, floodwater, flyswatter, freshwater, globe-trotter, groundwater, headwater, hot water, ice water, jerkwater, meltwater, rainwater, saltwater, sea otter, seawater, tap water, tidewater, tread water, white-water • above water, alma mater, holy water, in deep water, mineral water, river otter, running water, soda water, teeter-totter, tonic water, underwater • dead in the water, fish out of water, hell or high water

ottery \ät-ə-rē\ lottery, pottery, tottery, watery

ottid \ät-əd\ see OTTED

ottie \ät-ē\ see ATI[1]

otting \ät-iŋ\ jotting • globe-trotting, wainscoting
—also -ing forms of verbs listed at OT[1]

ottle \ät-ᵊl\ bottle, mottle, throttle, wattle • squeeze bottle • Aristotle, at full throttle, spin the bottle, vacuum bottle • Quetzalcoatl

otto[1] \ät-ō\ see ATO[1]

otto[2] \òt-ō\ see AUTO[1]

ottom \ät-əm\ see ATUM[1]

otty \ät-ē\ see ATI[1]

otun \ōt-ᵊn\ see OTON

oture \ō-chər\ see OACHER

otus \ōt-əs\ lotus, notice, Otis

oty \òt-ē\ see AUGHTY[1]

otyl \ät-ᵊl\ see OTTLE

ou[1] \ō\ see OW[1]

ou[2] \ü\ see EW[1]

ou[3] \aù\ see OW[2]

oubled \əb-əld\ see UBBLED

ouble \əb-əl\ see UBBLE

oubly \əb-lē\ see UBBLY[1]

oubt \aùt\ see OUT[3]

oubted \aùt-əd\ see OUTED

oubter \aùt-ər\ see OUTER[2]

ouc[1] \ü\ see EW[1]

ouc[2] \ük\ see UKE

ouc[3] \ùk\ see OOK[1]

ouce \üs\ see USE[1]

oucester[1] \äs-tər\ see OSTER[1]

oucester[2] \òs-tər\ see OSTER[2]

ouch[1] \üch\ see OOCH[1]

ouch[2] \üsh\ see OUCHE

ouch[3] \əch\ see UTCH

ouch[4] \aùch\ couch, crouch, grouch, ouch, pouch, slouch, vouch • studio couch

ouche \üsh\ swoosh, whoosh

ouchy[1] \əch-ē\ see UCHY

ouchy[2] \aù-chē\ grouchy, pouchy, slouchy

oud[1] \üd\ see UDE[1]

oud[2] \aùd\ boughed, bowed, cloud, crowd, loud, proud, shroud • aloud, becloud, do proud, enshroud, out loud, Saint Cloud, unbowed • funnel cloud, mushroom cloud, overcloud, overcrowd, thundercloud
—also -ed forms of verbs listed at OW[2]

ou'd \üd\ see UDE[1]

ouda \üd-ə\ see UDA

oudy \aùd-ē\ see OWDY

oue \ü\ see EW[1]

ouf \üf\ see OOF[1]

ouffe \üf\ see OOF[1]

oug \əg\ see UG

ouge[1] \üj\ see UGE[1]

ouge[2] \üzh\ see UGE[2]

ough[1] \ō\ see OW[1]

ough[2] \ü\ see EW[1]

ough[3] \aù\ see OW[2]

ough[4] \äk\ see OCK[1]

ough[5] \əf\ see UFF

ough[6] \òf\ see OFF[2]

ougham[1] \ōm\ see OME[1]

ougham[2] \üm\ see OOM[1]

oughed \aùd\ see OUD[2]

oughen \əf-ən\ see UFFIN

ougher \əf-ər\ see UFFER

oughie \əf-ē\ see UFFY

oughly \əf-lē\ see UFFLY

oughs \ōz\ see OSE[2]

ought[1] \òt\ bought, brought, caught, dot, fought, fraught, naught, ought, sought, taught, taut, thought, wrought

• distraught, forethought, hand-
wrought, onslaught, self-taught,
store-bought, unsought, untaught
• aeronaut, afterthought, aquanaut, argonaut, astronaut, cosmonaut, juggernaut, overwrought,
second thought

ought² \aut\ see OUT³

oughy¹ \ō-ē\ see OWY

oughy² \ü-ē\ see EWY

ouie \ü-ē\ see EWY

ouille \ü-ē\ see EWY

ouis \ü-ē\ see EWY

ouk \ük\ see UKE

ouki \ü-kē\ see OOKY¹

oul¹ \ōl\ see OLE¹

oul² \ül\ see OOL¹

oul³ \aul\ see OWL²

ould¹ \ōld\ see OLD¹

ould² \ud\ see OOD¹

oulder \ōl-dər\ see OLDER¹

ouldered \ōl-dərd\ shouldered
• round-shouldered
—*also* -ed *forms of verbs listed at*
OLDER¹

ouldest \ud-əst\ couldest,
shouldest, wouldest

ouldn't \ud-ᵊnt\ couldn't,
shouldn't, wouldn't

oule¹ \ü-lē\ see ULY

oule² \ül\ see OOL¹

ouled \ōld\ see OLD¹

oulee \ü-lē\ see ULY

ouleh¹ \ü-lə\ see ULA

ouleh² \ü-lē\ see ULY

ouli \ü-lē\ see ULY

oulie \ü-lē\ see ULY

ouling \au-liŋ\ see OWLING²

oulish \ü-lish\ see OOLISH

ou'll¹ \ül\ see OOL¹

ou'll² \ul\ see UL¹

oulle \ül\ see OOL¹

oulli \ü-lē\ see ULY

oully \au-lē\ see OWLY²

oult \ōlt\ see OLT¹

oum \üm\ see OOM¹

oun¹ \aun\ see OWN²

oun² \ün\ see OON¹

ounce \auns\ bounce, flounce,
ounce, pounce, trounce • an-
nounce, denounce, pronounce,
renounce • dead-cat bounce, fluid
ounce, mispronounce

ouncer \aun-sər\ bouncer • an-
nouncer

ound¹ \ünd\ wound • flesh wound
—*also* -ed *forms of verbs listed at*
OON¹

ound² \aund\ bound, crowned,
found, ground, hound, mound,
pound, round, sound, wound
• abound, aground, all-round,
around, astound, background,
bloodhound, campground,
chowhound, compound, con-
found, coonhound, dachshund,
deerhound, dumbfound, earth-
bound, eastbound, elkhound,
expound, fairground, fogbound,
foot-pound, foreground, foxhound, gain ground, greyhound,
Greyhound, hardbound, high
ground, homebound,
housebound, icebound, impound,
inbound, lose ground, newfound,
northbound, outbound, play-
ground, profound, rebound,
redound, renowned, resound,
rockbound, rock hound, snow-
bound, southbound, spellbound,
staghound, stone-ground, storm-
bound, surround, unbound, un-
sound, westbound, wolfhound,
year-round • aboveground,
Afghan hound, all-around, basset
hound, belowground, break new
ground, breeding ground, bring
around, common ground, dump-
ing ground, fool around, get
around, go around, hang around,
horse around, kick around, mess
around, muscle-bound, Nootka
Sound, off the ground, on the

ground, outward-bound, paper-bound, proving ground, Puget Sound, push around, runaround, screw around, spiral-bound, staging ground, stand one's ground, stick around, stomping ground, surround sound, turnaround, turn around, ultrasound, underground, wraparound • Albemarle Sound, English foxhound, Irish wolfhound, Long Island Sound, McMurdo Sound, merry-go-round, Prince William Sound, run rings around, Russian wolfhound, Scottish deerhound • happy hunting ground, run circles around, throw one's weight around
—*also* -ed *forms of verbs listed at* OWN[2]

oundary \aùn-drē\ see OUNDRY

ounded \aùn-dəd\ bounded, grounded, rounded • confounded, unbounded, unfounded, well-founded, well-grounded, well-rounded
—*also* -ed *forms of verbs listed at* OUND[2]

ounder \aùn-dər\ bounder, flounder, founder, grounder, pounder, sounder

ounding \aùn-diŋ\ grounding, sounding • astounding, high-sounding, resounding
—*also* -ing *forms of verbs listed at* OUND[2]

oundless[1] \ün-ləs\ see OONLESS

oundless[2] \aùn-ləs\ boundless, groundless

oundly \aùnd-lē\ roundly, soundly • profoundly

oundness \aùn-nəs\ roundness, soundness

oundry \aùn-drē\ boundary, foundry

ounds[1] \ünz\ see OONS

ounds[2] \aùnz\ zounds • out-of-bounds • by leaps and bounds

—*also* -s, -'s, *and* -s' *forms of nouns and* -s *forms of verbs listed at* OUND[2]

oundsman \aùnz-mən\ see OWNS-MAN

ounge \aùnj\ lounge, scrounge • cocktail lounge

ounger[1] \aùn-jər\ lounger, scrounger

ounger[2] \əŋ-gər\ see ONGER[1]

ounker \əŋ-kər\ see UNKER

ount[1] \änt\ see ANT[2]

ount[2] \aùnt\ count, fount, mount • account, amount, discount, dismount, recount, remount, surmount, viscount • body count, catamount, paramount, Rocky Mount, tantamount • call to account, checking account, expense account, on no account, savings account • Sermon on the Mount, take into account

ountable \aùnt-ə-bəl\ countable • accountable, discountable, surmountable • insurmountable, unaccountable

ountain \aùnt-ᵊn\ fountain, mountain • drinking fountain, soda fountain

ountie \aùnt-ē\ see OUNTY

ounting \aùnt-iŋ\ mounting • accounting
—*also* -ing *forms of verbs listed at* OUNT[2]

ounty \aùnt-ē\ bounty, county, Mountie

oup[1] \ōp\ see OPE

oup[2] \ü\ see EW[1]

oup[3] \üp\ see OOP

oupe[1] \ōp\ see OPE

oupe[2] \üp\ see OOP

ouper \ü-pər\ see OOPER

oupie \ü-pē\ see OOPY

ouple \əp-əl\ see UPLE[1]

ouplet \əp-lət\ see UPLET

oupy \ü-pē\ see OOPY

our[1] \ȯr\ see OR[1]

our² \ůr\ see URE¹
our³ \aůr\ see OWER²
our⁴ \är\ see AR³
our⁵ \ər\ see EUR¹
oura \ůr-ə\ see URA
ourable \ȯr-ə-bəl\ see ORABLE
ourbon \ər-bən\ see URBAN
ource \ȯrs\ see ORSE¹
ourceful \ȯrs-fəl\ see ORSEFUL
ourd \ȯrd\ see OARD
ourde \ůrd\ see URED¹
ou're¹ \ȯr\ see OR¹
ou're² \ü-ər\ see EWER¹
ou're³ \ůr\ see URE¹
ou're⁴ \ər\ see EUR¹
oured \ȯrd\ see OARD
ourer¹ \ȯr-ər\ see ORER
ourer² \ůr-ər\ see URER
ourg \ůr\ see URE¹
ourge¹ \ərj\ see URGE
ourge² \ȯrj\ see ORGE
ourger \ər-jər\ see ERGER
ouri \ůr-ē\ see URY¹
ourier¹ \ůr-ē-ər\ courier • couturier
ourier² \ər-ē-ər\ see URRIER
ouring¹ \ȯr-iŋ\ see ORING
ouring² \ůr-iŋ\ see URING
ourish \ər-ish\ flourish, nourish
• amateurish
ourist \ůr-əst\ see URIST
ourly \aůr-lē\ dourly, hourly,
sourly • half-hourly
ourn¹ \ȯrn\ see ORN¹
ourn² \ərn\ see URN
ournal \ərn-ᵊl\ see ERNAL
ournament \ȯr-nə-mənt\ see ORNA-
MENT
ourne \ȯrn\ see ORN¹
ourney¹ \ər-nē\ Bernie, Ernie,
gurney, journey, tourney • attorney • district attorney
ourney² \ȯr-nē\ see ORNY
ournful \ȯrn-fəl\ see ORNFUL
ourning \ȯr-niŋ\ see ORNING
ournment \ərn-mənt\ see ERNMENT
ours¹ \ȯrz\ see OORS
ours² \ärz\ see ARS

ours³ \aůrz\ ours • all hours
• after-hours
—also -s, -'s, and -s' forms of
nouns and -s forms of verbs listed
at OWER²
ours⁴ \ůr\ see URE¹
ourse \ȯrs\ see ORSE¹
ourt¹ \ȯrt\ see ORT¹
ourt² \ůrt\ see URT¹
ourth \ȯrth\ see ORTH¹
ourtier \ȯr-chər\ see ORCHER
ourtly \ȯrt-lē\ see ORTLY
oury \aůr-ē\ see OWERY
ous¹ \ü\ see EW¹
ous² \üs\ see USE¹
ousa¹ \ü-sə\ see USA¹
ousa² \ü-zə\ see USA²
ousal \aů-zəl\ spousal, tousle
• arousal, carousal
ouse¹ \üs\ see USE¹
ouse² \aůs\ blouse, douse, grouse,
house, Klaus, Laos, louse, mouse,
souse, spouse, Strauss • alehouse,
bathhouse, Bauhaus, birdhouse,
boathouse, book louse,
bunkhouse, clubhouse, court-
house, crab louse, deer mouse,
delouse, doghouse, dollhouse,
dormouse, espouse, farmhouse,
field house, field mouse, fire-
house, flophouse, full house, fun
house, greenhouse, guardhouse,
guesthouse, head louse, hothouse,
house mouse, icehouse, jailhouse,
keep house, lighthouse, long-
house, madhouse, nuthouse,
outhouse, penthouse, playhouse,
poorhouse, ranch house, road-
house, roughhouse, roundhouse,
row house, ruffed grouse, school-
house, smokehouse, statehouse,
steak house, storehouse,
teahouse, titmouse, tollhouse,
Toll House, town house, tree
house, warehouse, wheelhouse,
White House, wood louse, work-
house • boardinghouse, body

louse, cat and mouse, coffee-house, countinghouse, country house, customhouse, halfway house, house-to-house, manor house, meetinghouse, Mickey Mouse, motherhouse, on the house, open house, opera house, pocket mouse, powerhouse, rooming house, slaughterhouse, station house, sugarhouse, sum-merhouse, Westinghouse • bring down the house, man of the house

ouse³ \aůz\ blouse, browse, douse, dowse, drowse, house, mouse, rouse, spouse • arouse, carouse, delouse, espouse, rehouse, rough-house, warehouse
   —also -s, -'s, and -s' forms of nouns and -s forms of verbs listed at OW²

ouse⁴ \üz\ *see* USE²

ousel \aů-zəl\ *see* OUSAL

ouser \aů-zər\ mouser, schnauzer, trouser, wowser • carouser • rab-ble-rouser

ousin \əz-ᵊn\ *see* OZEN¹

ousing \aů-ziŋ\ housing, rousing • rabble-rousing
   —also -ing forms of verbs listed at OUSE³

ousle¹ \ü-zəl\ *see* USAL

ousle² \aů-zəl\ *see* OUSAL

ousse \üs\ *see* USE¹

ousseau \ü-sō\ *see* USOE

oust¹ \aůst\ Faust, joust, oust, roust
   —also -ed forms of verbs listed at OUSE²

oust² \üst\ *see* OOST

ouste \üst\ *see* OOST

ousy \aů-zē\ *see* OWSY

out¹ \ü\ *see* EW¹

out² \üt\ *see* UTE

out³ \aůt\ bout, clout, doubt, drought, flout, gout, grout, lout, out, pout, rout, route, scout, shout, snout, spout, sprout, stout, tout, trout • about, act out, all-out, back out, bailout, bail out, bawl out, bear out, beat out, blackout, black out, blot out, blowout, bombed-out, bow out, Boy Scout, breakout, break out, breechclout, bring out, brook trout, brownout, brown trout, bug out, burned-out, burnout, burn out, butt out, buy-out, buy out, campout, cast out, checkout, check out, chill out, clear out, closeout, come out, cookout, cop out, Cub Scout, cutout, cut out, devout, die out, dig out, dine out, dish out, dole out, downspout, draw out, dropout, drop out, dry out, dugout, eke out, en route, fade-out, fake out, fallout, fall out, farm out, far-out, fill out, find out, flake out, flameout, flame out, flat-out, flunk out, foldout, foul out, freak-out, freaked-out, get out, Girl Scout, give out, go out, grind out, gross-out, gross out, handout, hand out, hangout, hide-out, holdout, hold out, iron out, kick out, knockout, knock out, lake trout, layout, lights-out, line out, lock out, lookout, look out, lose out, make out, max out, miss out, no doubt, nose out, opt out, pan out, pass out, payout, phase-out, phase out, pick out, pig out, printout, print out, psych-out, pull out, punch out, put out, roll out, rub out, rule out, run out, sack out, Sea Scout, sea trout, sellout, sell out, set out, shell out, shoot-out, shout-out, shutout, shut out, sick-out, sign out, sit out, sleep out, smoke out, sold-out, spaced-out, space out, speak out, spell out, stakeout, stake out, standout, stand out, step out, stick out, stressed-out, strikeout, strike out, strung out, sweat out, takeout, take out, talk out, thought-out, throughout, throw out, time-out, trade route, tryout, try out, tune out, turnout, turn out, veg out, wait out, walkout, walk out, washout, wash out, watch out, way-out, wear out, weird out, whiteout, wigged-out, wimp out, wiped out, wipeout, wipe out, without, workout, work out, worn-out, write out, zone out, zonked-out • autoroute, bring about, brussels sprout, Cape Lookout, carryout, carry out, cast about, come about, cutthroat trout, down-and-out, duke it out, Eagle Scout, falling-out, figure out, gadabout, go about, hammer out, have it out, how about, just about, long-drawn-out, odd man out, out-and-out, rainbow trout, roustabout, runabout, rural route, sauerkraut, set about, speckled trout, spit it out, talent scout, waterspout • day in day out, eat one's heart out, knock-down dragout, stick one's neck out • technical knockout

oute[1] \üt\ see UTE

oute[2] \aủt\ see OUT[3]

outed \aủt-əd\ snouted
  • undoubted
  —*also* -ed *forms of verbs listed at* OUT[3]

outer[1] \üt-ər\ see UTER

outer[2] \aủt-ər\ doubter, outer, shouter, stouter • devouter

outh[1] \üth\ see OOTH[2]

outh[2] \aủth\ mouth, south • badmouth, Deep South, loudmouth, trench mouth • blabbermouth, cottonmouth, hand-to-mouth, motormouth, word-of-mouth
  • down in the mouth • from the horse's mouth • put one's foot in one's mouth

outherly \əth-ər-lē\ see OTHERLY

outhful \üth-fəl\ see UTHFUL

outi \üt-ē\ see OOTY[1]

outing \aủt-iŋ\ outing, scouting
  —*also* -ing *forms of verbs listed at* OUT[3]

outre \üt-ər\ see UTER

outrement \ü-trə-mənt\ see UTRIMENT

outs \aủts\ bean sprouts • hereabouts, on the outs, thereabouts, whereabouts
  —*also* -s, 's, *and* -s' *forms of nouns and* -s *forms of verbs listed at* OUT[3]

ou've \üv\ see OVE[3]

ouver \ü-vər\ see OVER[3]

oux \ü\ see EW[1]

ouy \ē\ see EE[1]

ouzel \ü-zəl\ see USAL

ov[1] \äf\ see OFF[1]

ov[2] \óf\ see OFF[2]

ova \ō-və\ nova • Jehovah
  • Casanova, supernova
  • Navratilova

ovable \ü-və-bəl\ movable, provable • disprovable, immovable, improvable, removable

ovah \ō-və\ see OVA

oval \ü-vəl\ approval, removal
  • disapproval

ove[1] \əv\ dove, glove, love, of, shove • above, as of, dream of, foxglove, in love, kind of, make love, out of, rock dove, short of, tough love, truelove • afoul of, ahead of, all kinds of, all sorts of, because of, become of, boxing glove, by means of, by way of, dispose of, get wind of, have none of, in case of, in light of, in place of, inside of, in spite of, instead of, in terms of, in view of, ladylove, make fun of, make use of, mourning dove, on top of, outside of, puppy love, turtledove, unheard-of, well-thought-of • alongside of, at the hands of, in advance of, in behalf of, in favor of, in the face of, in the light of, in the wake of, make the most of, on account of, on behalf of, on the heels of, push comes to shove, regardless of • at the mercy of, in defiance of, irrespective of

ove² \ōv\ clove, cove, dove, drove, grove, Jove, mauve, rove, stove, strove, trove, wove • alcove, cookstove, mangrove, woodstove • Franklin stove, interwove, treasure trove • potbellied stove

ove³ \üv\ groove, move, prove, you've • approve, disprove, improve, remove, reprove • disapprove, on the move

ovel¹ \äv-əl\ grovel, novel • graphic novel

ovel² \əv-əl\ grovel, hovel, shovel • steam shovel • power shovel

ovement \üv-mənt\ movement • improvement

oven \ō-vən\ cloven, coven, woven • Beethoven, handwoven, plainwoven • interwoven

over¹ \əv-ər\ cover, hover, lover, plover • bedcover, discover, dustcover, gill cover, ground cover, hardcover, recover, slipcover, softcover, uncover • blow one's cover, undercover

over² \ō-vər\ clover, Dover, Grover, over, rover • all over, blow over, boil over, bowl over, chew over, comb-over, crossover, flyover, get over, go over, hand over, hangover, holdover, hold over, in clover, knock over, layover, lay over, leftover, look over, moreover, once-over, Passover, pass over, pick over, popover, pullover, pull over, pushover, put over, red clover, rollover, run over, sea rover, spillover, stopover, strikeover, sweet clover, takeover, take over, talk over,

tide over, turnover, turn over, voice-over, walk over, warmed-over, watch over, work over • carryover, Strait of Dover • over and over

over³ \ü-vər\ Hoover, louver, mover • earthmover, maneuver, remover, Vancouver • people mover

over⁴ \äv-ər\ see AVER¹

overt \ō-vərt\ covert, overt

overy \əv-rē\ discovery, recovery

ovey \ə-vē\ covey • lovey-dovey

ovie \ü-vē\ see OOVY

ovo \ō-vō\ Provo • de novo

ow¹ \ō\ beau, blow, bow, bro, crow, do, doe, dough, floe, flow, foe, fro, glow, go, grow, hoe, Jo, joe, Joe, know, lo, low, mow, no, o, O, oh, owe, Poe, pro, roe, row, schmo, sew, show, slow, snow, so, sow, stow, Stowe, though, throe, throw, toe, tow, whoa, woe, yo • aglow, ago, airflow, air show, although, archfoe, argot, a throw, backhoe, Bardot, below, bestow, big toe, Bordeaux, bravo, callow, chateau, cockcrow, cornrow, corn snow, crossbow, Cousteau, Day-Glo, death row, Defoe, deathblow, elbow, fencerow, forego, forgo, freak show, free throw, game show, Glasgow, go-slow, gung ho, Hankow, heave-ho, hedgerow, hello, horse show, ice floe, ice show, inflow, in tow, Io, Jane Doe, jim crow, Joe Blow, John Doe, Juneau, kayo, KO, lie low, light show, longbow, Lu-chow, macho, mallow, Marlowe, marrow, merlot, minnow, mojo, Monroe, Moscow, mudflow, no-no, no-show, nouveau, oboe, outflow, outgrow, oxbow, plateau, pronto, quiz show, rainbow, red snow, regrow, repo, road show, Rousseau, scarecrow, sideshow, skid row, ski tow, Soho, so-so, sourdough, stone's throw, tableau, talk show, tiptoe, Thoreau, trade show, trousseau, uh-oh, van Gogh, wallow, widow, willow, winnow, yarrow • afterglow, aikido, Angelo, apropos, art deco, art nouveau, audio, barrio, bay window, Bilbao, black widow, blow-by-blow, bone marrow, Borneo, buffalo, Buffalo, bungalow, calico, cameo, centimo, CEO, Cicero, curio, do-si-do, domino, dynamo, embryo, Eskimo, French window, hammer throw, hammertoe, high and low, HMO, horror show, Idaho, in a row, indigo, in the know, Jericho, Lake Tahoe, little toe, long-ago, Longfellow, Mario, medico, Mexico, mistletoe, Monaco, Navajo, NCO, oleo, on tiptoe, overflow, overgrow, overthrow, patio, piccolo, Point Barrow, polio, pompano, portico, quid pro quo, radio, ratio, rococo, rodeo, Romeo, rose window, Scorpio, semipro, show window, sloppy joe, so-and-so, status quo, stereo, stop-and-go, studio, tallyho, tangelo, tic-tac-toe, TKO, to-and-fro, Tokyo, touch-and-go, tupelo, UFO, undergo, undertow, vertigo, video, zydeco • Antonio, Arapaho, arpeggio, at one's elbow, bull's-eye window, centesimo, clock radio, Geronimo, get-up-and-go, go with the flow, Guantánamo, home video, lothario, magnifico, medicine show, New Mexico, oregano, Ozark Plateau, picture window, politico, portfolio, pussy willow, Rosario, Sarajevo, scenario, simpatico, talk radio, tennis elbow • archipelago, braggadocio, dog and pony show, ex officio, generalissimo, impresario, oratorio, Paramaribo, variety show

ow² \aù\ bough, bow, brow, chow, ciao, cow, Dow, how, Howe, Lao, Mao, now, ow, plow, pow, prow, row, scow, slough, sow, Tao, thou, vow, wow • allow, and how, as how, avow, bowwow, cacao, cash cow, chowchow, chow chow, Cracow, Dachau, endow, eyebrow, Hankow, highbrow, hoosegow, Jungfrau, know-how, kowtow, Kraków, lowbrow, luau, Macao, mau-mau, meow, Moscow, nohow, Palau, powwow, sea cow, snowplow, somehow, Spandau • anyhow, cat's meow, disallow, disavow, here and now, Hu Jintao, Krakatau, middlebrow, sacred cow • crème de cacao, Guinea-Bissau • holier-than-thou, Oberammergau

ow³ \ôv\ see OFF²

owa \ō-və\ see OVA

owable¹ \ō-ə-bəl\ knowable, showable • unknowable

owable² \aù-ə-bəl\ plowable • allowable

owal¹ \ō-əl\ see OEL

owal² \aùl\ see OWL²

owan \ō-ən\ see OAN¹

oward¹ \ôrd\ see OARD

oward² \aùrd\ see OWERED

owd¹ \üd\ see UDE¹

owd² \aùd\ see OUD²

owdah \aùd-ə\ see AUDE³

owder \aùd-ər\ chowder, louder, powder, prouder • black powder, gunpowder, tooth powder • chili powder, curry powder, talcum powder

owdown \ō-daùn\ lowdown, showdown, slowdown

owdy \aùd-ē\ Audi, cloudy, dowdy, howdy, rowdy • cum laude • magna cum laude, summa cum laude

owe \ō\ see OW[1]
owed[1] \ōd\ see ODE
owed[2] \aud\ see OUD[2]
owel \aul\ see OWL[2]
oweling \au-liŋ\ see OWLING[2]
owell[1] \aul\ see OWL[2]
owell[2] \ō-əl\ see OEL
owen \ō-ən\ see OAN[1]
ower[1] \ȯr\ see OR[1]
ower[2] \aur\ bower, cower, dour, flour, flower, glower, hour, our, plower, power, scour, shower, sour, tower • air power, bellflower, bell tower, black power, brainpower, coneflower, cornflower, devour, disk flower, empower, firepower, fire tower, Glendower, great power, half hour, horsepower, man-hour, manpower, mayflower, moonflower, pasqueflower, ray flower, rush hour, safflower, sea power, starflower, state flower, strawflower, sunflower, wallflower, watchtower, wildflower, willpower, world power • candlepower, cauliflower, conning tower, cooling tower, Devils Tower, disempower, Eisenhower, flower power, gillyflower, happy hour, hydropower, ivory tower, overpower, passionflower, person-hour, quarter hour, staying power, superpower, sweet-and-sour, thundershower, trumpet flower, waterpower, water tower, whisky sour, zero hour • balance of power, eleventh hour, kilowatt-hour
ower[3] \ō-ər\ see OER[4]
owered \aurd\ coward, flowered, Howard, powered • high-powered • ivory-towered, underpowered
—*also* -ed *forms of verbs listed at* OWER[2]
owering \au-riŋ\ flowering, towering • nonflowering

—*also* -ing *forms of verbs listed at* OWER[2]
owery \aur-ē\ dowry, floury, flowery, Maori, showery
owhee \ō-ē\ see OWY
owie \au-ē\ Maui, zowie
owing \ō-iŋ\ see OING[1]
owl[1] \ōl\ see OLE[1]
owl[2] \aul\ bowel, foul, fowl, growl, howl, jowl, owl, prowl, scowl, towel, trowel, vowel, yowl • avowal, barn owl, barred owl, beach towel, befoul, horned owl, night owl, peafowl, screech owl, tea towel, wildfowl • disavowal, disembowel, guinea fowl, jungle fowl, on the prowl, snowy owl, spotted owl, Turkish towel, waterfowl • throw in the towel • neither fish nor fowl
owland \ō-lənd\ lowland, Poland, Roland
owledge \äl-ij\ college, knowledge • acknowledge
owler[1] \ō-lər\ see OLLER
owler[2] \au-lər\ growler, howler, prowler, scowler
owless \ō-ləs\ see OLUS
owline \ō-lən\ see OLON
owling[1] \ō-liŋ\ see OLLING
owling[2] \au-liŋ\ growling, howling, toweling
—*also* -ing *forms of verbs listed at* OWL[2]
owlock \äl-ək\ see OLOCH
owly[1] \ō-lē\ see OLY[1]
owly[2] \au-lē\ foully, growly, jowly
owman \ō-mən\ see OMAN
ow-me \ō-mē\ see OAMY
own[1] \ōn\ see ONE[1]
own[2] \aun\ Braun, brown, clown, crown, down, drown, frown, gown, noun, town • back down, bear down, boil down, boomtown, breakdown, break down, bring down, Cape Town, Charlestown, clampdown, clamp

down, closedown, comedown, come down, cooldown, countdown, count down, cow town, crackdown, crack down, crosstown, cut down, downtown, dress down, dumb down, facedown, first down, Freetown, Georgetown, ghost town, go down, hand down, hands-down, hold down, hometown, Jamestown, knockdown, knock down, lay down, letdown, let down, lie down, live down, look down, lowdown, markdown, mark down, meltdown, melt down, midtown, nightgown, nutbrown, phase down, pipe down, play down, pronoun, pull-down, renown, rubdown, rundown, set down, shakedown, shake down, shoot down, showdown, shutdown, shut down, slap down, slowdown, splashdown, splash down, strike down, strippeddown, sundown, swansdown, take down, tear down, thumbs-down, top-down, touchdown, touch down, trade down, turndown, turn down, uptown, Von Braun, wear down, weigh down, wind down, write down, Youngstown • Allentown, broken-down, Chinatown, common noun, dressing gown, eiderdown, go to town, hand-me-down, proper noun, shantytown, simmer down, thistledown, Tinseltown, trickledown, Triple Crown, tumbledown, up and down, upand-down, upside down, water down, watered-down • bring the house down, let one's hair down, man-about-town, nervous breakdown, put one's foot down

ownded \aún-dəd\ see OUNDED
ownding \aún-diŋ\ see OUNDING
owned¹ \ōnd\ see ONED¹
owned² \aúnd\ see OUND²
owner¹ \ō-nər\ see ONER¹
owner² \ü-nər\ see OONER
owner³ \aú-nər\ downer • downtowner
owness \ō-nəs\ see ONUS²
ownia \ō-nē-ə\ see ONIA¹
ownie \aú-nē\ see OWNY
owning \ō-niŋ\ see ONING²
ownish \aú-nish\ brownish, clownish
ownsman \aúnz-mən\ groundsman, townsman
owny \aú-nē\ brownie, browny, downy, townie
owper \ü-pər\ see OOPER
owry \aúr-ē\ see OWERY
owse \aúz\ see OUSE³
owser \aú-zər\ see OUSER
owster \ō-stər\ see OASTER
owsy \aú-zē\ blousy, blowsy, drowsy, frowsy, lousy, mousy
owth \ōth\ both, growth, loath, oath, quoth • old-growth, outgrowth • overgrowth, undergrowth • Hippocratic oath
owy \ō-ē\ blowy, Chloe, doughy, Joey, showy, snowy • echoey
owys \ō-əs\ see OIS³
ox \äks\ box, fox, Fox, Knox, lox, ox, pox • bandbox, black box, boom box, boondocks, Botox, cowpox, detox, dreadlocks, firebox, Fort Knox, gearbox, gray fox, hatbox, icebox, in-box, jewel box, jukebox, lockbox, mailbox, matchbox, musk ox, out-box, outfox, red fox, sandbox, smallpox, soapbox, squawk box, strongbox, toolbox, unbox, voice box, workbox, Xerox • arctic fox, ballot box, bobby socks, chatterbox, chicken pox, equinox, flying fox, music box, orthodox, Orthodox, paradox, sentry box, shadowbox, silver fox, tinderbox, window box, witness-box • dialog

box, Greek Orthodox, heterodox, idiot box, jack-in-the-box, Pandora's box, penalty box, unorthodox • Eastern Orthodox, safe-deposit box
—*also* -s, -'s, *and* -s' *forms of nouns and* -s *forms of verbs listed at* OCK[1]

oxer \äk-sər\ boxer, Boxer • kickboxer • bobby-soxer

oxie \äk-sē\ see OXY

oxy \äk-sē\ boxy, foxy, moxie, proxy • epoxy • orthodoxy • unorthodoxy

oy \òi\ boy, buoy, cloy, coy, joy, Joy, koi, oy, ploy, poi, Roy, soy, toy, Troy • ahoy, alloy, annoy, ball boy, batboy, B-boy, beachboy, bellboy, bell buoy, bok choy, borzoi, busboy, carboy, choirboy, convoy, cowboy, decoy, deploy, destroy, doughboy, employ, enjoy, envoy, Hanoi, homeboy, houseboy, killjoy, Leroy, life buoy, McCoy, newsboy, pageboy, page boy, playboy, plowboy, po'boy, Quemoy, Saint Croix, schoolboy, stock boy, Tolstoy, tomboy, viceroy • Adonai, altar boy, attaboy, bullyboy, cabin boy, corduroy, hoi polloi, Illinois, Iroquois, mama's boy, office boy, overjoy, paperboy, poster boy, Tinkertoy, whipping boy • delivery boy, Helen of Troy

oya \òi-ə\ see OIA

oyable \òi-ə-bəl\ employable, enjoyable • unemployable

oyal[1] \īl\ see ILE[1]

oyal[2] \òil\ see OIL

oyalist \òi-ə-ləst\ loyalist, royalist

oyalty \òil-tē\ loyalty, royalty • disloyalty

oyance \òi-əns\ annoyance, clairvoyance, flamboyance
—*also* -s, -'s, *and* -s' *forms of nouns listed at* OYANT

oyant \òi-ənt\ buoyant • clairvoyant, flamboyant

oyce \òis\ see OICE

oyd \òid\ see OID[1]

oyed \òid\ see OID[1]

oyer \òir\ foyer • destroyer

oyes \òiz\ see OISE[2]

oying \òiŋ\ see AWING

oyle \òil\ see OIL

oyless \òi-ləs\ joyless, Troilus

oyment \òi-mənt\ deployment, employment, enjoyment • redeployment, self-employment, unemployment

oyne \òin\ see OIN[1]

oyo \òi-ə\ see OIA

oyster \òi-stər\ see OISTER

oz[1] \əz\ see EUSE[1]

oz[2] \òz\ see AUSE[1]

oz[3] \ōz\ see OSE[2]

oze \ōz\ see OSE[2]

ozen[1] \əz-ᵊn\ cousin, dozen • first cousin • baker's dozen, second cousin • a dime a dozen

ozen[2] \ōz-ᵊn\ see OSEN

ozer \ō-zər\ see OSER[1]

ozily \ō-zə-lē\ see OSILY

ozo[1] \ō-sō\ see OSO[1]

ozo[2] \ō-zō\ see OSO[2]

ozy \ō-zē\ see OSY

ozzle \äz-əl\ Basel, Basil, nozzle, schnozzle

U

u \ü\ see EW[1]

ua \ä\ see A[1]

uable \ü-ə-bəl\ chewable, doable, viewable • renewable, undoable • nonrenewable

ual \ü-əl\ see UEL[1]

uan \ü-ən\ bruin, ruin, yuan

uancy \ü-ən-sē\ see UENCY

uant \ü-ənt\ see UENT

uart \ùrt\ see URT[1]

ub \əb\ chub, club, cub, drub, dub, flub, grub, hub, nub, pub, rub, schlub, scrub, shrub, snub, stub, sub, tub • bathtub, book club, brew pub, glee club, health club, hot tub, hubbub, nightclub, war club, washtub, yacht club • billy club, country club, overdub, service club, syllabub • Beelzebub

uba \ü-bə\ Cuba, scuba, tuba • Aruba, saxtuba

ubal \ü-bəl\ nubile, ruble, tubal

uban \ü-bən\ see EUBEN

ubbard \əb-ərd\ cupboard • Mother Hubbard

ubber \əb-ər\ blubber, rubber, scrubber • foam rubber, landlubber, nightclubber • moneygrubber

ubbery \əb-rē\ blubbery, rubbery, shrubbery

ubbily \əb-ə-lē\ bubbly, grubbily

ubbing \əb-iŋ\ drubbing, rubbing • *also* -ing *forms of verbs listed at* UB

ubble \əb-əl\ bubble, double, Hubble, rubble, stubble, trouble • abubble, redouble, soap bubble • body double, borrow trouble, daily double, on the double

ubbled \əb-əld\ bubbled, doubled, troubled • redoubled, untroubled

ubbly[1] \əb-lē\ bubbly, doubly, stubbly

ubbly[2] \əb-ə-lē\ see UBBILY

ubby \əb-ē\ chubby, clubby, grubby, hubby, scrubby, shrubby, stubby, tubby

ube \üb\ boob, cube, lube, rube, tube • boob tube, Danube, flashcube, jujube, test tube • bouillon cube, breathing tube, down the tube, inner tube

uben \ü-bən\ see EUBEN

ubens \ü-bənz\ Rubens —*also* -s, -'s, *and* -s' *forms of nouns listed at* EUBEN

uber \ü-bər\ goober, tuber

uberance \ü-brəns\ exuberance, protuberance

uberant \ü-brənt\ exuberant, protuberant • overexuberant

uberous \ü-brəs\ see UBRIS

ubic \ü-bik\ cubic • cherubic

ubile \ü-bəl\ see UBAL

uble \ü-bəl\ see UBAL

ubric \ü-brik\ Kubrick, rubric

ubrious \ü-brē-əs\ lugubrious, salubrious

ubris \ü-brəs\ hubris, tuberous

ubtile \ət-ᵊl\ see UTTLE

uby \ü-bē\ see OOBY

uca \ü-kə\ see OOKA

ucat \ək-ət\ see UCKET

ucca[1] \ü-kə\ see OOKA

ucca[2] \ək-ə\ see UKKA

uccal \ək-əl\ see UCKLE

ucci \ü-chē\ see OOCHY

uccor \ək-ər\ see UCKER

ucculence \ək-yə-ləns\ see UCULENCE

194

uce \üs\ see USE[1]

uced \üst\ see OOST

ucence \üs-ᵊns\ nuisance • translucence

ucer \ü-sər\ juicer • producer, seducer

uch¹ \ich\ see ITCH

uch² \ük\ see UKE

uch³ \əch\ see UTCH

uche¹ \ü-chē\ see OOCHY

uche² \üch\ see OOCH[1]

uche³ \üsh\ see OUCHE

ucher \ü-chər\ see UTURE

uchin \ü-shən\ see UTION

uchy \əch-ē\ duchy, touchy • archduchy, grand duchy

ucian \ü-shən\ see UTION

ucible \ü-sə-bəl\ crucible • deducible, inducible, producible, reducible • irreducible, reproducible

ucifer \ü-sə-fər\ crucifer, Lucifer

ucive \ü-siv\ see USIVE

uck¹ \ək\ buck, Buck, chuck, cluck, duck, guck, luck, muck, pluck, puck, Puck, schmuck, shuck, snuck, struck, stuck, suck, truck, tuck, yuck • awestruck, dead duck, dumbstruck, dump truck, fire truck, hard luck, lameduck, moonstruck, mukluk, potluck, roebuck, sawbuck, shelduck, stagestruck, starstruck, sunstruck, unstuck, upchuck, woodchuck • Daffy Duck, Habakkuk, horror-struck, Keokuk, ladder truck, megabuck, motortruck, muckamuck, nip and tuck, pass the buck, Peking duck, pickup truck, push one's luck, sitting duck, thunderstruck

uck² \ùk\ see OOK[1]

ukar \ək-ər\ see UCKER

ucker \ək-ər\ pucker, shucker, succor, sucker, trucker, tucker • bloodsucker, goatsucker, sapsucker, seersucker, shark sucker

ucket \ək-ət\ bucket, ducat

• lunch-bucket, Nantucket, Pawtucket, rust bucket • kick the bucket • drop in the bucket

uckle \ək-əl\ buckle, chuckle, knuckle, suckle, truckle • bareknuckle, pinochle, swashbuckle, unbuckle • honeysuckle

uckled \ək-əld\ cuckold, knuckled • bare-knuckled
—*also* -ed *forms of verbs listed at* UCKLE

uckling \ək-liŋ\ duckling, suckling • swashbuckling • ugly duckling
—*also* -ing *forms of verbs listed at* UCKLE

uckold \ək-əld\ see UCKLED

ucks \əks\ see UX[1]

uckus \ùk-əs\ ruckus, Sukkoth

ucky \ək-ē\ ducky, lucky, mucky, plucky, sucky, yucky • Kentucky, unlucky • happy-go-lucky

uct \əkt\ duct • abduct, bile duct, conduct, construct, deduct, destruct, induct, instruct, obstruct • aqueduct, deconstruct, reconstruct, self-destruct, viaduct
—*also* -ed *forms of verbs listed at* UCK[1]

uctable \ək-tə-bəl\ see UCTIBLE

uctible \ək-tə-bəl\ deductible, destructible • indestructible, nondeductible

uction \ək-shən\ suction • abduction, conduction, construction, deduction, destruction, induction, instruction, obstruction, production, reduction, seduction • coproduction, deconstruction, introduction, liposuction, mass production, reconstruction, reproduction, self-destruction

uctive \ək-tiv\ conductive, constructive, deductive, destructive, inductive, instructive, obstructive, productive, reductive, seductive • nonproductive, reconstructive, reproductive, self-destructive,

unconstructive, unproductive
• counterproductive
uctor \ək-tər\ conductor, instructor • nonconductor • semiconductor, superconductor
uculence \ək-yə-ləns\ succulence, truculence
ucy \ü-sē\ see UICY
ud¹ \əd\ blood, bud, crud, cud, dud, flood, Judd, mud, scud, spud, stud, thud • bad blood, blue blood, earbud, full-blood, half-blood, leaf bud, lifeblood, new blood, oxblood, pure-blood, redbud, rosebud, shed blood, smell blood, sweat blood • dragon's blood, flesh and blood, flower bud, in cold blood, in the bud • stick-in-the-mud
ud² \üd\ see UDE¹
ud³ \ud\ see OOD¹
uda \üd-ə\ Buddha, Gouda, Judah • Barbuda, Bermuda • barracuda
udah \üd-ə\ see UDA
udal \üd-ᵊl\ see OODLE
udd¹ \ud\ see OOD¹
udd² \əd\ see UD¹
udded \əd-əd\ see OODED¹
udder \əd-ər\ rudder, shudder, udder
uddha \üd-ə\ see UDA
uddhist \üd-əst\ see UDIST¹
uddie \əd-ē\ see UDDY¹
udding \əd-iŋ\ budding,
—also -ing forms of verbs listed at UD¹
uddle \əd-ᵊl\ cuddle, fuddle, huddle, muddle, puddle • befuddle
uddly \əd-lē\ cuddly, Dudley
uddy¹ \əd-ē\ bloody, buddy, Buddy, cruddy, muddy, ruddy, study • case study, work-study • buddy-buddy, fuddy-duddy, understudy
uddy² \ud-ē\ see OODY²
ude¹ \üd\ brood, crude, dude, feud, food, hued, Jude, lewd,

mood, nude, prude, rude, shrewd, snood, 'tude, who'd, you'd • allude, blood feud, collude, conclude, delude, denude, elude, exclude, exude, fast-food, Gertrude, health food, include, intrude, junk food, nonfood, plant food, postlude, preclude, prelude, protrude, seafood, seclude, subdued, unglued • altitude, amplitude, aptitude, attitude, certitude, comfort food, finger food, fortitude, frankenfood, gratitude, interlude, lassitude, latitude, longitude, magnitude, multitude, platitude, rectitude, servitude, solitude • beatitude, ineptitude, ingratitude, natural food, vicissitude
ude² \üd-ə\ see UDA
udel \üd-ᵊl\ see OODLE
udeness \üd-nəs\ see UDINOUS
udent \üd-ᵊnt\ prudent, student • imprudent, nonstudent
uder \üd-ər\ brooder, Tudor • intruder
—also -er forms of adjectives listed at UDE¹
udge¹ \əj\ budge, drudge, fudge, grudge, judge, nudge, sludge, smudge, trudge • adjudge, begrudge, misjudge, prejudge
udge² \üj\ see UGE¹
udgeon \əj-ən\ bludgeon • curmudgeon
udgie \əj-ē\ see UDGY
udgy \əj-ē\ budgie, pudgy, sludgy, smudgy
udi \ü-dē\ see OODY¹
udie \ü-dē\ see OODY¹
udinous \üd-nəs\ crudeness, rudeness, shrewdness • multitudinous
udist¹ \üd-əst\ Buddhist, nudist
—also -est forms of adjectives listed at UDE¹
udist² \ud-əst\ see OULDEST
udity \üd-ət-ē\ crudity, nudity

udley \əd-lē\ see UDDLY
udly \əd-lē\ see UDDLY
udo \üd-ō\ judo, pseudo
udor \üd-ər\ see UDER
udsman \ùdz-mən\ see OODSMAN
udu \üd-ü\ see OODOO
udy¹ \ü-dē\ see OODY¹
udy² \əd-ē\ see UDDY¹
ue¹ \ü\ see EW¹
ue² \ā\ see AY¹
ued \üd\ see UDE¹
ueghel \ü-gəl\ see UGAL
uel¹ \ü-əl\ crewel, cruel, dual, duel, fuel, gruel, jewel, Jewel • accrual, refuel, renewal, synfuel • biofuel, diesel fuel, fossil fuel
uel² \ül\ see OOL¹
uely \ü-lē\ see ULY
uence \ü-əns\ affluence, confluence, congruence, influence, pursuance • incongruence
—*also* -s, -'s *and* -s' *forms of nouns listed at* UENT
uency \ü-ən-sē\ fluency, truancy • congruency
ueness \ü-nəs\ see EWNESS
uent \ü-ənt\ fluent, truant • affluent, congruent, effluent • incongruent
uer \ü-ər\ see EWER¹
uerile \ùr-əl\ see URAL
ues \üz\ see USE²
uesman \üz-mən\ see EWSMAN
uesome \ü-səm\ gruesome, twosome
uesy \ü-zē\ see OOZY
uet \ü-ət\ bluet, cruet, suet • conduit, intuit
uette \et\ see ET¹
uey \ü-ē\ see EWY
uff \əf\ bluff, buff, cuff, duff, fluff, gruff, guff, huff, luff, muff, puff, rough, ruff, scruff, scuff, slough, snuff, stuff, tough • cream puff, earmuff, enough, feedstuff, foodstuff, french cuff, handcuff, hang tough, hot stuff, kid stuff, Pine Bluff, rebuff • blindman's buff,

call one's bluff, off-the-cuff, overstuff, powder puff, strut one's stuff, up to snuff
uffe¹ \üf\ see OOF¹
uffe² \ùf\ see OOF²
uffed \əft\ tuft
—*also* -ed *forms of verbs listed at* UFF
uffel \əf-əl\ see UFFLE
uffer \əf-ər\ bluffer, buffer, duffer, puffer, suffer • candlesnuffer, stocking stuffer
—*also* -er *forms of adjectives listed at* UFF
uffet \əf-ət\ buffet, tuffet
uffin \əf-ən\ muffin, puffin, roughen, toughen • English muffin, ragamuffin
uffle \əf-əl\ duffel, muffle, ruffle, scuffle, shuffle, snuffle, truffle • kerfuffle, reshuffle
uffled \əf-əld\ unruffled
—*also* -ed *forms of verbs listed at* UFFLE
uffly \əf-lē\ gruffly, roughly
uffy \əf-ē\ fluffy, huffy, puffy, scruffy, stuffy, toughie
ufi \ü-fē\ see OOFY
ufous \ü-fəs\ doofus, Rufus
uft \əft\ see UFFED
ufus \ü-fəs\ see UFOUS
ug \əg\ bug, chug, Doug, drug, dug, hug, jug, lug, mug, plug, pug, rug, shrug, slug, smug, snug, thug, tug, ugh • bear hug, bedbug, debug, earplug, firebug, fireplug, humbug, june bug, nondrug, prayer rug, sea slug, spark plug, stinkbug, throw rug, unplug, wall plug • antidrug, doodlebug, gateway drug, jitterbug, ladybug, lightning bug, litterbug, mealybug, pull the plug, scatter rug, shutterbug, toby jug, water bug, wonder drug • miracle drug, prescription drug • oriental rug
uga \ü-gə\ beluga, Tortuga • Chattanooga

ugal \ü-gəl\ Brueghel, bugle, frugal

ugar \ùg-ər\ see UGUR

uge[1] \üj\ huge, scrooge, stooge • deluge, refuge • centrifuge, subterfuge

uge[2] \üzh\ Bruges, luge, rouge • deluge, refuge • Baton Rouge

ugel \ü-gəl\ see UGAL

uges \üzh\ see UGE[2]

ugger[1] \əg-ər\ bugger, mugger, plugger, slugger, smugger, snugger • debugger, tree hugger

ugger[2] \ùg-ər\ see UGUR

uggery \əg-rē\ thuggery • skulduggery

uggie \əg-ē\ see UGGY

uggish \əg-ish\ sluggish, thuggish

uggle \əg-əl\ juggle, smuggle, snuggle, struggle

uggler \əg-lər\ juggler, smuggler

uggy \əg-ē\ buggy, muggy • beach buggy, dune buggy, swamp buggy • baby buggy, horse-and-buggy

ugh[1] \əg\ see UG

ugh[2] \ü\ see EW[1]

ughes \üz\ see USE[2]

ugle \ü-gəl\ see UGAL

ugli \ə-glē\ see UGLY

uglia \ùl-yə\ see ULIA

ugly \əg-lē\ smugly, snugly, ugly

ugn \ün\ see OON[1]

ugner \ü-nər\ see OONER

ugu \ü-gü\ fugu, goo-goo

ugur \ùg-ər\ booger, sugar • blood sugar, brown sugar, cane sugar • maple sugar

uhl \ül\ see OOL[1]

uhr[1] \ər\ see EUR[1]

uhr[2] \ùr\ see URE[1]

ührer \ùr-ər\ see URER

ui[1] \ā\ see AY[1]

ui[2] \ē\ see EE[1]

uice \üs\ see USE[1]

uiced \üst\ see OOST

uicer \ü-sər\ see UCER

uicy \ü-sē\ juicy, Lucy • Watusi

uid \ü-id\ druid, fluid

uidance \īd-ᵊns\ see IDANCE

uide \īd\ see IDE[1]

uided \īd-əd\ see IDED

uider \īd-ər\ see IDER[1]

uidon \īd-ᵊn\ see IDEN

uiker \ī-kər\ see IKER

uild \ild\ see ILLED

uilder \il-dər\ see ILDER[1]

uilding \il-diŋ\ see ILDING

uile \īl\ see ILE[1]

uiler \ī-lər\ see ILAR

uilleann \i-lən\ see ILLON

uilt \ilt\ see ILT

uimpe \amp\ see AMP[3]

uin[1] \ü-ən\ see UAN

uin[2] \ən\ see UN[1]

uin[3] \aⁿ\ see IN[4]

uing \ü-iŋ\ see OING[2]

uint \ü-ənt\ see UENT

uir \ùr\ see URE[1]

uirdly \ùr-lē\ see URELY

uisance \üs-ᵊns\ see UCENCE

uise[1] \üz\ see USE[2]

uise[2] \īz\ see IZE[1]

uiser \ü-zər\ see USER

uish \ü-ish\ see EWISH

uisne \ü-nē\ see OONY

uiste \is-tē\ see ICITY[2]

uit[1] \ü-ət\ see UET

uit[2] \üt\ see UTE

uitable \üt-ə-bəl\ see UTABLE

uite \üt\ see UTE

uited \üt-əd\ see OOTED[1]

uiter \üt-ər\ see UTER

uiting \üt-iŋ\ see UTING

uitless \üt-ləs\ see OOTLESS

uitor \üt-ər\ see UTER

uitous \ü-ət-əs\ circuitous, fortuitous, gratuitous

uits \üts\ see OOTS

uittle[1] \üt-ᵊl\ see UTILE

uittle[2] \ət-ᵊl\ see UTTLE

uity[1] \ü-ət-ē\ acuity, annuity, congruity, gratuity • ambiguity, continuity, incongruity, ingenuity • discontinuity

uity[2] \üt-ē\ see OOTY[1]

uk¹ \ük\ see UKE
uk² \ùk\ see OOK¹
uk³ \ək\ see UCK¹
ukar \ə-kər\ see UCKER
uke \ük\ cuke, duke, fluke, kook, Luke, nuke, Nuuk, puke, snook, spook, uke • archduke, Chinook, Dubuque, Farouk, grand duke, Kirkuk, rebuke • antinuke, Pentateuch
uki¹ \ü-kē\ see OOKY¹
uki² \ù-kē\ see OOKIE
ukka \ək-ə\ pukka, yucca
ukker \ək-ər\ see UCKER
ukkoth \ùk-əs\ see UCKUS
ul¹ \ùl\ bull, full, pull, wool, you'll • armful, bagful, bellpull, brimful, carful, chock-full, cupful, earful, eyeful, fistful, forkful, glassful, handful, houseful, in full, John Bull, mouthful, pailful, pit bull, plateful, potful, roomful, spoonful, steel wool, tankful, truckful, trunkful • barrelful, basketful, bellyful, bucketful, closetful, cock-and-bull, Istanbul, shovelful, Sitting Bull, tableful • dyed-in-the-wool
ul² \ül\ see OOL¹
ul³ \əl\ see ULL¹
ula \ü-lə\ Beulah, hula, moola • Missoula • Ashtabula, Pascagoula
ular \ü-lər\ see OOLER
ulch \əlch\ gulch, mulch
ule¹ \ü-lē\ see ULY
ule² \ül\ see OOL¹
ulean \ü-lē-ən\ Julian • Herculean
uled \üld\ see OOLED
ulep \ü-ləp\ see ULIP
uler \ü-lər\ see OOLER
ules \ülz\ Jules
—*also* -s, -'s, *and* -s' *forms of nouns and* -s *forms of verbs listed at* OOL¹
ulet \əl-ət\ see ULLET¹
uley¹ \ü-lē\ see ULY

uley² \ùl-ē\ see ULLY²
ulf \əlf\ golf, gulf, Gulf • engulf • Beowulf
ulgar \əl-gər\ see ULGUR
ulge \əlj\ bulge • divulge, indulge • overindulge
ulgur \əl-gər\ bulgur, vulgar
ulhas \əl-əs\ see ULLUS
uli \ùl-ē\ see ULLY²
ulia \ül-yə\ Julia • Apulia
ulie \ü-lē\ see ULY
ulip \ü-ləp\ julep, tulip • mint julep
ulish \ü-lish\ see OOLISH
ulk \əlk\ bulk, hulk, skulk, sulk, yolk
ulky \əl-kē\ bulky, sulky
ull¹ \əl\ cull, dull, gull, hull, lull, mull, null, scull, skull • annul, mogul, numskull, seagull • herring gull, laughing gull, monohull, multihull, Sitting Bull
ull² \ùl\ see UL¹
ulla¹ \ü-lə\ see ULA
ulla² \əl-ə\ see ULLAH
ullah \əl-ə\ Gullah, mullah, Sulla • medulla • ayatollah
ullan \əl-ən\ see ULLEN
ullard \əl-ərd\ see OLORED
ullate \əl-ət\ see ULLET¹
ulle \ül\ see OOL¹
ullein \əl-ən\ see ULLEN
ullen \əl-ən\ mullein, sullen
uller \əl-ər\ see OLOR¹
ulles \əl-əs\ see ULLUS
ullet¹ \əl-ət\ bullet, gullet, mullet • dodge a bullet, magic bullet, silver bullet
ullet² \ùl-ət\ bullet, pullet
ulley \ùl-ē\ see ULLY²
ullis \əl-əs\ see ULLUS
ullitt \ùl-ət\ see ULLET²
ullus \əl-əs\ Dulles • Catullus
ully¹ \əl-ē\ gully, sully
ully² \ùl-ē\ bully, fully, gully, pulley, woolly
ulp \əlp\ gulp, pulp • wood pulp
ulse \əls\ dulse, pulse • convulse, impulse, repulse

ulsion \əl-shən\ compulsion, convulsion, emulsion, expulsion, impulsion, propulsion, repulsion, revulsion • jet propulsion, self-propulsion

ulsive \əl-siv\ compulsive, convulsive, impulsive, propulsive, repulsive • anticonvulsive

ult \əlt\ cult • adult, consult, exult, insult, occult, result, subcult, tumult • catapult, difficult •

ultant \əlt-ᵊnt\ consultant, exultant, resultant

ultch \əlch\ see ULCH

ultery \əl-trē\ see ULTRY

ultry \əl-trē\ sultry • adultery

ulture \əl-chər\ culture, vulture • subculture • agriculture, aquaculture, counterculture, horticulture, turkey vulture

ulu \ü-lü\ lulu, Sulu, Zulu • Honolulu

uly \ü-lē\ coolie, coolly, duly, Julie, newly, Thule, truly • Grand Coulee, unduly, unruly, yours truly

um¹ \əm\ bum, chum, come, crumb, drum, dumb, from, glum, gum, hum, mum, numb, plum, plumb, rum, scum, slum, some, strum, sum, swum, them, thrum, thumb, yum • bass drum, bay rum, beach plum, become, dumdum, eardrum, green thumb, ho-hum, how come, humdrum, income, outcome, pond scum, side drum, snare drum, steel drum, succumb, therefrom, to come, Tom Thumb, tom-tom, yum-yum • apart from, aside from, bubblegum, chewing gum, kettledrum, kingdom come, overcome, rule of thumb, sugarplum, Tweedledum •

um² \ùm\ broom, groom, room • ballroom, barroom, bathroom, bedroom, chat room, checkroom, classroom, cloakroom, coatroom, courtroom, darkroom, headroom, homeroom, lunchroom, men's room, mushroom, push broom, rec room, restroom, schoolroom, stateroom, sunroom, washroom, weight room, workroom • breathing room, dining room, dressing room, elbow room, family room, ladies' room, locker room, sitting room, standing room, waiting room, wiggle room

um³ \üm\ see OOM¹

uma \ü-mə\ puma, Yuma • Montezuma, Petaluma

uman \ü-mən\ crewman, human, Newman, Truman, Yuman • acumen, illumine, inhuman, nonhuman, prehuman, subhuman • superhuman

umanous \ü-mə-nəs\ see UMINOUS

umb \əm\ see UM¹

umbar \əm-bər\ see UMBER¹

umbed \əmd\ unplumbed
—*also* -ed *forms of verbs listed at* UM¹

umbel \əm-bəl\ see UMBLE

umber¹ \əm-bər\ Humber, lumbar, lumber, number, slumber, umber • call number, cucumber, encumber, outnumber, prime number • sea cucumber • atomic number, 800 number, serial number

umber² \əm-ər\ see UMMER

umbered \əm-bərd\ numbered • unnumbered
—*also* -ed *forms of verbs listed at* UMBER¹

umberland \əm-bər-lənd\ Cumberland • Northumberland

umbing \əm-iŋ\ see OMING¹

umble \əm-bəl\ bumble, crumble, fumble, grumble, humble, jumble, mumble, rumble, stumble, tumble • rough-and-tumble

umbler \əm-blər\ bumbler, grumbler, tumbler

umbling \əm-bliŋ\ tumbling
—*also* -ing *forms of verbs listed at*
UMBLE

umbly[1] \əm-blē\ crumbly, grumbly,
humbly, mumbly, rumbly

umbly[2] \əm-lē\ dumbly, numbly

umbness \əm-nəs\ numbness
• alumnus

umbo \əm-bō\ gumbo, jumbo
• Colombo • mumbo jumbo

umbria \əm-brē-ə\ Cumbria
• Northumbria

ume \üm\ see OOM[1]

umed \ümd\ see OOMED

umely \ü-mə-lē\ see OOMILY

umen \ü-mən\ see UMAN

umer \ü-mər\ bloomer, Bloomer,
boomer, humor, roomer, rumor,
Sumer, tumor • consumer, cos-
tumer • baby boomer, gallows
humor

umerous \üm-rəs\ see UMOROUS

umerus \üm-rəs\ see UMOROUS

umey \ü-mē\ see OOMY

umf \əmf\ see UMPH

umi \ü-mē\ see OOMY

umin \ü-mən\ see UMAN

umine \ü-mən\ see UMAN

uming \ü-miŋ\ blooming
• everblooming, time-consuming,
unassuming
—*also* -ing *forms of verbs listed at*
OOM[1]

uminous \ü-mə-nəs\ luminous
• bituminous, voluminous

ummary \əm-ə-rē\ see UMMERY

ummate \əm-ət\ see UMMET

ummel \əm-əl\ see OMMEL[2]

ummell \əm-əl\ see OMMEL[2]

ummer \əm-ər\ bummer, drummer,
mummer, plumber, strummer,
summer • latecomer, midsummer,
newcomer • Indian summer
—*also* -er *forms of adjectives listed
at* UM[1]

ummery \əm-ə-rē\ summary, sum-
mery • Montgomery

ummet \əm-ət\ plummet, summit

ummie \əm-ē\ see UMMY

ummit \əm-ət\ see UMMET

ummox \əm-əks\ flummox, lum-
mox

ummy \əm-ē\ chummy, crummy,
dummy, gummy, mommy,
mummy, rummy, scummy,
slummy, tummy, yummy • gin
rummy

umness \əm-nəs\ see UMBNESS

umnus \əm-nəs\ see UMBNESS

umor \ü-mər\ see UMER

umorous \üm-rəs\ humerus, hu-
morous, numerous

umous \ü-məs\ humus • posthu-
mous

ump \əmp\ bump, chump, clump,
dump, grump, hump, jump, lump,
plump, pump, rump, slump,
stump, sump, thump, trump, ump
• air pump, broad jump, heat
pump, high jump, long jump, ski
jump, speed bump, sump pump
• bungee jump, vacuum pump
• hop skip and jump

umper \əm-pər\ bumper, dumper,
jumper, pumper, stumper • broad
jumper, high jumper, long
jumper, ski jumper, smoke
jumper, tub-thumper • bungee
jumper • bumper-to-bumper

umph \əmf\ humph • galumph,
harrumph

umpish \əm-pish\ lumpish, plump-
ish

umpkin \əŋ-kən\ see UNKEN

umple \əm-pəl\ crumple, rumple

umps \əms\ dumps, mumps
• goose bumps
—*also* -s, -'s, *and* -s' *forms of
nouns and* -s *forms of verbs listed
at* UMP

umption \əm-shən\ gumption
• assumption, consumption, pre-
sumption, resumption

umptious \əm-shəs\ bumptious,

scrumptious, sumptuous • presumptuous

umptuous¹ \əm-chəs\ sumptuous • presumptuous

umptuous² \əm-shəs\ see UMPTIOUS

umpus \əm-pəs\ see OMPASS

umpy \əm-pē\ bumpy, dumpy, grumpy, jumpy, lumpy, stumpy

umus \ü-məs\ see UMOUS

umy \ü-mē\ see OOMY

un¹ \ən\ bun, done, Donne, fun, gun, hon, Hun, none, nun, one, pun, run, shun, son, spun, stun, sun, ton, won • A-1, air gun, begun, big gun, blowgun, Bull Run, burp gun, Chaplin, dry run, earned run, end run, first-run, flashgun, godson, grandson, handgun, hard-won, hired gun, home run, homespun, long run, outdone, outgun, outrun, popgun, redone, rerun, short run, shotgun, six-gun, speargun, spray gun, squirt gun, stepson, stun gun, top gun, trial run, undone, V-1, welldone, zip gun • Algonquin, antigun, Bofors gun, Browning gun, Gatling gun, hit-and-run, jump the gun, kiloton, machine-gun, machine gun, megaton, midnight sun, one-on-one, one-to-one, on the run, overdone, overrun, pellet gun, radar gun, ride shotgun, riot gun, smoking gun, squirrel gun, tommy gun, underdone, water gun • son of a gun, submachine gun

un² \ün\ see OON¹

una \ü-nə\ Luna, tuna • Altoona, kahuna, vicuña

uña¹ \ü-nə\ see UNA

uña² \ün-yə\ see UNIA

unal \ün-ᵊl\ communal, tribunal

unar \ü-nər\ see OONER

unary \ü-nə-rē\ buffoonery, festoonery, lampoonery

unc \ənk\ see UNK

uncan \ən-kən\ see UNKEN

unce \əns\ dunce, once
—*also* -s, -'s, *and* -s' *forms of nouns and* -s *forms of verbs listed at* ONT¹

unch \ənch\ brunch, bunch, crunch, hunch, lunch, munch, punch, scrunch • box lunch, free lunch, keypunch • counterpunch, one-two punch, out to lunch, rabbit punch, sucker punch

unche \ənch\ see UNCH

uncher \ən-chər\ cowpuncher, keypuncher • counterpuncher, number cruncher

unchy \ən-chē\ crunchy, punchy

uncle \əŋ-kəl\ uncle • carbuncle, granduncle, great-uncle, say uncle

unct \əŋt\ adjunct, defunct
—*also* -ed *forms of verbs listed at* UNK

unction \əŋ-shən\ function, junction • compunction, conjunction, dysfunction, injunction, malfunction

uncture \əŋ-chər\ juncture, puncture • acupuncture

und¹ \ənd\ fund • dachshund, hedge fund, refund, rotund, slush fund, trust fund • cummerbund, underfund • mutual fund
—*also* -ed *forms of verbs listed at* UN¹

und² \aund\ see OUND²

undae \ən-dē\ see UNDI

undant \ən-dənt\ abundant, redundant • overabundant, superabundant

unday \ən-dē\ see UNDI

undays \ən-dēz\ Mondays, Sundays, undies
—*also* -s *and* -s' *forms of nouns listed at* UNDI

under \ən-dər\ blunder, funder, plunder, thunder, under, wonder • asunder, down under, go under, plow under, snow under

• knuckle under, steal one's thunder • build a fire under

underous \ən-drəs\ thunderous, wondrous

undi \ən-dē\ Monday, sundae, Sunday • Bay of Fundy, salmagundi • coatimundi

undies \ən-dēz\ see UNDAYS

undle \ən-dᵊl\ bundle, trundle

undy \ən-dē\ see UNDI

une \ün\ see OON[1]

uneau \ü-nō\ see UNO

uneless \ün-ləs\ see OONLESS

uner \ü-nər\ see OONER

unes \ünz\ see OONS

ung[1] \əŋ\ clung, dung, flung, hung, lung, rung, slung, sprung, strung, stung, sung, swung, tongue, wrung, young • among, black lung, far-flung, forked tongue, hamstrung, high-strung, iron lung, low-slung, unsung, with young • Aqua-Lung, bite one's tongue, egg foo yong, hold one's tongue, mother tongue

ung[2] \ůŋ\ Jung, Sung

ungal \ən-gəl\ see UNGLE

unge \ənj\ grunge, lunge, plunge, sponge • expunge • take the plunge

unger[1] \ən-jər\ plunger, sponger

unger[2] \əŋ-gər\ see ONGER[1]

ungle \əŋ-gəl\ bungle, fungal, jungle • asphalt jungle

ungous \əŋ-gəs\ fungus • humongous

ungry \ən-grē\ see ONGERY

ungus \əŋ-gəs\ see UNGOUS

ungy \ən-jē\ grungy, spongy

unha \ü-nə\ see UNA

uni \ü-nē\ see OONY

unia \ün-yə\ petunia, vicuña

unic \ü-nik\ eunuch, Munich, Punic, runic, tunic

unich \ü-nik\ see UNIC

union \ən-yən\ bunion, onion • Paul Bunyan

unis \ü-nəs\ see EWNESS

unish[1] \ən-ish\ Hunnish, punish

unish[2] \ü-nish\ see OONISH

unity \ü-nət-ē\ unity • community, disunity, immunity, impunity • opportunity

unk \əŋk\ bunk, chunk, clunk, drunk, dunk, flunk, funk, gunk, hunk, junk, monk, plunk, punk, shrunk, skunk, slunk, spunk, stunk, sunk, thunk, trunk • chipmunk, debunk, Podunk, preshrunk, punch-drunk, slam dunk • cyberpunk, steamer trunk

unked \əŋt\ see UNCT

unken \ən-kən\ Duncan, drunken, pumpkin, shrunken, sunken

unker \ən-kər\ bunker, clunker, hunker, junker • debunker, spelunker

unkie \ən-kē\ see UNKY

unkin \ən-kəm\ see UNCAN

unky \ən-kē\ chunky, clunky, donkey, flunky, funky, gunky, hunky, junkie, junky, monkey, skunky, spunky • grease monkey

unless \ən-ləs\ runless, sunless

unn \ən\ see UN[1]

unned \ənd\ see UND[1]

unnel \ən-ᵊl\ funnel, tunnel • wind tunnel

unner \ən-ər\ gunner, runner, stunner • base runner, forerunner, front-runner, gunrunner, roadrunner, rumrunner • machine gunner

unnery \ən-rē\ gunnery, nunnery

unning \ən-iŋ\ cunning, running, stunning • baserunning, gunrunning, rum-running • blockade-running, in the running • hit the ground running, out of the running

—also -ing forms of verbs listed at UN[1]

unnion \ən-yən\ see UNION

unnish \ən-ish\ see UNISH[1]

unny \ən-ē\ bunny, funny, honey, money, runny, sonny, sunny • blood money, Bugs Bunny, dust bunny, pin money, prize money, seed money, smart money, unfunny • for one's money, funny money, on the money, pocket money, spending money • run for one's money

uno \ü-nō\ Bruno, Juneau, Juno • numero uno

unt \ənt\ see ONT[1]

untal \ənt-ᵊl\ see UNTLE

unter \ənt-ər\ bunter, hunter, punter • foxhunter, headhunter, witch-hunter • bounty hunter, fortune hunter

unting \ənt-iŋ\ bunting • foxhunting, head-hunting, witch-hunting —*also* -ing *forms of verbs listed at* ONT[1]

untle \ənt-ᵊl\ frontal • disgruntle

unwale \ən-ᵊl\ see UNNEL

uny \ü-nē\ see OONY

unyan \ən-yən\ see UNION

uoy[1] \ü-ē\ see EWY

uoy[2] \òi\ see OY

uoyance \ü-əns\ see OYANCE

uoyant \òi-ənt\ see OYANT

up \əp\ cup, pup, sup, up, yup • act up, add up, backup, back up, bang-up, bear up, beat-up, beat up, blowup, blow up, bone up, bound up, breakup, break up, bring up, brush up, buck up, buildup, build up, built-up, bulk up, buy up, catch-up, chalk up, checkup, choose up, clam up, cleanup, clean up, close-up, close up, come up, cough up, crack-up, curl up, cut up, dial-up, dial up, dig up, doll up, do up, draw up, dream up, dress up, dried-up, drive-up, drum up, dry up, dustup, face up, fed up, fill up, fix up, flare-up, foul-up, foul up, frame-up, gang up, gear up, getup, get up, giddap, give up, grown-up, grow up, hang-up, hang up, hard up, heads-up, hiccup, hitch up, holdup, hold up, hole up, hookup, hook up, hung up, hyped-up, juice up, keep up, lay-up, lead-up, leg up, letup, let up, line up, linkup, lockup, look up, louse up, made-up, makeup, make up, markup, matchup, mix-up, mixed-up, mop-up, one-up, pass up, pay up, pickup, pick up, pileup, pinup, play up, pop-up, pull-up, pump up, push-up, rack up, rake up, ramp up, re-up, ring up, roll up, roundup, round up, run-up, scare up, screwup, screw up, setup, set up, sew up, shakeup, shape up, shook-up, show up, shut up, sign up, sit-up, size up, slipup, slip up, smashup, souped-up, speak up, speedup, spiffed-up, spit up, stack up, stand-up, start-up, steam up, step up, stepped-up, stickup, stick up, strike up, sum up, sunup, take up, talk up, teacup, throw up, thumbs-up, tie-up, toss-up, touch-up, trade up, trumped-up, tune-up, turn up, use up, wait up, wake up, warm-up, washed-up, windup, work up, wrap-up • belly-up, bottom-up, buckle up, bundle up, buttercup, butter up, cover-up, cover up, Dixie cup, double up, follow-up, giddyup, higher-up, hurry up, lighten up, live it up, measure up, open up, pick-me-up, power up, runner-up, shoot-'em-up, suction cup • sunny-side up

upboard \əb-ərd\ see UBBARD

upe \üp\ see OOP

upel \ü-pəl\ see UPLE[2]

uper \ü-pər\ see OOPER

upi \ü-pē\ see OOPY

upid \ü-pəd\ Cupid, stupid

upil \ü-pəl\ see UPLE[2]

uple

uple[1] \əp-əl\ couple, supple ∘ quadruple, quintuple, sextuple, uncouple

uple[2] \ü-pəl\ pupil, scruple ∘ quadruple, quintuple, sextuple

uplet \əp-lət\ couplet ∘ quadruplet, quintuplet, sextuplet

uplicate \ü-pli-kət\ duplicate ∘ quadruplicate

upor \ü-pər\ see OOPER

uppance \əp-əns\ threepence, twopence

upper \əp-ər\ supper, upper ∘ Last Supper, Lord's Supper ∘ builder-upper, fixer-upper

uppie \əp-ē\ see UPPY

upple[1] \üp-əl\ see UPLE[2]

upple[2] \əp-əl\ see UPLE[1]

uppy \əp-ē\ guppy, puppy, yuppie ∘ hush puppy, mud puppy

upt \əpt\ abrupt, bankrupt, corrupt, disrupt, erupt ∘ developed, interrupt

—also -ed forms of verbs listed at UP

uq \ük\ see UKE

uque \ük\ see UKE

ur[1] \ȯr\ see OR[1]

ur[2] \ùr\ see URE[1]

ur[3] \ər\ see EUR[1]

ura \ùr-ə\ Jura, Kura ∘ bravura, tempura ∘ coloratura

urable \ùr-ə-bəl\ curable, durable ∘ endurable, incurable, insurable ∘ unendurable, uninsurable

urae \ùr-ē\ see URY[1]

urah \ùr-ə\ see URA

ural \ùr-əl\ mural, neural, plural, puerile, rural, Ural ∘ extramural, intramural, semirural

urance \ùr-əns\ assurance, endurance, insurance ∘ health insurance, life insurance, reassurance, self-assurance

urate \ùr-ət\ curate, turret

urb \ərb\ see ERB

urban \ər-bən\ bourbon, Durban, turban, turbine, urban ∘ steam turbine, suburban, wind turbine

urber \ər-bər\ Berber ∘ disturber

urbia \ər-bē-ə\ Serbia ∘ exurbia, suburbia

urbine \ər-bən\ see URBAN

urble \ər-bəl\ see ERBAL

urch \ərch\ birch, church, lurch, perch, search ∘ Christchurch, research

urchly \ərch-lē\ churchly, virtually

urd[1] \ùrd\ see URED[1]

urd[2] \ərd\ see IRD

urder \ərd-ər\ see ERDER

urdle \ərd-ᵊl\ curdle, girdle, hurdle

urdy \ərd-ē\ birdie, sturdy, wordy ∘ hurdy-gurdy, Mesa Verde, Monteverdi

ure[1] \ùr\ Boer, boor, cure, dour, ewer, fewer, lure, moor, Moore, poor, pure, Ruhr, sewer, skewer, sure, tour, your, you're ∘ abjure, allure, amour, assure, brochure, cocksure, conjure, contour, demure, detour, dirt-poor, endure, ensure, Exmoor, for sure, grandeur, impure, insure, land-poor, manure, mature, obscure, procure, secure, tenure, unmoor, unsure, velour ∘ amateur, aperture, connoisseur, curvature, epicure, forfeiture, haute couture, immature, insecure, manicure, overture, pedicure, portraiture, premature, reassure, saboteur, signature, sinecure, soup du jour, temperature, to be sure, troubadour, Yom Kippur ∘ caricature, entrepreneur, expenditure, imprimatur, investiture, literature, miniature, musculature, nomenclature

ure[2] \ùr-ē\ see URY[1]

urean \ùr-ē-ən\ see URIAN

ureau \ùr-ō\ see URO

ured[1] \ùrd\ gourd, Kurd ∘ assured, steward ∘ self-assured ∘ out of one's gourd, underinsured

—also -ed *forms of verbs listed at* URE[1]

ured[2] \ərd\ *see* IRD

urely \u̇r-lē\ poorly, purely, surely • securely • prematurely

ureous \u̇r-ē-əs\ *see* URIOUS

urer \u̇r-ər\ führer, furor, juror • insurer
—also -er *forms of adjectives listed at* URE[1]

urety \u̇r-ət-ē\ *see* URITY

urey \u̇r-ē\ *see* URY[1]

urf \ərf\ serf, surf, turf • windsurf ∘ Astroturf, bodysurf, channel surf, surf and turf

urgative \ər-gə-tiv\ *see* URGATIVE

urge \ərj\ dirge, merge, purge, splurge, surge, urge, verge • converge, diverge, emerge, resurge, submerge, upsurge • reemerge

urgence \ər-jəns\ *see* ERGENCE

urgency \ər-jən-sē\ *see* ERGENCY

urgent \ər-jənt\ urgent • convergent, detergent, divergent, emergent, insurgent, resurgent • counterinsurgent

urgeon \ər-jən\ burgeon, sturgeon, surgeon, virgin • tree surgeon • plastic surgeon

urger[1] \ər-gər\ burger, burgher • cheeseburger, hamburger, Limburger • Luxembourger, veggie burger

urger[2] \ər-jər\ *see* ERGER

urgery \ərj-rē\ *see* ERJURY

urgh[1] \ər-ə\ *see* OROUGH[1]

urgh[2] \ər-ō\ *see* URROW[1]

urgher \ər-gər\ *see* URGER[1]

urgic \ər-jik\ *see* ERGIC

urgical \ər-ji-kəl\ surgical • liturgical • metallurgical

urgor \ər-gər\ *see* URGER[1]

urgy \ər-jē\ clergy • dramaturgy, metallurgy

uri \u̇r-ē\ *see* URY[1]

urial \er-ē-əl\ *see* ARIAL

urian \u̇r-ē-ən\ Arthurian, centurion, Manchurian, Missourian • Canterburian, epicurean

urible \u̇r-ə-bəl\ *see* URABLE

urie \u̇r-ē\ *see* URY[1]

urier[1] \er-ē-ər\ *see* ERRIER

urier[2] \u̇r-ē-ər\ *see* OURIER[1]

uriere \u̇r-ē-ər\ *see* OURIER[1]

uring \u̇r-iŋ\ during, mooring, touring • alluring, enduring
—also -ing *forms of verbs listed at* URE[1]

urion \u̇r-ē-ən\ *see* URIAN

urious \u̇r-ē-əs\ curious, furious, spurious ∘ incurious, injurious, luxurious

uris \u̇r-əs\ *see* URUS

urist \u̇r-əst\ jurist, purist, tourist • manicurist, pedicurist • caricaturist
—also -est *forms of adjectives listed at* URE[1]

urity \u̇r-ət-ē\ purity • impurity, maturity, obscurity, security • immaturity, insecurity • Social Security

urk \ərk\ *see* ORK[1]

urka \ər-kə\ burka, circa, Gurkha

urke \ərk\ *see* ORK[1]

urker \ər-kər\ *see* ORKER[1]

urkey \ər-kē\ *see* ERKY

urkha \ər-kə\ *see* URKA

urki \ər-kē\ *see* ERKY

urky \ər-kē\ *see* ERKY

url \ərl\ *see* IRL

urled \ərld\ *see* ORLD

urlin \ər-lən\ *see* ERLIN

urling \ər-liŋ\ hurling, sterling
—also -ing *forms of verbs listed at* IRL

urlish \ər-lish\ churlish, girlish

urly \ər-lē\ burly, curly, early, pearly, squirrely, surly, swirly, twirly, whirly

urman \ər-mən\ *see* ERMAN

urn \ərn\ Bern, burn, churn, earn, fern, learn, spurn, stern, tern, turn, urn, yearn • adjourn, astern, concern, discern, downturn, heartburn, Hepburn, intern, in turn, kick turn, Lucerne, nocturne, return, sojourn, sunburn, unlearn, upturn, U-turn, windburn • Arctic tern, in return, out of turn, overturn, slash-and-burn, taciturn, unconcern • at every turn, from stem to stern • point of no return

urnable \ər-nə-bəl\ burnable • discernible, returnable
• indiscernible, nonreturnable

urnal \ərn-ᵊl\ see ERNAL

urne \ərn\ see URN

urned \ərnd\ burned • concerned, sunburned, unearned, unlearned, windburned
—*also* -ed *forms of verbs listed at* URN

urner \ər-nər\ burner, earner • afterburner

urney \ər-nē\ see OURNEY[1]

urnian \ər-nē-ən\ see ERNIAN

urnish \ər-nish\ burnish, furnish

urnt \ərnt\ see EARNT

uro \ùr-ō\ bureau, euro, Euro
• politburo, travel bureau, weather bureau

uror \ùr-ər\ see URER

urore \ùr-ər\ see URER

urous \ùr-əs\ see URUS

urp \ərp\ burp, chirp, perp, slurp, twerp • Antwerp, usurp

urr \ər\ see EUR[1]

urra¹ \ùr-ə\ see URA

urra² \ər-ə\ see OROUGH[1]

urragh \ər-ə\ see OROUGH[1]

urral \ər-əl\ see ERRAL

urrant \ər-ənt\ see URRENT

urray \ər-ē\ see URRY

urre \ər\ see EUR[1]

urred \ərd\ see IRD

urrence \ər-əns\ deterrence, occurrence, recurrence, transference
—*also* -s, -'s, *and* -s' *forms of nouns listed at* URRENT

urrent \ər-ənt\ currant, current, weren't • concurrent, crosscurrent, deterrent, recurrent, rip current • countercurrent, undercurrent

urret \ùr-ət\ see URATE

urrey \ər-ē\ see URRY

urrian \ùr-ē-ən\ see URIAN

urrie \ər-ē\ see URRY

urrier \ər-ē-ər\ blurrier, courier, furrier, worrier

urring \ər-iŋ\ stirring
—*also* -ing *forms of verbs listed at* EUR[1]

urrish \ər-ish\ see OURISH

urro¹ \ər-ə\ see OROUGH[1]

urro² \ər-ō\ see URROW[1]

urrow¹ \ər-ō\ borough, burgh, burro, burrow, furrow, thorough
• Marlborough

urrow² \ər-ə\ see OROUGH[1]

urry \ər-ē\ blurry, curry, flurry, furry, hurry, Murray, scurry, surrey, Surrey, worry • in a hurry

ursary \ərs-rē\ cursory, nursery
• day nursery • anniversary

urse \ərs\ see ERSE

ursed \ərst\ see URST

ursery \ərs-rē\ see URSARY

ursion \ər-zhən\ see ERSION[1]

ursive \ər-siv\ see ERSIVE

ursory \ərs-rē\ see URSARY

urst \ərst\ burst, cursed, first, Hearst, thirst, worst • accursed, at first, cloudburst, feetfirst, headfirst, knockwurst, outburst, starburst, sunburst • liverwurst, microburst
—*also* -ed *forms of verbs listed at* ERSE

ursy¹ \ər-sē\ see ERCY

ursy² \əs-ē\ see USSY

urt¹ \ùrt\ Frankfurt

urt² \ərt\ see ERT[1]

urtain \ərt-ᵊn\ see ERTAIN

urtal \ərt-ᵊl\ see ERTILE

urter \ərt-ər\ see ERTER

urtive \ərt-iv\ see ERTIVE
urtle \ərt-ᵊl\ see ERTILE
urton \ərt-ᵊn\ see ERTAIN
urus \ùr-əs\ Arcturus, sulfurous • Epicurus
urve \ərv\ see ERVE
urved \ərvd\ see ERVED
urvy \ər-vē\ curvy, nervy, scurvy • topsy-turvy
ury[1] \ùr-ē\ Curie, fury, jury • grand jury, Missouri
ury[2] \er-ē\ see ARY[1]
urze \ərz\ see ERS[1]
urzy \ər-zē\ see ERSEY
us[1] \əs\ bus, cuss, fuss, Gus, muss, plus, pus, Russ, thus, truss, us • airbus, discuss, school bus, surplus • blunderbuss, minibus, motor bus, trolleybus
us[2] \ü\ see EW[1]
us[3] \üsh\ see OUCHE
us[4] \üz\ see USE[2]
usa[1] \ü-sə\ Sousa • Medusa • Appaloosa, Tuscaloosa
usa[2] \ü-zə\ Sousa • Medusa • Arethusa
usable \ü-zə-bəl\ usable • excusable, reusable, unusable • inexcusable, nonreusable
usae \ü-sē\ see UICY
usal \ü-zəl\ bamboozle, perusal, refusal
usc \əsk\ see USK
uscan \əs-kən\ Tuscan • Etruscan
uscle \əs-əl\ see USTLE
use[1] \üs\ Bruce, deuce, goose, juice, loose, moose, mousse, noose, puce, ruse, Russ, schuss, Seuss, sluice, spruce, truce, use, Zeus • abstruse, abuse, adduce, blue spruce, burnoose, caboose, chartreuse, conduce, cut loose, deduce, diffuse, disuse, excuse, footloose, hang loose, induce, misuse, mongoose, obtuse, Orpheus, papoose, Perseus, produce, profuse, Proteus, recluse, reduce,

refuse, reuse, Sanctus, seduce, slip noose, snow goose, Theseus, turn loose, vamoose • Belarus, Betelgeuse, cook one's goose, fast and loose, flag of truce, introduce, mass-produce, Mother Goose, Odysseus, overuse, Prometheus, reproduce, Syracuse • Canada goose, hypotenuse
use[2] \üz\ blues, booze, bruise, choose, cruise, Druze, fuse, Hughes, lose, Meuse, muse, news, ooze, ruse, schmooze, snooze, use, whose • abuse, accuse, amuse, bad news, chartreuse, confuse, defuse, diffuse, enthuse, excuse, infuse, masseuse, misuse, peruse, refuse, reuse, short fuse, suffuse, transfuse • Betelgeuse, disabuse, Newport News, overuse, p's and q's, Santa Cruz, Syracuse, Veracruz • Goody Two-shoes, hypotenuse
—*also* -s, -'s, *and* -s' *forms of nouns and* -s *forms of verbs listed at* EW[1]
used \üzd\ used • confused • underused
—*also* -ed *forms of verbs listed at* USE[2]
user \ü-zər\ boozer, bruiser, cruiser, loser, user • abuser, accuser, end user • battle cruiser, cabin cruiser
ush[1] \əsh\ blush, brush, crush, flush, gush, hush, lush, mush, plush, rush, shush, slush, squush, thrush • bulrush, bum's rush, gold rush, hairbrush, hush-hush, nailbrush, onrush, paintbrush, sagebrush, scrub brush, song thrush, straight flush, toothbrush, wood thrush • Hindu Kush, royal flush, underbrush
ush[2] \ùsh\ bush, Bush, mush, push, shush, squoosh, swoosh, whoosh • ambush, bell push, rosebush,

spicebush, thornbush • burning
bush, Hindu Kush • beat around
the bush

usher[1] \əsh-ər\ crusher, gusher,
usher
—*also* -er *forms of adjectives listed
at* USH[1]

usher[2] \ush-ər\ pusher • ambusher

ushi \ush-ē\ see USHY[2]

ushing \əsh-iŋ\ onrushing, un-
blushing
—*also* -ing *forms of verbs listed at*
USH[1]

ushy[1] \əsh-ē\ brushy, gushy,
mushy, plushy, slushy

ushy[2] \ush-ē\ bushy, cushy, mushy,
pushy, sushi

usi \ü-sē\ see UICY

usian \ü-zhən\ see USION

usible[1] \ü-sə-bəl\ see UCIBLE

usible[2] \ü-zə-bəl\ see USABLE

usie \ü-zē\ see OOZY

usil \ü-zəl\ see USAL

using \əs-iŋ\ busing • antibusing
—*also* -ing *forms of verbs listed at*
US[1]

usion \ü-zhən\ fusion • allusion,
collusion, conclusion, confusion,
contusion, delusion, exclusion,
illusion, inclusion, infusion, intru-
sion, profusion, protrusion, seclusion, transfusion, Venusian
• Andalusian, disillusion, maloc-
clusion • foregone conclusion
• optical illusion

usive \ü-siv\ abusive, allusive,
conclusive, conducive, delusive,
effusive, elusive, exclusive, inclusive, intrusive, reclusive • all-
inclusive, inconclusive,
unobtrusive

usk \əsk\ brusque, dusk, husk,
musk, tusk

usker \əs-kər\ busker • cornhusker

uskie \əs-kē\ see USKY

uskin \əs-kən\ see USCAN

usky \əs-kē\ dusky, husky, musky

uso \ü-sō\ see USOE

usoe \ü-sō\ Rousseau, trousseau,
whoso • Caruso • Robinson Crusoe

usque \əsk\ see USK

uss[1] \us\ puss, wuss • chartreuse,
sourpuss • glamour-puss, octopus,
platypus

uss[2] \üs\ see USE[1]

uss[3] \əs\ see US[1]

ussate \əs-ət\ see USSET

usse \üs\ see USE[1]

ussel \əs-əl\ see USTLE

ussell \əs-əl\ see USTLE

usset \əs-ət\ gusset, russet

ussia \əsh-ə\ Prussia, Russia • Be-
lorussia

ussian \əsh-ən\ see USSION

ussing \əs-iŋ\ see USING

ussion \əsh-ən\ Prussian, Russian
• concussion, discussion, percus-
sion • Belorussian, repercussion

ussle \əs-əl\ see USTLE

ussy \əs-ē\ fussy, mussy

ust[1] \əst\ bust, crust, dust, gust,
just, lust, must, rust, thrust, trust
• adjust, august, bloodlust, dis-
gust, distrust, encrust, entrust, in
trust, leaf rust, mistrust, moon-
dust, piecrust, robust, sawdust,
stardust, unjust • antitrust, bite
the dust, cosmic dust, readjust,
upper crust, wanderlust
—*also* -ed *forms of verbs listed at*
US[1]

ust[2] \əs\ see US[1]

ust[3] \üst\ see OOST

ustable \əs-tə-bəl\ see USTIBLE

ustard \əs-tərd\ custard, mustard
—*also* -ed *forms of verbs listed at*
USTER

usted \əs-təd\ busted • disgusted
• maladjusted, well-adjusted
—*also* -ed *forms of verbs listed at*
UST[1]

uster \əs-tər\ bluster, buster, cluster, Custer, duster, fluster, luster,
muster • adjuster, blockbuster,

crop duster, gangbuster, lackluster, pass muster • broncobuster, filibuster

ustful \əst-fəl\ lustful, trustful • distrustful, mistrustful

usth \əst\ see UST[1]

ustible \əs-tə-bəl\ adjustable, combustible • incombustible

ustin \əs-tən\ Justin • Augustine

ustine \əs-tən\ see USTIN

ustle \əs-əl\ bustle, hustle, muscle, mussel, Russell, rustle, trestle, tussle • corpuscle, outhustle, outmuscle

ustor \əs-tər\ see USTER

ustrious \əs-trē-əs\ illustrious, industrious

usty \əs-tē\ busty, crusty, dusty, gusty, lusty, musty, rusty, trusty

usy \iz-ē\ see IZZY

ut[1] \ət\ but, butt, cut, glut, gut, hut, jut, mutt, nut, putt, rut, shut, smut, soot, strut, what • abut, all but, beechnut, brush cut, buzz cut, catgut, chestnut, clean-cut, clear-cut, crew cut, crosscut, doughnut, haircut, jump cut, kick butt, lug nut, peanut, pignut, pine nut, precut, putt-putt, rebut, shortcut, somewhat, walnut, wing nut, woodcut • betel nut, brazil nut, butternut, coconut, hazelnut, lychee nut, scuttlebutt, undercut, uppercut • director's cut, open-and-shut

ut[2] \ü\ see EW[1]

ut[3] \üt\ see UTE

ut[4] \u̇t\ see OOT[1]

utable \üt-ə-bəl\ suitable • immutable, inscrutable • executable, indisputable, irrefutable, substitutable

utal \üt-ᵊl\ see UTILE

utan \üt-ᵊn\ gluten, Newton, Putin, Teuton • Rasputin • highfalutin

utant \üt-ᵊnt\ mutant • disputant, pollutant

utch \əch\ clutch, crutch, dutch, Dutch, hutch, much, such, touch • and such, as such, retouch, soft touch, so much, too much • a bit much, common touch, Midas touch, overmuch, pretty much, such and such

utchy \əch-ē\ see UCHY

ute \üt\ boot, brute, butte, chute, coot, cute, flute, fruit, hoot, jute, Jute, loot, lute, moot, mute, newt, root, rout, route, scoot, shoot, snoot, soot, suit, toot, Ute • acute, astute, bear fruit, Beirut, breadfruit, Canute, commute, compute, cube root, deaf-mute, dilute, dispute, en route, flight suit, grapefruit, hip boot, hirsute, impute, jackboot, jumpsuit, lawsuit, minute, offshoot, Paiute, pantsuit, playsuit, pollute, pursuit, reboot, recruit, refute, salute, Silk Route, snowsuit, spacesuit, sport-ute, square root, star fruit, statute, strong suit, sunsuit, sweat suit, swimsuit, take root, taproot, to boot, tracksuit, trade route, transmute, tribute, uproot, wet suit • absolute, Aleut, arrowroot, attribute, autoroute, bathing suit, birthday suit, bitterroot, bodysuit, business suit, constitute, contribute, destitute, disrepute, dissolute, execute, follow suit, gingerroot, hot pursuit, institute, kiwifruit, leisure suit, malamute, overshoot, parachute, passion fruit, persecute, point-and-shoot, prosecute, resolute, rural route, substitute, troubleshoot • electrocute, forbidden fruit, reconstitute, redistribute, telecommute

uted \üt-əd\ see OOTED[1]

utee \üt-ē\ see OOTY[1]

utely \üt-lē\ acutely, minutely • absolutely, resolutely

uten \üt-ᵊn\ see UTAN
uteness \üt-nəs\ cuteness, muti-
nous
utenous \üt-nəs\ see UTENESS
uteous \üt-ē-əs\ beauteous, du-
teous
uter \üt-ər\ cuter, neuter, hooter,
looter, pewter, scooter, suitor,
tutor • commuter, computer,
freebooter, jump shooter,
peashooter, polluter, recruiter,
sharpshooter, six-shooter, straight
shooter, trapshooter • motor
scooter, persecutor, prosecutor,
troubleshooter • microcomputer,
minicomputer, telecommuter
utes \üts\ see OOTS
uteus \üt-ē-əs\ see UTEOUS
uth¹ \üt\ see UTE
uth² \üth\ see OOTH²
uther \ə-thər\ see OTHER¹
uthful \üth-fəl\ truthful, youthful
• untruthful
uthless \üth-ləs\ ruthless, toothless
uti \üt-ē\ see OOTY¹
utian \ü-shən\ see UTION
utical \üt-i-kəl\ cuticle • pharma-
ceutical
uticle \üt-i-kəl\ see UTICAL
utie \üt-ē\ see OOTY¹
utiful \üt-i-fəl\ beautiful, dutiful
utile \üt-ᵊl\ brutal, futile, tootle
utin \üt-ᵊn\ see UTAN
utine \üt-ᵊn\ see UTAN
uting \üt-iŋ\ sharpshooting, trap-
shooting
—also -ing forms of verbs listed at
UTE
utinous¹ \üt-ᵊn-əs\ glutinous, muti-
nous
utinous² \üt-nəs\ see UTENESS
utiny \üt-ᵊn-ē\ mutiny, scrutiny
ution \ü-shən\ Aleutian, Confu-
cian, dilution, locution, pollution,
solution • absolution, attribution,
constitution, contribution, desti-
tution, dissolution, distribution,

elocution, evolution, execution,
institution, persecution, prosecu-
tion, resolution, restitution, retri-
bution, revolution, substitution
• electrocution, joint resolution,
redistribution
utionary \ü-shə-ner-ē\ evolutionary, revolutionary
utist \üt-əst\ cutest, flutist • abso-
lutist
utl \ü-t-ᵊl\ see UTILE
utland \ət-lənd\ Jutland, Rutland
utlass \ət-ləs\ cutlass, gutless
utless \ət-ləs\ see UTLASS
utney \ət-nē\ chutney, gluttony
uton \üt-ⁿ\ see UTAN
utor \üt-ər\ see UTER
utriment \ü-trə-mənt\ nutriment
• accoutrement
uts \əts\ see UTZ
utsy \ət-sē\ gutsy, klutzy
utt \ət\ see UT¹
uttal \ət-ᵊl\ see UTTLE
utte \üt\ see UTE
uttee \ət-ē\ see UTTY
utter¹ \ət-ər\ butter, clutter, cutter,
flutter, gutter, mutter, putter,
shutter, splutter, sputter, stutter,
utter • aflutter, haircutter, stone-
cutter, woodcutter • bread and
butter, cookie-cutter, paper cutter
utter² \ut-ər\ see OOTER¹
uttery \ət-ə-rē\ buttery, fluttery
utti¹ \üt-ē\ see OOTY¹
utti² \ut-ē\ see OOTY²
utting \ut-iŋ\ see OOTING¹
uttle \ət-ᵊl\ scuttle, shuttle, subtle
• rebuttal, space shuttle
utton \ət-ᵊn\ button, glutton, mut-
ton, Sutton • hot-button, push-
button, unbutton • belly button,
on the button, panic button
uttony \ət-nē\ see UTNEY
utty \ət-ē\ gutty, nutty, putty,
rutty, smutty
uture \ü-chər\ future, moocher,
suture • wave of the future

uty \üt-ē\ see OOTY[1]

utz \əts\ klutz, nuts • blood-and-guts, spill one's guts
  —*also -s, -'s, and -s' forms of nouns and -s forms of verbs listed at* UT[1]

utzy \ət-sē\ see UTSY

uu \ü\ see EW[1]

uvian \ü-vē-ən\ Peruvian, Vesuvian • antediluvian

uvion \ü-vē-ən\ see UVIAN

ux[1] \əks\ crux, flux, tux • big bucks, deluxe, influx • Benelux, megabucks,
  —*also -s, -'s, and -s' forms of nouns and -s forms of verbs listed at* UCK[1]

ux[2] \uks\ see OOKS[2]

uxe[1] \üks\ see OOKS[1]

uxe[2] \uks\ see OOKS[2]

uxe[3] \əks\ see UX[1]

uxion \ək-shən\ see UCTION

uy \ī\ see Y[1]

uygur \ē-gər\ see EAGER

uyot \ē-ō\ see IO[2]

uyp \īp\ see IPE

uz[1] \üts\ see OOTS

uz[2] \uz\ see USE[2]

uze \üz\ see USE[2]

uzz \əz\ see EUSE[1]

uzzi \ü-zē\ see OOZY

uzzle \əz-əl\ guzzle, muzzle, nuzzle, puzzle • crossword puzzle, jigsaw puzzle

uzzler \əz-lər\ guzzler, muzzler, puzzler • gas-guzzler

uzzy \əz-ē\ fuzzy, muzzy, scuzzy

Y

y[1] \ī\ aye, Bligh, buy, by, bye, chai, cry, die, dry, dye, eye, fie, fly, fry, guy, Guy, hi, high, i, I, lie, lye, my, nigh, pi, pie, ply, pry, rye, scythe, shy, sigh, sky, Skye, sly, spry, spy, sty, Thai, thigh, thy, tie, try, vie, why, wry, wye, Y • air-dry, ally, anti, apply, awry, aye-aye, Bacchae, Baha'i, banzai, Belgae, belie, black eye, blackfly, black tie, blow-dry, blowfly, bone-dry, bonsai, botfly, Brunei, buckeye, bull?s-eye, bye-bye, cockeye, come by, comply, cow pie, crane fly, cream pie, cross-eye, decry, deep-fry, deerfly, defy, Delphi, deny, drip-dry, drive-by, drop by, Dubai, Eli, espy, face fly, firefly, flyby, fly high, freeze-dry, fruit fly, gadfly, get by, GI, glass eye, go by, good-bye, gun-shy, Haggai, Hawkeye, hereby, hi-fi, hog-tie, horn fly, horsefly, house-fly, imply, jai alai, July, Karzai, Kaui, Kenai, knee-high, Lehigh, let fly, Levi, magpie, Masai, mayfly, medfly, mind's eye, Mumbai, nearby, necktie, outcry, panfry, pigsty, pinkeye, Popeye, pop fly, potpie, put by, quasi, rabbi, red-eye, rely, reply, retry, rib eye, run dry, sand fly, sci-fi, screw eye, semi, shanghai, Shanghai, shut-eye, Sinai, sky-high, small-fry, stand by, standby, stir-fry, string tie, supply, swear by, test-fly, thereby, tie-dye, tongue-tie, Transkei, twist tie, two-ply, untie, vat dye, Versailles, whereby, whitefly, white tie, wise guy • abide by, Adonai, alibi, alkali, amplify, beautify, bolo tie, butterfly, by-and-by, by the bye, calcify, certify, Chou En-lai, citify, clarify, classify, codify, crucify, cut-and-dry, cutie-pie, DIY, damselfly, dandify, deify, dignify, do-or-die, dragonfly, eagle eye, edify, evil eye, falsify, fortify, Gemini, gentrify, glorify, gratify, Haggai, high and dry, horrify, junior high, justify, kiss good-bye, liquefy, Lorelei, lullaby, magnify, Malachi, misapply, modify, mollify, mortify, Mount Sinai, multi-ply, multiply, mummify, mystify, nazify, notify, nuclei, nullify, occupy, on standby, on the fly, ossify, overbuy, overfly, overlie, pacify, Paraguay, passerby, petrify, preachify, prettify, private eye, prophesy, purify, putrefy, qualify, quantify, ratify, RBI, reapply, rectify, resupply, robber fly, runner's high, Russify, samurai, sanctify, satisfy, scarify, Seeing Eye, senior high, shepherd's pie, shoofly pie, signify, simplify, specify, speechify, stratify, stultify, stupefy, sweetie pie, Tenebrae, terrify, testify, tsetse fly, tumble dry, typify, uglify, underlie, unify, Uruguay, verify, vilify, vivify, yuppify, zombify • aniline dye, a priori, beatify, decertify, declassify, demystify, detoxify, disqualify, dissatisfy, diversify, electric eye, electrify, exemplify, Helvetii, humidify, identify, intensify, misclassify, money supply, oversupply, personify, preoccupy, revivify, see eye to eye, solidify, undersupply, water supply • dehumidify, misidentify, oversimplify • in the blink of an eye, modus operandi

y² \ē\ see EE¹
yable \ī-ə-bəl\ see IABLE¹
yad \ī-əd\ dryad, naiad, triad • jeremiad
yan \ī-ən\ see ION¹
yant \ī-ənt\ see IANT
yatt \ī-ət\ see IET
yber \ī-bər\ see IBER
ybia \i-bē-ə\ see IBIA
yce \īs\ see ICE¹
yche \ī-kē\ see IKE¹
ycin \īs-ᵊn\ see ISON¹
ycle¹ \ī-kəl\ cycle, Michael • cell cycle, life cycle, recycle, song cycle • business cycle, carbon cycle, Exercycle, kilocycle, megacycle, motorcycle, unicycle
ycle² \ik-əl\ see ICKLE
ycler \ik-lər\ see ICKLER
yde \īd\ see IDE¹
ydia \i-dē-ə\ see IDIA
ydian \id-ē-ən\ see IDIAN
ydney \id-nē\ see IDNEY
ye \ī\ see Y¹
yeable \ī-ə-bəl\ see IABLE¹
yed \īd\ see IDE¹
yer \īr\ see IRE¹
yeth \ī-əth\ see IATH¹
yfe \īf\ see IFE¹
yg \ig\ see IG
ygamous \ig-ə-məs\ see IGAMOUS
ygamy \ig-ə-mē\ see IGAMY
ygian \i-jən\ Phrygian, pidgin, pigeon, smidgen • clay pigeon, religion, rock pigeon, stool pigeon, wood pigeon • homing pigeon • carrier pigeon, passenger pigeon
ying \ī-iŋ\ crying, flying, lying, trying • high-flying, low-lying, outlying, undying • terrifying, underlying
—also -ing *forms of verbs listed at* Y¹
yke \īk\ see IKE²
ylan \il-ən\ see ILLON
yle \īl\ see ILE¹

ylem \ī-ləm\ see ILUM
yler \ī-lər\ see ILAR
ylet \ī-lət\ see ILOT
ylic \il-ik\ see ILIC
yling \ī-liŋ\ see ILING[1]
yllable \il-ə-bəl\ see ILLABLE
yllic \il-ik\ see ILIC
yllis \il-əs\ see ILLUS
yllo[1] \ē-lō\ see ILO[2]
yllo[2] \ī-lō\ see ILO[1]
ylum \ī-ləm\ see ILUM
ylus \ī-ləs\ see ILUS
yly \ī-lē\ dryly, highly, shyly, slyly,
  smiley, Wiley, wily, wryly
ym \im\ see IM[1]
ymbal \im-bəl\ see IMBLE
ymboi \im-bəl\ see IMBLE
yme \īm\ see IME[1]
ymen \ī-mən\ see IMEN
ymer \ī-mər\ see IMER[1]
ymic \im-ik\ gimmick, mimic
ymie \ī-mē\ see IMY
ymion \im-ē-ən\ see IMIAN
ymity \im-ət-ē\ see IMITY
ymn \im\ see IM[1]
ymph \imf\ lymph, nymph
ynah \ī-nə\ see INA[1]
ynast \ī-nəst\ see INIST[1]
ynch[1] \inch\ see INCH
ynch[2] \iŋk\ see INK
yness \ī-nəs\ see INUS[1]
ynic \in-ik\ see INIC
ynical \in-i-kəl\ see INICAL
ynn \in\ see IN[1]
ynth \inth\ see INTH
ynx \iŋs\ see INX
yp \ip\ see IP
ypal \ī-pəl\ disciple • archetypal,
  prototypal
ype \īp\ see IPE
yper \ī-pər\ see IPER
yph \if\ see IFF
yphen \ī-fən\ hyphen, siphon
yphic \if-ik\ see IFIC
yphony \if-ə-nē\ see IPHONY
yping \ī-piŋ\ see IPING
ypo \ī-pō\ hypo, typo

ypse \ips\ see IPS
ypsy \ip-sē\ gypsy, Gypsy, tipsy
ypt \ipt\ see IPT
yptian \ip-shən\ see IPTION
yptic \ip-tik\ cryptic, triptych
  • ecliptic, elliptic • apocalyptic
yra \ī-rə\ Ira, Lyra, Myra • Elmira,
  Elvira, hegira, Palmyra
yrant \ī-rənt\ see IRANT
yre \īr\ see IRE[1]
yria \ir-ē-ə\ see ERIA[1]
yriad \ir-ē-əd\ see ERIOD
yric \ir-ik\ see ERIC[2]
yrical \ir-i-kəl\ see ERICAL[2]
yrie \ir-ē\ see EARY
yril \ir-əl\ see ERAL[1]
yrna \ər-nə\ see ERNA
yro[1] \ī-rō\ Cairo, gyro, Gyro, tyro
yro[2] \ir-ō\ see ERO[3]
yron \īr-ən\ see IREN
yros \ī-rəs\ see IRUS
yrrh \ər\ see EUR[1]
yrrhic \ir-ik\ see ERIC[2]
yrrhus \ir-əs\ see EROUS
yrtle \ərt-ᵊl\ see ERTILE
yrup \ər-əp\ see IRRUP
yrupy \ər-ə-pē\ see IRRUPY
yrus \ī-rəs\ see IRUS
ysch \ish\ see ISH[1]
ysia \ish-ə\ see ITIA[1]
ysian[1] \is-ē-ən\ Odyssean
  • Dionysian
ysian[2] \ish-ən\ see ITION
ysian[3] \izh-ən\ see ISION
ysian[4] \ī-sē-ən\ see ISCEAN[1]
ysical \iz-i-kəl\ physical, quizzical
  • nonphysical • metaphysical
ysm \iz-əm\ see ISM
ysmal \iz-məl\ dismal • abysmal,
  baptismal • cataclysmal
yson \īs-ᵊn\ see ISON[1]
yss \is\ see ISS
yssean \is-ē-ən\ see YSIAN[1]
yst \ist\ see IST[2]
ystal \is-tᵊl\ see ISTAL
yster \ī-stər\ see EISTER[1]
ystery \is-trē\ see ISTORY

ystic \is-tik\ see ISTIC

ystical \is-ti-kəl\ see ISTICAL

ysus¹ \ē-səs\ see ESIS

ysus² \ī-səs\ see ISIS

yte \īt\ see ITE¹

ythe¹ \ī\ see Y¹

ythe² \īth\ see ITHE¹

ytic \it-ik\ see ITIC

ytical \it-i-kəl\ see ITICAL

ytton \it-ᵊn\ see ITTEN

yx \iks\ see IX¹

yze \īz\ see IZE¹